VOLKSWAGEN
BEETLE & GHIA
1961-1979
SHOP MANUAL

By
ERIC JORGENSEN

JEFF ROBINSON
Editor and Publisher

CLYMER PUBLICATIONS

World's largest publisher of books
devoted exclusively to automobiles and motorcycles

12860 MUSCATINE STREET · P.O. BOX 20 · ARLETA, CALIFORNIA 91331

FIRST EDITION
First Printing December, 1972

SECOND EDITION
Revised to include 1973-1974 models
First Printing May, 1974

THIRD EDITION
Revised to include 1975-1976 models
First Printing April, 1976

FOURTH EDITION
Revised by Jim Combs to include 1977 models
First Printing March, 1977

FIFTH EDITION
Revised by Ed Scott to include 1978-1979 models
First Printing October, 1979

SIXTH EDITION
First Printing November, 1982
Second Printing February, 1983
Third Printing July, 1983
Fourth Printing September, 1983

Printed in U.S.A.

ISBN: 0-89287-144-X

Production Coordinator, Mike Heimowitz

*COVER: Photographed by Michael Brown Photographic Productions, Los Angeles, California. Assisted b
Ryfle and Kimm Frew. Car courtesy of Volkswagen of America.*

CONTENTS

VOLKSWAGEN
BEETLE & GHIA
1961-1979
SHOP MANUAL

QUICK REFERENCE DATA

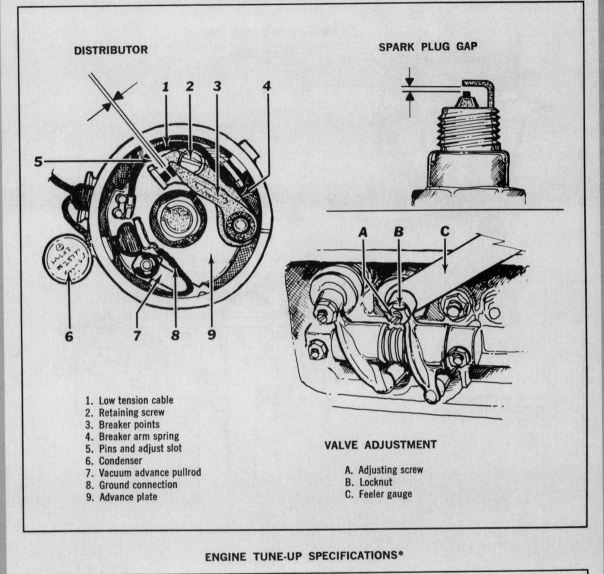

DISTRIBUTOR

SPARK PLUG GAP

1. Low tension cable
2. Retaining screw
3. Breaker points
4. Breaker arm spring
5. Pins and adjust slot
6. Condenser
7. Vacuum advance pullrod
8. Ground connection
9. Advance plate

VALVE ADJUSTMENT

A. Adjusting screw
B. Locknut
C. Feeler gauge

ENGINE TUNE-UP SPECIFICATIONS*

Valve Clearance	
Long studs	Intake: 0.008 in. (0.2mm) Exhaust: 0.012 in. (0.3mm)
Short studs	
Through 1971	Intake and Exhaust: 0.004 in. (0.1mm)
1972-ON	Intake and Exhaust: 0.006 in. (0.15mm)
Spark Plug Gap	0.024-0.028 in. (0.6-0.7mm)
Spark Plug Type	
1961-1974	Bosch W175 T1, Champion L88A, Beru 145/14
1975-ON	Bosch W145 M1, Champion L288, Beru 145/14/L
Breaker Point Gap	0.016 in. (0.4mm)

*Ignition timing may vary from these specifications due to varying exhaust emission standards. Always use the timing specification listed on the emission control sticker located in the engine compartment.

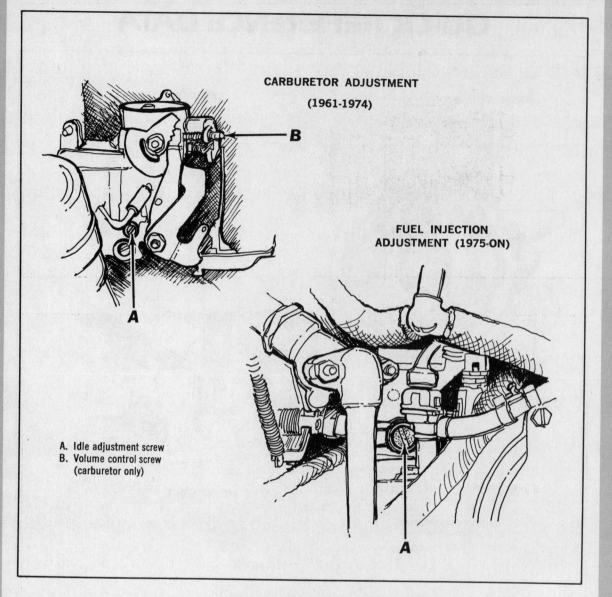

CARBURETOR ADJUSTMENT
(1961-1974)

B

FUEL INJECTION
ADJUSTMENT (1975-ON)

A. Idle adjustment screw
B. Volume control screw
(carburetor only)

A

A

EXHAUST EMISSION LEVELS
(1968-1977 ONLY)

Year	Carbon Monoxide (CO)	Hydrocarbons (PPM[1])
1968 & 1969	2-3.5%	400 maximum
1970	2-4%	400 maximum
1971 & 1972	1.5-3%	400 maximum
1973	0.7-1.5%	400 maximum
1974	0.7-1.5%	400 maximum
1975-ON	$1.1 \pm 0.1\%$	400 maximum
1. Parts per million		

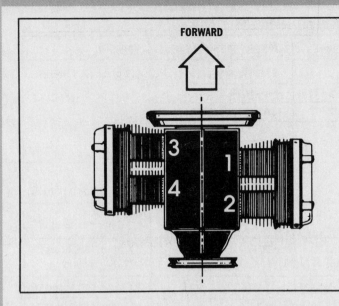

FORWARD

FIRING ORDER 1-4-3-2

IGNITION TIMING

1961-1965	1200 engine ①	10° BTDC ②
1966	1300 engine ①	7.5° BTDC ②
1967	1500 engine ①	7.5° BTDC ②
1968 and 1969	1500 engine	TDC @ 900 rpm ③
1970	1600 engine	TDC @ 900 rpm ③
1971-1973	1600 engine	5° ATDC @ 900 rpm ④
1974	1600 engine	7.5° BTDC @ 800-900 rpm ③ ⑥ 7.5° BTDC @ 900-1,000 rpm ③ ⑦ 5° ATDC @ 800-900 rpm ④ ⑤
1975-ON	1600 engine	5° ATDC @ 800-850 rpm ④ ⑧ TDC @ 850-1,000 rpm ④ ⑦

① Without exhaust emission control
② Static timing point; engine not running
③ Vacuum advance disconnected
④ Vacuum advance connected
⑤ California vehicle, manual transmission
⑥ Manual transmission (except Calif.)
⑦ Automatic Stick Shift
⑧ All manual transmissions

Table 4   RECOMMENDED LUBRICANTS AND FUEL

	Temperature Range	Recommended Type	Capacity
Engine oil	Below —13°F	SAE 5W(MS)	5.3 pints (2.5 liters)
	Between —13°F & 13°F	SAE 10W(MS)	
	Between 5°F & 40°F	SAE 20W-20(MS)	
	Between 40°F & 86°F	SAE 30(MS)	
	Above 68°F	SAE 40(MS)	
Manual transaxle & Automatic Stick Shift (except torque converter)	Above 0°F	Gear Oil SAE 90	Manual: 5.3 pints (2.5 liters)
	Between 0°F & —13°F	Gear Oil SAE 80	
	Below —13°F	ATF (DEXRON)	Automatic: 6.3 pints (3 liters)
Automatic Stick Shift torque converter	All temperatures	ATF (DEXRON)	7.6 pints (3.6 liters)
Fuel	— — —	91 octane (regular) ③	10.6 gal. (40 liters) ①
			11.1 gal. (42 liters) ②

① All except Super Beetle   ② Super Beetle   ③ 1975-ON — unleaded only

TIRE PRESSURES

Model	Persons	Pressure Front	Rear
Bettle and Karmann Ghia	1-2	16 psi	24 psi
	3-5	17 psi	26 psi
Super Beetle and Convertible	1-2	16 psi	27 psi
	3-5	19 psi	27 psi

Note: Pressures are for standard 5.60-15 bias ply tires. Add 1 psi to all pressures for 155SR-15 radials. Add 3 psi to all pressures for long, high-speed trips.

- NOTES -

XIV

INTRODUCTION

This detailed, comprehensive manual covers the Volkswagen Beetle and Karmann Ghia from 1961 to the present. Changes in exterior appearance has been limited to refinements in better driver visibility and safety related items. Mechanically, the changes have been far more reaching with a steady increase in engine displacement and horsepower from 1200cc and 40hp to 1600cc with 60hp. In 1968, 2 transmissions were offered; the 4-speed fully synchronized, available from 1961, and the new Automatic Stick Shift.

With the introduction of the Automatic Stick Shift, VW dropped the single joint swing axle in favor of a double joint axle with diagonal trailing arms similar to the 911 Porsche.

Even the front suspension has changed. For the Super Beetle, Volkswagen switched to its own version of the MacPherson strut suspension. On 1974 Super Beetles, VW introduced negative steering roll radius which vastly improved steering stability.

The expert text in this manual gives complete information on maintenance, tune-up, repair, and overhaul. Hundreds of photos and drawings guide you through every step. The book includes all you need to know to keep your Volkswagen running right.

Where repairs are practical for the owner/mechanic, complete procedures are given. Equally important, difficult jobs are pointed out. Such operations are usually more economically performed by a dealer or independent garage.

A shop manual is a reference. You want to be able to find information fast. As in all Clymer books, this one is designed with this in mind. All chapters are thumb tabbed. Important items are extensively indexed at the rear of the book. Finally, all the most frequently used specifications and capacities are summarized on the blue *Quick Reference* pages at the front of this manual.

General specifications, chassis number information and identifications numbers are explained in detail in the *Appendix* at the end of this manual.

Keep the book handy. Carry it in your glove box. It will help you to better understand your VW, lower repair and maintenance costs, and generally improve your satisfaction with your vehicle.

CHAPTER ONE

GENERAL INFORMATION

The troubleshooting, tune-up, maintenance, and step-by-step repair procedures in this book are written for the owner and home mechanic. The text is accompanied by useful photos and diagrams to make the job as clear and correct as possible.

Troubleshooting, tune-up, maintenance, and repair are not difficult if you know what tools and equipment to use and what to do. Anyone not afraid to get their hands dirty, of average intelligence, and with some mechanical ability can perform most of the procedures in this book.

In some cases, a repair job may require tools or skills not reasonably expected of the home mechanic. These procedures are noted in each chapter and it is recommended that you take the job to your dealer, a competent mechanic, or machine shop.

MANUAL ORGANIZATION

This chapter provides general information and safety and service hints. Also included are lists of recommended shop and emergency tools as well as a brief description of troubleshooting and tune-up equipment.

Chapter Two provides methods and suggestions for quick and accurate diagnosis and repair of problems. Troubleshooting procedures discuss typical symptoms and logical methods to pinpoint the trouble.

Chapter Three explains all periodic lubrication and routine maintenance necessary to keep your vehicle running well. Chapter Three also includes recommended tune-up procedures, eliminating the need to constantly consult chapters on the various subassemblies.

Subsequent chapters cover specific systems such as the engine, transmission, and electrical systems. Each of these chapters provides disassembly, repair, and assembly procedures in a simple step-by-step format. If a repair requires special skills or tools, or is otherwise impractical for the home mechanic, it is so indicated. In these cases it is usually faster and less expensive to have the repairs made by a dealer or competent repair shop. Necessary specifications concerning a particular system are included at the end of the appropriate chapter.

When special tools are required to perform a procedure included in this manual, the tool is illustrated either in actual use or alone. It may be possible to rent or borrow these tools. The inventive mechanic may also be able to find a suitable substitute in his tool box, or to fabricate one.

The terms NOTE, CAUTION, and WARNING have specific meanings in this manual. A NOTE provides additional or explanatory information. A CAUTION is used to emphasize areas where equipment damage could result if proper precautions are not taken. A WARNING is used to stress those areas where personal injury or death could result from negligence, in addition to possible mechanical damage.

SERVICE HINTS

Observing the following practices will save time, effort, and frustration, as well as prevent possible injury.

Throughout this manual keep in mind two conventions. "Front" refers to the front of the vehicle. The front of any component, such as the transaxle, is that end which faces toward the front of the vehicle. The "left" and "right" sides of the vehicle refer to the orientation of a person sitting in the vehicle facing forward. For example, the steering wheel is on the left side. These rules are simple, but even experienced mechanics occasionally become disoriented.

Most of the service procedures covered are straightforward and can be performed by anyone reasonably handy with tools. It is suggested, however, that you consider your own capabilities carefully before attempting any operation involving major disassembly of the engine.

Some operations, for example, require the use of a press. It would be wiser to have these performed by a shop equipped for such work, rather than to try to do the job yourself with makeshift equipment. Other procedures require precision measurements. Unless you have the skills and equipment required, it would be better to have a qualified repair shop make the measurements for you.

Repairs go much faster and easier if the parts that will be worked on are clean before you begin. There are special cleaners for washing the engine and related parts. Brush or spray on the cleaning solution, let it stand, then rinse it away with a garden hose. Clean all oily or greasy parts with cleaning solvent as you remove them.

WARNING
Never use gasoline as a cleaning agent. It presents an extreme fire hazard. Be sure to work in a well-ventilated area when using cleaning solvent. Keep a fire extinguisher, rated for gasoline fires, handy in any case.

Much of the labor charge for repairs made by dealers is for the removal and disassembly of other parts to reach the defective unit. It is frequently possible to perform the preliminary operations yourself and then take the defective unit in to the dealer for repair, at considerable savings.

Once you have decided to tackle the job yourself, make sure you locate the appropriate section in this manual, and read it entirely. Study the illustrations and text until you have a good idea of what is involved in completing the job satisfactorily. If special tools are required, make arrangements to get them before you start. Also, purchase any known defective parts prior to starting on the procedure. It is frustrating and time-consuming to get partially into a job and then be unable to complete it.

Simple wiring checks can be easily made at home, but knowledge of electronics is almost a necessity for performing tests with complicated electronic testing gear.

During disassembly of parts keep a few general cautions in mind. Force is rarely needed to get things apart. If parts are a tight fit, like a bearing in a case, there is usually a tool designed to separate them. Never use a screwdriver to pry apart parts with machined surfaces such as cylinder head and valve cover. You will mar the surfaces and end up with leaks.

Make diagrams wherever similar-appearing parts are found. You may think you can remember where everything came from — but mistakes are costly. There is also the possibility you may get sidetracked and not return to work for days or even weeks — in which interval, carefully laid out parts may have become disturbed.

Tag all similar internal parts for location, and mark all mating parts for position. Record number and thickness of any shims as they are removed. Small parts such as bolts can be identified by placing them in plastic sandwich bags that are sealed and labeled with masking tape.

Wiring should be tagged with masking tape and marked as each wire is removed. Again, do not rely on memory alone.

When working under the vehicle, do not trust a hydraulic or mechanical jack to hold the vehicle up by itself. Always use jackstands. See **Figure 1**.

Disconnect battery ground cable before working near electrical connections and before disconnecting wires. Never run the engine with the battery disconnected; the alternator could be seriously damaged.

Protect finished surfaces from physical damage or corrosion. Keep gasoline and brake fluid off painted surfaces.

Frozen or very tight bolts and screws can often be loosened by soaking with penetrating oil like Liquid Wrench or WD-40, then sharply striking the bolt head a few times with a hammer and punch (or screwdriver for screws). Avoid heat unless absolutely necessary, since it may melt, warp, or remove the temper from many parts.

Avoid flames or sparks when working near a charging battery or flammable liquids, such as brake fluid or gasoline.

No parts, except those assembled with a press fit, require unusual force during assembly. If a part is hard to remove or install, find out why before proceeding.

Cover all openings after removing parts to keep dirt, small tools, etc., from falling in.

When assembling two parts, start all fasteners, then tighten evenly.

The clutch plate, wiring connections, brake shoes, drums, pads, and discs should be kept clean and free of grease and oil.

When assembling parts, be sure all shims and washers are replaced exactly as they came out.

Whenever a rotating part butts against a stationary part, look for a shim or washer. Use new gaskets if there is any doubt about the condition of old ones. Generally, you should apply gasket cement to one mating surface only, so the parts may be easily disassembled in the future. A thin coat of oil on gaskets helps them seal effectively.

Heavy grease can be used to hold small parts in place if they tend to fall out during assembly. However, keep grease and oil away from electrical, clutch, and brake components.

High spots may be sanded off a piston with sandpaper, but emery cloth and oil do a much more professional job.

Carburetors are best cleaned by disassembling them and soaking the parts in a commercial carburetor cleaner. Never soak gaskets and rubber parts in these cleaners. Never use wire to clean out jets and air passages; they are easily damaged. Use compressed air to blow out the carburetor, but only if the float has been removed first.

Take your time and do the job right. Do not forget that a newly rebuilt engine must be broken in the same as a new one. Refer to your owner's manual for the proper break-in procedures.

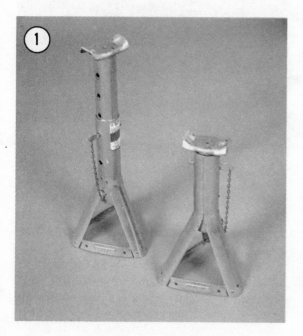

SAFETY FIRST

Professional mechanics can work for years and never sustain a serious injury. If you observe a few rules of common sense and safety, you can enjoy many safe hours servicing your vehicle. You could hurt yourself or damage the vehicle if you ignore these rules.

1. Never use gasoline as a cleaning solvent.
2. Never smoke or use a torch in the vicinity of

flammable liquids such as cleaning solvent in open containers.

3. Never smoke or use a torch in an area where batteries are being charged. Highly explosive hydrogen gas is formed during the charging process.

4. Use the proper sized wrenches to avoid damage to nuts and injury to yourself.

5. When loosening a tight or stuck nut, be guided by what would happen if the wrench should slip. Protect yourself accordingly.

6. Keep your work area clean and uncluttered.

7. Wear safety goggles during all operations involving drilling, grinding, or use of a cold chisel.

8. Never use worn tools.

9. Keep a fire extinguisher handy and be sure it is rated for gasoline (Class B) and electrical (Class C) fires.

EXPENDABLE SUPPLIES

Certain expendable supplies are necessary. These include grease, oil, gasket cement, wiping rags, cleaning solvent, and distilled water. Also, special locking compounds, silicone lubricants, and engine cleaners may be useful. Cleaning solvent is available at most service stations and distilled water for the battery is available at most supermarkets.

SHOP TOOLS

For proper servicing, you will need an assortment of ordinary hand tools (**Figure 2**).

As a minimum, these include:

a. Combination wrenches
b. Sockets
c. Plastic mallet
d. Small hammer
e. Snap ring pliers
f. Gas pliers
g. Phillips screwdrivers
h. Slot (common) screwdrivers
i. Feeler gauges
j. Spark plug gauge
k. Spark plug wrench
l. Torque wrench

Special tools necessary are shown in the chapters covering the particular repair in which they are used.

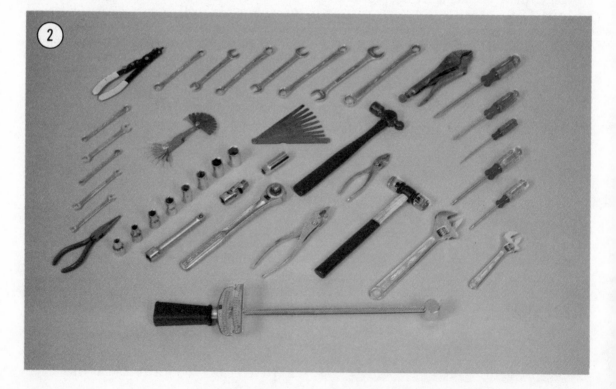

Engine tune-up and troubleshooting procedures require other special tools and equipment. These are described in detail in the following sections.

EMERGENCY TOOL KIT

A small emergency tool kit kept in the trunk is handy for road emergencies which otherwise could leave you stranded. The tools listed below and shown in **Figure 3** will let you handle most roadside repairs.

a. Combination wrenches

b. Crescent (adjustable) wrench

c. Screwdrivers — common and Phillips

d. Pliers — conventional (gas) and needle nose

e. Vise Grips

f. Hammer — plastic and metal

g. Small container of waterless hand cleaner

h. Rags for cleanup

i. Silver waterproof sealing tape (duct tape)

j. Flashlight

k. Emergency road flares — at least four

l. Spare drive belts (cooling fan, alternator, etc.)

TROUBLESHOOTING AND TUNE-UP EQUIPMENT

Voltmeter, Ohmmeter, and Ammeter

For testing the ignition or electrical system, a good voltmeter is required. For automotive use, an instrument covering 0-20 volts is satisfac-

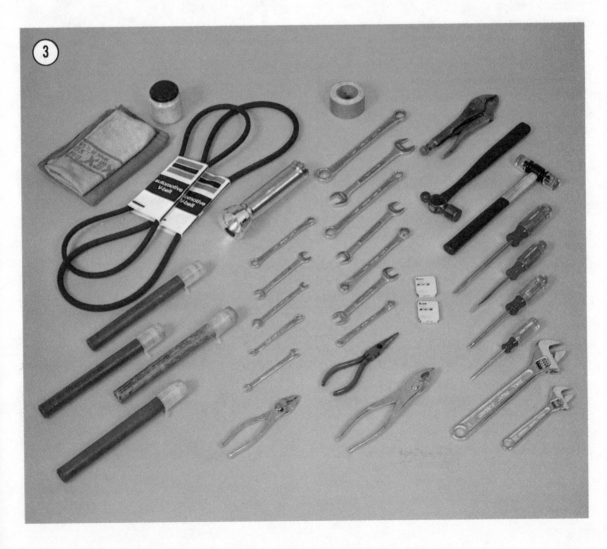

tory. One which also has a 0-2 volt scale is necessary for testing relays, points, or individual contacts where voltage drops are much smaller. Accuracy should be ± ½ volt.

An ohmmeter measures electrical resistance. This instrument is useful for checking continuity (open and short circuits), and testing fuses and lights.

The ammeter measures electrical current. Ammeters for automotive use should cover 0-50 amperes and 0-250 amperes. These are useful for checking battery charging and starting current.

Several inexpensive VOM's (volt-ohm-milliammeter) combine all three instruments into one which fits easily in any tool box. See **Figure 4**. However, the ammeter ranges are usually too small for automotive work.

Hydrometer

The hydrometer gives a useful indication of battery condition and charge by measuring the specific gravity of the electrolyte in each cell. See **Figure 5**. Complete details on use and interpretation of readings are provided in the electrical chapter.

Compression Tester

The compression tester measures the compression pressure built up in each cylinder. The results, when properly interpreted, can indicate general cylinder and valve condition. See **Figure 6**.

Most compression testers have long flexible extensions built-in or as accessories. Such an extension is necessary since the spark plug holes are deep inside the metal air cooling covers.

Vacuum Gauge

The vacuum gauge (**Figure 7**) is one of the easiest instruments to use, but one of the most difficult for the inexperienced mechanic to interpret. The results, when interpreted with other findings, can provide valuable clues to possible trouble.

To use the vacuum gauge, connect it to a vacuum hose that goes to the intake manifold. Attach it either directly to the hose or to a T-fitting installed into the hose.

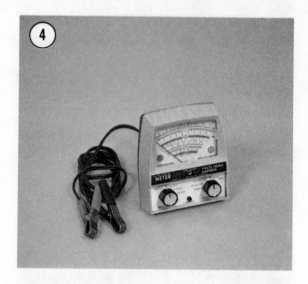

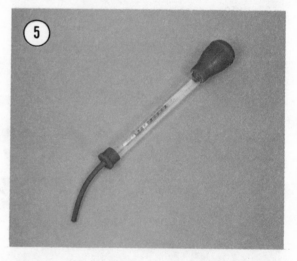

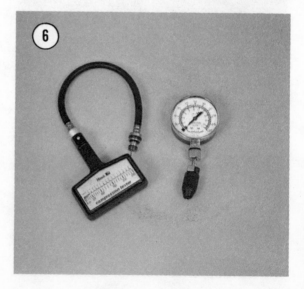

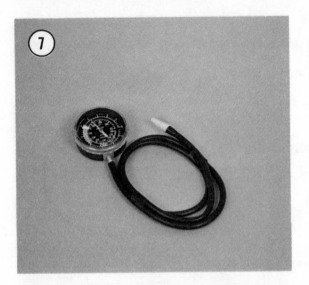

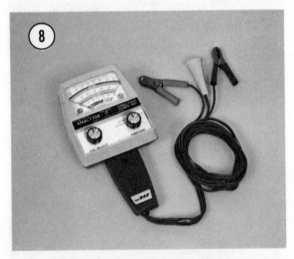

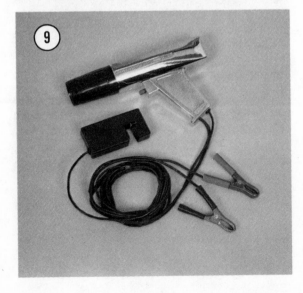

NOTE: *Subtract one inch from the reading for every 1,000 ft. elevation.*

Fuel Pressure Gauge

This instrument is invaluable for evaluating fuel pump performance. Fuel system troubleshooting procedures in this manual use a fuel pressure gauge. Usually a vacuum gauge and fuel pressure gauge are combined.

Dwell Meter (Contact Breaker Point Ignition Only)

A dwell meter measures the distance in degrees of cam rotation that the breaker points remain closed while the engine is running. Since this angle is determined by breaker point gap, dwell angle is an accurate indication of breaker point gap.

Many tachometers intended for tuning and testing incorporate a dwell meter as well. See **Figure 8**. Follow the manufacturer's instructions to measure dwell.

Tachometer

A tachometer is necessary for tuning. See **Figure 8**. Ignition timing and carburetor adjustments must be performed at the specified idle speed. The best instrument for this purpose is one with a low range of 0-1,000 or 0-2,000 rpm for setting idle, and a high range of 0-4,000 or more for setting ignition timing at 3,000 rpm. Extended range (0-6,000 or 0-8,000 rpm) instruments lack accuracy at lower speeds. The instrument should be capable of detecting changes of 25 rpm on the low range.

Strobe Timing Light

This instrument is necessary for tuning, as it permits very accurate ignition timing. The light flashes at precisely the same instant that No. 1 cylinder fires, at which time the timing marks on the engine should align. Refer to Chapter Three for exact location of the timing marks for your engine.

Suitable lights range from inexpensive neon bulb types ($2-3) to powerful xenon strobe lights ($20-40). See **Figure 9**. Neon timing lights are difficult to see and must be used in dimly lit areas. Xenon strobe timing lights can be used

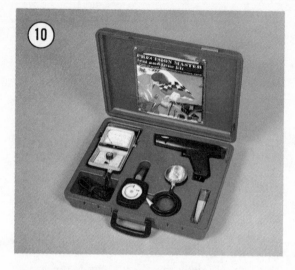

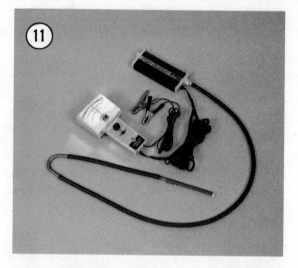

outside in bright sunlight. Both types work on
this vehicle; use according to the manufacturer's instructions.

Tune-up Kits

Many manufacturers offer kits that combine
several useful instruments. Some come in a convenient carry case and are usually less expensive
than purchasing one instrument at a time.
Figure 10 shows one of the kits that is available.
The prices vary with the number of instruments
included in the kit.

Exhaust Gas Analyzer

Of all instruments described here, this is the
least likely to be owned by a home mechanic.
This instrument samples the exhaust gases from
the tailpipe and measures the thermal conductivity of the exhaust gas. Since different
gases conduct heat at varying rates, thermal
conductivity of the exhaust is a good indication
of gases present.

An exhaust gas analyzer is vital for accurately checking the effectiveness of exhaust
emission control adjustments. They are relatively expensive to buy ($70 and up), but must
be considered essential for the owner/mechanic

to comply with today's emission laws. See
Figure 11.

Fire Extinguisher

A fire extinguisher is a necessity when working on a vehicle. It should be rated for both
Class B (flammable liquids — gasoline, oil,
paint, etc.) and *Class C* (electrical — wiring,
etc.) type fires. It should always be kept within
reach. See **Figure 12**.

CHAPTER TWO

TROUBLESHOOTING

Troubleshooting can be a relatively simple matter if it is done logically. The first step in any troubleshooting procedure must be defining the symptoms as closely as possible. Subsequent steps involve testing and analyzing areas which could cause the symptoms. A haphazard approach may eventually find the trouble, but in terms of wasted time and unnecessary parts replacement, it can be very costly.

The troubleshooting procedures in this chapter analyze typical symptoms and show logical methods of isolation. These are not the only methods. There may be several approaches to a problem, but all methods must have one thing in common — a logical, systematic approach.

STARTING SYSTEM

The starting system consists of the starter motor and the starter solenoid. The ignition key controls the starter solenoid, which mechanically engages the starter with the engine flywheel, and supplies electrical current to turn the starter motor.

Starting system troubles are relatively easy to find. In most cases, the trouble is a loose or dirty electrical connection. **Figures 1 and 2** provide routines for finding the trouble.

CHARGING SYSTEM

The charging system consists of the alternator (or generator on older vehicles), voltage regulator, and battery. A drive belt driven by the engine crankshaft turns the alternator which produces electrical energy to charge the battery. As engine speed varies, the voltage from the alternator varies. A voltage regulator controls the charging current to the battery and maintains the voltage to the vehicle's electrical system at safe levels. A warning light or gauge on the instrument panel signals the driver when charging is not taking place. Refer to **Figure 3** for a typical charging system.

Complete troubleshooting of the charging system requires test equipment and skills which the average home mechanic does not possess. However, there are a few tests which can be done to pinpoint most troubles.

Charging system trouble may stem from a defective alternator (or generator), voltage regulator, battery, or drive belt. It may also be caused by something as simple as incorrect drive belt tension. The following are symptoms of typical problems you may encounter.

1. *Battery dies frequently, even though the warning lamp indicates no discharge* — This can be caused by a drive belt that is slightly too

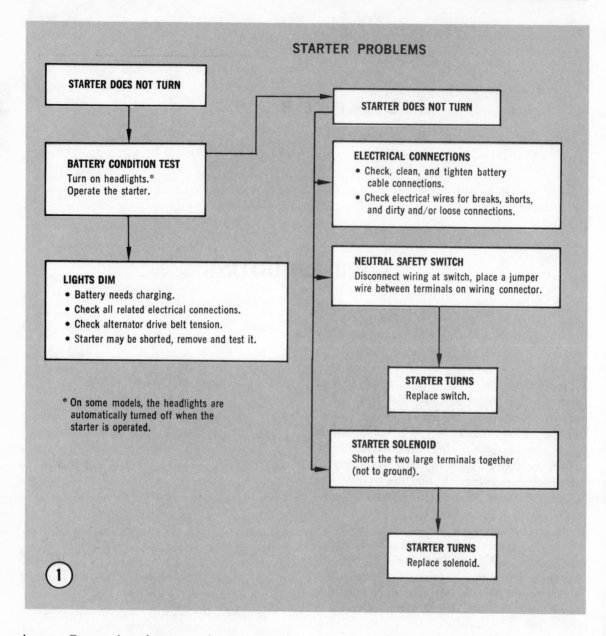

STARTER PROBLEMS

STARTER DOES NOT TURN

BATTERY CONDITION TEST
Turn on headlights.*
Operate the starter.

LIGHTS DIM
• Battery needs charging.
• Check all related electrical connections.
• Check alternator drive belt tension.
• Starter may be shorted, remove and test it.

* On some models, the headlights are automatically turned off when the starter is operated.

STARTER DOES NOT TURN

ELECTRICAL CONNECTIONS
• Check, clean, and tighten battery cable connections.
• Check electrical wires for breaks, shorts, and dirty and/or loose connections.

NEUTRAL SAFETY SWITCH
Disconnect wiring at switch, place a jumper wire between terminals on wiring connector.

STARTER TURNS
Replace switch.

STARTER SOLENOID
Short the two large terminals together (not to ground).

STARTER TURNS
Replace solenoid.

①

loose. Grasp the alternator (or generator) pulley and try to turn it. If the pulley can be turned without moving the belt, the drive belt is too loose. As a rule, keep the belt tight enough that it can be deflected about ½ in. under moderate thumb pressure between the pulleys (**Figure 4**). The battery may also be at fault; test the battery condition.

2. *Charging system warning lamp does not come on when ignition switch is turned on* — This may indicate a defective ignition switch, battery, voltage regulator, or lamp. First try to

start the vehicle. If it doesn't start, check the ignition switch and battery. If the car starts, remove the warning lamp; test it for continuity with an ohmmeter or substitute a new lamp. If the lamp is good, locate the voltage regulator and make sure it is properly grounded (try tightening the mounting screws). Also, the alternator (or generator) brushes may not be making contact. Test the alternator (or generator) and voltage regulator.

3. *Alternator (or generator) warning lamp comes on and stays on* — This usually indicates

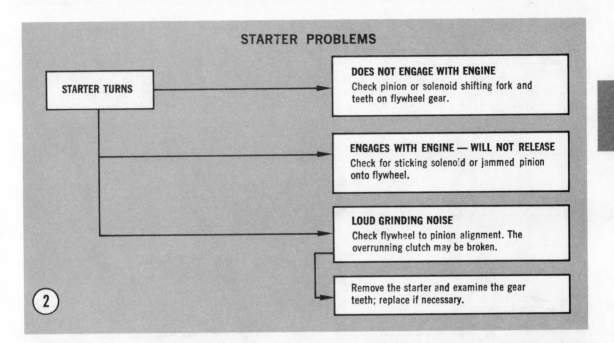

STARTER PROBLEMS

STARTER TURNS

DOES NOT ENGAGE WITH ENGINE
Check pinion or solenoid shifting fork and teeth on flywheel gear.

ENGAGES WITH ENGINE — WILL NOT RELEASE
Check for sticking solenoid or jammed pinion onto flywheel.

LOUD GRINDING NOISE
Check flywheel to pinion alignment. The overrunning clutch may be broken.

Remove the starter and examine the gear teeth; replace if necessary.

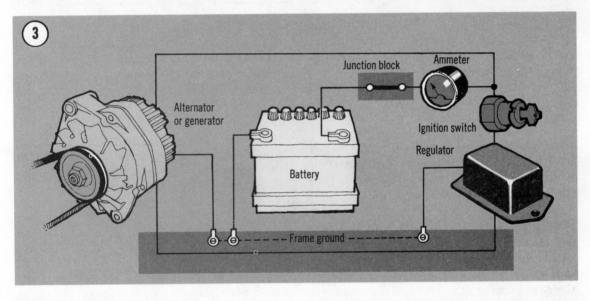

that no charging is taking place. First check drive belt tension (**Figure 4**). Then check battery condition, and check all wiring connections in the charging system. If this does not locate the trouble, check the alternator (or generator) and voltage regulator.

4. *Charging system warning lamp flashes on and off intermittently* — This usually indicates the charging system is working intermittently. Check the drive belt tension (**Figure 4**), and check all electrical connections in the charging

system. Check the alternator (or generator). *On generators only*, check the condition of the commutator.

5. *Battery requires frequent additions of water, or lamps require frequent replacement* — The alternator (or generator) is probably overcharging the battery. The voltage regulator is probably at fault.

6. *Excessive noise from the alternator (or generator)* — Check for loose mounting brackets and bolts. The problem may also be

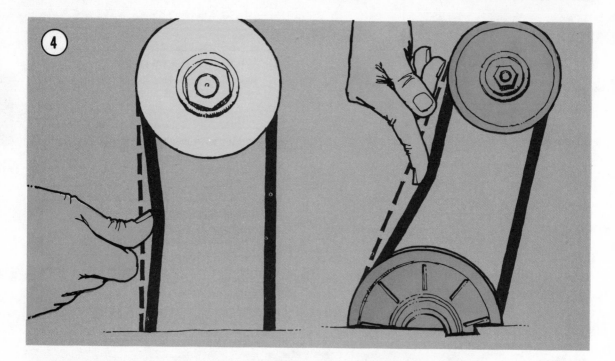

worn bearings or the need of lubrication in some cases. If an alternator whines, a shorted diode may be indicated.

IGNITION SYSTEM

The ignition system may be either a conventional contact breaker type or an electronic ignition. See electrical chapter to determine which type you have. **Figures 5 and 6** show simplified diagrams of each type.

Most problems involving failure to start, poor performance, or rough running stem from trouble in the ignition system, particularly in contact breaker systems. Many novice troubleshooters get into trouble when they assume that these symptoms point to the fuel system instead of the ignition system.

Ignition system troubles may be roughly divided between those affecting only one cylinder and those affecting all cylinders. If the trouble affects only one cylinder, it can only be in the spark plug, spark plug wire, or portion of the distributor associated with that cylinder. If the trouble affects all cylinders (weak spark or no spark), then the trouble is in the ignition coil, rotor, distributor, or associated wiring.

In order to get maximum spark, the ignition coil must be wired correctly. Make sure that the double wire from the battery is attached to terminal No. 15 on the ignition coil and that the single wire from the distributor is attached to terminal No. 1 on the ignition coil.

The troubleshooting procedures outlined in **Figure 7** (breaker point ignition) or **Figure 8** (electronic ignition) will help you isolate ignition problems fast. Of course, they assume that the battery is in good enough condition to crank the engine over at its normal rate.

ENGINE PERFORMANCE

A number of factors can make the engine difficult or impossible to start, or cause rough running, poor performance and so on. The majority of novice troubleshooters immediately suspect the carburetor or fuel injection system. In the majority of cases, though, the trouble exists in the ignition system.

The troubleshooting procedures outlined in **Figures 9 through 14** will help you solve the majority of engine starting troubles in a systematic manner.

Some tests of the ignition system require running the engine with a spark plug or ignition coil wire disconnected. The safest way to do this is to disconnect the wire with the engine

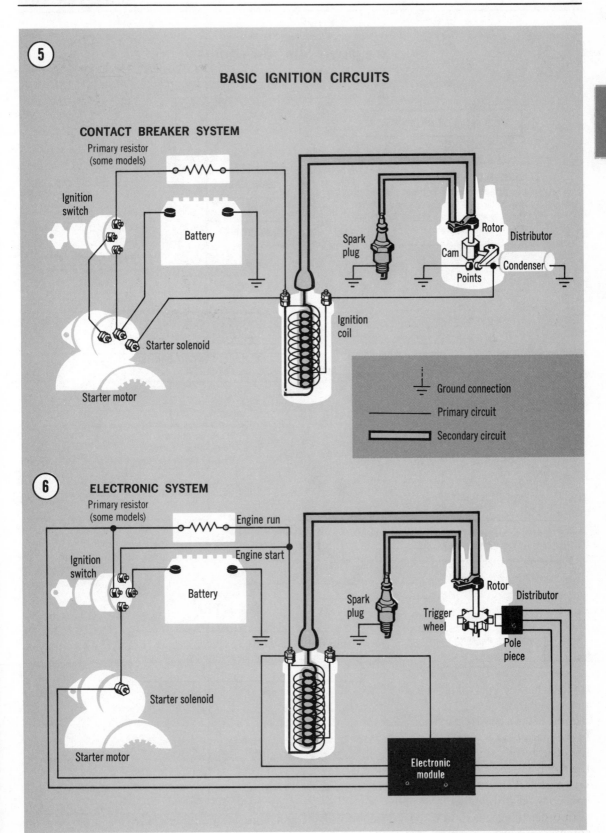

BASIC IGNITION CIRCUITS

⑤

CONTACT BREAKER SYSTEM

Primary resistor (some models)

Ignition switch

Battery

Spark plug

Rotor

Distributor

Cam

Points

Condenser

Ignition coil

Starter solenoid

Starter motor

Ground connection

Primary circuit

Secondary circuit

⑥

ELECTRONIC SYSTEM

Primary resistor (some models)

Ignition switch

Engine run

Engine start

Battery

Spark plug

Rotor

Distributor

Trigger wheel

Pole piece

Starter solenoid

Starter motor

Electronic module

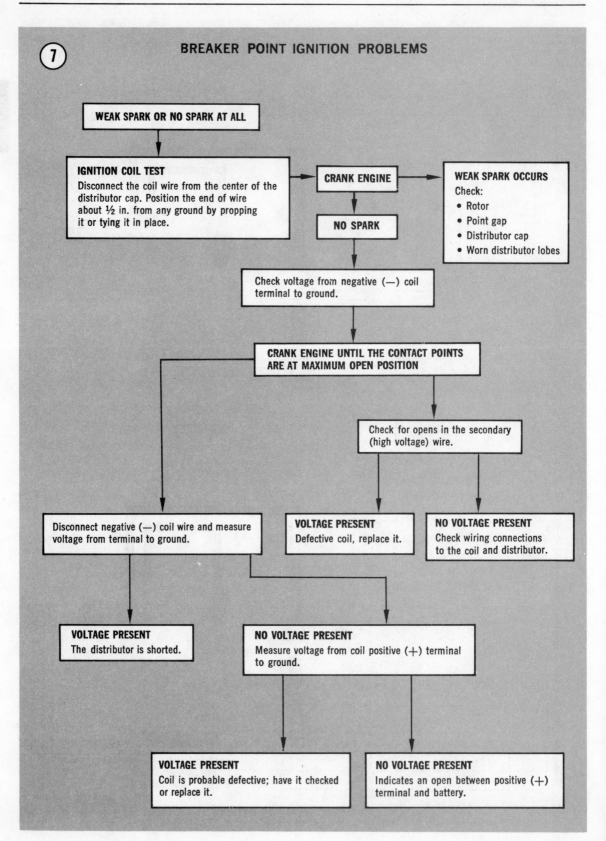

BREAKER POINT IGNITION PROBLEMS

⑦

WEAK SPARK OR NO SPARK AT ALL

IGNITION COIL TEST
Disconnect the coil wire from the center of the distributor cap. Position the end of wire about ½ in. from any ground by propping it or tying it in place.

CRANK ENGINE

NO SPARK

WEAK SPARK OCCURS
Check:
• Rotor
• Point gap
• Distributor cap
• Worn distributor lobes

Check voltage from negative (—) coil terminal to ground.

CRANK ENGINE UNTIL THE CONTACT POINTS ARE AT MAXIMUM OPEN POSITION

Check for opens in the secondary (high voltage) wire.

Disconnect negative (—) coil wire and measure voltage from terminal to ground.

VOLTAGE PRESENT
Defective coil, replace it.

NO VOLTAGE PRESENT
Check wiring connections to the coil and distributor.

VOLTAGE PRESENT
The distributor is shorted.

NO VOLTAGE PRESENT
Measure voltage from coil positive (+) terminal to ground.

VOLTAGE PRESENT
Coil is probable defective; have it checked or replace it.

NO VOLTAGE PRESENT
Indicates an open between positive (+) terminal and battery.

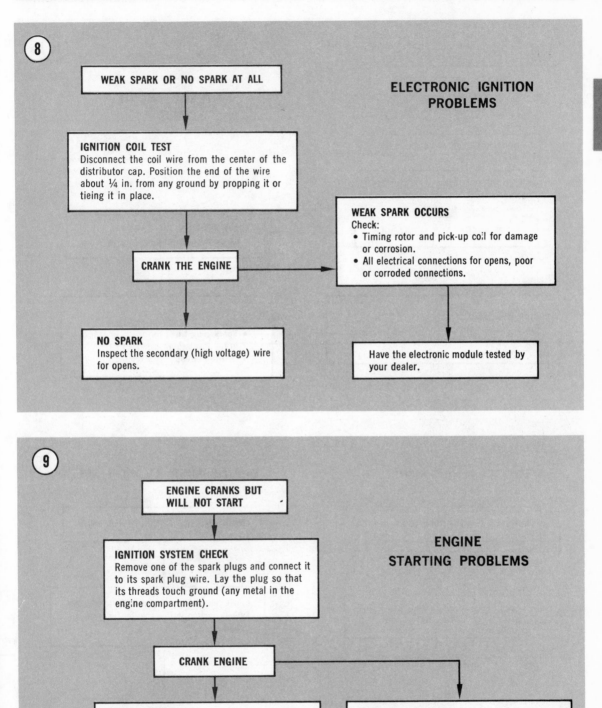

8

WEAK SPARK OR NO SPARK AT ALL

ELECTRONIC IGNITION PROBLEMS

2

IGNITION COIL TEST
Disconnect the coil wire from the center of the distributor cap. Position the end of the wire about ¼ in. from any ground by propping it or tieing it in place.

CRANK THE ENGINE

WEAK SPARK OCCURS
Check:
• Timing rotor and pick-up coil for damage or corrosion.
• All electrical connections for opens, poor or corroded connections.

NO SPARK
Inspect the secondary (high voltage) wire for opens.

Have the electronic module tested by your dealer.

9

ENGINE CRANKS BUT WILL NOT START

ENGINE STARTING PROBLEMS

IGNITION SYSTEM CHECK
Remove one of the spark plugs and connect it to its spark plug wire. Lay the plug so that its threads touch ground (any metal in the engine compartment).

CRANK ENGINE

SPARK OCCURS
Check:
• Fouled spark plugs.
• Spark plug wires to the wrong cylinder.
• Fuel system, refer to **Fuel System** section in this chapter for further details.

NO SPARK
Refer to **Ignition System** section in this chapter for further details.

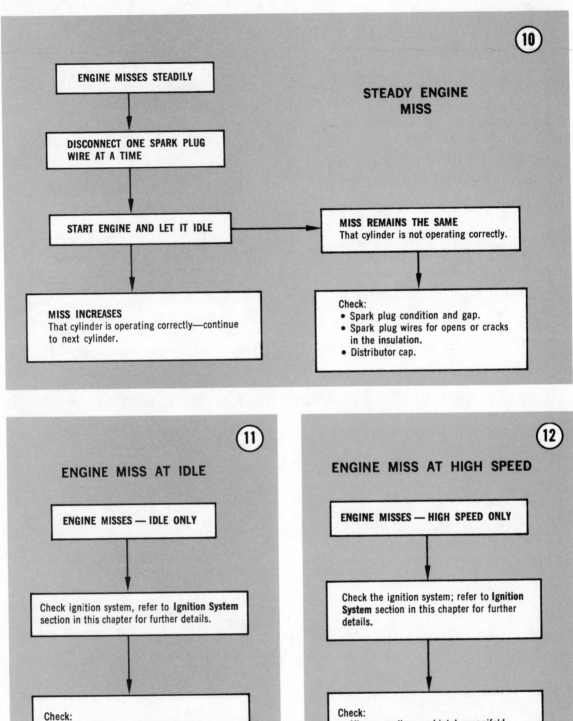

⑩

ENGINE MISSES STEADILY

STEADY ENGINE
MISS

DISCONNECT ONE SPARK PLUG
WIRE AT A TIME

START ENGINE AND LET IT IDLE → MISS REMAINS THE SAME
That cylinder is not operating correctly.

MISS INCREASES
That cylinder is operating correctly—continue
to next cylinder.

Check:
• Spark plug condition and gap.
• Spark plug wires for opens or cracks
  in the insulation.
• Distributor cap.

⑪

ENGINE MISS AT IDLE

ENGINE MISSES — IDLE ONLY

Check ignition system, refer to **Ignition System**
section in this chapter for further details.

Check:
• Carburetor idle adjustment.
• Vacuum lines and intake manifold for leaks.
  Run a compression test; one cylinder may
  have a defective valve or broken ring(s).

⑫

ENGINE MISS AT HIGH SPEED

ENGINE MISSES — HIGH SPEED ONLY

Check the ignition system; refer to **Ignition
System** section in this chapter for further
details.

Check:
• All vacuum lines and intake manifold
  for leaks.
• Fuel system, refer to **Fuel System** section in
  this chapter for further details.

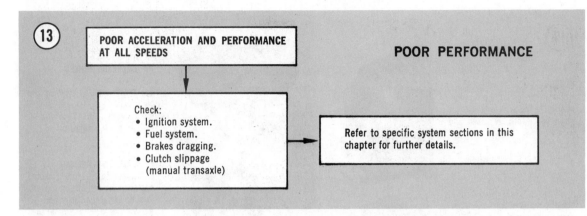

⑬ POOR ACCELERATION AND PERFORMANCE AT ALL SPEEDS

POOR PERFORMANCE

Check:
- Ignition system.
- Fuel system.
- Brakes dragging.
- Clutch slippage (manual transaxle)

Refer to specific system sections in this chapter for further details.

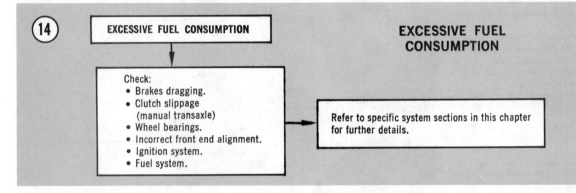

⑭ EXCESSIVE FUEL CONSUMPTION

EXCESSIVE FUEL CONSUMPTION

Check:
- Brakes dragging.
- Clutch slippage (manual transaxle)
- Wheel bearings.
- Incorrect front end alignment.
- Ignition system.
- Fuel system.

Refer to specific system sections in this chapter for further details.

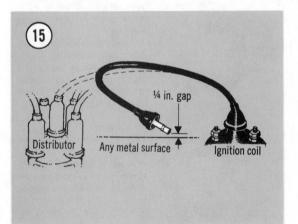

⑮ ¼ in. gap

Distributor   Any metal surface   Ignition coil

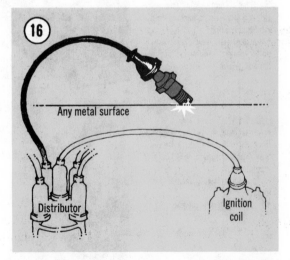

⑯ Any metal surface

Distributor   Ignition coil

stopped, then prop the end of the wire next to a metal surface as shown in **Figures 15 and 16**.

WARNING
Never disconnect a spark plug or ignition coil wire while the engine is running. The high voltage in an ignition system, particularly the newer high-energy electronic ignition systems could cause serious injury or even death.

Spark plug condition is an important indication of engine performance. Spark plugs in a properly operating engine will have slightly pitted electrodes, and a light tan insulator tip. **Figure 17** shows a normal plug, and a number of others which indicate trouble in their respective cylinders.

⑰

NORMAL
- Appearance—Firing tip has deposits of light gray to light tan.
- Can be cleaned, regapped and reused.

CARBON FOULED
- Appearance—Dull, dry black with fluffy carbon deposits on the insulator tip, electrode and exposed shell.
- Caused by—Fuel/air mixture too rich, plug heat range too cold, weak ignition system, dirty air cleaner, faulty automatic choke or excessive idling.
- Can be cleaned, regapped and reused.

OIL FOULED
- Appearance—Wet black deposits on insulator and exposed shell.
- Caused by—Excessive oil entering the combustion chamber through worn rings, pistons, valve guides or bearings.
- Replace with new plugs (use a hotter plug if engine is not repaired).

LEAD FOULED
- Appearance — Yellow insulator deposits (may sometimes be dark gray, black or tan in color) on the insulator tip.
- Caused by—Highly leaded gasoline.
- Replace with new plugs.

LEAD FOULED
- Appearance—Yellow glazed deposits indicating melted lead deposits due to hard acceleration.
- Caused by—Highly leaded gasoline.
- Replace with new plugs.

OIL AND LEAD FOULED
- Appearance—Glazed yellow deposits with a slight brownish tint on the insulator tip and ground electrode.
- Replace with new plugs.

FUEL ADDITIVE RESIDUE
- Appearance — Brown-colored, hardened ash deposits on the insulator tip and ground electrode.
- Caused by—Fuel and/or oil additives.
- Replace with new plugs.

WORN
- Appearance — Severely worn or eroded electrodes.
- Caused by—Normal wear or unusual oil and/or fuel additives.
- Replace with new plugs.

PREIGNITION
- Appearance — Melted ground electrode.
- Caused by—Overadvanced ignition timing, inoperative ignition advance mechanism, too low of a fuel octane rating, lean fuel/air mixture or carbon deposits in combustion chamber.

PREIGNITION
- Appearance—Melted center electrode.
- Caused by—Abnormal combustion due to overadvanced ignition timing or incorrect advance, too low of a fuel octane rating, lean fuel/air mixture, or carbon deposits in combustion chamber.
- Correct engine problem and replace with new plugs.

INCORRECT HEAT RANGE
- Appearance—Melted center electrode and white blistered insulator tip.
- Caused by—Incorrect plug heat range selection.
- Replace with new plugs.

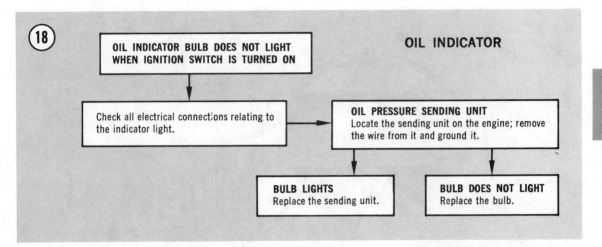

2

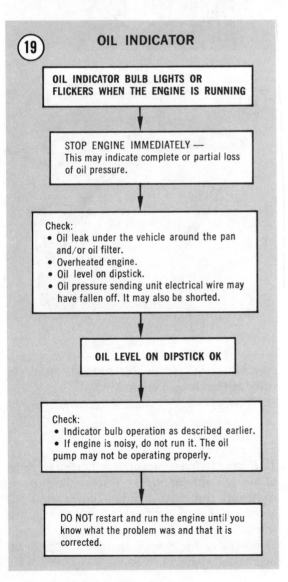

ENGINE OIL
PRESSURE LIGHT

Proper oil pressure to the engine is vital. If oil pressure is insufficient, the engine can destroy itself in a comparatively short time.

The oil pressure warning circuit monitors oil pressure constantly. If pressure drops below a predetermined level, the light comes on.

Obviously, it is vital for the warning circuit to be working to signal low oil pressure. Each time you turn on the ignition, but before you start the vehicle, the warning light should come on. If it doesn't, there is trouble in the warning circuit, not the oil pressure system. See **Figure 18** to troubleshoot the warning circuit.

Once the engine is running, the warning light should stay off. If the warning light comes on or acts erratically while the engine is running there is trouble with the engine oil pressure system. *Stop the engine immediately*. Refer to **Figure 19** for possible causes of the problem.

FUEL SYSTEM
(CARBURETTED)

Fuel system problems must be isolated to the fuel pump (mechanical or electric), fuel lines, fuel filter, or carburetor(s). These procedures assume the ignition system is working properly and is correctly adjusted.

1. *Engine will not start* — First make sure that fuel is being delivered to the carburetor. Remove the air cleaner, look into the carburetor throat, and operate the accelerator

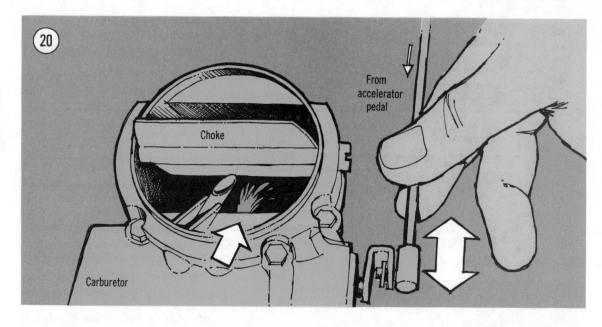

linkage several times. There should be a stream of fuel from the accelerator pump discharge tube each time the accelerator linkage is depressed (**Figure 20**). If not, check fuel pump delivery (described later), float valve, and float adjustment. If the engine will not start, check the automatic choke parts for sticking or damage. If necessary, rebuild or replace the carburetor.

2. *Engine runs at fast idle* — Usually this is caused by a defective automatic choke heater element. Ensure that the heater wire is connected and making good contact. Check the idle speed, idle mixture, and decel valve (if equipped) adjustment.

3. *Rough idle or engine miss with frequent stalling* — Check idle mixture and idle speed adjustments.

Poor idle may also be caused by a defective or dirty electromagnetic cutoff valve. Check that the electromagnetic cutoff valve wire is connected to the valve (on the carburetor) and making good contact. If it is, turn the ignition switch on, disconnect the wire and touch it to the valve terminal. If the valve is working, there should be a slight click heard each time the wire touches. If the valve is defective, turn the small setscrew on the end of the valve fully counterclockwise. This permanently opens the valve,

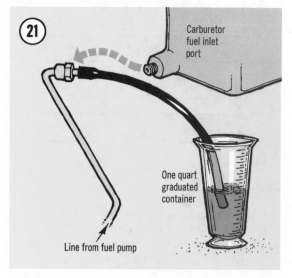

permitting the car to idle properly until the valve can be cleaned or replaced.

NOTE: *The engine may "diesel" in this condition. Replace the valve as soon as possible.*

4. *Engine "diesels" (continues to run) when ignition is switched off* — Check idle mixture (probably too rich), ignition timing, and idle speed (probably too fast). Check the throttle solenoid (if equipped) and electromagnetic cutoff valve for proper operation. Check for overheated engine.

5. *Stumbling when accelerating from idle* —
Check the idle speed and mixture adjustments.
Check the accelerator pump.

6. *Engine misses at high speed or lacks power*
— This indicates possible fuel starvation.
Check fuel pump pressure and capacity as
described in this chapter. Check float needle
valves. Check for a clogged fuel filter or air
cleaner.

7. *Black exhaust smoke* — This indicates a
badly overrich mixture. Check idle mixture and
idle speed adjustment. Check choke setting.
Check for excessive fuel pump pressure, leaky
floats, or worn needle valves.

8. *Excessive fuel consumption* — Check for
overrich mixture. Make sure choke mechanism
works properly. Check idle mixture and idle
speed. Check for excessive fuel pump pressure,
leaky floats, or worn float needle valves.

FUEL SYSTEM
(FUEL INJECTED)

Troubleshooting a fuel injection system requires more thought, experience, and know-
how than any other part of the vehicle. A
logical approach and proper test equipment are
essential in order to successfully find and fix
these troubles.

It is best to leave fuel injection troubles to
your dealer. In order to isolate a problem to the
injection system make sure that the fuel pump
is operating properly. Check its performance as
described later in this section. Also make sure
that fuel filter and air cleaner are not clogged.

FUEL PUMP TEST
(MECHANICAL AND ELECTRIC)

1. Disconnect the fuel inlet line where it enters
the carburetor or fuel injection system.

2. Fit a rubber hose over the fuel line so fuel
can be directed into a graduated container with
about one quart capacity. See **Figure 21**.

3. To avoid accidental starting of the engine,
disconnect the secondary coil wire from the
coil.

4. Crank the engine for about 30 seconds.

5. If the fuel pump supplies the specified
amount (refer to the fuel chapter later in this

book), the trouble may be in the carburetor or
fuel injection system. The fuel injection system
should be tested by your dealer.

6. If there is no fuel present or the pump cannot supply the specified amount, either the fuel
pump is defective or there is an obstruction in
the fuel line. Replace the fuel pump and/or inspect the fuel lines for air leaks or obstructions.

7. Also pressure test the fuel pump by installing a T-fitting in the fuel line between the fuel
pump and the carburetor. Connect a fuel pressure gauge to the fitting with a short tube
(**Figure 22**).

8. Reconnect the secondary coil wire, start the
engine, and record the pressure. Refer to the fuel
chapter later in this book for the correct pressure. If the pressure varies from that specified,
the pump should be replaced.

9. Stop the engine. The pressure should drop
off very slowly. If it drops off rapidly, the
outlet valve in the pump is leaking and the
pump should be replaced.

EMISSION CONTROL SYSTEMS

Major emission control systems used on
nearly all U.S. models include the following:

 a. Positive crankcase ventilation (PCV)

 b. Thermostatic air cleaner

 c. Air injection reaction (AIR)

 d. Fuel evaporation control

 e. Exhaust gas recirculation (EGR)

Emission control systems vary considerably
from model to model. Individual models contain variations of the five systems described
here. In addition, they may include other
special systems. Use the index to find specific
emission control components in other chapters.

Many of the systems and components are
factory set and sealed. Without special expensive test equipment, it is impossible to adjust
the systems to meet state and federal requirements.

Troubleshooting can also be difficult without
special equipment. The procedures described
below will help you find emission control parts
which have failed, but repairs may have to be
entrusted to a dealer or other properly equipped
repair shop.

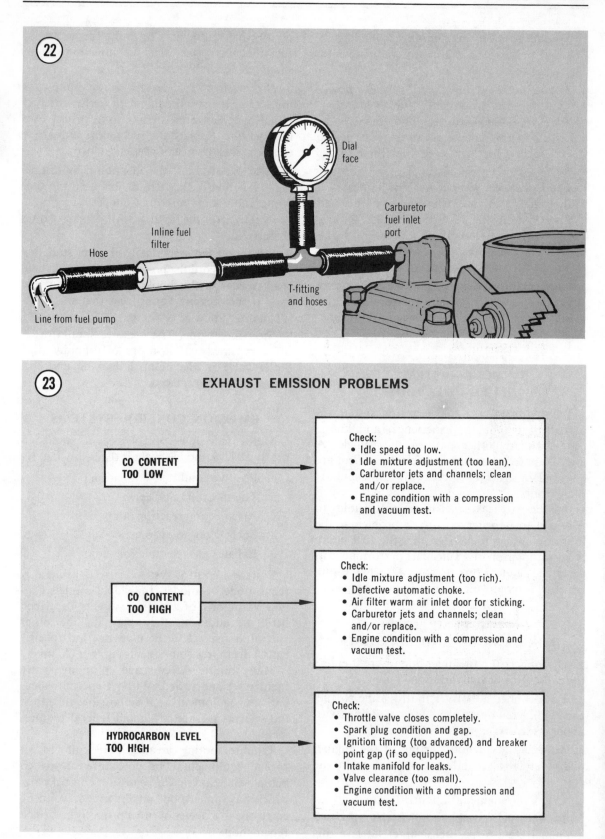

22

Dial face

Carburetor fuel inlet port

Inline fuel filter

Hose

T-fitting and hoses

Line from fuel pump

23

EXHAUST EMISSION PROBLEMS

CO CONTENT TOO LOW →

Check:
- Idle speed too low.
- Idle mixture adjustment (too lean).
- Carburetor jets and channels; clean and/or replace.
- Engine condition with a compression and vacuum test.

CO CONTENT TOO HIGH →

Check:
- Idle mixture adjustment (too rich).
- Defective automatic choke.
- Air filter warm air inlet door for sticking.
- Carburetor jets and channels; clean and/or replace.
- Engine condition with a compression and vacuum test.

HYDROCARBON LEVEL TOO HIGH →

Check:
- Throttle valve closes completely.
- Spark plug condition and gap.
- Ignition timing (too advanced) and breaker point gap (if so equipped).
- Intake manifold for leaks.
- Valve clearance (too small).
- Engine condition with a compression and vacuum test.

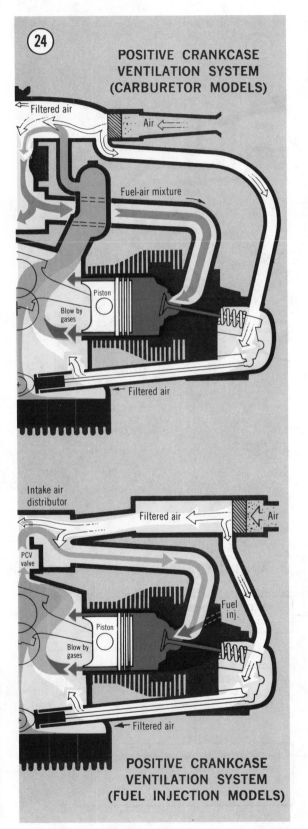

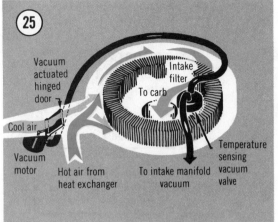

With the proper equipment, you can test the carbon monoxide and hydrocarbon levels. **Figure 23** provides some sources of trouble if the readings are not correct.

Positive Crankcase Ventilation

Fresh air drawn from the air cleaner housing scavenges emissions (e.g., piston blow-by) from the crankcase, then the intake manifold vacuum draws emissions into the intake manifold. They can then be reburned in the normal combustion process. **Figure 24** shows a typical system.

Thermostatic Air Cleaner

The thermostatically controlled air cleaner maintains incoming air to the engine at a predetermined level, usually about 100°F or higher. It mixes cold air with heated air from the exhaust manifold region. The air cleaner includes a temperature sensor, vacuum motor, and a hinged door. See **Figure 25**.

The system is comparatively easy to test. See **Figure 26** for the procedure.

Air Injection Reaction System

The air injection reaction system reduces air pollution by oxidizing hydrocarbons and carbon monoxide as they leave the combustion chamber. See **Figure 27**.

The air injection pump, driven by the engine, compresses filtered air and injects it at the exhaust port of each cylinder. The fresh air mixes with the unburned gases in the exhaust and pro-

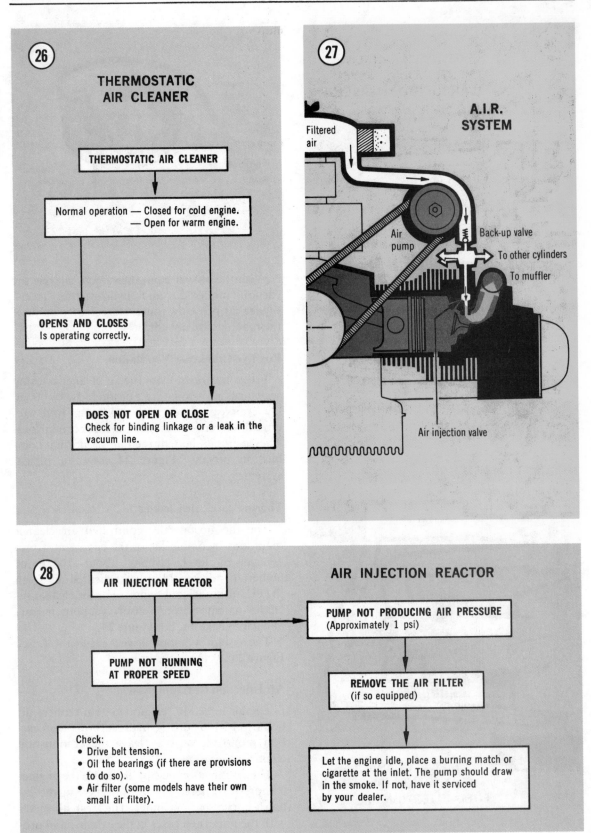

(26)

THERMOSTATIC AIR CLEANER

THERMOSTATIC AIR CLEANER

Normal operation — Closed for cold engine.
— Open for warm engine.

OPENS AND CLOSES
Is operating correctly.

DOES NOT OPEN OR CLOSE
Check for binding linkage or a leak in the vacuum line.

(27)

A.I.R. SYSTEM

Filtered air

Air pump

Back-up valve

To other cylinders

To muffler

Air injection valve

(28)

AIR INJECTION REACTOR

AIR INJECTION REACTOR

PUMP NOT PRODUCING AIR PRESSURE
(Approximately 1 psi)

PUMP NOT RUNNING AT PROPER SPEED

REMOVE THE AIR FILTER
(if so equipped)

Check:
• Drive belt tension.
• Oil the bearings (if there are provisions to do so).
• Air filter (some models have their own small air filter).

Let the engine idle, place a burning match or cigarette at the inlet. The pump should draw in the smoke. If not, have it serviced by your dealer.

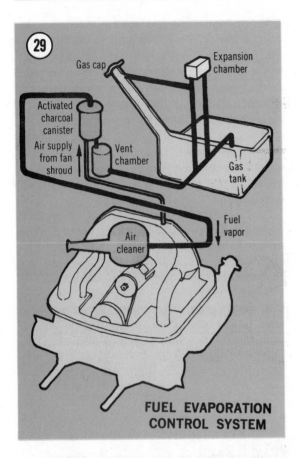

FUEL EVAPORATION CONTROL SYSTEM

motes further burning. A check valve prevents exhaust gases from entering and damaging the air pump if the pump becomes inoperative, e.g., from a drive belt failure.

Figure 28 explains the testing procedure for this system.

Fuel Evaporation Control

Fuel vapor from the fuel tank passes through the liquid/vapor separator to the carbon canister. See **Figure 29**. The carbon absorbs and stores the vapor when the engine is stopped. When the engine runs, manifold vacuum draws the vapor from the canister. Instead of being released into the atmosphere, the fuel vapor takes part in the normal combustion process.

Exhaust Gas Recirculation

The exhaust gas recirculation (EGR) system is used to reduce the emission of nitrogen oxides (NOx). Relatively inert exhaust gases are introduced into the combustion process to slightly reduce peak temperatures. This reduction in temperature reduces the formation of NOx.

Figure 30 provides a simple test of this system.

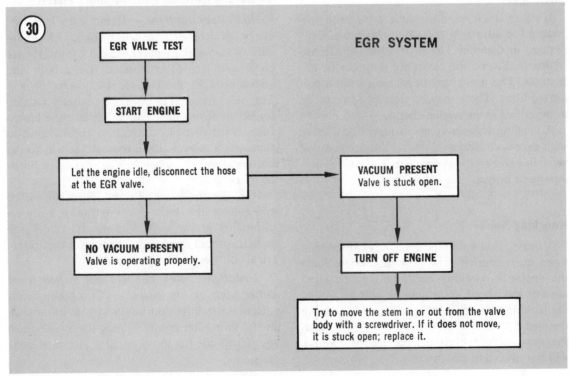

ENGINE NOISES

Often the first evidence of an internal engine trouble is a strange noise. That knocking, clicking, or tapping which you never heard before may be warning you of impending trouble.

While engine noises can indicate problems, they are sometimes difficult to interpret correctly; inexperienced mechanics can be seriously misled by them.

Professional mechanics often use a special stethoscope which looks similar to a doctor's stethoscope for isolating engine noises. You can do nearly as well with a "sounding stick" which can be an ordinary piece of doweling or a section of small hose. By placing one end in contact with the area to which you want to listen and the other end near your ear, you can hear sounds emanating from that area. The first time you do this, you may be horrified at the strange noises coming from even a normal engine. If you can, have an experienced friend or mechanic help you sort the noises out.

Clicking or Tapping Noises

Clicking or tapping noises usually come from the valve train, and indicate excessive valve clearance.

If your vehicle has adjustable valves, the procedure for adjusting the valve clearance is explained in Chapter Three. If your vehicle has hydraulic lifters, the clearance may not be adjustable. The noise may be coming from a collapsed lifter. These may be cleaned or replaced as described in the engine chapter.

A sticking valve may also sound like a valve with excessive clearance. In addition, excessive wear in valve train components can cause similar engine noises.

Knocking Noises

A heavy, dull knocking is usually caused by a worn main bearing. The noise is loudest when the engine is working hard, i.e., accelerating hard at low speed. You may be able to isolate the trouble to a single bearing by disconnecting the spark plugs one at a time. When you reach the spark plug nearest the bearing, the knock will be reduced or disappear.

Worn connecting rod bearings may also produce a knock, but the sound is usually more "metallic." As with a main bearing, the noise is worse when accelerating. It may even increase further just as you go from accelerating to coasting. Disconnecting spark plugs will help isolate this knock as well.

A double knock or clicking usually indicates a worn piston pin. Disconnecting spark plugs will isolate this to a particular piston, however, the noise will *increase* when you reach the affected piston.

A loose flywheel and excessive crankshaft end play also produce knocking noises. While similar to main bearing noises, these are usually intermittent, not constant, and they do not change when spark plugs are disconnected.

Some mechanics confuse piston pin noise with piston slap. The double knock will distinguish the piston pin noise. Piston slap is identified by the fact that it is always louder when the engine is cold.

ELECTRICAL ACCESSORIES

Lights and Switches (Interior and Exterior)

1. *Bulb does not light* — Remove the bulb and check for a broken element. Also check the inside of the socket; make sure the contacts are clean and free of corrosion. If the bulb and socket are OK, check to see if a fuse has blown. The fuse panel (**Figure 31**) is usually located under the instrument panel. Replace the blown fuse. If the fuse blows again, there is a short in that circuit. Check that circuit all the way to the battery. Look for worn wire insulation or burned wires.

If all the above are all right, check the switch controlling the bulb for continuity with an ohmmeter at the switch terminals. Check the switch contact terminals for loose or dirty electrical connections.

2. *Headlights work but will not switch from either high or low beam* — Check the beam selector switch for continuity with an ohmmeter at the switch terminals. Check the switch contact terminals for loose or dirty electrical connections.

Cover

Fuse panel

Fuse

2

3. *Directional signals will not self-cancel* — Check the self-cancelling mechanism located inside the steering column.

4. *Directional signals flash slowly* — Check the condition of the battery and the alternator (or generator) drive belt tension (**Figure 4**). Check the flasher unit and all related electrical connections.

Windshield Wipers

1. *Wipers do not operate* — Check for a blown fuse and replace it. Check all related terminals for loose or dirty electrical connections. Check continuity of the control switch with an ohmmeter at the switch terminals. Check the linkage and arms for loose, broken, or binding parts. Straighten out or replace where necessary.

2. *Wiper motor hums but will not operate* — The motor may be shorted out internally; check and/or replace the motor. Also check for broken or binding linkage and arms.

3. *Wiper arms will not return to the stowed position when turned off* — The motor has a special internal switch for this purpose. Have it inspected by your dealer. Do not attempt this yourself.

3. *Brake light switch inoperative* — On mechanically operated switches, usually mounted near the brake pedal arm, adjust the switch to achieve correct mechanical operation. Check the switch for continuity with an ohmmeter at the switch terminals. Check the switch contact terminals for loose or dirty electrical connections.

4. *Back-up lights do not operate* — Check light bulb as described earlier. Locate the switch, normally located near the shift lever. Adjust switch to achieve correct mechanical operation. Check the switch for continuity with an ohmmeter at the switch terminals. Bypass the switch with a jumper wire; if the lights work, replace the switch.

Directional Signals

1. *Directional signals do not operate* — If the indicator light on the instrument panel burns steadily instead of flashing, this usually indicates that one of the exterior lights is burned out. Check all lamps that normally flash. If all are all right, the flasher unit may be defective. Replace it with a good one.

2. *Directional signal indicator light on instrument panel does not light up* — Check the light bulbs as described earlier. Check all electrical connections and check the flasher unit.

Interior Heater

1. *Heater fan does not operate* — Check for a blown fuse.. Check the switch for continuity with an ohmmeter at the switch terminals. Check the switch contact terminals for loose or dirty electrical connections.

2. *Heat output is insufficient* — Check that the heater door(s) and cable(s) are operating correctly and are in the open position. Inspect the heat ducts; make sure that they are not crimped or blocked.

3. *Exhaust fumes in passenger compartment* — Open all windows and inspect heat exchangers and heating system immediately.

WARNING
Do not continue to operate the vehicle with deadly carbon monoxide fumes present in the passenger compartment.

COOLING SYSTEM

Engine cooling is provided by an engine driven fan which draws in outside air for the cylinders and cylinder heads. Thermostatically controlled air flaps limit the amount of cold air when engine is cold to provide rapid warm up.

If the engine is running abnormally hot, check fan drive condition and tension, air control ring adjustment and/or air control thermostat.

If overheating is extreme, the engine will have to be removed and the cooling duct system removed and inspected.

CLUTCH

All clutch troubles except adjustments require removal of the engine/transaxle assembly to identify and cure the problem.

1. *Slippage* — This is most noticeable when accelerating in a high gear at relatively low speed. To check slippage, park the vehicle on a level surface with the handbrake set. Shift to 2nd gear and release the clutch as if driving off. If the clutch is good, the engine will slow and stall. If the clutch slips, continued engine speed will give it away.

Slippage results from insufficient clutch pedal free play, oil or grease on the clutch disc, worn pressure plate, or weak springs. Also check for binding in the clutch cable and lever arm which may prevent full engagement.

CAUTION
This is a severe test. Perform this test only when slippage is suspected, not periodically.

2. *Drag or failure to release* — This trouble usually causes difficult shifting and gear clash, especially when downshifting. The cause may be excessive clutch pedal free play, warped or bent pressure plate or clutch disc, excessive clutch cable guide sag, broken or loose linings, lack of lubrication in gland nut bearing or felt ring. Also check condition of main shaft splines.

3. *Chatter or grabbing* — A number of things can cause this trouble. Check tightness of

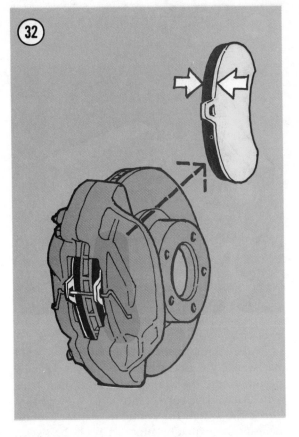

engine mounts and engine-to-transmission mounting bolts. Check for worn or misaligned pressure plate and misaligned release plate, or excessive cable guide sag.

4. *Other noises* — Noise usually indicates a dry or defective release or pilot bearing. Check the bearings and replace if necessary. Also check all parts for misalignment and uneven wear.

MANUAL TRANSAXLE

Transaxle troubles are evident when one or more of the following symptoms appear:

a. Difficulty changing gears

b. Gears clash when downshifting

c. Slipping out of gear

d. Excessive noise in NEUTRAL

e. Excessive noise in gear

f. Oil leaks

Transaxle repairs, except for one oil seal, are not possible without expensive special tools.

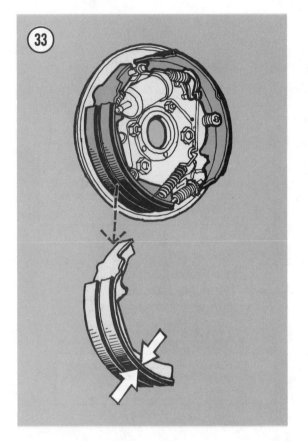

The main shaft oil seal, however, is easily replaced after removing the engine.

Transaxle troubles are sometimes difficult to distinguish from clutch troubles. Eliminate the clutch as a source of trouble before installing a new or rebuilt transaxle.

AUTOMATIC AND SEMI-AUTOMATIC TRANSAXLE

Most automatic and semi-automatic transaxle repairs require considerable specialized knowledge and tools. It is impractical for the home mechanic to invest in the tools, since they cost more than a properly rebuilt transmission.

Check fluid level and condition frequently to help prevent future problems. If the fluid is orange or black in color or smells like varnish, it is an indication of some type of damage or failure within the transmission. Have the transmission serviced by your dealer or competent automatic transmission service facility.

Refer to transaxle chapter for specific troubleshooting procedures.

BRAKES

Good brakes are vital to the safe operation of the vehicle. Performing the maintenance specified in Chapter Three will minimize problems with the brakes. Most importantly, check and maintain the level of fluid in the master cylinder, and check the thickness of the linings on the disc brake pads (**Figure 32**) or drum brake shoes (**Figure 33**).

If trouble develops, **Figures 34 through 36** will help you locate the problem. Refer to the brake chapter for actual repair procedures.

STEERING AND SUSPENSION

Trouble in the suspension or steering is evident when the following occur:

   a. Steering is hard

   b. Vehicle pulls to one side

   c. Vehicle wanders or front wheels wobble

   d. Steering has excessive play

   e. Tire wear is abnormal

Unusual steering, pulling, or wandering is usually caused by bent or otherwise misaligned suspension parts. This is difficult to check without proper alignment equipment. Refer to the suspension chapter in this book for repairs that you can perform and those that must be left to a dealer or suspension specialist.

If your trouble seems to be excessive play, check wheel bearing adjustment first. This is the most frequent cause. Then check ball-joints as described below. Finally, check tie rod end ball-joints by shaking each tie rod. Also check steering gear, or rack-and-pinion assembly to see that it is securely bolted down.

TIRE WEAR ANALYSIS

Abnormal tire wear should be analyzed to determine its causes. The most common causes are the following:

   a. Incorrect tire pressure

   b. Improper driving

   c. Overloading

   d. Bad road surfaces

   e. Incorrect wheel alignment

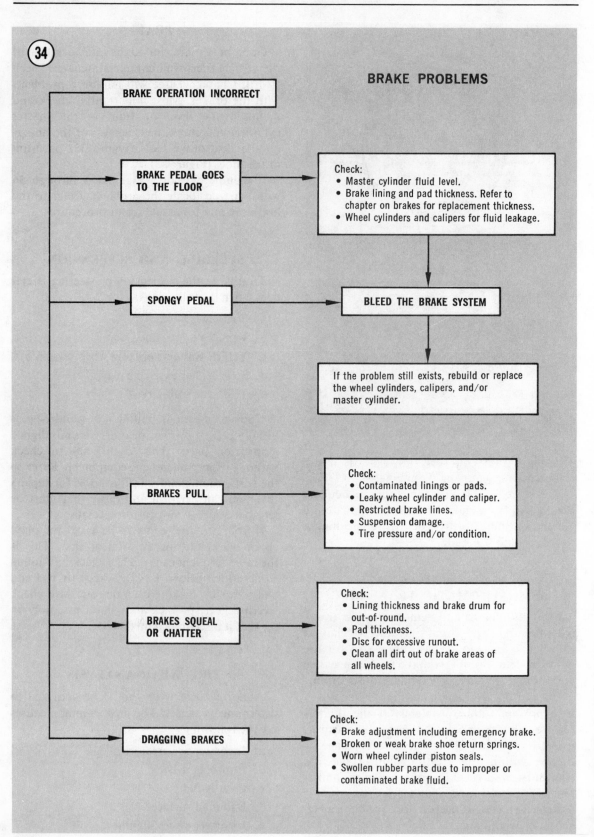

(34)

BRAKE PROBLEMS

BRAKE OPERATION INCORRECT

BRAKE PEDAL GOES TO THE FLOOR → Check:
- Master cylinder fluid level.
- Brake lining and pad thickness. Refer to chapter on brakes for replacement thickness.
- Wheel cylinders and calipers for fluid leakage.

SPONGY PEDAL → BLEED THE BRAKE SYSTEM

If the problem still exists, rebuild or replace the wheel cylinders, calipers, and/or master cylinder.

BRAKES PULL → Check:
- Contaminated linings or pads.
- Leaky wheel cylinder and caliper.
- Restricted brake lines.
- Suspension damage.
- Tire pressure and/or condition.

BRAKES SQUEAL OR CHATTER → Check:
- Lining thickness and brake drum for out-of-round.
- Pad thickness.
- Disc for excessive runout.
- Clean all dirt out of brake areas of all wheels.

DRAGGING BRAKES → Check:
- Brake adjustment including emergency brake.
- Broken or weak brake shoe return springs.
- Worn wheel cylinder piston seals.
- Swollen rubber parts due to improper or contaminated brake fluid.

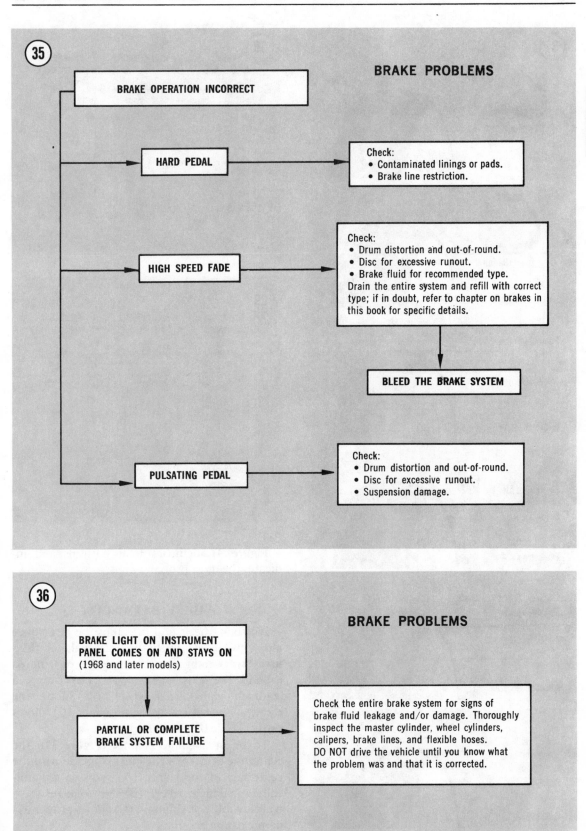

35

BRAKE PROBLEMS

BRAKE OPERATION INCORRECT

HARD PEDAL → Check:
• Contaminated linings or pads.
• Brake line restriction.

HIGH SPEED FADE → Check:
• Drum distortion and out-of-round.
• Disc for excessive runout.
• Brake fluid for recommended type.
Drain the entire system and refill with correct type; if in doubt, refer to chapter on brakes in this book for specific details.

→ BLEED THE BRAKE SYSTEM

PULSATING PEDAL → Check:
• Drum distortion and out-of-round.
• Disc for excessive runout.
• Suspension damage.

36

BRAKE PROBLEMS

BRAKE LIGHT ON INSTRUMENT PANEL COMES ON AND STAYS ON (1968 and later models)

↓

PARTIAL OR COMPLETE BRAKE SYSTEM FAILURE →

Check the entire brake system for signs of brake fluid leakage and/or damage. Thoroughly inspect the master cylinder, wheel cylinders, calipers, brake lines, and flexible hoses.
DO NOT drive the vehicle until you know what the problem was and that it is corrected.

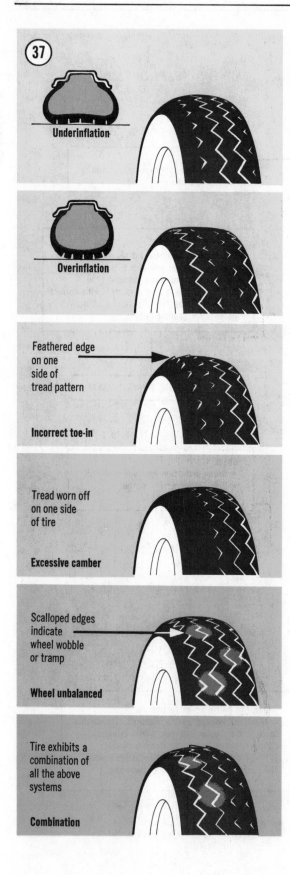

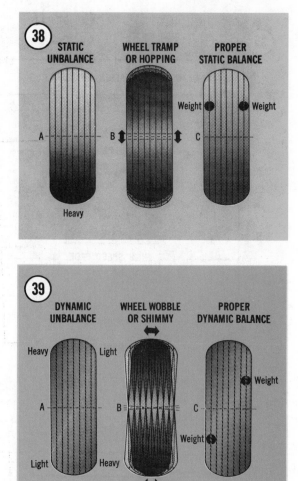

Figure 37 identifies wear patterns and indicates the most probable causes.

WHEEL BALANCING

All four wheels and tires must be in balance along two axes. To be in static balance (**Figure 38**), weight must be evenly distributed around the axis of rotation. (A) shows a statically unbalanced wheel; (B) shows the result — wheel tramp or hopping; (C) shows proper static balance.

To be in dynamic balance (**Figure 39**), the centerline of the weight must coincide with the centerline of the wheel. (A) shows a dynamically unbalanced wheel; (B) shows the result — wheel wobble or shimmy; (C) shows proper dynamic balance.

CHAPTER THREE

LUBRICATION, MAINTENANCE, AND TUNE-UP

To ensure good performance, dependability and safety, regular preventive maintenance is necessary. This chapter outlines periodic lubrication and maintenance for a car driven by an average owner. A car driven more than average may require more frequent attention, but even without use, rust, dirt and corrosion cause unnecessary damage. Whether performed by the owner or a Volkswagen dealer, regular routine attention helps avoid expensive repairs.

The recommended schedule in this chapter includes routine checks which are easily performed at each fuel stop, periodic checks to be performed at each oil change, and periodic maintenance to prevent future trouble. The last part of this chapter suggests a simplified engine tune-up procedure which simplifies this important task. **Table 1** summarizes all periodic maintenance required in an easy-to-use form.

ROUTINE CHECKS

The following simple checks should be performed at each fueling stop.

1. Check engine oil level. See **Figure 1**. Level should be between the 2 marks on the dipstick, but never below. Top up if necessary.

2. Check battery electrolyte level. It should be even with the top of the vertical separators. Top up with *distilled* water.

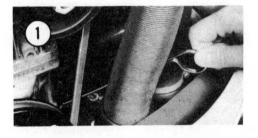

3. Check that brake fluid level is at the top mark. See **Figure 2**. Use brake fluid clearly marked SAE 7OR3, SAE J1703 (which supercedes 7OR3), DOT 3, or DOT 4 only.

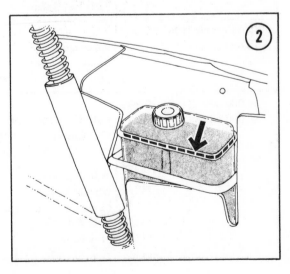

Table 1   LUBRICATION AND MAINTENANCE SUMMARY

Interval	Item	Check Fluid Level	Replace	Lube	Inspect and/or Clean	Check and/or Adjust
Fuel stop	Engine oil	X				
	Battery electrolyte	X				
	Brake fluid	X				
	Windshield washer	X				
	Tire pressure					X
3,000 miles (1961-1974)						
5,000 miles (1975-on)	Engine oil		X			
	Body mechanisms			X		
6,000 miles (1961-1974)						
15,000 miles (1975-on)	Clutch					X
	Transaxle oil	X				
	Torque converter	X				
	Front suspension			X		
	Compression					X
	Distributor		X			
	Carburetor (1961-1974)		X			
	Breaker points (1961-1974)				X	X
	Spark plugs (1961-1974)				X	X
	Ball-joint seals				X	
	Brake linings				X	
	Fuel filter				X	
	Valve clearance					X
	Crankcase ventilation hoses				X	
	Ball-joint or kingpin play					X
	Front end alignment					X
	Fan belt					X
	Exhaust system					X
12,000 miles (1961-1974)						
15,000 miles (1975-on)	Spark plugs	X				X
	Breaker points	X				X
	EGR valve (1972-1976)	X				
24,000 miles (1961-1974)						
15,000 miles (1975-on)	EGR filter (1972-1976)		X			
	EGR valve (1972-1976)					X
30,000 miles (1961-on)	Transmission oil		X			
	Wheel bearings			X	X	X
	Constant velocity joints (1968-on)			X	X	
	Air cleaner		X			

Table 2   TIRE PRESSURES

Model	Persons	Pressure Front	Rear
Beetle and	1-2	16 psi	24 psi
Karmann Ghia	3-5	17 psi	26 psi
Super Beetle and	1-2	16 psi	27 psi
Convertible	3-5	19 psi	27 psi

Note: Pressures are for standard 5.60-15 bias ply tires. Add 1 psi to all pressures for 155SR-15 radials. Add 3 psi to all pressures for long, high-speed trips.

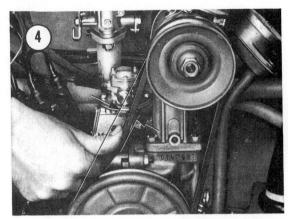

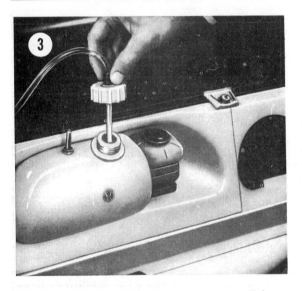

4. Check fan belt tension and condition. Tension is correct when the belt can be depressed 1/2 to 3/4 in. (10-15 mm) under slight thumb pressure.

5. Check tire pressure when tires are cold. See **Table 2**.

6. Check windshield washer container level. See **Figure 3**.

PERIODIC CHECKS

These checks are performed less frequently than routine checks. Recommended intervals are discussed below and are summarized in **Table 1**. Many require that the automobile be on a hoist or jackstands.

> *WARNING*
> *Do not use the tire jack when working under the car. Use only jackstands made specifically for this purpose.*

Fan Belt

Since fan belt tension affects engine cooling and electrical charging, it is important to check it frequently. When correct, the belt should deflect about 0.6 in. (15 mm) when pressed midway between the crankshaft and generator pulleys. See **Figure 4**. In addition, it should be possible to crank the engine over by turning the generator pulley nut with a wrench. If the belt slips, it is too loose. Check the condition of the belt also. If worn or cracked, replace it.

To adjust or replace the belt, hold a screwdriver in the cutout in the pulley as shown in **Figure 5**. Remove the nut on the end of the pulley. If installing a new belt, remove the crankshaft pulley cover plate, then remove the old belt. Install the new belt and then the pulley cover plate.

Belt tension is adjusted by varying the number of shims between the pulley halves. Decreasing the number tightens the belt, increasing the number loosens the belt. Store extra shims on the outside of the pulley, under the pulley nut. See **Figure 6**.

Adjust belt tension carefully. If it is too loose, the engine can overheat and the battery may not charge. If too tight, belt life will be low and the generator bearings will wear prematurely.

A new fan belt using different material was introduced in early 1971. New belts are identified with either "D.A." or "XDA" part numbers. Deflection should be 0.25 in. instead of 0.6 in.

Table 3   EXHAUST EMISSION LEVELS
(1968 AND LATER)

Year	Carbon Monoxide (CO)	Hydrocarbons (PPM ①)
1968 & 1969	2-3.5%	400 maximum
1970	2-4%	400 maximum
1971 & 1972	1.5-3%	400 maximum
1973	0.7-1.5%	400 maximum
1974	0.7-1.5%	400 maximum
1975 and later	1.1 ± 0.1%	400 maximum
① Parts per million		

Compression Check

Every **6,000** (1961-1974) or **15,000** (1975-on) miles, check cylinder compression.

Many automotive books describe a "dry" compression test and a "wet" compression test. Usually these tests must be interpeted together to isolate the trouble in cylinders or valves.

Unfortunately, the wet compression test is unreliable when performed on a VW. To perform it, about one tablespoon is poured into the spark plug hole before checking compression. Since VW cylinders are horizontal, oil does not spread evenly over the piston crown–a necessity for this test.

Only the dry compression test should be performed on the VW. To perform the test:

1. Warm the engine to normal operating temperature. Ensure that the choke valve and throttle valve are completely open.
2. Remove the spark plugs.
3. Connect the compression tester to one cylinder following the manufacturer's instructions.
4. Have an assistant crank the engine over until there is no further rise in pressure.
5. Remove the tester and record the reading.
6. Repeat Steps 3-5 for each cylinder.

When interpeting the results, actual readings are not as important as the difference between readings. All readings should be from about 132 to 162 psi (9 to 11 kg/cm^2). Readings below 100 psi (7 kg/cm^2) indicate that an engine overhaul is due. A maximum difference of 21 psi (1.5 kg/cm^2) between any 2 cylinders is acceptable. Greater

differences indicate worn or broken rings, leaky or sticky valves or combination of all. Compare with vacuum gauge reading to isolate the trouble more closely.

Engine Compartment Check

Every **6,000** (1961-1974) or **15,000** miles, check entire engine compartment for leaking or deteriorated oil and fuel lines. Check electrical wiring for breaks in insulation caused by deterioration or chafing. Check for loose or missing nuts, bolts and screws.

Exhaust Emission Control Check

After every engine tune-up (see later section), check carbon monoxide (CO) content of exhaust gas. Use a good quality exhaust gas analyzer, following the manufacturer's instructions. With engine idling, CO content should be within values shown in **Table 3**.

NOTE
Some 1977 models are equipped with high altitude kits, consisting of a new deceleration valve and a 2-way switch. Whenever the vehicle is operated at "low" altitudes (below 4,000 feet.) or "high" altitudes (above 4,000 ft.) the switch should be set accordingly to the LOW or HIGH position. Whenever the switch is changed, the CO value of the exhaust gases must be readjusted to specifications.

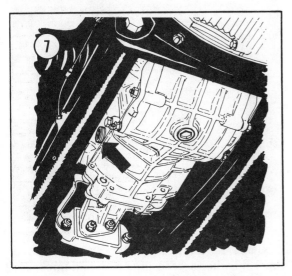

Manual Transaxle

Every **6,000** (1961-74) or **15,000** (1975-on) miles, check the oil level in the transaxle. To do this, remove the filler plug (**Figure 7**) and ensure the oil level reaches to the bottom of the opening. If the level is low, top up with gear oil recommended in **Table 4**.

CAUTION
Do not overfill. Before replacing plug, let any excess oil drain out. Excess oil can damage seals.

While the car is jacked up, check the transmission throughly for leaks and mounting bolt tightness. See Chapter Nine for bolt location and recommended torque value.

Automatic Stick Shift

Every **6,000** (1961-1974) or **15,000** miles, check the oil level in the transaxle in the same manner as for the manual transaxle. In addition, check the automatic transmission fluid for the torque converter. Check level on dipstick as shown in **Figure 8** at the right side of the engine compartment with the engine off.

Table 4   RECOMMENDED LUBRICANTS AND FUEL

	Temperature Range	Recommended Type	Capacity
Engine oil	Below —13°F	SAE 5W(MS)	5.3 pints (2.5 liters)
	Between —13°F & 13°F	SAE 10W(MS)	
	Between 5°F & 40°F	SAE 20W-20(MS)	
	Between 40°F & 86°F	SAE 30(MS)	
	Above 68°F	SAE 40(MS)	
Manual transaxle & Automatic Stick Shift (except torque converter)	Above 0°F	Gear Oil SAE 90	Manual: 5.3 pints (2.5 liters)
	Between 0°F & —13°F	Gear Oil SAE 80	
	Below —13°F	ATF (DEXRON)	Automatic: 6.3 pints (3 liters)
Automatic Stick Shift torque converter	All temperatures	ATF (DEXRON)	7.6 pints (3.6 liters)
Fuel	— — —	91 octane (regular) ③	10.6 gal. (40 liters) ①
			11.1 gal. (42 liters) ②

① All except Super Beetle   ② Super Beetle   ③ 1975-ON — unleaded only

Level should be between the 2 marks and never below the lowest mark. Top up if necessary.

Steering and Suspension

Every **6,000** (1961-1974) or **15,000** miles (1975-on), check ball-joint and tie rod end dust seals. Check tie rods for tightness and damage. Check steering gear free play and adjust if necessary as described in Chapter Eleven. Check tire wear which may indicate damaged or worn suspension parts. See Chapter Eleven to check for kingpin or ball-joint play.

On 1961-1965 cars, check the steering gear oil level every **3,000** miles by removing the filler plug on top of the steering gear case. The plug is accessible through an inspection plate in back of the spare tire on the left side. Oil level should reach to the bottom of filler hole threads. Top up with SAE 90 transmission oil.

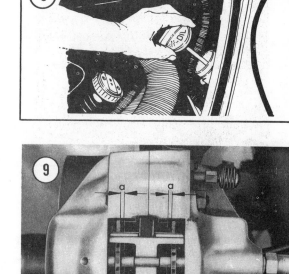

> *CAUTION*
> *Overfilling can cause seal damage and leaks.*

It is not necessary to check steering gear lubricant level on 1966 and later cars and no filler plug is provided. Check the housing for external leaks. Top cover leaks may be repaired as described in Chapter Eleven. Other leaks indicate internal damage which involves repair by a VW dealer. See Chapter Eleven.

Brakes

Every **6,000** (1961-1974) or **15,000** (1975-on) miles, check brake lining thickness. This is a simple job on the Beetle and 1961-1966 Karmann Ghias. After jacking the car up and removing the wheel, look through the brake inspection/ adjustment holes in the brake drum (1961-1967) or backing plate (1968-on). If linings are less than 1/16 in. (1.6 mm) thick, replace them. See Chapter Twelve. Bonded lining wear limit is 0.040 in. (1 mm) remaining thickness.

Check disc brake pads on 1967 and later Karmann Ghias at the same interval. To do this, jack up the front of the car and remove the front wheels. Measure brake pad thickness (a) in **Figure 9**. If (a) is 0.08 in. (2 mm) or less, replace all 4 pads (both wheels). See Chapter Twelve.

Check foot and handbrake adjustments which are also described in Chapter Twelve.

Warning Light

The engine or Automatic Stick Shift could unknowingly be seriously damaged if a warning light burns out and is unable to inform the driver of the malfunction. Therefore, it is good practice to check the warning lights often. Replace them *immediately* if burned out.

To check the engine oil pressure light and generator warning light, simply turn the ignition on without starting the engine. If either lamp does not light, replace it.

If oil pressure light doesn't go on after replacement, check oil pressure switch by grounding the wire connected to it. If light works, replace switch. If light remains out,

check connections and conditions of all leads.

To check the ATF temperature warning lamps, jack the rear of the car on jackstands until the tires clear the ground. Apply the handbrake and start the engine. Shift to DRIVE 1. Remove the wire from DRIVE 1 temperature sender (see Chapter Nine for location) and ground the wire. The lamp on the speedometer should light. Reconnect the wire. Shift to DRIVE 2 and repeat the procedure as in DRIVE 1. If the warning lamp fails to light in either or both ranges, see Chapter Three, *Automatic Stick Shift Troubleshooting*.

Windshield Wiper Blades

Long exposure to weather and road film hardens the rubber wiper blades and destroys their effectiveness. When blades smear or otherwise fail to clean the windshield, they should be replaced.

Tire Inspection

At least every **5,000** miles, check the condition of all tires. Volkswagen recommends replacing tires with tread less than 0.04 in. (1 mm). Check local road regulations; many states specify minimum tread depths. Ensure that tire wear is even over the whole surface. If not, see *Tire Wear Analysis* in Chapter Three. Check lug nuts for tightness.

Tire Rotation

While periodic tire rotation improves tire mileage slightly, there are several disadvantages. Unless you rotate tires yourself, the cost of rotation is greater than the savings in tires. In addition, once a tire has worn to the pattern in one position, it can cause unusual handling problems until it wears into the pattern in the new position. Volkswagen no longer recommends periodic tire rotation. Fortunately, the VW gets relatively good tire mileage without rotation.

PERIODIC MAINTENANCE

Engine Oil Change

The oil change interval varies depending on the type of driving you do. For normal driving, including some city traffic, change oil at interval specified in **Table 1**. If driving is primarily short distances with considerable stop-and-go city traffic, change oil twice as often as specified. Change oil every 6-8 weeks if driving amounts to only a few hundred miles per month. In arctic climates with temperatures frequently below -13° F (-25° C) change oil every **750-1000** miles.

Any oil used must be rated FOR API SERVICE SE. Non-detergent oils are not recommended. See **Table 4** for recommended oil grades.

To drain engine oil, remove the drain plug in the center of the oil strainer cover. Oil should always be drained when hot. Let oil drain for at least 10 minutes. When oil has drained, remove nuts securing the oil strainer and and remove the strainer. See **Figure 10**. Clean all strainer parts in solvent, then reinstall them with a new gasket. Do not overtighten nuts. Install the drain plug. Remove the oil filler cap (see **Figure 11**) and add 5.3 pints (2.5 liters) of a suitable oil

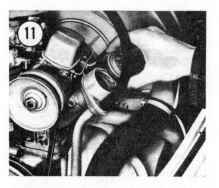

selected from **Table 4**. Check level on dipstick. The level should be between the marks or slightly above the top mark.

Oil Bath Air Cleaner

Change the air cleaner oil at the same time as the engine oil, using the same grade. Fill to the mark provided; on small air cleaners this takes about 0.6 pints (0.28 liters), on larger ones about 0.9 pints (0.41 liters).

To change the oil, remove the air cleaner as described in Chapter Six. Clean all sludge from the bottom part with solvent. The top part usually does not require cleaning unless conditions are very dusty or oil level has been neglected for long periods. Reinstall the air cleaner, and fill to the mark with oil.

Paper Air Cleaner

To replace the paper cartridge, release the clips on the air cleaner housing and lift the cover away. Remove the old element and install a new one. Make sure the cover is properly aligned when installing it and make sure that the clips are securely fastened.

Fuel Filter

Clean the fuel filter every **6,000** (1961-1974) or **15,000** (1975-on) miles. To do this, remove the plug shown in **Figure 12** and remove the filter. Clean filter in solvent such as benzine and blow dry. Install the filter and plug.

Front Suspension Lubrication

Lubrication varies depending on type of suspension and year. Lubricate 1961-1965 models every **3,000** miles, 1966-1974 models every **6,000** miles and 1975-on models every **15,000** miles. Regardless of mileage, lubricate at least once a year.

On 1961-1962 models, there are grease fittings on tie rod ends, 2 per wheel on the king pin links and 4 on the axle tubes (see **Figure 13**). From 1963-1965, tie rods do not have fittings and require no lubrication. On 1966-on models with ball-joint suspensions, only the 4 front axle fittings are provided; no other lubrication is required. Super Beetles require no lubrication.

Wipe each grease fitting with a clean cloth. Inject fresh lithium grease until it emerges from extremities of lubricated part. Do not get grease on rubber parts such as tires or brake hoses; wipe accidental spills off immediately.

NOTE
Raise the front of the car when lubricating to ensure that grease reaches all points.

Distributor Lubrication

Every **6,000** (1961-1974) or **15,000** (1975-on) miles, apply a thin coat of high temperature grease to contact surfaces of the breaker cam. If there is a felt wick under the rotor (Bosch distributors) apply one drop of oil every **3,000** miles.

CAUTION
Do not get grease or oil on breaker points. Dirty points burn and pit rapidly.

Carburetor

Every **6,000** (1961-1974) or **15,000** (1975-on) miles, lubricate the carburetor controls and linkages with powdered graphite. See **Figure 14**. Never use oil, which collects dust and may lead to dangerous throttle sticking.

On models *without* a fuel filter, the idle volume control screw whould be removed at this time and blown clean with compressed air. See Chapter Six for location on your carburetor.

Body Maintenance

Every **6,000** (1961-1974) or **15,000** (1975-on) miles, lightly grease front and rear hood locks with molybendum disulfide-based grease. Apply 1-2 drops of oil to door hinges. Lubricate striker plates with a non-staining stick lube such as Door Ease.

Lubricate lock tumblers by applying a thin coat of Lubriplate, lock oil or graphite to the key. Insert the key and work the lock several times. Wipe the key clean.

Clean front seat runners once a year and grease with Lubriplate.

Exhaust System

Every **6,000** (1961-1974) or **15,000** (1975-on) miles, examine the muffler and tailpipes for rust, holes and other damage. Replace any damaged parts.

Clutch

Every **6,000** (1961-1974) or **15,000** (1975-on) miles, check clutch pedal play on manual shift cars. Depress pedal by hand. Free play should be 1/2-3/4 in. See Chapter Eight for adjustment procedure.

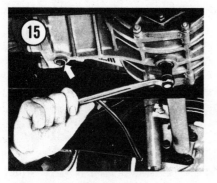

On Automatic Stick Shifts, check clutch adjustment and gearshift switch adjustment as described in Chapter Nine.

Transaxle Oil Change

Every 30,000 miles, change oil in either the manual transaxle or Automatic Stick Shift. It is not necessary to change automatic transmission fluid for the torque converter in Automatic Stick Shift models.

Transaxle oil must be at normal operating temperature before draining. Remove both magnetic drain plugs (see **Figure 15**) and let oil drain for at least 10-15 minutes. Install the drain plugs and remove the filler plug. Fill the transaxle slowly as shown in **Figure 16**. It is good practice to fill with 2 or 3 pints, wait a few minutes, then add the rest. Use 5.3 pints (2.5 liters) of an oil listed in **Table 4**.

CAUTION
Do not overfill. See oil level check in previous section.

Catalytic Converter

All cars delivered in California must have a catalytic converter. This converter must be replaced every 30,000 miles. To do this, remove the mounting bolts from the flange, loosen the clamp and pull the converter out. Install the new converter with new gaskets. Tighten mounting bolts and clamp securely.

Exhaust Gas Recirculator (EGR)

Many Beetles since 1972 have a special exhaust gas recirculation system to reduce oxides of nitrogen. See Chapter Five for

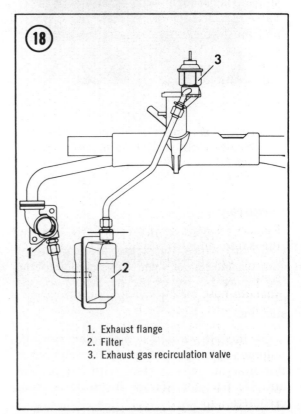

1. Exhaust flange
2. Filter
3. Exhaust gas recirculation valve

specific years and models and a complete description of each system.

On 1972 models, replace the recirculating valve every **12,000** miles. See **Figure 17**.

A slightly different system is used on 1973 models. Replace the filter element (2, **Figure 18**) every **24,000** miles. At the same interval, remove the recirculating valve, but keep the vacuum hose connected. Start the engine. It should stall at idle; if not, the line between the valve base and the intake manifold is clogged and must be cleaned. Restart the engine and run it at 2,000-3,000 rpm. The pin in the valve should retract at least 0.16 in. (4 mm) and return at idle; if not, replace the valve.

NOTE
The cooling coil on 1972 models may be replaced with the filter element used on later models. Follow procedure in Chapter Five.

All 1974 models have some form of EGR. Replace filter element every **24,000** miles. At the same interval, check operation of the system. On all models, except those originally sold in California, run engine at idle, pull the vacuum hose off the EGR valve and connect the back hose from the intake air temperature regulator in its place. Engine speed should drop noticeably or stall; if not, either the valve or hose is blocked.

To check 1971 California models, simply observe the pin in the EGR valve. See **Figure 19**. It should retract when the engine is run about 2,000 rpm and return at idle. Replace the valve if necessary.

California Automatic Stick Shift models for 1974 have a throttle valve switch to control EGR. To check the switch, run the engine at idle and operate the switch by hand. Engine speed should drop or stall. If speed doesn't change, the switch, 2-way valve or connecting wires are faulty. See Chapter Five for replacement and adjustment.

All 1975-on models have EGR which must be serviced every **15,000** miles. A special elapsed time odometer located in the luggage compartment lights and EGR indicator on the instrument panel every **15,000** miles as a reminder. When this occurs, the EGR filter must be replaced and the system must be checked for proper operation.

NOTE
There is no EGR filter on models equipped with a catalytic converter (sold in California).

To check the system, follow the procedure for 1974 systems sold outside California. After checking the system, press the reset button on the EGR elapsed time odometer.

Other Emission Control Systems

Harmful emissions are minimized by 3 additional systems:
   a. Crankcase ventilation.
   b. Exhaust emission control (since 1968).
   c. Fuel evaporative control (since 1970).

The crankcase ventilation system scavenges emissions (e.g., piston blow-by) from the crankcase and directs them to the air intake. Eventually they can be reburned in the normal combustion process.

Exhaust emission control is more complex. Harmful exhaust emissions consist mainly of carbon monoxide and unburned hydrocarbons. The relative amount of these emissions depends on the carburetor air/fuel mixture ratio, ignition timing, engine temperature and condition. Exhaust emission control, therefore, depends largely on proper ignition and carburetor adjustment.

Even with a properly tuned engine, excessive emissions are produced when the rear wheels drive the engine, e.g., when coasting downhill or decelerating. Special throttle positioners and exhaust recirculation techniques described in Chapter Five and Chapter Six ensure adequate air/fuel mixture to minimize unburned fuel and nitrogen oxides in the exhaust.

The fuel evaporation control eliminates emission of fuel vapor into the atmosphere. Fuel vapor forms in the fuel tank of a car parked in the hot sun. The vapor is stored until the engine is started and the vapor can be burned in the engine. Chapter Six describes the system in detail.

Wheel Bearings

Every **30,000** miles, clean, pack and adjust front wheel bearings. See *Front Brake Drum Removal/Installation* in Chapter Twelve for cleaning and packing procedures. See Chapter Eleven for adjustment procedure.

Constant Velocity Joints

Every **30,000** miles, clean and pack the rear axle constant velocity joints. To do this, follow procedures in Chapter Ten under *Constant Velocity Joints, Removal and Installation.*

ENGINE TUNE-UP

In order to maintain a car in proper running condition, the engine must receive periodic tune-ups.

On 1961-1974 models, perform these procedures every **6,000** miles. However, every **12,000** miles, spark plugs and breaker points should be replaced, not merely cleaned.

On 1975 and later models, perform these procedures every **15,000** miles. At this interval, replace the plugs and points; do not clean and reinstall them.

Since different systems in an engine interact to affect overall performance, tune-up must be accomplished in the following order:
1. Valve clearance adjustment.

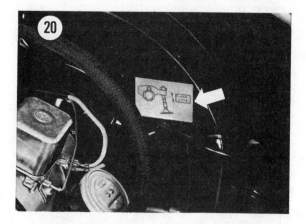

2. Ignition adjustment and timing.
3. Carburetor adjustment.

Valve Clearance Adjustment

This is a series of simple mechanical adjustments which should be performed while the engine is cold. Valve clearance for your engine must be carefully determined. If the clearance is too small, the valves may be burned or distorted. Large clearance results in excessive noise. In either case, engine power is reduced.

Normally a sticker with correct valve clearances is pasted on the fan housing (**Figure 20**). If the sticker is missing or unreadable, determine valve clearance as follows:

1. Determine if the rocker arm shaft support studs are long or short. To do this, feel under the engine between pushrod tubes for the bottom end of the studs. If you feel the stud, the engine has long studs. If you cannot feel the stud, the engine has short studs.

> *NOTE*
> *Check all 4 studs. You may have an engine with long studs on one end and short on the other. Short stud conversion kits are available to replace long studs. This must always be done to both cylinder heads.*

2. If the engine has long studs, valve clearances are as follows:
   Exhaust–0.012 in. (0.3 mm).
   Intake–0.008 in. (0.2 mm).
3. If the engine has short studs, determine valve clearance from **Table 5**.

Table 5   ENGINE TUNE-UP SPECIFICATIONS*

Valve Clearance
  Long studs   Intake: 0.008 in. (0.2mm)   Exhaust: 0.012 in. (0.3mm)
  Short studs
    Through 1971   Intake and Exhaust: 0.004 in. (0.1mm)
    1972-ON   Intake and Exhaust: 0.006 in. (0.15mm)

Ignition Timing

1961-1965	1200 engine ①	10° BTDC ②
1966	1300 engine ①	7.5° BTDC ②
1967	1500 engine ①	7.5° BTDC ②
1968 and 1969	1500 engine	TDC @ 900 rpm ③
1970	1600 engine	TDC @ 900 rpm ③
1971-1973	1600 engine	5° ATDC @ 900 rpm ④
1974	1600 engine	7.5° BTDC @ 800-900 rpm ③ ⑥ 7.5° BTDC @ 900-1,000 rpm ③ ⑦ 5° ATDC @ 800-900 rpm ④ ⑤
1975-ON	1600 engine	5° ATDC @ 800-850 rpm ④ ⑧ TDC @ 850-1,000 rpm ④ ⑦

Spark Plug Gap   0.024-0.028 in. (0.6-0.7mm)

Spark Plug Type
  1961-1974   Bosch W175 T1, Champion L88A, Beru 145/14
  1975-ON   Bosch W145 M1, Champion L288, Beru 145/14/L

Breaker Point Gap   0.016 in. (0.4mm)

*Ignition timing may vary from these specifications due to varying exhaust emission standards. Always use the timing specification listed on the emission control sticker located in the engine compartment.

① Without exhaust emission control   ⑤ California vehicle, manual transmission
② Static timing point; engine not running   ⑥ Manual transmission (except Calif.)
③ Vacuum advance disconnected   ⑦ Automatic Stick Shift
④ Vacuum advance connected   ⑧ All manual transmissions

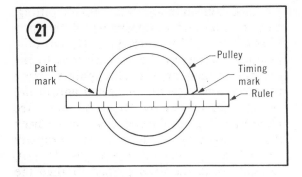

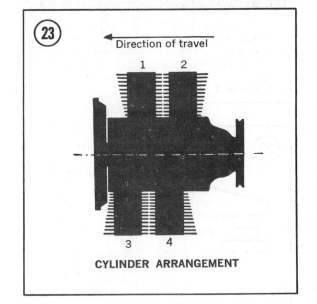

Adjust valves in the following order: 1-2-3-4. First, remove both rocker arm covers and the spark plugs. This makes the engine much easier to turn by hand; and plugs require cleaning or replacement at this time anyway. Rotate the crankshaft pulley. There should be a paint mark exactly 180° from the TDC timing mark. If not, make one. Measure across the pulley as shown in **Figure 21** to accurately locate the mark.

To adjust the valves, rotate the crankshaft so that piston No. 1 is at TDC on its compression stroke. This is evident when the timing mark on the pulley aligns with the crankcase seam and the rotor points to the notch on the distributor. See **Figure 22**.

> *NOTE*
> *On most cars, the pulley mark is not exactly at TDC, but the slight difference is not significant for valve adjustment.*

> *NOTE*
> *Intake valves are on top; exhaust valves are on the bottom.*

Adjust valve clearance for cylinder No. 1, which is the right front cylinder. See **Figure 23**. Loosen the locknut on the adjusting screw, insert a feeler gauge and adjust to clearance given above. Tighten locknut and recheck the clearance to be sure it has not changed.

Rotate the crankshaft pulley 180° *counterclockwise* (backward) until the paint mark aligns with the crankcase seam. Adjust valves for cylinder No. 2. Rotate the pulley 180° counterclockwise and adjust cylinder No. 3. Rotate the pulley another 180° counterclockwise and adjust cylinder No. 4.

When finished, install rocker arm covers with new gasket.

Ignition Adjustment and Timing

Once valve clearance is properly adjusted, work on the ignition system. Examine spark plugs and compare their appearance to the examples given in Chapter Two. Electrode appearance is a good indication of performance in each cylinder and permits early recognition of trouble. Clean the plugs, regap them and reinstall using new gaskets. Remove plugs in order. That way, you will know which cylinder is malfunctioning, should such be the case.

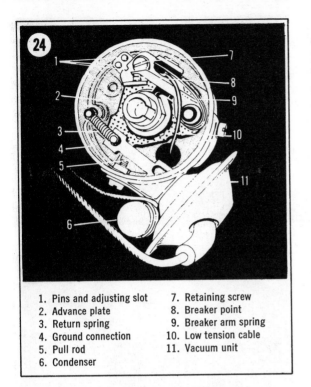

1. Pins and adjusting slot
2. Advance plate
3. Return spring
4. Ground connection
5. Pull rod
6. Condenser
7. Retaining screw
8. Breaker point
9. Breaker arm spring
10. Low tension cable
11. Vacuum unit

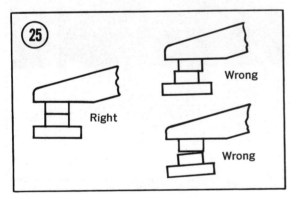

CAUTION
Ensure the rubber seals on the spark plug wires are in good condition and seal properly. Replace them if necessary. These seals prevent the loss of cooling air.

Next remove the distributor cap and wipe off any dirt or corrosion. Remove the rotor. This is a good time to lubricate the distributor as discussed earlier in this chapter.

Check distributor rotor resistance at this time. Maximum allowable is 10,000 ohms. Excessive resistance may be the cause of hard starting or high speed miss.

Check breaker points for signs of pitting, discoloration and misalignment. If this is a **12,000** (1961-1974) or **15,000** (1975-on) mile tune-up, disconnect the primary lead to the distributor and remove the points. Note carefully how they are connected and install new points in exactly the same way. See **Figure 24**. Replace the condenser also. Check that the contacts on the points are properly aligned as shown in **Figure 25**. If not, carefully bend the *fixed* contact to align the contacts.

Carefully rotate the distributor body or the crankshaft pulley until a high cam lobe opens the points to the maximum gap. Loosen the screw holding the points, insert a feeler gauge in the gap and adjust to 0.016 in. (0.4 mm). Tighten the retaining screw. More accurate measurement is possible by measuring dwell angle which should be 44-50°. Connect dwell meter following the manufacturer's instructions.

Reconnect the primary wire and install the rotor and distributor cap. Ensure that all wires are connected properly. Tighten the distributor housing clamp screw.

After adjusting breaker gap, set the ignition timing. On 1961-1967 cars without exhaust emission control, either a test lamp or stroboscopic timing light may be used. Emission control cars may only be timed with a strobe.

Static Test Lamp Method (1961-1967)

1. Remove distributor cap.
2. Crank engine over by hand until timing mark indicated in **Table 5** aligns with the crankcase seam and the rotor points to the No. 1 mark on the distributor housing clamp rim.
3. Loosen the distributor housing clamp screw.
4. Connect one test lamp lead to ignition coil terminal 1 and the other lead to the ground.

NOTE
Use a lamp (6-12 volts) which matches your electrical system.

5. Switch ignition on.

6. Rotate distributor body clockwise until the contact points close (lamp off). Slowly rotate distributor counterclockwise until points just begin to open (lamp on). Tighten distributor clamp screw in this position.

7. Reinstall the distributor cap and disconnect the test lamp.

Stroboscopic Timing Method (1968-on)

1. Select proper timing mark for your engine (**Table 5**). Mark the notch with white chalk or paint for better visibility.

2. Connect the timing light to cylinder No. 1 (**Figure 23**) following the manufacturer's instructions.

3. Run engine at specified speed. See **Table 4**.

> *NOTE*
> *Determine from **Table 4** if vacuum hose to advance must be connected or not.*

4. Loosen the distributor housing and turn it until the timing notch on the pulley, illuminated by the timing light, aligns with the crankcase seam. See **Figure 26**. Tighten the distributor in this position.

Carburetor Adjustment

Adjustments are basically the same for all carburetors. On 1961-1967 carburetors (without exhaust emission control), adjust idle speed to 850 rpm with a tachometer. See **Figure 27**. Turn idle mixture screw in slowly until engine speed begins to drop, then back the screw out about 1/4-1/3 turn. See **Figure 28**.

The procedure is the same for 1968-1970 exhaust emission control carburetors, except turn the idle mixture screw in until engine speed drops, then back the screw out until engine speed is maximum. Readjust idle speed to 850 rpm if it has changed. Automatic Stick Shifts must be in NEUTRAL for the adjustment.

> *CAUTION*
> *Idle mixture on 34PICT (1971-1974) carburetors is factory set and must not be adjusted.*

AFC Fuel Injection Adjustments

There are 2 adjustments to the AFC system:
   a. Idle speed.
   b. Carbon monoxide (CO) content.

To adjust the idle speed, warm the engine to operating temperature. Turn the idle adjustment screw (**Figure 29**) to idle speed specified in **Table 5** or on the emission sticker in the engine compartment.

After adjusting the carburetor, adjust the throttle positioner as described in Chapter Six.

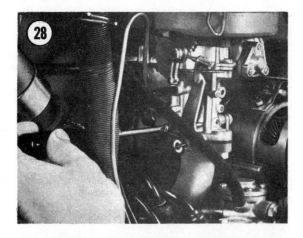

To adjust CO content, you must have an analyzer capable of measuring CO and hydrocarbons (HC). Do not attempt this adjustment without the analyzer as emission output is very sensitive to small changes in the adjustment.

On vehicles without a catalytic converter, insert the analyzer probe well into the exhaust pipe and adjust CO and HC (**Figure 30**) to specifications in **Table 3** or the emission sticker in the engine compartment.

On vehicles with a catalytic converter, measurement must be made with the special probe connected ahead of the catalytic converter to the tap on the left side of the muffler assembly. Measurement cannot be made with a probe at the exhaust pipe, since the catalytic converter reduces CO and HC to unmeasureable levels.

VW DIAGNOSIS AND MAINTENANCE

An important part of VW's "total service concept" is their VW diagnosis.

When you go to a dealer, your car receives a thorough examination in a special stall equipped for this purpose. A trained diagnostician checks items on VW Diagnosis test report (**Figure 31**). He indicates repairs and maintenance needed, depending on mileage and condition of the car. Since he is a top mechanic in addition to a diagnostician, he can explain each item to you if necessary.

When the diagnosis is complete, you receive a copy of the test report and a cost estimate. VW will repair the items after getting your approval, or of course you may fix them yourself. In either case, you know exactly the condition of your car and have the opportunity to keep it in top shape.

You should also consider VW Diagnosis when buying a used VW. Insist on a test report when buying from a VW dealer. If you buy from someone else, the small cost of having a diagnosis done may save you from a painful mistake.

NOTE
Some 1977 models are equipped with high altitude kits, consisting of a new deceleration valve and a 2-way switch. Whenever the vehicle is operated at "low" altitudes (below 4,000 ft.) or "high" altitudes (above 4,000 feet) the switch should be set accordingly to the LOW or HIGH position. Whenever the switch is changed, the CO value of the exhaust gases must be readjusted to specifications.

31

VW Diagnosis

We have noted the items that need to be adjusted, repaired or replaced, in addition to the factory-recommended maintenance listed in your Volkswagen Maintenance Record. Your Service Advisor will be glad to review the results of our diagnosis with you.

Engine and Clutch
Fan belt
Distributor contact points

Dwell angle   40°   50°   60°

Ignition timing
Spark plugs   Cylinders 1 2 3 4
Compression
Carburetor preheating flaps
Throttle positioner or switch
Crankcase ventilation
Air intake flaps and bellows
Exhaust system
Clutch pedal free play
Automatic stick shift servo rod clearance
Automatic stick shift lever contacts
Engine oil level (disregard if oil is changed)
Engine oil leaks

Rear Axle and Transmission
Axle boots or drive shaft boots
Rear axle, final drive and transmission leaks
Automatic transmission fluid leaks
Shock absorbers   left   right

Compression Test

Cyl.	Compression Lbs./Sq. Inch
1	
2	
3	
4	
5	
6	

Repair Order No.:

Chassis No.:

Customer's Name

Front Axle and Steering
Tie rods and tie rod ends
Upper torsion arms and play
King and link pins
Ball joints   upper left   upper right
                   lower left   lower right
Steering damper
Shock absorbers   left   right
Steering gear play
Steering gear box leaks

Camber of front wheels
                + 2 +
                  1
        left   0   right
                  1
                − 2 −

Toe-in/toe out of front wheels   − 2 1 0 1 2 +

Wheels, Brakes, Tires
Brake system leaks and damages
Brake pedal stroke
Brake pedal free play
Hand brake adjustment
Brake fluid level

Brake linings or pads   front   rear
                             L R   L R   Spare
Tire condition
(Tire pressures corrected as needed)

Electrical System
Functioning of electrical equipment (headlights adjusted as needed)
Cranking system
Charging system
Wiper blades
Windshield washer
Battery condition (electrolyte level corrected as needed)

                9.6 10   11   12
Battery voltage 0
                   4.6 5   5.5   6

Test Drive
Foot brake   Hand brake   Clutch   Heating system

Date:

Diagnostician's Signature:

VW Maintenance & Repair Analysis

Operation No.	▲	Description	Labor Estimate	Parts Estimate
		Factory-recommended VW Maintenance	$	$
W MA1k		Adjust clutch free play		
W B1k		Adjust brakes		
W E62c		Replace points		
W E70c		Replace plugs	N/C	
W EB36c		Replace wiper blades		

▲ = Urgently required

The above indicated maintenance and repair work is required on your vehicle to obtain the best performance and safe operation. Please indicate with your signature that the nature and importance of each listed item has been explained to you.

Customer's Signature:

CHAPTER FOUR

ENGINE

Four versions of the 4-cylinder, air-cooled overhead valve engine were used since 1961. All 4 engines are similar in design, varying mainly in their specifications. From 1961-1965, Volkswagen used a 40 hp, 1200cc engine. In 1966, the company introduced a 50 hp, 1300cc engine which required a new crankshaft, cylinders, heads, and crankcase with replaceable camshaft bearing shells. The 53 hp, 1500cc engine powered the Beetle from 1967-1969 and is basically the 1300cc design with a larger bore and modified flywheel. A 1600cc engine has been used since 1970. **Figures 1 and 2** show views of a typical engine.

Volkswagen frequently makes minor engine design changes during a production run. For this reason, *always* order engine parts by year, chassis number, and engine number. *Never* substitute engine parts from one engine in another unless the parts are obviously identical or you have experience with that particular substitution. Design changes are often very subtle, and incorrect substitutions can be disastrous.

This chapter includes repair procedures for the 1200, 1300, 1500, and 1600cc engines. Few repairs other than fuel and ignition system troubles are possible with the engine installed. If in doubt, refer to the procedure in question to determine if the engine must be removed.

Tightening torques are given in **Table 1**; engine specifications are given in **Table 2**. Both will be found at the end of the chapter.

ENGINE REMOVAL

1. Prop the engine compartment lid up, or remove it.

2. Drain engine oil.

3. Put the transmission in neutral and chock the front tires.

4. Disconnect ground strap from the battery.

5. Remove air cleaner.

6a. On 1961-1966 voltage regulators, mounted on the generator, disconnect the small wire and mark it 61. Disconnect the large wire (or wires) and mark it B+51. Disconnect and mark the ignition coil wires.

6b. On 1967 and later models, disconnect 3 wires from the generator or alternator. Mark them in accord with the labels stamped on the generator. Disconnect and mark the ignition coil wires.

7. Disconnect the oil pressure switch wire located on the crankcase under the distributor.

NOTE: *The following 4 steps apply only to carburetted models.*

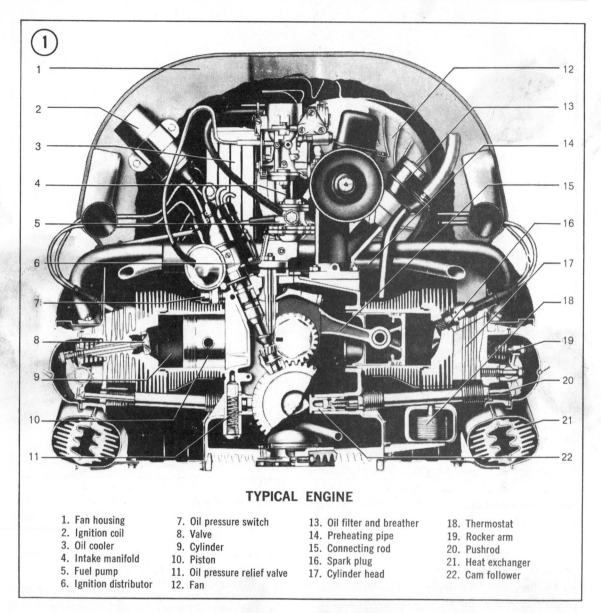

TYPICAL ENGINE

1. Fan housing	7. Oil pressure switch	13. Oil filter and breather	18. Thermostat
2. Ignition coil	8. Valve	14. Preheating pipe	19. Rocker arm
3. Oil cooler	9. Cylinder	15. Connecting rod	20. Pushrod
4. Intake manifold	10. Piston	16. Spark plug	21. Heat exchanger
5. Fuel pump	11. Oil pressure relief valve	17. Cylinder head	22. Cam follower
6. Ignition distributor	12. Fan		

8. Disconnect electrical wire for the automatic choke on the right side of the carburetor and mark it 01. Disconnect wire from electromagnetic cutoff jet near the choke and mark it 02.

9. Disconnect throttle cable to carburetor.

10a. On 1968 and 1969 manual shift models, disconnect the vacuum hose on the throttle positioner shown in **Figure 3**. Remove 3 screws and pull off the retaining ring and throttle positioner. Disconnect the pull rod at the carburetor.

10b. On 1970-1972 manual shift models, disconnect vacuum line between operating and control parts of throttle positioner (4, **Figure 4**).

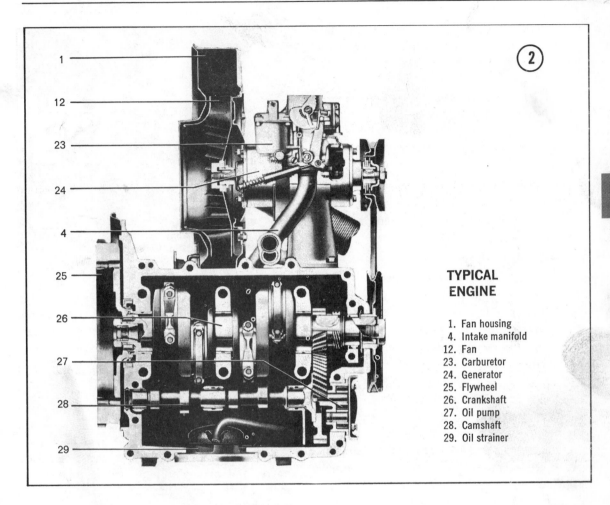

**TYPICAL
ENGINE**

1. Fan housing
4. Intake manifold
12. Fan
23. Carburetor
24. Generator
25. Flywheel
26. Crankshaft
27. Oil pump
28. Camshaft
29. Oil strainer

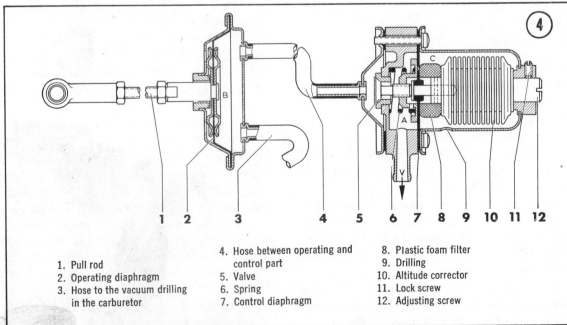

1. Pull rod
2. Operating diaphragm
3. Hose to the vacuum drilling
   in the carburetor

4. Hose between operating and
   control part
5. Valve
6. Spring
7. Control diaphragm

8. Plastic foam filter
9. Drilling
10. Altitude corrector
11. Lock screw
12. Adjusting screw

11. Pull the woven fuel line off the copper tube leading to the fuel pump. Plug the woven fuel line so it doesn't leak.

NOTE: *The following 2 steps apply to fuel injected models only.*

12. Disconnect and mark electrical cables connected to the following components:
   a. Throttle valve switch
   b. Injectors
   c. Cylinder head temperature sensor
   d. Cold start valve
   e. Auxiliary air regulator
   f. Intake air sensor potentiometer

13. Pull fuel return line off pressure regulator. Pull fuel line off injector distributor pipe and clamp end to prevent fuel leakage.

14. Raise the rear of the car and block it up on jackstands.

15. From underneath the car, pull off the flexible heater hoses. Disconnect the heater control cables located near the 2 lower engine mounting bolts.

16. On 1974 and later models, disconnect push-on connector between the TDC sensor in the right crankcase half and computer diagnosis socket.

NOTE: *The following 5 steps apply only to cars equipped with Automatic Stick Shift.*

17. Disconnect the electrical wires from the control valve mounted on the left side of the engine compartment. Mark them with masking tape for reconnection later.

18. Disconnect 2 vacuum lines for the control valve from the carburetor and intake manifold or intake air sensor.

19. Disconnect the line between the fluid reservoir (under the right rear fender) and the oil pump at the union nut. See **Figure 5**. Seal the line with a spare union nut which has been blocked with solder.

20. Disconnect the oil pressure line between the oil pump and the torque converter at the union nut. Position the line so it doesn't leak.

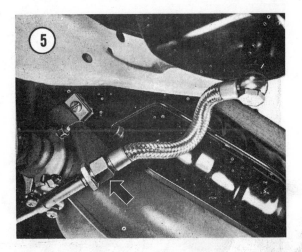

21. Remove screws securing the torque converter to the drive plate. Hand-turn the engine with the fan belt until each screw is accessible through one of the transmission case openings, then remove the screw.

NOTE: *Remaining steps apply to all models unless specified otherwise.*

22. On 1961-1966 models, remove the rear cover plate. To do this, disconnect the hoses between the fan housing and heat exchanger (1963-1966 models), remove the fan pulley cover, and preheater pipe sealing plates. Remove 6 screws securing the rear cover plate and then the plate.

23. Loosen the distributor, and turn vacuum advance inward to provide additional clearance.

24. Remove both lower engine mounting nuts with a 17mm wrench as shown in **Figure 6**.

25. Slide a garage-type floor jack under the engine and raise it so that it contacts the center bottom of the crankcase. Raise it far enough to put slight pressure on the engine.

26. If an assistant is available, have him hold the upper engine mounting nuts with a 17mm box wrench while you unscrew the bolt from underneath the car. See **Figure 7**. The nuts are accessible by reaching behind the fan shroud; you'll have to feel around for them as they are not visible. If an assistant is not available, hold the nut with Vise Grips, wedged so the nut cannot turn.

27. Roll the engine *straight* backward until the clutch release plate clears the main drive shaft.

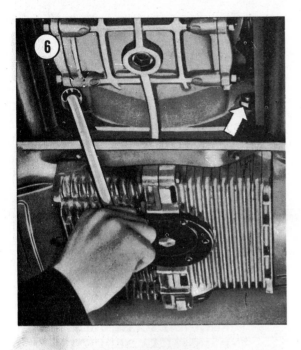

CAUTION
Do not let the engine tilt or let engine weight put any load on the drive shaft. Either the drive shaft or clutch parts can be seriously damaged.

28. Lower the engine slowly, making sure the clutch release plate remains clear of the drive shaft until the engine can be withdrawn.

29. If the car is equipped with the Automatic Stick Shift, secure the torque converter with a retainer plate as shown in **Figure 8**.

ENGINE INSTALLATION

1. Clean the transmission case and engine flange thoroughly.

2. On Automatic Stick Shift cars, remove the temporary retaining strap installed during the removal.

3. On manual shift cars, make sure the clutch plate is properly centered (see Chapter Eight). Inspect the clutch release bearing and release plate for wear and cracks. Replace them if necessary.

4. Lubricate the starter shaft bushing with universal bearing grease. Put ⅓ oz. of universal grease in the gland nut.

5. Apply molybdenum disulphide powder or heavy duty grease to the main drive shaft spline and the plastic ring on the clutch release bearing. Use a clean cloth or a brush.

6. Put the transmission in gear to steady the main drive shaft.

7. Lift the engine into place with a garage-type floor jack.

8. Rotate the engine crankshaft with the fan belt so that the clutch plate hub lines up with the main drive shaft splines. Take care that the gland nut needle bearing, clutch release bearing, and main drive shaft are not damaged when pushing the engine forward.

CAUTION
Do not let the engine tilt or let engine weight put any load on the drive shaft.

*Either the drive shaft or the clutch
parts can be seriously damaged.*

9. Guide the lower engine mounting studs into
position, then push the engine firmly against the
transmission until it is flush all the way around.

10. Install the upper engine mounting bolts and
nuts and tighten slightly. Install the lower
mounting nuts and tighten slightly. Then tighten
all bolts and nuts. Pull the floor jack out.

11. Install the rear cover plate on 1961-1966
models.

NOTE: *The following 3 steps apply
only to Automatic Stick Shift cars.*

12. Install 4 screws which secure the torque
converter to the drive plate. Tighten them to 22
ft.-lb. Be careful not to drop any screws into
the transmission case. The engine must be removed to get them out.

13. Reconnect the oil pressure line for the
torque converter and the oil suction line for the
fluid reservoir.

14. Reconnect the vacuum lines for the control
valve to the carburetor and intake manifold or
intake air sensor. Reconnect electrical wires to
control valve.

NOTE: *The following 3 steps apply
only to carburetted models.*

15. Install the throttle positioner (1968 and
1969 manual shift cars only) and reconnect its
vacuum line. On 1970 and later manual shift
cars, simply reconnect the vacuum line between
the control and operating units.

16. Reconnect the electrical wires for the electromagnetic cutoff jet and automatic choke.

17. Reconnect the woven fuel line to the copper
line leading to the fuel pump.

NOTE: *The following 3 steps apply
only to fuel injected models.*

18. Reconnect wires to injection components
listed in Step 12, *Engine Removal.*

19. Reconnect fuel return line to pressure
regulator.

20. Reconnect fuel line to fuel distributor pipe.

NOTE: *Remaining steps apply to all
models unless otherwise specified.*

21. Reconnect electrical wires to oil pressure
switch, alternator or generator, ignition coil,
and TDC sensor.

22. Reconnect the flexible heater hoses and
heater control cables.

23. Reconnect the accelerator cable and adjust
it (see Chapter Six).

24. Install air cleaner.

25. Adjust clutch free play (Chapter Eight).

26. Add 2½ quarts of engine oil.

27. Check the transmission fluid level in Automatic Stick Shift cars and top up if necessary.

28. Reconnect the battery ground strap.

ENGINE DISASSEMBLY
AND ASSEMBLY SEQUENCES

The following sequences are designed so that
the engine need not be disassembled any further
than necessary. Unless otherwise indicated, procedures for major assemblies in these sequences
are included in this chapter. The procedures are
arranged in the approximate order in which they
are performed.

To perform a step, turn to the procedure for
the major assembly indicated, e.g., cylinder
head, and perform the removal and inspection
procedures. Move to the next step, perform the
removal and inspection procedures, etc., until
the engine is disassembled. To reassemble, reverse the disassembly sequence and perform the
installation procedure for the major assembly
involved.

Decarbonizing or Valve Service

1. Remove cover plates and fan housing.

2. Remove valve rocker assemblies.

3. Remove cylinder heads.

4. Remove and inspect valves, guides, and seats.

5. Assembly is the reverse of these steps.

Valve and Ring Service

1. Perform Steps 1-4 for valve service.

2. Remove cylinders.

3. Remove rings. It is not necessary to remove the pistons unless they are damaged.

4. Assembly is the reverse of these steps.

General Overhaul Sequence

1. Remove cover plates and fan housing.

2. Remove oil cooler.

3. Remove muffler and heater assemblies (Chapter Five).

4. Remove distributor (Chapter Seven), fuel pump (Chapter Six), and distributor drive gear.

5. Remove clutch assembly (Chapter Eight) and flywheel.

6. Remove valve rocker assemblies.

7. Remove cylinder heads.

8. Remove cylinders and pistons.

9. Remove oil pump and oil strainer.

10. Disassemble crankcase.

11. Remove camshaft, crankshaft, and connecting rods.

12. Assembly is the reverse of these steps.

COVER PLATE DISASSEMBLY/ASSEMBLY

Refer to **Figure 9** to identify cover plates discussed below.

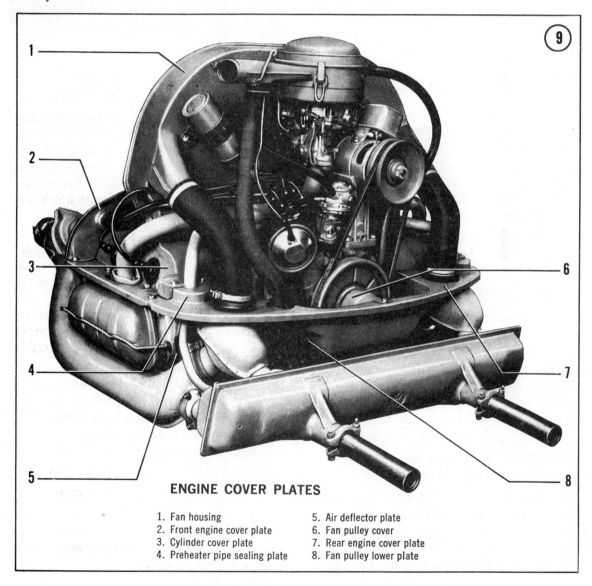

ENGINE COVER PLATES

1. Fan housing
2. Front engine cover plate
3. Cylinder cover plate
4. Preheater pipe sealing plate
5. Air deflector plate
6. Fan pulley cover
7. Rear engine cover plate
8. Fan pulley lower plate

1. Remove hoses between fan housing and heat exchangers (1963 and later).

2. Remove front engine cover plate (2).

3. Remove crankshaft pulley cover (6).

4. Remove preheater pipe sealing plates (4).

5. On 1966 and later models, remove rear engine cover plate (7).

6. Remove intake manifold with carburetor attached.

7. Loosen generator pulley nut and remove the fan belt.

8. Disconnect the wire from the ignition coil to the distributor. Mark it 15.

9. Remove distributor cap and pull spark plug connectors off.

10. Remove screws on both sides of the fan housing.

11a. On 1961-1964 models, unhook the air control ring spring and remove bolts securing the ring to the fan housing. See **Figure 10**.

that any weather stripping fits over and under mating cover plates. See **Figure 12**.

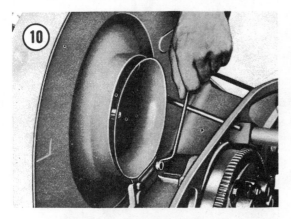

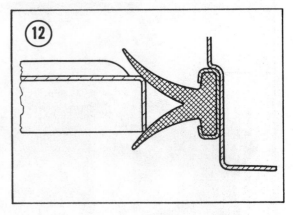

11b. On 1965 and later models, remove the air control thermostat screw (see **Figure 11**) and unscrew the thermostat from the control rod.

12. Pull the fan housing straight up complete with generator.

13. Remove rear air deflector plate (5), and the lower air ducts (not shown).

14. Lift cylinder plates (3) off.

15. Remove crankshaft pulley.

16. Remove lower crankshaft pulley plate (8).

17. Assembly is the reverse of these steps. Refer to Chapter Five for air control thermostat adjustment (all models) after reassembly. Ensure

OIL COOLER

The oil cooler can be replaced with the engine installed. If the engine is in the car, remove the fan housing following the procedure in Chapter Five. If the oil cooler has been leaking, check the oil pressure relief valve(s) for damage causing high oil pressure. Bulging cores are a sign of pressure damage. The distortion, in turn, can restrict air flow and lead to engine overheating. Replace cooler.

If non-detergent oil has been used, and you wish to change to detergent oil, discard the old oil cooler and install a new one. Otherwise, particles in the old cooler will work loose and could clog a vital oil passage.

Removal

1. Remove the oil cooler retaining nuts. If the engine is in the car, use an offset wrench as shown in **Figure 13** for 1961-1970 oil coolers. On 1971 and later oil coolers, all nuts are on the front of the cooler. See **Figure 14**.

2. Pull the oil cooler off and remove the rubber seals. See **Figure 15**.

3. Pour solvent in the cooler and let it soak upside down. Pour the solvent out and flush with clean solvent.

4. Check that no ribs touch each other, and that no parts are loose.

Installation

1. Install new seals on the bracket.

2. Install the oil cooler and nuts. Tighten all .nuts evenly. The oil cooler must be vertical, not leaning to one side.

DISTRIBUTOR DRIVE SHAFT

The distributor drive shaft may be removed with the engine installed.

Removal

1. If the engine will not be disassembled, remove the distributor cap, and turn the engine so the rotor points toward the notch on the distributor housing rim. This puts piston No. 1 at TDC of its compression stroke.

> NOTE: *Do not turn the engine over after removing the distributor. If you do, see* Valve Adjustment, *Chapter Two, to reset piston No. 1 to* TDC.

2. Remove the distributor (see Chapter Seven) and fuel pump (see Chapter Six).

3. Remove the spring on top of the distributor drive shaft.

4. Extract the drive shaft with a special tool by rotating it to the left and lifting up simultaneously. One method which works well is shown in **Figure 16**.

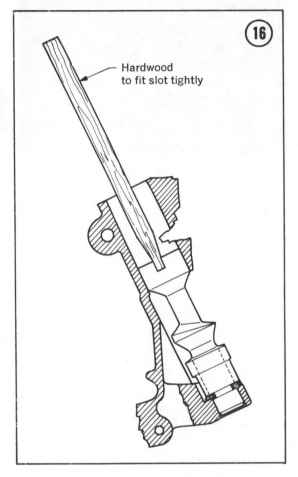

Hardwood
to fit slot tightly

5. Reach down in the crankcase through the distributor drive shaft hole with a magnet, and lift out the thrust washer(s).

CAUTION

Do not drop the washers into the crankcase if you do not intend to disassemble the crankcase. Occasionally it is possible to fish them out if dropped; usually it means splitting the crankcase.

Inspection

Check the distributor drive gear and fuel pump eccentric for wear. If the distributor drive gear is worn, you should also check the crankshaft gear. This means completely disassembling the engine.

Installation

This procedure should be performed after the engine is completely assembled, with the exception of the distributor and fuel pump.

1. Ensure that piston No. 1 is at TDC on the compression stroke. If you have not disassembled the engine, or turned the engine over since distributor removal, it should be correct. Otherwise, see *Valve Adjustment,* Chapter Two, to set piston No. 1 correctly.

2. Insert a small wire rod (e.g., coat hanger wire) to the bottom of the distributor shaft hole.

3. Apply universal grease to thrust washer(s), and slide them down the wire rod (see **Figure 17**). Do not move the rod until the washers are in place; the rod keeps the washers from dropping into the crankcase. Look into the hole and check that the washers are all the way down and centered, then remove the rod. Grease holds the washers in place.

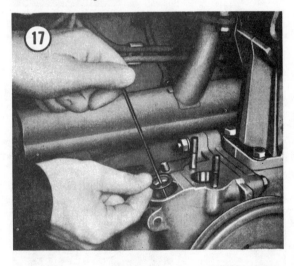

4. Oil the distributor drive shaft and insert it so the slot is perpendicular to the crankcase seam. See **Figure 18**. Push the shaft down with a large screwdriver until you are certain it is seated in the thrust washers.

5. Turn the crankshaft by hand and watch the distributor drive shaft. If the shaft turns, it is seated properly.

6. Insert the wire rod into the hole in the distributor drive shaft. Slide the small spring over the rod into the shaft. See **Figure 19**. Remove the rod.

7. Install the fuel pump and distributor (see respective chapters).

FLYWHEEL

Removal

1. Remove the clutch pressure plate and clutch disc. See Chapter Eight.

2. Mark the relationship between the flywheel and crankshaft.

3. Hold the flywheel in a special retainer; remove the gland nut and spring washer. It is torqued to 217 ft.-lb. (30 mkg) and on the 1600cc engine to 253 ft.-lb. (35 mkg), so a wrench with breaker bar is necessary. If a special flywheel retainer is not obtainable, bolt

a 3-4 ft. angle iron or 2 x 4 between 2 clutch bolt holes on the flywheel as shown in **Figure 20**.

4. Pull the flywheel off. Don't lose any of the metal dowels on the end of the crankshaft.

CAUTION
Do not damage TDC *sensor dowel pins on 1974 and later flywheels. Height of pins must not differ more than 0.004 in. (0.1mm).*

Inspection

1. Check the dowel holes in the flywheel and crankshaft. If they are out-of-round, have new holes drilled in a different spot.

2. Check the locating dowels. Replace them if they are marred.

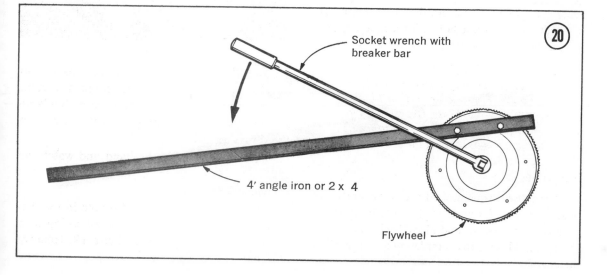

3. On 1974 and later flywheels, check TDC sensor dowels. Height must not vary more than 0.004 in. (0.1mm).

4. Check the flywheel teeth for wear or damage. If the teeth are damaged only slightly, up to 0.08 in. may be machined off the clutch side. Rechamfer the edges of the teeth.

5. Check the gland nut bearing for wear. Replace if necessary.

6. Remove the paper or metal gasket and note which you have, so a proper replacement can be made. No gasket is used on 1966 (from engine No. FO 741385) to 1974 flywheels; a rubber seal is used instead.

Installation

1. Set cylinder No. 1 to TDC on 1974 and later engines.

2. Lubricate the outer surfaces of the front crankcase oil seal.

3a. On 1961-1973 engines, reinstall the flywheel on the crankshaft using all 4 dowels, and a new paper or metal gasket, depending on the type removed above. If the crankshaft, flywheel, or clutch is new, note that the heaviest points are marked. The crankshaft is marked with a spot of paint and a 5mm hole on the flywheel end. The flywheel and clutch may be marked with a painted line on the outer edge. If all 3 parts have a mark, install them so the marks are distributed 120° from each other. If only 2

have a mark, install them so the marks are 180° from each other.

3b. On 1974 and later engines, install flywheel so that TDC sensor pins are on the right side of the engine.

4. Install the gland nut and tighten to 217 ft.-lb. (30 mkg). On the 1600cc engine, torque to 253 ft.-lb. (35 mkg). Use a 2 x 4 or angle iron to keep the flywheel from rotating when tightening. See **Figure 21**.

5. Check crankshaft end play using a procedure applicable to your engine (see *Crankshaft End Play*).

6. Check flywheel runout. The easiest method is to attach a dial indicator (**Figure 22**), rotate the flywheel and note the reading variation or runout. A more tedious method requires the threaded stock and flat bar used for end play measurement (see **Figure 23**). Set the bar 0.012 in. from the face of the flywheel. Mark off the rim of the flywheel in about 6 equal segments. Rotate flywheel so each segment is near the flat bar and measure the gap. When all 6 gaps are recorded, determine that no 2 gaps are more than 0.012 in. apart. If they are, the flywheel must be machined true or replaced.

DRIVE PLATE

The drive plate for the Automatic Stick Shift is attached to the crankshaft with a gland nut in the same manner as the flywheel.

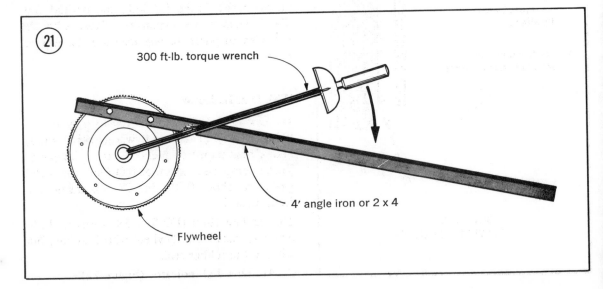

(21)

300 ft-lb. torque wrench

4' angle iron or 2 x 4

Flywheel

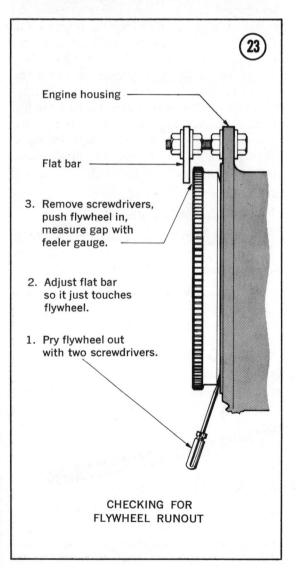

3. Remove screwdrivers,
   push flywheel in,
   measure gap with
   feeler gauge.

2. Adjust flat bar
   so it just touches
   flywheel.

1. Pry flywheel out
   with two screwdrivers.

Engine housing

Flat bar

CHECKING FOR
FLYWHEEL RUNOUT

A special retaining ring shown in **Figure 24** is required to hold the drive plate while removing the gland nut. The nut is torqued to 282 ft.-lb. (39 mkg). Rather than improvise a ring and risk warping the drive plate, take the entire engine to a VW dealer and let him remove it. Later when the engine is reassembled, let the dealer reinstall the drive plate.

CRANKSHAFT END PLAY

Crankshaft end play must be adjusted any time the engine is completely disassembled, and should be checked any time the engine is removed for whatever purpose.

Two methods are used to check end play. By far the easiest is the dial indicator method, but dial indicators are expensive. Those who do not wish to purchase one may use the second method.

With Dial Indicator

1a. On 1961-1966 engines (up to engine No. FO 741 384), install the flywheel with 2 shims and a new paper or metal gasket. The paper gasket compresses to about 0.006 in.; the metal gasket to about 0.019 in. Do not install the front oil seal.

1b. On late 1966 (FO 741 385—on) to 1974 engines, install the flywheel with 2 shims, but without the rubber seal.

2. Attach a dial indicator (Figure 22).

3. Move the crankshaft back and forth. Read the end play on the dial indicator. Record this figure.

4. Calculate the thickness of the 3rd shim by subtracting the desired end play (see specifications for your engine) from the figure recorded in the previous step.

5. Remove the flywheel, install a 3rd shim as calculated above, and reinstall the flywheel. On 1961-1966 engines, reuse the paper or metal gasket. On engines since late 1966, use a new rubber seal.

6. Remeasure the end play. If it is correct, remove the flywheel and install the front oil seal (see procedure later in this chapter). Reinstall the flywheel. If end play is not correct, change one of the shims and remeasure.

Without Dial Indicator

1. Install the flywheel as described in Step 1a or 1b of the dial indicator method above.

2. Attach a 5 in. length of ⅜ in. threaded stock to the crankcase with 2 nuts. See Figure 23.

3. Attach a piece of flat bar stock to the threaded stock with 2 nuts. Leave the nuts loose.

4. With a large screwdriver, carefully pry between the flywheel and crankcase to move the crankshaft all the way forward. Have someone hold the screwdriver in this position.

5. Adjust the flat bar stock on the threaded rod until it just touches the surface of the flywheel. Tighten the nuts in this position.

6. Remove the screwdriver and push the flywheel back.

7. Insert a feeler gauge between the flat bar stock and the flywheel. This is end play; record this figure.

8. Calculate the thickness of the 3rd shim and install it and the flywheel as described in Steps 4-6 of the dial indicator method.

FRONT OIL SEAL

The oil seal normally leaks a small amount of oil which lubricates the seal lips and prevents them from burning. This leaking causes a thin smear of oil to coat the transmission case. This smear does not indicate a defective seal. Replace the seal if leaking appears excessive or if the seal is removed for any reason; never reuse a seal.

Removal

1. Remove flywheel using the procedure given previously.

2. Carefully pry the old seal out with a screwdriver or other sharp object. See **Figure 25**. Don't nick the crankcase surface. Discard the oil seal.

3. Leave all end play shims in the crankcase.

Installation

1. If oil seal replacement is part of an engine overhaul, adjust crankshaft end play as described earlier before installing the oil seal. Otherwise, end play adjustment is desirable, but not necessary.

2. Clean the recess between the crankcase and crankshaft. If necessary, chamfer the edges of the crankcase opening slightly so that the oil seal seats without damage. Carefully clean out any metal flakes.

3. Ensure that proper end play shims are in place, and install oil seal with the closed side out. One method is to put the seal in place and gently tap it with a hammer using a small block of wood and working slowly and evenly around the seal until it is flush with the bottom of the

crankcase recess. Another method requires a special tool, shown in **Figure 26**, which presses the seal in evenly. This is easily improvised with a metal plate, large nut, and bolt to fit the hole in the end of the crankshaft.

4. Reinstall flywheel as described previously.

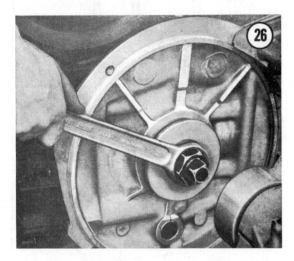

TDC SENSOR (1974-ON)

The TDC sensor is located in the right crankcase half. See **Figure 27**. The flywheel must be removed to replace the sensor.

1. Cut wire off at sensor.

2. Drive old sensor out of the crankcase toward the inside.

3. Install new sensor in as far as it will go with an old piston pin and a rubber mallet. Do not damage inner ring of sensor.

NOTE: *Use special oversize sensor (Part No. 113 919 101A) for replacement.*

VALVE ROCKER ASSEMBLY

Removal

1. Clean away all road dirt around the valve covers.

2. Pry the valve cover holder down and remove the valve cover.

3. Remove the 2 rocker shaft support nuts and keep them separate from other hardware (see **Figure 28**). These are copper plated and must be used to reinstall the rocker shaft.

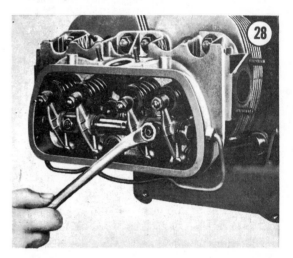

4. Pull off the rocker shaft with rocker arms.

5. Remove the stud seals on 1966 and later cylinder heads.

6. Remove all 4 pushrods and store them so that they may be reinstalled in exactly the same place. See **Figure 29**.

Rocker Shaft Disassembly/Assembly

1. Mark the rocker arms so they may be reinstalled in the same position.

2. Remove end clips from rocker arm shaft.

3. Slide all the parts off the shaft.

4. Clean all parts in solvent. Examine the bearing surfaces of the shaft and rocker arms. Small irregularities may be removed with crocus cloth. Check the rocker arm seats and ball sockets for wear.

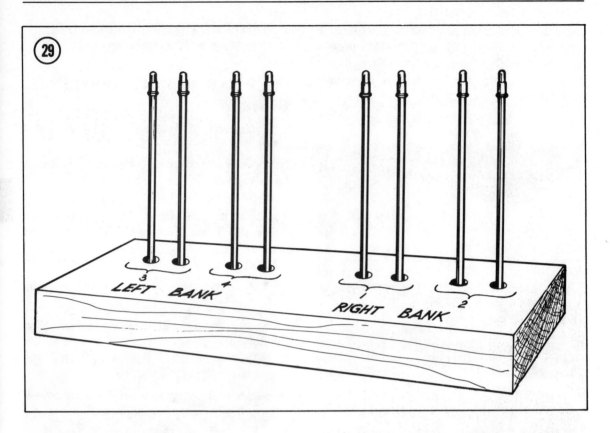

5. Coat all parts with assembly lubricant and reassemble as shown in **Figure 30** (1961-1965) or **Figure 31** (1966 on).

Installation

1. Roll each pushrod on a flat surface to check for bends.

2. Install pushrods in the cylinder head.

3. Install new stud seals on 1966 and later cylinder heads. Most gasket kits provide 2 types of seals: donut-shaped and flat. If there is a recessed groove around the stud, use the flat seals. Otherwise use the donut-shaped seals.

4. Install the rocker shaft assembly. Note that the chamfered edge of the 1966 and later rocker shaft support points outward (away from the head) and the slot points upward (**Figure 32**).

5. Ensure that the pushrod ball ends are centered in the rocker arm sockets. In addition, make sure that the rocker arm adjusting screws contact the valves slightly off center as shown in **Figure 33**.

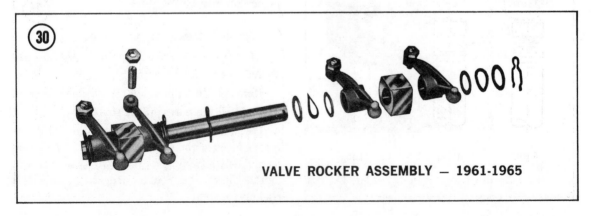

VALVE ROCKER ASSEMBLY — 1961-1965

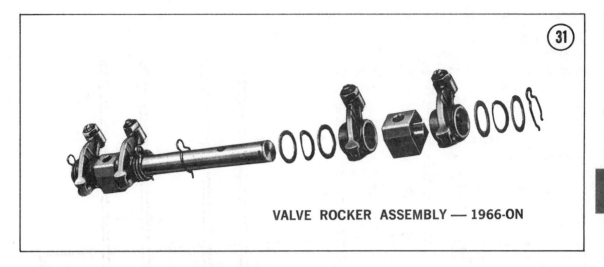

VALVE ROCKER ASSEMBLY — 1966-ON

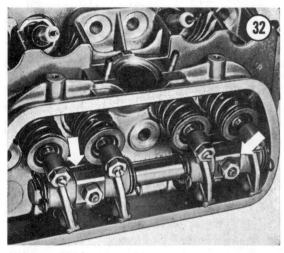

6. Tighten both nuts on the rocker shaft studs to 18 ft.-lb. (2.5 mkg).

7. Adjust intake and exhaust valves. See Chapter Two.

8. Clean all traces of old gasket from the valve covers.

9. Hold new gaskets in place on the valve covers with grease. Install the cover.

CYLINDER HEADS

Removal

1. Remove the valve rocker assembly as described previously.

2. Loosen all 8 cylinder head nuts (**Figure 34** for location). Remove the nuts and washers. Keep all head washers separate from other hardware; they are special and are available only from a Volkswagen dealer if lost.

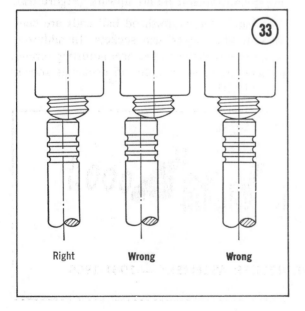

Right   Wrong   Wrong

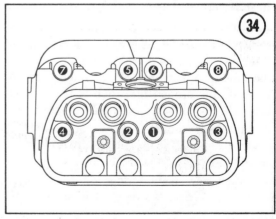

3. Pull the cylinder head off. If it is stuck, carefully pry the head and cylinders apart. In particularly tough cases, tap on the exhaust manifold studs with a hammer and block of wood. Never hammer on the fragile fins.

4. On 1961-1965 cylinders, remove the copper sealing rings from the shoulders of the cylinders. There is no sealing ring or gasket on 1966 or later engines.

5. If performing a valve job, it is unnecessary to remove cylinders. Tie them on with soft wire.

Inspection

1. Without removing the valves, remove all carbon deposits from the combustion chambers with a wire brush. A blunt screwdriver or chisel may be used if care is taken not to damage the head or valves.

2. After all carbon is removed from the combustion chamber, both valves, intake and exhaust ports, clean the entire head with solvent.

3. Clean away all carbon on the piston crown. Do not remove the carbon ridge at the top of the cylinder bore.

4. Check for cracks in the combustion chamber and exhaust ports. Cracked heads must be replaced.

5. Check all studs for tightness. If a stud can't be tightened, have a machinist drill the hole out and install a Heli-coil threaded insert.

6. Push the valve stem ends sideways with your thumb. If there is any play, the valve guides are probably worn. Replace them as described later if there is any doubt.

Installation

1. Stretch the pushrod tubes to dimensions shown in **Figure 35**. This can be done by hand. First insert a dowel or rod in the tube to keep the tube from bending. Then stretch each end out until the proper dimension is reached. Do this carefully so the tubes are not cracked.

2. Install new rubber seals on both ends of all pushrod tubes. The beveled edge of the seal should face toward the end of the tube.

3. Install new sealing rings on the cylinder shoulders (1961-1965 only). The narrow edge faces out.

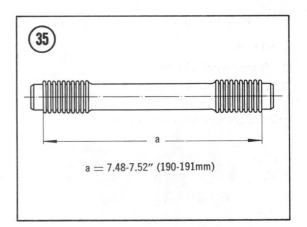

a = 7.48-7.52" (190-191mm)

4. Place the head on the studs and push it in slightly.

5. Install the inner pushrod tubes and push the head in further.

6. Install the outer tubes and push the head as far as it will go.

7. Turn all tubes so that the seams are facing upward.

8. Install at least one head nut and washer. If the washer won't fit at this time, install the nut without it. Tighten the nut until the other washers and nuts can be installed. Then be sure to install a washer under the first nut. Remember these are special thick washers which are available only from VW dealers.

9. Tighten the nuts to 7 ft.-lb. (1 mkg) in the order shown in Figure 34.

10. Tighten the nuts to 22-23 ft.-lb. (3.0-3.2 mkg) in the order shown in **Figure 36**.

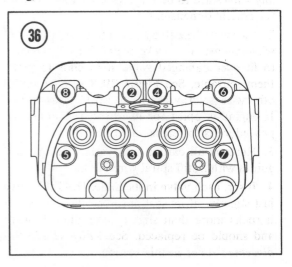

VALVES AND VALVE SEATS

Removal

1. Remove cylinder head.

2. Compress springs with a valve spring compression tool, remove the valve keepers and release compression. See **Figure 37**.

3. Remove the valve spring caps, springs, oil deflector rings (1966 and later only), and valves.

CAUTION
Remove any burrs from valve stem grooves before removing valves. Otherwise the valve guides will be damaged.

Inspection

1. Clean valves with a wire brush and solvent. Discard burned, warped, or cracked valves. If any valves are to be refaced, refer to **Figure 38** for critical dimensions.

2. Measure the valve stems for wear. Compare with specifications. VW dealers have small caps to fit over damaged valve stem ends to make them reusable. See **Figure 39**. Use caps on an otherwise healthy engine to avoid disassembly. If engine is apart for overhaul, recommended procedure is to reface valve stems.

3. Remove all carbon and varnish from valve guides with a stiff spiral wire brush.

4. Insert each valve in its guide. Hold the valve just slightly off its seat and rock it sideways. If it rocks more than slightly, the guide is worn and should be replaced. See *Valve Guide Replacement* later in this section.

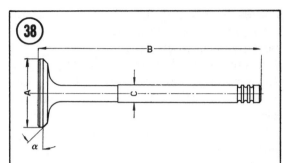

INTAKE VALVES

Engine	A	B	C	α
1200	31.5	112	7.94-7.95	44°
1300	33.0	112	7.94-7.95	44°
1500	35.5	112	7.94-7.95	44°
1600	35.6	112	7.94-7.95	44°

All dimensions in millimeters.

EXHAUST VALVES

Engine	A	B	C	α
1200	30.0	112	7.91-7.92	45°
1300	30.0	112	7.91-7.92	45°
1500	32.0	112	7.91-7.92	45°
1600				
to 1974	32.1	112	7.91-7.92	45°
1975 on	30.1	112	8.91-8.92	45°

* All dimensions in millimeters.

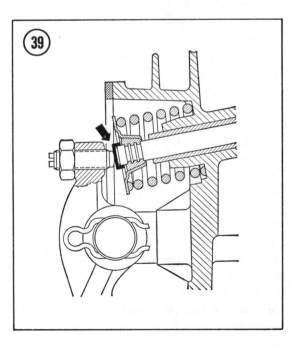

5. Measure the valve spring heights. All should be of equal length with no bends or other distortion. Replace defective springs.

6. Test valve springs under load. Springs should compress to 1.22 in. (31mm) with a 126 ± 8.8 lb. (57 ± 4 kg) load. Replace any which fail this test.

7. Check the valve keepers. If they are reusable, grind the joining faces until it is still possible to turn the valve while holding the keeper halves pressed together. New keepers must be ground in the same manner.

8. Inspect valve seats. If worn or burned, they must be reconditioned. This should be performed by the dealer or local machine shop, although the procedure is described later in this section. Seats and valves in near perfect condition can be reconditioned by lapping with fine carborundum paste. Lapping, however, is always inferior to precision grinding.

Installation

Refer to **Figure 40** (1961-1965) or **Figure 41** (1966 and later) for the following procedure.

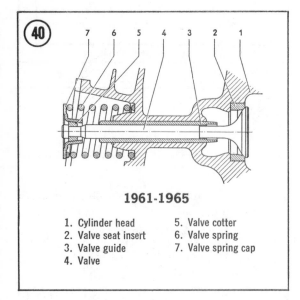

1961-1965

1. Cylinder head	5. Valve cotter
2. Valve seat insert	6. Valve spring
3. Valve guide	7. Valve spring cap
4. Valve	

1. Coat the valve stems with molybdenum disulphide paste and insert them into the cylinder head.

2. Install oil deflector rings with sleeves (1966 and later).

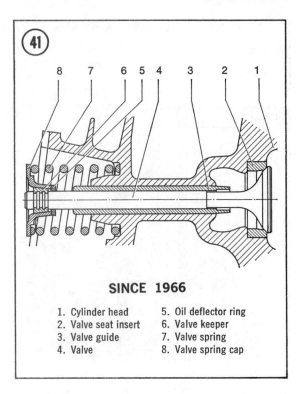

SINCE 1966

1. Cylinder head	5. Oil deflector ring
2. Valve seat insert	6. Valve keeper
3. Valve guide	7. Valve spring
4. Valve	8. Valve spring cap

3. Install valve springs with close-pitched coils next to cylinder head.

4. Install valve spring caps, compress springs, and install valve keepers.

Valve Guide Replacement

When valve guides are worn so that there is excessive stem-to-guide clearance or valve tipping, they must be replaced. Replace all guides even if only one is worn. VW recommends dealer replacement since he has special equipment using liquid air to do the job. The following procedure is for use by properly equipped machine shops unfamiliar with VW's.

1. Measure the exact distance valve guides extend above cylinder head. See **Figure 42**.

2. If the guide has a flanged top, drill it away with a ½ in. drill.

3. Drill valve guides with a 27/64 in. (12mm) bit to loosen them in their seats. See **Figure 43**. Be sure that the head is clamped at proper angle.

4. Place punch with a pilot in the guide. See **Figure 44**. The punch diameter should be a few thousandths of an inch smaller than the guide diameter so that the punch does not bind in the

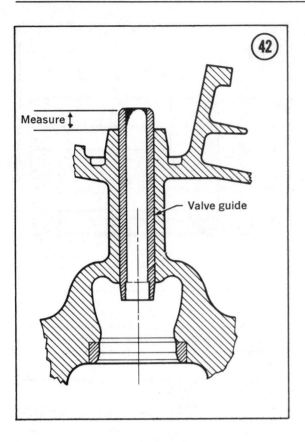

Measure

Valve guide

42

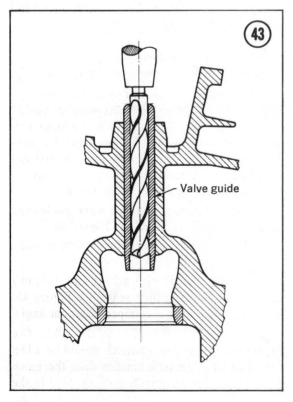

Valve guide

43

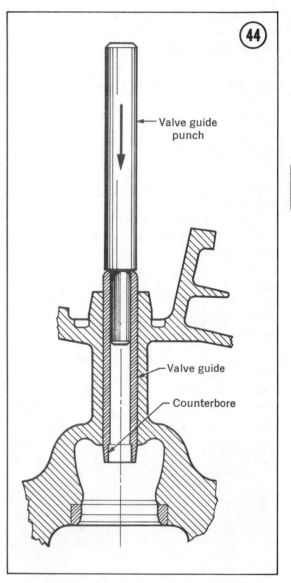

Valve guide
punch

Valve guide

Counterbore

44

guide hole. Hold the punch firmly, and drive the valve guide out.

5. Accurately measure the valve guide bore.

> NOTE: *Driving the old guide out increases the bore.*

6. Turn oversize valve guides down to 0.001-0.002 in. (0.03-0.06mm) larger than the measured valve guide bore.

7. Lubricate valve guides with Lubriplate and press it into cylinder head from the rocker area side. Guides should protrude the exact distance above the head measured in Step 1.

NOTE: *Chill valve guides in a freezer if possible to shrink them and make insertion easier.*

8. Ream the guides with a broach or fine boring mill to 0.3140-0.3156 in. (8.00-8.02mm).

Valve Seat Reconditioning

This job is best left to your dealer or local machine shop. They have the special equipment and knowledge required for this exacting job. The following procedure is provided in the event you are not near a dealer and the local machine shop is not familiar with VW's.

Valve seats are shrunk into the cylinder heads. Damaged or burned seats may be reconditioned until the edge of the top 15° chamfer reaches the outer edge of the valve seat. After this point is reached, the cylinder head must be replaced.

1. Using a 45° valve seat cutter or special stone, cut the 45° face. Don't take off any more metal than necessary to provide a clean, concentric seat. See **Figures 45 and 46**.

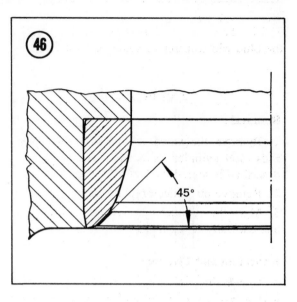

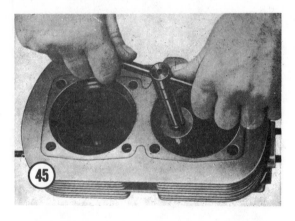

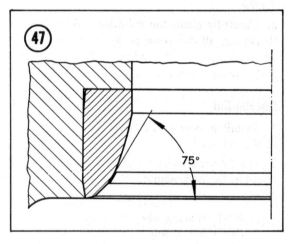

2. Slightly chamfer the bottom of the 45° seat with a 75° cutter or stone. See **Figure 47**.

3. Narrow the width of the 45° valve seat by cutting the top of the seat with a 15° cutter or stone. See **Figure 48**. The specification table at the end of this chapter shows intake and exhaust seat width for your engine.

4. Coat the corresponding valve face with Prussian blue.

5. Insert the valve into the guide.

6. Rotate the valve under light pressure about one-quarter turn.

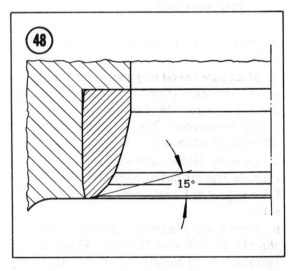

7. Lift the valve out. If the valve seats properly, the blue will transfer to valve seat face evenly.

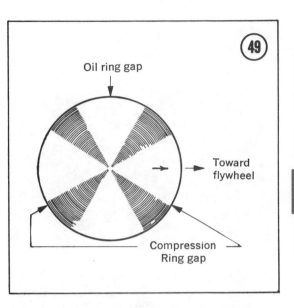

CYLINDERS

Removal

1. Remove the valve rocker assembly, push-rods, and cylinder head using the procedures described earlier.

2. Remove air deflector plate below cylinders.

3. Mark the cylinder numbers on each cylinder and carefully lift them out.

Inspection and Cleaning

1. Check the bore for wear. If worn, replace with a matched cylinder and piston of the same displacement.

2. Carefully clean the cylinder inside and out. Brush out all dirt from between the fins. Clean away any dirt on the cylinder sealing surfaces, and remove the old gasket on the crankcase end.

Installation

1. Install a new gasket on the crankcase end of the cylinder.

2. Rotate the crankshaft until the desired piston is out as far as possible.

> **CAUTION**
> *While rotating the crankshaft, watch that skirts of any exposed pistons do not catch on the crankcase. This will crack the piston.*

3. Apply a heavy coat of assembly lubricant to the piston.

4. Make sure the oil ring gap is straight up. The other 2 ring gaps should be evenly spaced 120° apart. See **Figure 49**. Compress the rings with a ring compressor. The compressor must be a 2-piece breakaway type so it can be removed.

5. Liberally oil the cylinder bore and slide the cylinder over the piston. See **Figure 50**. Be careful not to break any cooling fins against the studs.

6. When both cylinders on one side are in place, clip the air deflector in place (**Figure 51**). If necessary, bend the plate so that it fits tightly against the cylinders and won't rattle loose later on.

7. Install cylinder head as described previously.

PISTONS, PINS, AND RINGS

Removal

1. Remove the cylinder head and cylinders as described previously.

2. Mark the piston to make sure it is reinstalled in the same cylinder. See **Figure 52**. Counting from the flywheel, pistons are numbered 1, 2 on the right bank and 3, 4 on the left bank.

3. Rotate the crankshaft until the desired piston is out as far as it goes.

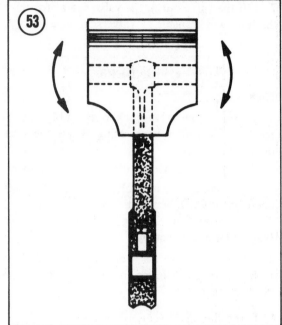

CAUTION
While rotating the crankshaft, watch that skirts of any exposed pistons do not catch on the crankcase. This will crack the piston.

4. Before removing the piston pin, hold the connecting rod tightly and rock the piston as shown in **Figure 53**. Any rocking movement (do not confuse with sliding motion) indicates wear in the piston pin, rod bushing, piston pin bore, or

more likely, a combination of all three. Mark the piston, pin, and rod for further examination later.

5. Remove the snap rings at each end of the piston pin.

6. Turn the engine so that the crankshaft is vertical, and place wet rags around the oily areas of the crankcase.

7. Heat the piston and pin with a small butane torch. The piston pin will probably drop right out, but may need coaxing with a metal rod. Heat the piston to 176°F (80°C), i.e., until it is too warm to touch, but not excessively hot.

Inspection

1. Clean piston thoroughly in solvent. Scrape carbon deposits from the top of the piston and ring grooves. Don't damage the piston.

2. Examine each ring groove for burrs, dented edges, and side wear. Pay particular attention to the top compression ring groove as it usually wears more than the others.

3. Weigh each piston. The difference in weight between any 2 pistons in the same engine must not exceed 10 grams. If necessary, file metal off the heaviest pistons at the point indicated in **Figure 54**.

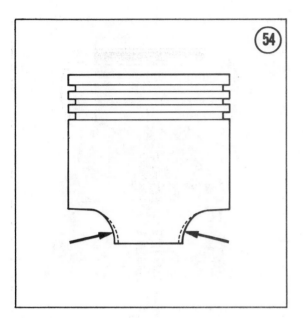

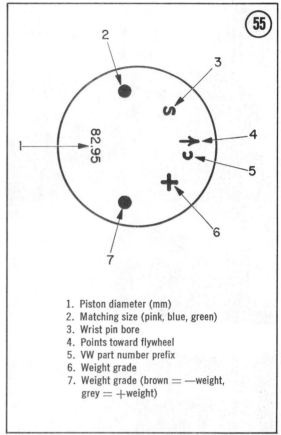

1. Piston diameter (mm)
2. Matching size (pink, blue, green)
3. Wrist pin bore
4. Points toward flywheel
5. VW part number prefix
6. Weight grade
7. Weight grade (brown = —weight, grey = +weight)

4. If the damage, wear, or weight of a piston suggests replacement, replace it with a size and weight comparable to others in the engine. **Figure 55** shows markings on the top of each VW piston used to identify its size, weight range, and assembly operation.

> NOTE: *Although pistons since 1970 are of the same diameter, 1972 and later pistons have recessed crowns and are not interchangeable with 1970-1971 pistons.*

5. Measure any parts marked in Step 4, *Piston Removal,* with a micrometer to determine which part or parts are worn. Any machinist can do this for you if you do not have micrometers.

6. When replacing a piston pin, select a size compatible with the piston pin bore. Piston pin bore is stamped on the top of the piston (see Figure 55 again). Piston pins are painted black or white to match piston markings (S = black, W = white).

Piston Clearance

VW discourages using a feeler gauge to check piston clearance and therefore does not provide specifications to do so. The following procedure is the "hard way," but certainly adequate.

1. Make sure the piston and cylinder walls are clean and dry.

2. Measure the inside diameter of the cylinder bore at a point 0.4-0.6 in. (10-15mm) from the upper edge. See **Figure 56**.

3. Measure the outside diameter of the piston at the bottom of the skirt. See **Figure 57**.

4. If the difference in the 2 readings is near 0.008 in. (0.2mm) or the engine oil consumption is greater than one quart in 600 miles (one liter/1,000 km), the piston/cylinder combination requires overhaul. If cylinder bore is excessive, replace the cylinder and piston. If the piston is worn or damaged you may replace the piston only. Choose one which is the correct size and weight.

Piston Ring Fit and Installation

Engines built in 1967 (1500cc) beginning with engine No. HO 823 800 have additional oil passages drilled in the crankshaft. This causes more oil to be pumped to the connecting rod bearings and requires different rings. To

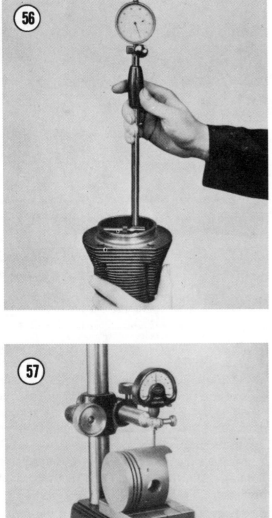

be 0.010-0.016 in. (0.25-0.40mm). If the gap is smaller, hold a small file in a vise, grip the ends of the ring with your hands and enlarge the gap. See **Figure 59**.

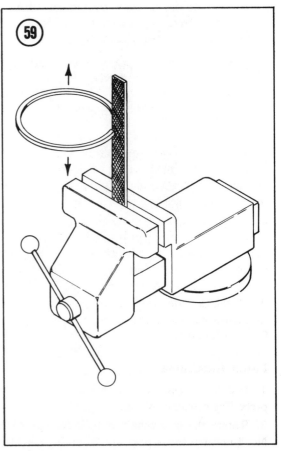

avoid trouble, order new rings by chassis number and engine number. Even though the rings for earlier engine numbers fit, *they must not be interchanged*. To avoid trouble, always order parts by chassis and engine number.

1. Check the ring gap of each ring. To check a ring, insert it in the bottom of the cylinder bore, and square it with the wall by tapping with a piston. The ring should be about 0.2 in. Insert a feeler gauge as shown in **Figure 58**. A compression ring gap should be 0.012-0.018 in. (0.30-0.45mm) while an oil ring gap should

2. Roll each ring around its piston groove as shown in **Figure 60** to check for binding.

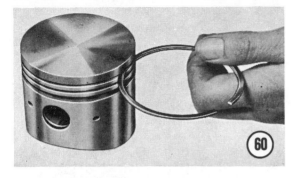

3. With a ring expander tool, carefully install oil ring, then 2 compression rings (**Figure 61**). The compression ring side marked TOP *must* be up.

4. Check the side clearance of the ring as shown in **Figure 62**. Compare with the specifications for your engine.

Piston Installation

1. Install the rings on all 4 pistons using the preceding procedures.

2. Rotate the crankshaft until connecting rod No. 1 is out as far as possible. Counting from the

flywheel, rods are numbered 1, 2 on the right bank, and 3, 4 on the left bank.

3. Starting with piston No. 1, install an end lock (snap ring) in the piston pin hole nearest the alignment arrow.

4. Coat the connecting rod bushing, piston pin and piston holes with assembly lubricant.

5. Place the piston over the connecting rod *with the top arrow pointing toward the flywheel.* Insert the piston pin and tap it with a plastic hammer until it starts into the connecting rod bushing. If it doesn't slide in easily, heat the piston until it is warm to the touch, but not too hot. Continue to drive the piston pin in. While hammering hold the piston so that the rod does not have to take any shock. Otherwise, it may be bent. Drive pin in until it touches end lock.

6. Insert the other end lock.

7. Rotate the crankshaft until connecting rod No. 2 is out as far as it will go.

CAUTION
While rotating the crankshaft watch that skirts of any exposed pistons do not catch on the crankcase. This will crack the piston.

8. Repeat Steps 3-9 for piston No. 2, No. 3, and No. 4. When all are installed, check that all arrows on the pistons point toward the flywheel.

OIL PUMP

Different oil pumps are used on manual and Automatic Stick Shift cars. Manual shift cars have a single gear-type pump for engine oil. Automatic Stick Shift cars have an additional transmission oil pump mounted on the engine oil pump.

Engine oil pumps for 1600cc engines (1970-on) are larger than earlier pumps. However, repair procedures are identical. Oil pumps can be replaced with the engine installed in the car.

Removal

1. If the engine is still in the car, remove rear cover plate, crankcase pulley, and lower fan pulley plate.

2. Remove oil pump cover nuts. Remove cover and gasket.

3a. On single pumps (manuals) remove the gears (3, **Figure 63**).

3b. On dual pumps (automatics) remove the transmission oil pump gears (7 & 8), plate (10), engine oil gears (13 & 14), and gasket (15). See **Figure 64**.

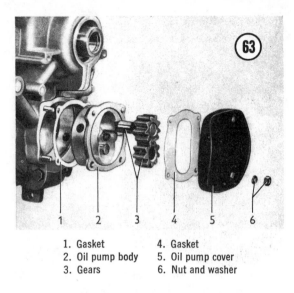

1. Gasket	4. Gasket
2. Oil pump body	5. Oil pump cover
3. Gears	6. Nut and washer

4. Mark the crankcase and oil pump body on the outside edge to aid reassembly. Do not mark on the sealing surface of the pump body.

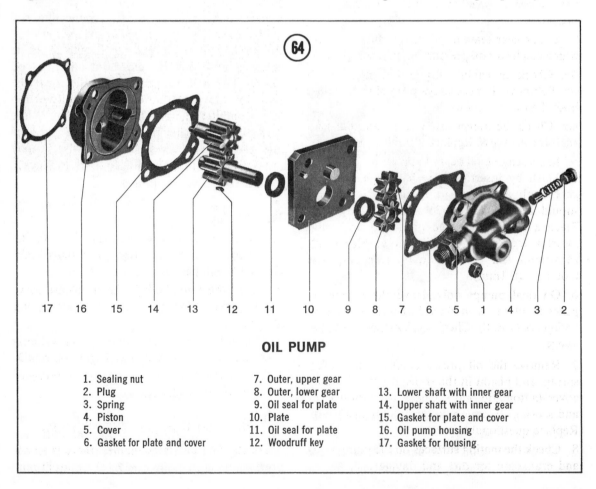

OIL PUMP

1. Sealing nut	7. Outer, upper gear
2. Plug	8. Outer, lower gear
3. Spring	9. Oil seal for plate
4. Piston	10. Plate
5. Cover	11. Oil seal for plate
6. Gasket for plate and cover	12. Woodruff key

13. Lower shaft with inner gear
14. Upper shaft with inner gear
15. Gasket for plate and cover
16. Oil pump housing
17. Gasket for housing

5. Remove the oil pump body with an extractor. See **Figure 65**.

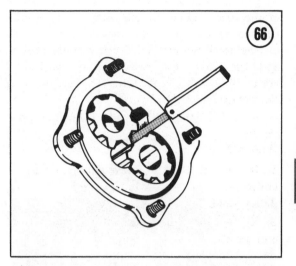

Inspection

1. Clean all parts thoroughly in solvent.

2. Check oil pump cover and plate (automatics) for excessive wear or scoring. Replace it if necessary.

3. Check gear seats in oil pump body for wear which can lower oil pressure to dangerous levels.

4a. Check the engine oil pump idler gear shaft for tightness. If necessary, peen the oil pump body lightly or replace it.

4b. Check the transmission oil pump idler gear shaft for tightness. Replace it if the shaft is loose.

5. Install engine oil gears in pump body. Check backlash by inserting a feeler gauge between gear teeth as shown in **Figure 66**; backlash should be 0.0012-0.0031 in. (0.03-0.08mm). Place a square over the oil pump body and insert a feeler gauge as shown in **Figure 67**. Maximum end play without cover gasket is 0.004 in. (0.1mm).

6. On dual pumps only, leave the engine oil gears in place as in Step 5. Install plate (10) and gears (7 & 8). Check backlash with a feeler gauge.

7. Remove the oil pressure relief valve plug, spring, and piston in the transmission oil pump cover (automatic only). Check for piston wear and scoring. Examine the spring for distortion. Replace questionable parts.

8. Check the mating surfaces on the pump body and crankcase for dirt and damage.

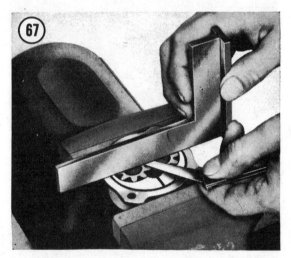

Installation

1. Clean all parts in solvent just prior to installation, even though they were thoroughly cleaned for inspection.

2. Install the pump body in the crankcase using a new gasket. Line up the marks made during removal.

3. Coat all internal parts with assembly lubricant and assemble pump as in Figure 62 or 63.

4. Install the transmission oil pump pressure relief valve parts (2, 3, & 4).

OIL PRESSURE RELIEF VALVES

On all 1961 and later engines, there is an oil pressure relief valve located on the bottom rear of the engine near the oil pump. Since 1970, there is an additional oil pressure relief valve on the bottom front of the engine near the flywheel.

Removal

Refer to **Figure 68** for the following procedure.

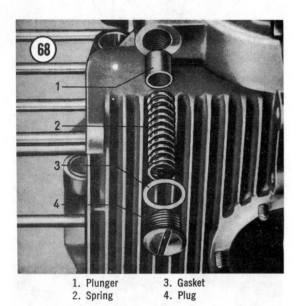

1. Plunger   3. Gasket
2. Spring   4. Plug

1. Remove the plug (4) and gasket (3).
2. Remove the spring (2) and piston (1). If the piston is stuck, thread a 10mm tap lightly into it and pull it out.

Inspection

1. Check the crankcase bore and piston for signs of scoring or seizure. Dress the bore with crocus cloth and replace the piston if necessary.
2. Measure the spring length. Unloaded length should be 2.44-2.52 in. (62-64mm).

Installation

Install the piston, spring, new gasket, and plug in the order shown in Figure 68.

OIL STRAINER

The oil strainer can be removed with the engine installed.

Removal

1. Drain engine oil.
2. Remove 6 nuts securing the cover plate and remove the plate.
3. Remove oil strainer and 2 gaskets.

Inspection

1. Check that the oil suction pipe is tight and centered in the large hole. If not, the engine must be dismantled and the right crankcase half peened. See *Crankcase Inspection*.

2. Clean all parts in solvent and remove all traces of old gasket.

3. Check that cover plate is not bent. Straighten or replace if necessary.

Installation

1. See **Figure 69**. Install all parts in the order shown. Note that a different strainer is used from 1968 and later. There is no difference in installation.

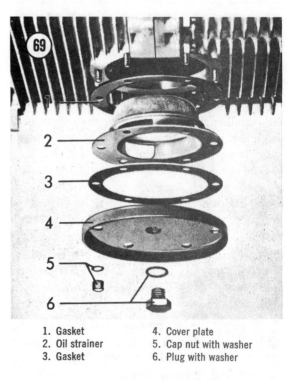

1. Gasket   4. Cover plate
2. Oil strainer   5. Cap nut with washer
3. Gasket   6. Plug with washer

2. Secure cover plate with 6 nuts and new washers. Do not overtighten, or the plate will bend and cause leaks.

CRANKCASE

Disassembly

Remove the oil pressure switch.

Remove the oil filler by pulling off the connecting hose, and unscrewing the internal threaded ring (see **Figure 70**).

3. Remove the 6 bolts securing the oil strainer on the bottom of the crankcase. Pull off the cover, 2 gaskets and strainer. See Figure 69.

4. Tip the crankcase so that it leans on the left half cylinder studs. Remove all 13mm nuts. Loosen the 6 large nuts (17mm).

5. Pull the oil pump out, and remove all 6 large nuts.

6. Check carefully all around the crankcase for any remaining nuts.

7. Loosen the right half of the crankcase by tapping with a rubber hammer or block of wood. Keep pulling upward on the crankcase half and tapping with the hammer until the right half is free. See **Figure 71**. Four valve lifters will fall out, so watch for them.

CAUTION
Never try to pry the crankcase halves apart with a screwdriver or similar object or you will damage the sealing surfaces.

8. Remove the camshaft end seal, shown in **Figure 72**, and lift the camshaft out.

9. Lift the crankshaft out.

10. Remove the center crankshaft bearing inserts. On 1966 and later engines, remove the camshaft bearing inserts; there are none on earlier engines.

11. Remove the oil pressure relief valves as described in an earlier procedure.

Inspection

1. Clean and flush both halves of the crankcase with solvent. Blow out oil passages with air. Remove all traces of old sealing compound on mating faces.

2. Check both crankcase halves for cracks and other damage. Mating and sealing surfaces should be free of nicks and scratches or they will leak.

3. The oil suction pipe in the right half must be centered over the large hole and must be tight.

Refer to **Figure 73**. If not, center it and peen the crankcase around the pipe. To do this, note where the pipe goes through the camshaft bearing web (right-hand arrow in Figure 73). Peen all around the pipe on the side of the web opposite the arrow.

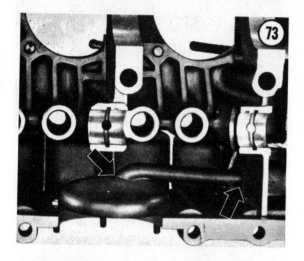

Note that bearing No. 3, which fits in the le crankcase half, has shoulders to support axi loads from the camshaft. Refer to **Figure 75**.

4. Check all studs in the crankcase for looseness. If any cannot be tightened, have a machinist install a Heli-coil insert.

5. Inspect all bearing bores (crankshaft and camshaft) for burrs. Remove with a file. Flush out any metal particles.

6. Ensure that TDC sensor wire on 1974 and later crankcases is undamaged by the cleaning solvent. If necessary, replace the TDC sensor as described earlier in this chapter.

Assembly

1. Coat the cam followers (tappets) with assembly lubricant and insert them in the crankcase halves. The followers for the right half may be coated with heavy grease to hold them in place during Step 18.

2. Insert crankshaft bearing dowel pins in the left case half. See **Figure 74**.

3. Install crankshaft bearing inserts for No. 2 bearing in crankcase halves. Ensure that the inserts fit properly on the dowels. Coat the bearings with assembly lubricant.

4. On 1966 and later engines, install camshaft bearing inserts in the crankcase halves. Make sure the tangs on the bearings fit in the notches.

5. Coat the inside of No. 1 and No. 4 main bearings and crankshaft journals with assembly lubricant.

6. Slide No. 1 bearing (with thrust flanges) onto the flywheel end of the crankshaft with the dowel pin hole closest to the flywheel end.

7. Slide No. 4 bearing onto the timing gear (rear) end of the crankshaft with slot inside the bearing facing toward the timing gear end.

8. Slide the oil slinger onto the rear of the crankshaft so the concave side faces toward the rear.

Lift the crankshaft assembly by connecting
ods No. 1 and No. 2. Place the crankshaft on
e main bearing holders as shown in **Figure 76**.
onnecting rods No. 3 and No. 4 must protrude
rough the corresponding cylinder holes.

10. Take the weight off one bearing at a time,
otate it until the pencil mark on the bearing
s in its original position. There will be a slight
click and the crankshaft should drop into place.
Do this for each bearing, making sure each bearing seats in its dowel. Keep checking until none
of the bearings rotate or move back and forth.

11. Turn the crankshaft until the centerpunched
marks on the timing gear face toward the camshaft bearings.

12. Coat camshaft journals and bearing surfaces with assembly lubricant.

13. Install the camshaft so that the camshaft
gear tooth marked "O" fits between the crankshaft gear teeth marked with centerpunches. See
Figure 77. This alignment is *very important* as
it establishes the valve timing.

14. Install the camshaft end seal using VW
sealing compound.

NOTE: *On Automatic Stick Shift cars,
install the seal so the open end faces
out. Others should be installed with the
open end facing the camshaft.*

15. Again check that the main bearings and
cam bearings are seated. Lubricate all exposed
crankshaft and camshaft journals and bearings.

16. Install new rubber seals over the crankcase
studs on 1968 and later engines. Late 1967
engines (from HO 398 526) also use these seals.

17. Spread VW sealing compound on the crankcase mating surfaces. Do not get any on bearings.

18. Hold connecting rods No. 1 and No. 2 up.
Tip the right case half over the left and slide it
down on the studs.

19. Install some of the center washers and nuts
hand-tight. On 1967 engines from HO 230 323
to HO 398 525, 2 large center nuts on either
side of bearing No. 2 have plastic rings pressed
into them. Install these sealing nuts *without
washers*. Before going any further, check that
no cam followers (tappets) have slipped out.

20. Install the rest of the washers and nuts
hand-tight.

CAUTION
*The tightening sequence described in
the next 4 steps is very important.
Throughout the process, turn the
crankshaft occasionally. If there is any
binding, stop; take the case apart and
find the trouble. Usually it is a main
bearing off its dowel pin.*

21. Torque the 2 small nuts on either side of
the camshaft end seal to 10 ft.-lb. (1.4 mkg);
then to 14 ft.-lb. (2.0 mkg).

22. Torque the 2 large center nuts to 20 ft.-lb.
(2.8 mkg); then to 25 ft.-lb. (3.5 mkg).

23. Torque all other large nuts to 20 ft.-lb.
(2.8 mkg); then to 25 ft.-lb. (3.5 mkg).

24. Torque all remaining small nuts to 10 ft.-lb., then to 14 ft.-lb.

CRANKSHAFT

Removal

1. When the right half of the crankcase has been removed, lift the crankshaft out.

2. Remove the bearing inserts from the crankcase halves. Mark each on its back as it is removed so that it may be reinstalled in the same position.

Gear and Bearing Disassembly

Refer to **Figure 78** for the following procedure.

1. Slide the oil thrower and No. 4 main bearing off of the crankshaft.

2. Remove the snap ring on the rear of the crankshaft.

3. With a large gear puller, pull on the bottom of the innermost (timing) gear. Remove the distributor drive and timing gears. Save the 2 Woodruff keys.

4. Slide No. 3 main bearing off.

5. Slide No. 1 main bearing off the front of the crankshaft.

Gear and Bearing Assembly

Refer again to Figure 78 for the following procedure.

1. Fit No. 1, 3, and 4 main bearings in the left case half. Make sure the bearings fit properly in the dowels. Mark their depth on the bearings to help position the bearings correctly on the crankshaft.

2. Wipe No. 3 bearing journal clean. Coat journal and No. 3 bearing with assembly lubricant. Note the hole in No. 3 bearing is offset. Slide No. 3 bearing on the crankshaft so the hole is close to the flywheel end of crankshaft.

3. Lay the crankshaft vertically on a piece of wood with the flywheel end down.

4. Insert the large Woodruff key in the crankshaft slot. Fit the timing gear over the crankshaft with the centerpunched timing marks

facing up (toward the rear of the shaft). Ali the timing gear slot with the Woodruff key.

5. Tap lightly around the gear with a hamm and dull punch until the gear engages the Woo ruff key. The key must be flat, not canted in t timing gear slot.

6. Heat the timing gear with a small butar torch for a few minutes. Do not heat the beari or the crankshaft. After 3 or 4 minutes, fit length of 2 in. pipe over the crankshaft and dri the gear into position.

7. Slide the spacer ring in place and align i slot with both Woodruff key slots.

8. Insert the small Woodruff keys in the cran shaft. Slide the brass distributor drive gear ov the crankshaft and align it with the Woodru key. Tap the gear down slightly over the Woo ruff key in the same manner as the timing gea

9. Heat the distributor drive gear for or minute, then drive it down with a length of pip until it is against the spacer ring.

10. Spread the snap ring with snap ring plie and slide it over the crankshaft into the groov cut for it. Don't nick or scratch the No. bearing journal.

11. Leave the No. 1 and No. 4 bearings off unt ready to install the crankshaft. See *Crankcas Assembly.*

Inspection

1. Check connecting rod end play, then remov all connecting rods. Both procedures are de scribed under *Connecting Rod Removal* below

2. Clean the crankshaft thoroughly with solvent Clean the oil holes with rifle type brushes; flus thoroughly and blow dry with air. Lightly oil al journal surfaces immediately to prevent rust.

3. Carefully inspect each journal for scratches ridges, scoring, nicks, etc. Very small nicks and scratches may be removed with crocus cloth More serious damage must be removed by grinding; a job for a machine shop.

4. If the surface finish on all journals is satis factory, take the crankshaft to your dealer o local machine shop. They can check for out of-roundness, taper and wear on the journals They will also check crankshaft alignment and inspect for cracks.

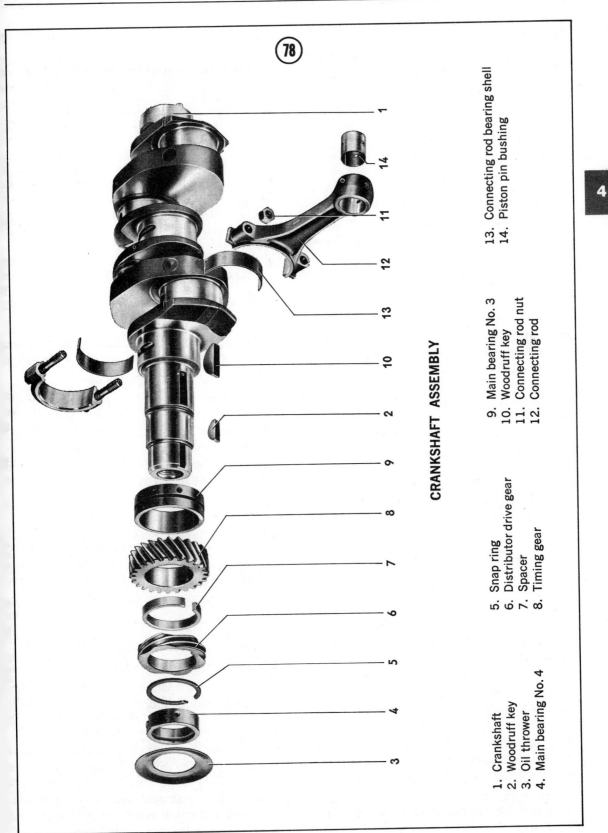

78

CRANKSHAFT ASSEMBLY

1. Crankshaft
2. Woodruff key
3. Oil thrower
4. Main bearing No. 4

5. Snap ring
6. Distributor drive gear
7. Spacer
8. Timing gear

9. Main bearing No. 3
10. Woodruff key
11. Connecting rod nut
12. Connecting rod

13. Connecting rod bearing shell
14. Piston pin bushing

4

Installation

Installation is simply a matter of setting the crankshaft in place after the crankcase is prepared. See *Crankcase Assembly*.

CONNECTING RODS

Removal

1. Remove the crankshaft from the engine. Clamp it down or have someone hold it.

2. File very small marks on each rod to indicate its position for reassembly. For example, make one mark on rod No. 1, two marks on rod No. 2, etc. The rods are numbered 3, 1, 4, 2 from the flywheel end of the crankshaft.

3. Insert a feeler gauge between the side of the rod and the crank throw (see **Figure 79**). If this gap (the connecting rod end play) is greater than 0.016 in., mark the rod for replacement.

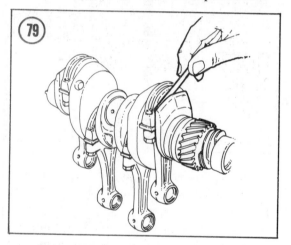

4a. On 1961-1966 (FO 451 420) engines, remove the connecting rod bolts and pull off the rod caps.

4b. On engines since late 1966 (from FO 451 421), remove the connecting rod nuts only, and pull off the rod cap. *Do not* remove the bolts from the rod cap.

5. Remove the bearing inserts from the rod and cap. Mark the back of the insert with rod number for later inspection and reassembly. Do not mix up the bearings.

6. Install the caps on the rods to keep them together.

Inspection

1. Discard any rods with excessive end play (see Step 3 above).

2. Check each rod for obvious damage such as cracks or burns. If either of the bolts or a 1966 and later rod cap is damaged, the entire rod must be replaced.

3. Check the piston pin bushing for wear or scoring. At room temperature a piston pin may slide through with light finger pressure. This does not indicate excessive wear, even though other pins are a drive fit, as long as there is no rocking (see *Piston Removal*, Step 4).

4. Take rods to a machine shop. Have their alignment checked for twisting and bending.

5. Weigh each rod on a scale. They should be within 1/3 oz. (10 grams) of each other. If not, find the lightest rod, and lighten the others as required to match it. You can remove up to 8 grams total by filing or grinding metal away from the points indicated in **Figure 80**.

6. Examine the bearing inserts for wear, scoring, or burning. They are reusable if in good condition. Make a note of the bearing size (if any) stamped on the back of the insert if the bearing is to be discarded; a previous owner may have used undersize bearings.

Installation

1. Remove the rod cap from the rod and *discard the bolts* (1961-1966) *or nuts* (1966 on). You must use new bolts or nuts. Do not remove the bolt from 1966 (FO 451 421) and later rods.

2. Carefully match the number on the side of each rod to its associated rod cap.

3. Install the bearing inserts in the rods and caps. Press the bearings in with your thumbs on the ends of the bearing. Don't press down on the middle of the bearing. Be sure that the tangs on the bearings fit into the notches on the rods and caps.

CAUTION
The bearing ends will extend slightly above the cap or rod. See **Figure 81**. *Do not file any part of the rod, cap, or bearing for a different fit.*

4. Oil the nuts and rod cap bolts lightly.

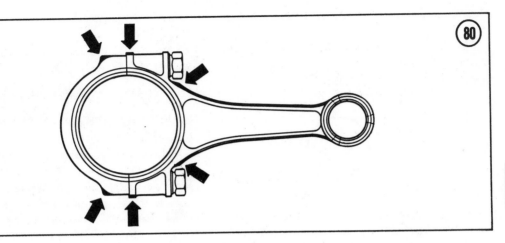

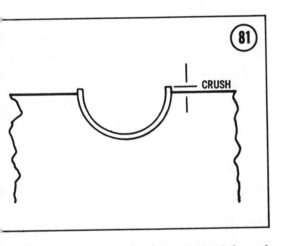

CRUSH

5. Cut a piece of Plastigage the width of the rod bearing. Assemble the rod cap on the crank throw for cylinder No. 3 (the one closest to the flywheel) with the Plastigage inserted between the rod cap and the crank throw. Make sure the forge mark on the rod faces up as shown in **Figure 82**. Tighten the nuts to 22-25 ft.-lb. (3.0-3.4 mkg).

6. Remove the bearing cap and measure the width of the flattened Plastigage wire following the manufacturer's instructions. This is the bearing clearance. Compare it to the specifications for your engine. If it is not right, make sure that you have installed the proper bearings.

7. Remove the strip of Plastigage, coat the bearing and crank throw with assembly lubricant, and reassemble the rod on the corresponding crank throw.

8. Check that the rod rotates freely 180° through its own weight alone.

9. Measure the rod end play with a feeler gauge (see *Removal*, Step 3). Compare with the specifications.

10. Repeat Steps 5-9 for each rod. Be sure you assemble each rod with the forge mark up, and on the crank throw originally used for that rod. Also ensure that the rod and cap number are aligned.

11. Peen the bolt head or nut into the slot on the rod to lock it in place. See **Figure 83**.

CAMSHAFT

Removal

1. When the right half of the crankcase has been removed, lift the camshaft out.

2. Remove the camshaft bearing inserts from the 1966 and later crankcase halves, and mark

7. Check the cam followers (tappets), which ar removed when splitting the crankcase, for wea and scoring.

Installation

Installation is simply a matter of setting th camshaft in place after the crankcase is pre pared. See *Crankcase Assembly*.

each on the back as it is removed so that it may be reinstalled in the same position.

Inspection

1. Check bearing journals and cam lobes for wear. The cam lobes should not be scored and the edges should be square. Slight damage may be removed with a silicon carbide oilstone. Use 100-120 grit initially, then polish them with a 280-320 grit.

2. Check camshaft runout at the center bearing. See **Figure 84**. Runout must not exceed 0.0008 in. (0.02mm).

3. Examine timing gear rivets, and check for gear looseness.

4. Check the timing gear teeth for wear and proper tooth contact.

5. Chamfer all edges of the bearing bores slightly to prevent seizure due to bearing pressure.

6. Check the bearing inserts for wear, scoring or burns. Replace if necessary.

Table 1   TIGHTENING TORQUES

	foot-pounds	mkg
Connecting rods	22-25	3-3.5
Crankcase halves (large nuts)	25	3.5
Crankcase halves (small nuts)	14	2.0
Cylinder head nuts	23	3.2
Rocker shaft nuts	14-18	2-2.5
Oil pump cover nuts	14	2.0
Oil drain plug	25	3.5
Flywheel gland nut		
except 1600 engine	217	30
1600 engine	253	
Oil strainer nuts	5	0.7
Flywheel gland nut	217	30
Pressure plate bolts	18	2.5
Engine mounting bolts	22	3
Torque converter to drive plate	18	2.5
Crankshaft pulley	29-36	4-5
Spark plugs	22-29	3-4
Generator pulley	40-47	5.5-6.5

Table 2   ENGINE SPECIFICATIONS — 1200, 1300

	1200 (1961-1965)		1300 (1966)	
PE	TOLERANCE (NEW)	WEAR LIMIT	TOLERANCE (NEW)	WEAR LIMIT
ENERAL				
Number of cylinders	4		4	
Bore, inch (mm)	3.03 (77)		3.03 (77)	
Stroke, inch (mm)	2.52 (64)		2.72 (69)	
Displacement, inch (mm)	72.7 (1192)		78.4 (1285)	
Compression ratio	7.0:1		7.3:1	
Firing order	1-4-3-2		1-4-3-2	
Output (SAE) bhp @ rpm	41.5 @ 3900		50 @ 4600	
Torque (SAE) foot-pounds				
@ rpm	65 @ 2400		69 @ 2600	
Weight (dry) lbs (kg)	237 (108)		244 (111)	
YLINDERS				
Bore, inch (mm)	3.03 (77)		3.03 (77)	
Cylinder/piston clearance				
Out-of-round inch (mm)	0.0015-0.0019 (0.04-0.05)	0.008 (0.20)	0.0015-0.0019 (0.04-0.05)	0.008 (0.20)
inch (mm)	0.0004 (0.01)		0.0004 (0.01)	
Oversizes available mm	0.5, 1		0.5, 1	
ISTONS				
Material	light alloy		light alloy	
Weight, + (gray) grams	285-310		306-318	
− (brown) grams	280-302		298-310	
Permissible weight deviation				
in same engine	5	10 max	5	10 max
PISTON RINGS				
Number per piston	3		3	
Compression	2		2	
Oil Control	1		1	
Ring end gap				
Compression inch (mm)	0.012-0.018 (0.30-0.45)	0.035 (0.90)	0.012-0.018 (0.30-0.45)	0.035 (0.90)
Oil Control inch (mm)	0.010-0.016 (0.25-0.40)	0.037 (0.95)	0.010-0.016 (0.25-0.40)	0.037 (0.95)
Ring side clearance				
Top compression				
inch (mm)	0.0027-0.0035 (0.07-0.09)	0.0047 (0.12)	0.0027-0.0035 (0.07-0.09)	0.0047 (0.12)
Bottom compression				
inch (mm)	0.0019-0.0027 (0.05-0.07)	0.0039 (0.10)	0.0019-0.0027 (0.05-0.07)	0.0039 (0.10)
Oil Control inch (mm)	0.0012-0.0019 (0.03-0.05)	0.0039 (0.10)	0.0012-0.0019 (0.03-0.05)	0.0039 (0.10)
PISTON PINS				
Diameter inch (mm)	0.7871-0.7874 (19.996-20.000)		0.8658-0.8661 (21.996-22.000)	
Clearance in rod bushing				
inch (mm)	0.0004-0.0008 (0.01-0.02)	0.0016 (0.04)	0.0004-0.0008 (0.01-0.02)	0.0016 (0.04)
CRANKSHAFT				
Number of main bearings	4		4	
Main bearing journal diameter				
Bearings 1-3 inch (mm)	2.1640-2.1648 (54.97-54.99)		2.1640-2.1648 (54.97-54.99)	
Bearing 4 inch (mm)	1.5739-1.5748 (39.98-40.00)		1.5739-1.5748 (39.98-40.00)	
Connecting rod journal				
diameter, inch (mm)	2.1640-2.1648 (54.97-54.99)		2.1644-2.1653 (54.98-55.00)	
Main bearing clearances				
Bearings 1 & 3	0.0016-0.0047 (0.04-0.10)	0.007 (0.18)	0.0016-0.0047 (0.04-0.10)	0.007 (0.18)
Bearing 2	0.0011-0.0035 (0.03-0.09)	0.0066 (0.17)	0.0011-0.0035 (0.03-0.09)	0.0066 (0.17)
Bearing 4	0.0019-0.004 (0.05-0.10)	0.0074 (0.19)	0.0019-0.004 (0.05-0.10)	0.0074 (0.19)

4

Table 2   ENGINE SPECIFICATIONS — 1200, 1300 (continued)

	1200 (1961-1965)		1300 (1966)	
	TOLERANCE (NEW)	WEAR LIMIT	TOLERANCE (NEW)	WEAR LIMIT
End play inch (mm)	0.0027-0.0051 (0.07-0.13)	0.006 (0.15)	0.0027-0.0051 (0.07-0.13)	0.006 (0.15)
Permissible out-of-round				
Main bearing journal				
inch (mm)		0.0011 (0.03)		0.0011 (0.03)
Connecting rod journal				
inch (mm)		0.0011 (0.03)		0.0011 (0.03)
CONNECTING RODS				
Weight deviation in same				
engine, grams	5	10 max	5	10 max
Weight + (black or gray)				
grams	507-515		592-600	
— (white or brown)				
grams	487-495		580-588	
Side clearance inch (mm)	0.004-0.016 (0.1-0.4)	0.028 (0.7)	0.004-0.016 (0.1-0.4)	0.028 (0.7)
Connecting rod bearing				
clearance inch (mm)	0.0008-0.0031 (0.02-0.08)	0.006 (0.15)	0.0008-0.0031 (0.02-0.08)	0.006 (0.15)
Piston pin bushing diameter,				
inch (mm)	0.7877-0.7880 (20.008-20.017)		0.8664-0.8667 (22.008-22.017)	
CAMSHAFT				
Number of bearings	3		3	
Bearing diameter inch (mm)	0.9837-0.9842 (24.99-25.00)		0.9837-0.9842 (24.99-25.00)	
Bearing clearance inch (mm)	0.0008-0.0019 (0.02-0.05)	0.0047 (0.12)	0.0008-0.0019 (0.02-0.05)	0.0047 (0.12)
End play inch (mm)	0.0016-0.0051 (0.04-0.13)	0.0063 (0.16)	0.0016-0.0051 (0.04-0.13)	0.0063 (0.16)
TIMING GEARS				
Backlash inch (mm)	0.0000-0.0019 (0.00-0.05)		0.0000-0.0019 (0.00-0.05)	
VALVES — INTAKE				
Head diameter inch (mm)	1.239 (31.5)		1.299 (33.0)	
Stem diameter inch (mm)	0.3125-0.3129 (7.94-7.95)	0.3109 (7.90)	0.3125-0.3129 (7.94-7.95)	0.3109 (7.90)
Valve guide inside diameter				
inch (mm)	0.3149-0.3156 (8.00-8.02)		0.3149-0.3156 (8.00-8.02)	
Valve face angle	45°		45°	
Valve seat angle	45°		45°	
VALVES — EXHAUST				
Head diameter inch (mm)	1.181 (30.0)		1.181 (30.0)	
Stem diameter inch (mm)	0.3114-0.3118 (7.91-7.92)	0.3109 (7.90)	0.3114-0.3118 (7.91-7.92)	0.3109 (7.90)
Valve guide inside diameter				
inch (mm)	0.3149-0.3156 (8.00-8.02)		0.3149-0.3156 (8.00-8.02)	
Valve face angle	45°		45°	
Valve seat angle	45°		45°	
VALVE SPRINGS				
Length inch (mm)	1.305 (33.4)		1.220 (31.0)	
@ load lbs (kg)	@ 90-103 lbs (40.8-46.8)		@ 117-135 (53.2-61.2)	
OIL SYSTEM				
Oil pressure (SAE 30 @ 158°F)				
and 2500 rpm	42 psi (3 kg/cm²)	28 psi	42 psi (3 kg/cm²)	28 psi
Oil pressure relief valve spring		(2 kg/cm²)		(2 kg/cm²)
Length inch (mm)	0.928 (23.6)		0.928 (23.6)	
@ load lbs (kg)	@ 17 (7.75)		@ 17 (7.75)	
Oil pump				
Gear shaft end play				
(no gaskets) inch (mm)		0.004 (0.1)		0.004 (0.1)
Gear backlash inch (mm)	0.0012-0.0031 (0.03-0.08)		0.0012-0.0031 (0.03-0.08)	

Table 2   ENGINE SPECIFICATIONS — 1500, 1600 (continued)

PE	1500 (1967-1969)		1600 (1970-ON)	
	TOLERANCE (NEW)	WEAR LIMIT	TOLERANCE (NEW)	WEAR LIMIT
NERAL				
Number of cylinders	4		4	
Bore, inch (mm)	3.27 (83)		3.36 (85.5)	
Stroke, inch (mm)	2.72 (69)		2.72 (69)	
Displacement, inch (mm)	91.1 (1493)		96.6 (1584)	
Compression ratio	7.5:1		7.5:1 [1] [2] 7.3:1 [3]	
Firing order	1-4-3-2		1-4-3-2	
Output (SAE) bhp @ rpm	53 @ 4200		57 @ 4400 [1] 60 @ 4400 [2]	
			46 @ 4000 [4] 48 @ 4200 [5]	
Torque (SAE) ft.-lb. @ rpm	78 @ 2600		81.7 @ 3000 [1], [2]	
			73.1 @ 2800 [5] 72.0 @ 2000 [4]	
Weight (dry) lbs (kg)	250 (114)		264 (120)	
LINDERS				
Bore, inch (mm)	3.27 (83)		3.36 (85.5)	
Cylinder/piston clearance				
inch (mm)	0.0015-0.0019 (0.04-0.05)	0.008 (0.20)	0.0016-0.0024 (0.04-0.06)	0.008 (0.20)
Out-of-round inch (mm)	0.0004 (0.01)		0.0004 (0.01)	
Oversizes available mm	0.5, 1		0.5, 1	
STONS				
Material	light alloy		light alloy	
Weight, + (gray) grams	378-388		406-418 [1], [2] 410-420 [6]	
— (brown) grams	370-380		398-410 [1], [2] 402-412 [6]	
Permissible weight deviation				
in same engine	5	10 max	5	10 max
STON RINGS				
Number per piston	3		3	
Compression	2		2	
Oil Control	1		1	
Ring end gap				
Compression inch (mm)	0.012-0.018 (0.30-0.45)	0.035 (0.90)	0.012-0.018 (0.30-0.45)	0.035 (0.90)
Oil Control inch (mm)	0.010-0.016 (0.25-0.40)	0.037 (0.95)	0.010-0.016 (0.25-0.40)	0.037 (0.95)
Ring side clearance				
Top compression				
inch (mm)	0.0027-0.0035 (0.07-0.09)	0.0047 (0.12)	0.0027-0.0039 (0.07-0.10)	0.0047 (0.12)
Bottom compression				
inch (mm)	0.0019-0.0027 (0.05-0.07)	0.0039 (0.10)	0.0019-0.0027 (0.05-0.07)	0.0039 (0.10)
Oil Control in (mm)	0.0012-0.0019 (0.03-0.05)	0.0039 (0.10)	0.0012-0.0019 (0.03-0.05)	0.0039 (0.10)
STON PINS				
Diameter inch (mm)	0.8658-0.8661 (21.996-22.000)		0.8658-0.8661 (21.996-22.000)	
Clearance in rod bushing				
inch (mm)	0.0004-0.0008 (0.01-0.02)	0.0016 (0.04)	0.0004-0.0008 (0.01-0.02)	0.0016 (0.04)
RANKSHAFT				
Number of main bearings	4		4	
Main bearing journal diameter				
Bearings 1-3 inch (mm)	2.1640-2.1648 (54.97-54.99)		2.1640-2.1648 (54.97-54.99)	
Bearing 4 inch (mm)	1.5739-1.5748 (39.98-40.00)		1.5739-1.5748 (39.98-40.00)	
Connecting rod journal				
diameter, inch (mm)	2.1644-2.1653 (54.98-55.00)		2.1644-2.1653 (54.98-55.00)	
Main bearing clearances				
Bearings 1 & 3	0.0016-0.004 (0.04-0.10)	0.007 (0.18)	0.0016-0.004 (0.04-0.10)	0.007 (0.18)
Bearing 2	0.001-0.0035 (0.03-0.09)	0.0066 (0.17)	0.001-0.0035 (0.03-0.09)	0.0066 (0.17)
Bearing 4	0.002-0.004 (0.05-0.10)	0.0074 (0.19)	0.002-0.004 (0.05-0.10)	0.0074 (0.19)

4

[1] 1970   [2] 1971   [3] 1972-ON   [4] 1972-ON   [5] 1975-ON   [6] After Aug., 1971

Table 2   ENGINE SPECIFICATIONS — 1500, 1600 (continued)

	1500 (1967-1969)		1600 (1970-ON)	
	TOLERANCE (NEW)	WEAR LIMIT	TOLERANCE (NEW)	WEAR LIMIT
End play inch (mm)	0.0027-0.0051 (0.07-0.13)	0.006 (0.15)	0.0027-0.0051 (0.07-0.13)	0.006 (0.15)
Permissible out-of-round				
Main bearing journal				
inch (mm)		0.0011 (0.03)		0.0011 (0.03)
Connecting rod journal				
inch (mm)		0.0011 (0.03)		0.0011 (0.03)
CONNECTING RODS				
Weight deviation in same				
engine, grams	5	10 max	5	10 max
Weight + (black or gray)				
grams	592-600		592-600	
— (white or brown)				
grams	580-588		580-588	
Side clearance inch (mm)	0.004-0.016 (0.1-0.4)	0.028 (0.7)	0.004-0.016 (0.1-0.4)	0.028 (0.7)
Connecting rod bearing				
clearance inch (mm)	0.0008-0.0031 (0.02-0.08)	0.006 (0.15)	0.0008-0.0028 (0.02-0.07)	0.006 (0.15)
Piston pin bushing diameter,				
inch (mm)	0.8664-0.8667 (22.008-22.017)		0.8664-0.8667 (22.008-22.017)	
CAMSHAFT				
Number of bearings	3		3	
Bearing diameter inch (mm)	0.9837-0.9842 (24.99-25.00)		0.9837-0.9842 (24.99-25.00)	
Bearing clearance inch (mm)	0.0008-0.0019 (0.02-0.05)	0.0047 (0.12)	0.0008-0.0019 (0.02-0.05)	0.0047 (0.12)
End play inch (mm)	0.0016-0.0051 (0.04-0.13)	0.0063 (0.16)	0.0016-0.0051 (0.04-0.13)	0.0063 (0.16)
TIMING GEARS				
Backlash inch (mm)	0.0000-0.0019 (0.00-0.05)		0.0000-0.0019 (0.00-0.05)	
VALVES — INTAKE				
Head diameter inch (mm)	1.397 (35.5)		1.40 (35.6)	
Stem diameter inch (mm)	0.3125-0.3129 (7.94-7.95)	0.3109 (7.90)	0.3125-0.3129 (7.94-7.95)	0.3109 (7.90)
Valve guide inside diameter				
inch (mm)	0.3149-0.3156 (8.00-8.02)		0.3149-0.3156 (8.00-8.02)	
Valve face angle	44°		44°	
Valve seat angle	44°		44°	
VALVES — EXHAUST				
Head diameter inch (mm)	1.259 (32.0)		1.26 (32.1)/1.19 (30.1)**	
Stem diameter inch (mm)	0.3114-0.3118 (7.91-7.92)	0.3109 (7.90)	0.3114-0.3118 (7.91-7.92)*	0.3109 (7.90)*
Valve guide inside diameter				
inch (mm)	0.3149-0.3156 (8.00-8.02)		0.3149-0.3156 (8.00-8.02)*	
Valve face angle	45°		45°	
Valve seat angle	45°		45°	
VALVE SPRINGS				
Length inch (mm)	1.220 (31.0)		1.220 (31.0)	
@ load lbs (kg)	@ 117-135 (53.2-61.2)		@ 117-135 (53.2-61.2)	
OIL SYSTEM				
Oil pressure (SAE 30 @ 158°F)	42 psi (2 kg/cm²)	28 psi	28 psi (2kg/cm²)	28 psi
and 2500 rpm		(2 kg/cm²)		(2 kg/cm²)
Oil pressure relief valve spring				
Length inch (mm)	0.928 (23.6)		1.73 (44.1)	
@ load lbs (kg)	@ 17 (7.75)		@ 12.3-16.1 (5.6-7.3)	
Oil pressure control				
valve spring				
Length inch (mm)	——	——	0.79 (20.2)	
@ load lbs (kg)	——	——	@ 6.8-8.4 (3.1-3.8)	
Oil pump				
Gear shaft end play				
(no gaskets) inch (mm)		0.004 (0.1)		0.004 (0.1)
Gear backlash inch (mm)	0.0012-0.0031 (0.03-0.08)		0.0012-0.0031 (0.03-0.08)	

* Add 1.00mm for 1975-on.   ** 1975-on.

CHAPTER FIVE

COOLING, HEATING, AND EXHAUST SYSTEMS

The cooling, heating, and exhaust systems on Beetle or Karmann Ghia are very closely related. A large fan on the front end of the generator provides cooling air to the engine. Sheet metal cover plates direct the air from the fan housing around the cylinders and cylinder heads. Cooling air temperature is thermostatically controlled.

When the engine is cold, an air control ring limits the intake of cold air to the fan housing in 1961-1964 models. Since 1965, air control flaps limit the outflow of cold air from the fan housing to the engine. Both methods permit rapid engine warm up in any weather by limiting the cooling effect of the fan. Once the engine is warm, the thermostat permits the maximum volume of cool air to be admitted.

Two different heating systems are used. On 1961 and 1962 models, heated air, which cooled the engine, is directed into the passenger area. This system should be watched closely for exhaust leaks, since dangerous carbon monoxide could be blown directly into the passenger area. If you smell exhaust fumes, open the windows and investigate immediately.

Heaters on 1963 and later models differ importantly from the earlier system. Large hoses direct fresh air from the fan housing through heat exchangers and into the passenger area. Exhaust gases pass through a separate area in the heat exchanger and warm the air. There is

less chance of exhaust leaks contaminating the heated air. Models from 1975 have improved heat exchangers, but service procedures are the same.

The exhaust system is very straightforward. On 1961 and 1962 cars, exhaust gases pass through exhaust pipes to the muffler. On 1963 and later models, exhaust gases pass through heat exchangers to the muffler. A portion of the exhaust gases are tapped off through the preheater pipe to warm the intake manifold.

Many Beetles produced since 1972 have a unique exhaust recirculation system to cut nitrogen oxides in the exhaust gases. In 1972, only Automatic Stick Shift cars for California had exhaust gas recirculation (EGR). In 1973, all California Beetles and all U.S./Canadian Beetles with Automatic Stick Shift were equipped with EGR. Since 1974, all Beetles have EGR.

Figure 1 shows the 1972 EGR system. Exhaust gases pass from a special take-off point on the muffler into the cooling coil (2) and filter (3). During partial engine loads, intake manifold vacuum opens the recirculation valve (1) which admits the cooled, clean exhaust gases into the intake manifold. Addition of this gas lowers combustion chamber temperatures, thereby reducing the emission of oxides of nitrogen in the exhaust.

Later systems are similar to 1972, except that a filter element replaces the cooling coil.

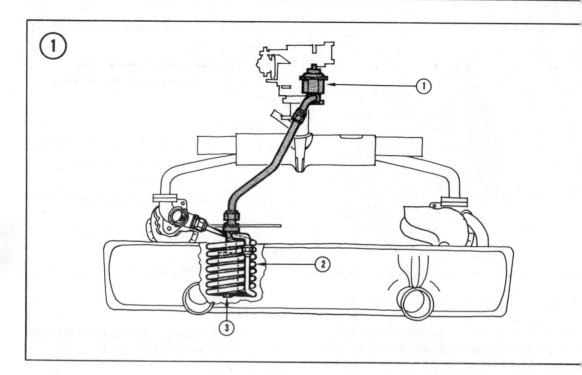

All 1975 and later models sold in California have a catalytic converter inserted between the engine and the muffler. This device consists of a platinum plated ceramic honeycomb element inside a stainless steel housing. When hot exhaust gases reach the platinum catalyst, a chemical reaction occurs which reduces harmful exhaust emissions.

CAUTION
Cars with a catalytic converter must use only unleaded fuel. As few as 2 tankfuls of leaded fuel can destroy the catalytic converter.

COOLING SYSTEM

Fan Housing Removal/Installation

This procedures permits removal while the engine is installed. If the engine is not installed, the fan housing is removed by performing Steps 10 through 12 of *Engine Disassembly*.

1. Remove the fan belt as described in Chapter Two. Do not attempt to pry the belt over the pulley.

2. Disconnect the negative battery cable.

3. Remove the rear hood as described in Chapter Thirteen.

4. Remove heater hoses between fan housin and heat exchangers (1963 on).

5a. On 1961-1966 cars, disconnect the sma wire from the voltage regulator (mounted c generator) and mark it 61. Disconnect the larg wire(s) and mark it B+(51). Disconnect ar mark ignition coil wires.

5b. On 1967 and later cars, disconnect 3 wir from the generator. Mark them with labels marked on the generator.

6. Disconnect the oil pressure switch wire. T oil pressure switch is located on the crankca near the distributor.

7. Remove the carburetor (or intake air senso following the procedure in Chapter Six.

8. Pull the accelerator cable out the front of t fan housing.

9. Remove the distributor cap and pull wires o the spark plugs.

10. Remove strap securing generator to pedestal.

11. Remove screws on both sides and at the re of the fan housing.

12a. On 1961-1964 models, unhook the a control ring spring and remove bolts securi the ring to the fan housing. See **Figure 2**.

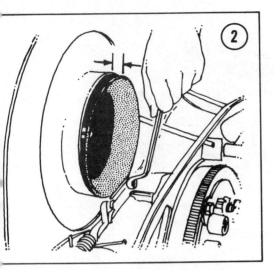

2b. On 1965 and later models, remove the air control thermostat screw (see **Figure 3**) and screw the thermostat from the control rod.

3. Pull the fan housing off, complete with generator and fan.

4. Installation is the reverse of these steps. Adjust the air control ring (1961-1964) or thermostat (1965 on) as described later in this chapter.

Fan Housing Disassembly / Assembly (1965 on)

Refer to **Figure 4** for the following procedure.
1. Unhook connecting link return spring (3).

2. Remove 8 screws securing the control flap housings (1 and 7).

3. Pull both control flap housings out.

4. Assembly is the reverse of disassembly.

Fan Removal

1. Remove fan housing as described previously.

2. Make small marks on the fan housing and fan cover to aid reassembly.

3. Remove 4 screws securing fan cover to fan housing.

4. Remove generator and fan assembly.

5. Remove the fan nut.

6. Pull off fan, thrust washer, shims, and hub.

Fan Installation

1. Place the fan hub on the generator shaft. Be sure the Woodruff key is properly seated.

2. Insert shims.

3. Place fan in position.

4. Install fan nut and tighten to 40-47 ft.-lb. (5.5-6.5 mkg).

5. Check the distance from fan to cover (a, **Figure 5**). It should be 0.08 in. (2.0mm). If not, remove the nut; vary the number of shims under the thrust washer. Install the thrust washer, any unused shims, and retorque the nut. Measure distance (a) again. Readjust if necessary.

6. Install fan cover assembly in the fan housing.

7. Install the fan housing.

8. Adjust fan belt tension. See Chapter Two.

CAUTION
Polarize the generator as described in Chapter Seven before connecting any generator or voltage regulator wires. Otherwise the voltage regulator can be seriously damaged. Do not polarize alternator, if so equipped.

Air Control Ring Adjustment (1961-1964)

If the engine is installed, warm the engine and check that the upper edge of the air control is about 0.78 in. (20mm) from the fan housing (see Figure 2). If not, adjust as described below. Note this procedure also applies to engines which are not yet installed.

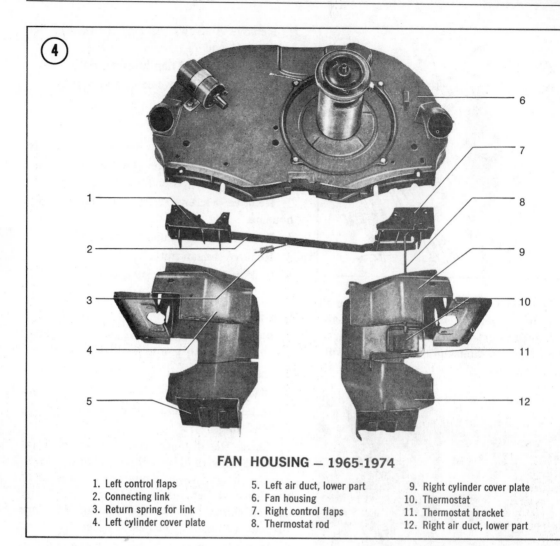

FAN HOUSING — 1965-1974

1. Left control flaps	5. Left air duct, lower part	9. Right cylinder cover plate
2. Connecting link	6. Fan housing	10. Thermostat
3. Return spring for link	7. Right control flaps	11. Thermostat bracket
4. Left cylinder cover plate	8. Thermostat rod	12. Right air duct, lower part

1. Loosen the clamp bolt on the ring operating lever (1, Figure 2).

2a. If the engine is installed, warm the engine until the upper end of the thermostat touches the upper stop on the bracket. The thermostat is mounted on the right side between the pushrod tubes for cylinders 1 and 2.

2b. If the engine is not installed, remove the bolt securing the thermostat to its bracket. Have an assistant lift the thermostat until its upper end touches the upper stop on the bracket.

3. Pull the air control ring away from the fan housing about 0.78 in. (20mm) as measured with a steel rule. See Figure 2.

4. Tighten the clamp bolt on the ring operating lever while holding the ring in this position.

NOTE: *Remaining steps apply only if engine is not installed.*

5. Install and tighten the bolt securing t thermostat to its bracket.

6. Ensure the air control ring rests agair rubber stop on fan housing with slight preloa

7. Check adjustment again once the engine installed and warmed up.

Air Control Thermostat Adjustment (1965 on)

This procedure may be performed with t engine installed or not installed. The engi should be cold.

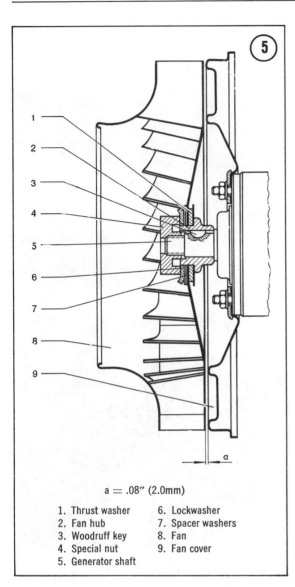

a = .08″ (2.0mm)

1. Thrust washer
2. Fan hub
3. Woodruff key
4. Special nut
5. Generator shaft
6. Lockwasher
7. Spacer washers
8. Fan
9. Fan cover

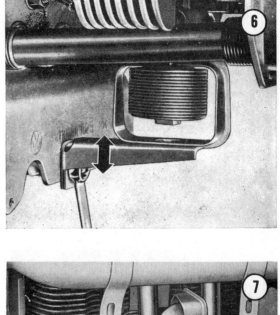

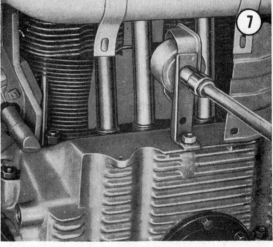

HEATING SYSTEM

Heater Cable Replacement

1. If thermostat has been removed, screw it onto the connecting rod (8, Figure 4).

2. Loosen nut securing the thermostat bracket to the crankcase.

3. Open the control flaps with connecting rod.

4. Move the thermostat bracket in the slot until the upper end of the thermostat touches the upper part of the bracket. See **Figure 6**. Tighten the bracket nut.

5. Move the thermostat back and forth to ensure that the flaps work.

6. Install and tighten the bolt securing the thermostat to the bracket. See **Figure 7**.

Two cables are permanently joined at the lever end so that both heater flaps operate simultaneously. The cables are replaced together, not individually.

1. Loosen the clamp nuts securing the cable ends to the heat exchanger or junction box lever. See **Figure 8**.

2. Pull cable ends out of the clamps.

3. Pull sealing plugs out of the guide tubes and slide them off the cables. See **Figure 9**.

4a. On 1961 and 1962 models, remove the threaded cap and pull out the knob with cable. See **Figure 10**.

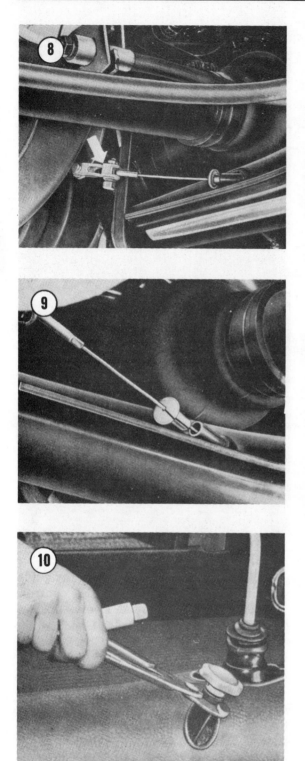

lever and friction discs. Disconnect cable from lever. Pull cable out from the lever end. See **Figure 12**.

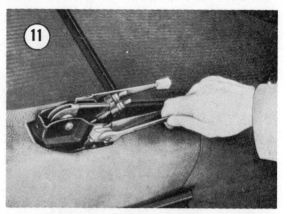

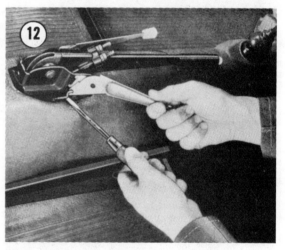

5. Check all parts for wear or damage. Replace if necessary.

6. Grease the new cable lightly with universal grease and push the ends into the guide tubes.

> NOTE: *On 1961 and 1962 models, the longer cable goes into the right-hand guide tube.*

7a. On 1961 and 1962 models, hook the new cable onto the heater control knob assembly. Turn the knob counterclockwise to the stop, then 3 turns clockwise before installation. Install the heater control knob assembly.

4b. On 1963 and later models, remove handbrake cover. Remove nut securing the right operating lever (see **Figure 11**). Remove the

7b. On 1963 and later models, hook cable on operating lever. Install the lever with friction discs. Install the handbrake cover.

8. Install sealing plugs on cables and push them into the guide tubes.

9. Clamp cables to heater flap clamps. Ensure the flaps open and close fully when operating the lever.

> NOTE: *You can alter the force required to operate the heater flaps by adjusting the tightness of the mounting nut.*

EXHAUST SYSTEM

Figure 13 shows the complete exhaust system for 1961-1971. Different mufflers are used on later models. In 1972, a different muffler was used to reverse the flow of preheating gases for the intake manifold. See **Figure 14**. The 1972-1973 muffler may be installed on earlier models if the 1972-1973 warm air pickup pipe is also used. In 1974, the intake manifold received a second preheating pipe. This required a new muffler with larger flanges to accept the new intake manifold. See **Figure 15**. Also, the 1974 tailpipes are larger than on previous years.

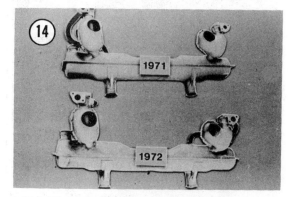

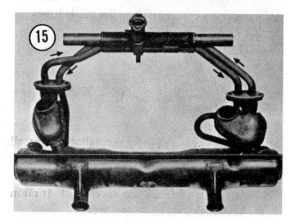

Two different mufflers are used on 1975 and later models: a short muffler on vehicles equipped with a catalytic converter and a long muffler on all other models.

Muffler Replacement (1961-1974)

1. Remove clamps between muffler and heat exchanger (1963-1974 only). See **Figure 16**.

2. Remove warm air channel clamps. See **Figure 17**.

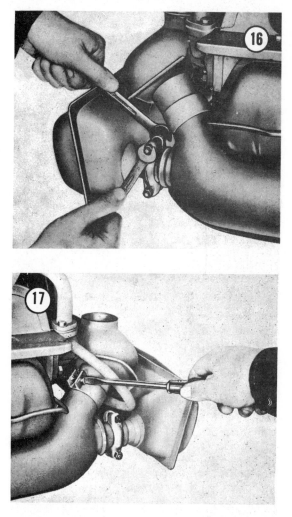

3. On EGR-equipped models, remove exhaust recirculation coil/filter as described in the next section.

4. If engine is installed, remove small cover plate around preheater pipes. See **Figure 18**. Also remove rear cover plate (**Figure 19**).

⑬

EXHAUST SYSTEM — 1962-ON

1. Clamp washer
2. E-clip
3. M 5 bolt
4. Air hose from fan housing
5. Hose clamp
6. Air hose grommet
7. Air hose connecting pipe
8. M 8 self-locking nut
9. Left preheating pipe gasket
10. Exhaust pipe flange gasket (2)
11. Flexible heated air duct
12. Heat exchanger
13. Heater flap lever
14. Flap lever return spring
15. Pin
16. Cable connecting link
17. Cable retaining pin
18. E-clip
19. Flat clamp
20. Tailpipe retaining ring (2)
21. Heat exchanger seal
22. M 6 nut
23. Clamp
24. M 6 bolt (2)
25. Tailpipe seal
26. Tailpipe
27. Right preheating pipe gasket
28. Muffler

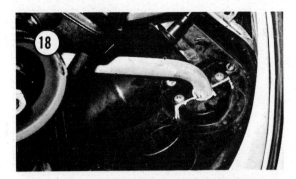

5. Remove muffler flange nuts and preheater pipe flange screws. See **Figure 20**.

6. Pull muffler off. Remove all gaskets.

7. Examine the muffler and tailpipes carefully for leaks or damage. Replace if necessary.

8. Installation is the reverse of these steps. Use new gaskets. See WARNING under *Heater Junction Box Replacement*.

9. Adjust tailpipe length from tip to muffler to 8-9/32 in. (210mm) on 1961-1973 models and 8-7/8 in. (226mm) on 1974 models. See (a), **Figure 21**.

> NOTE: *Tailpipe length affects exhaust flow and engine back pressure.*

Muffler Replacement (1975 on)

1. Remove bolts securing EGR take-off pipe to muffler assembly.

2. Remove bolts securing each end of muffler assembly to the heat exchangers.

3. Lower the muffler.

4. Installation is the reverse of these steps.

> NOTE: *The catalytic converter can be reused with the new muffler if the converter is still in good condition. Re-*

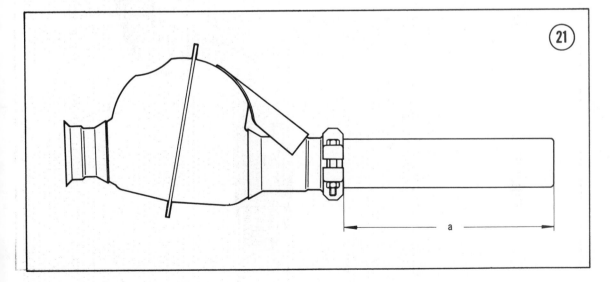

*move the bolts and clamps holding the
converter to the old muffler and install
it on the new one.*

EXHAUST RECIRCULATION
SYSTEM

This system consists of a recirculation valve
and a cooling coil/filter (1972) or replaceable
filter element (1973 on).

On 1972 models, the recirculation valve must
be replaced every 12,000 miles as described in
Chapter Two. The cooling coil need only be
replaced if damaged or defective (leaking).

On 1973-1974 models, the filter element
must be replaced every 24,000 miles; on 1975
and later models, every 15,000 miles. The recirculation valve must be checked at the same
interval. See Chapter Two.

To replace the cooling coil (1972) or filter
element (1973 on), disconnect the union nuts
at each end of the coil or filter. Remove the coil
or filter and install a new one.

CHAPTER SIX

FUEL SYSTEMS

This chapter describes 2 fuel systems:

a. Carburetted (1961-1974)

b. Fuel injected (1975 on)

Specifications (**Table 1**) for the carburetted system are at the end of the chapter. In addition, this chapter describes the fuel evaporative control system required since 1970. Adjustments are described in Chapter Two under *Engine Tune-up*.

CARBURETTED FUEL SYSTEM

The fuel system consists of a front-mounted fuel tank connected through a line to the fuel pump. An eccentric cam on the distributor drive shaft operates the mechanical fuel pump which delivers fuel to a Solex downdraft carburetor.

A variety of carburetors are found on 1961 to 1974 models. All work on the same general principles. Refer to **Figure 1** for the following discussion. The figure shows a 30 PICT-2 (1968 and 1969) which is typical of all carburetors in this chapter.

All carburetted VW's use an oil bath air cleaner which removes dust and dirt particles from the carburetor air. In addition, air cleaners from 1961-1974 have means to control the temperature of air introduced to the carburetor.

Air Cleaner Removal/Installation

1. Remove the air preheater hose(s).

2. Remove the oil breather tube.

3a. On 1968-1970 air cleaners, disconnect the automatic preheater cable.

3b. On 1972-1974 air cleaners, disconnect the vacuum line near the base of the carburetor. See **Figure 2**.

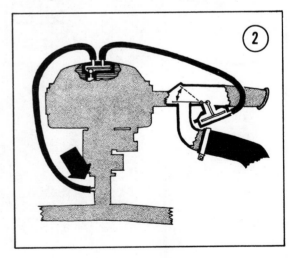

4. Loosen the clamp at the bottom of the air cleaner and pull the air cleaner off. Keep it level; it contains oil.

①

1. Float
2. Fuel line
3. Float lever
4. Float needle valve
5. Float needle
6. Pilot jet
7. Gasket
8. Pilot air drilling
9. Ball check valve in power fuel system
10. Air correction jet with emulsion tube
11. Power fuel tube
12. Float bowl vent tube
13. Choke valve
14. Bimetal spring
15. Operating lever
16. Accelerator pump discharge tube
17. Diaphragm rod
18. Vacuum diaphragm
19. Pump lever
20. Pump diaphragm
21. Spring
22. Pushrod spring
23. Ball check valve for accelerator pump
24. Pump connector rod
25. Main jet
26. Volume control screw
27. Fuel metering screw*
28. Bypass port
29. Idle port
30. Throttle valve
31. Discharge arm
32. Vacuum drilling
33. Ball check valve in accelerator pump drilling
34. Jet in vacuum drilling
35. Vacuum connection
36. Diaphragm spring

*Caution: Do not change the adjustment of this screw.

30 PICT-2 CARBURETOR

5. Installation is the reverse of these steps. See Chapter Two for cleaning.

Carburetor Types

Six different Solex downdraft carburetors were used from 1961-1974. They are so similar, however, that the same procedures apply with only minor differences. Following is a brief description of each.

28 PICT (1961-1963)

This is the first VW carburetor equipped with an automatic choke. A vacuum piston opens the choke butterfly slightly when the engine starts. This model has a power fuel system. See 30 PICT-2 description.

28 PICT-1 (1964 and 1965)

This model is the same as the 28 PICT except that a vacuum diaphragm replaces the vacuum piston and there is no power fuel system. See 30 PICT-2 description.

30 PICT-1 (1966 and 1967)

The 30 PICT-1 is similar to the 28 PICT-1 except that it has a larger venturi. There is no power fuel system. See 30 PICT-2 description.

30 PICT-2 (1968 and 1969)

This carburetor is similar to the 30 PICT-1, except that it has a power fuel system which draws fuel directly from the float chamber under full load, high speed conditions.

30 PICT-3 (1970)

This model is similar to the 30 PICT-2 except that redesigned idling permits the throttle to completely close at idle, while idle speed is controlled by air bypass around the throttle.

34 PICT-3 and 34 PICT-4 (1971-1974)

These 2 carburetors are similar to the 30 PICT-3, except a bypass mixture cutoff valve replaces the pilot jet cutoff valve, and the venturi is larger. Although all 1971-1974 carburetors are 34 PICT types, differing choke parts prevents interchangeability.

Carburetor Removal/Installation

1. Remove air cleaner as described previously.

2. Pull the fuel line and vacuum line off the carburetor. See **Figure 3**.

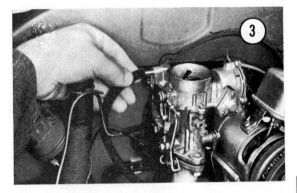

3. Disconnect the electrical wires to the automatic choke and pilot jet cutoff valve (1961-1970) or bypass mixture cutoff valve (1971-1974).

4. Disconnect the accelerator cable from the throttle linkage. Remove both carburetor mounting nuts (**Figure 4**) and pull the carburetor off.

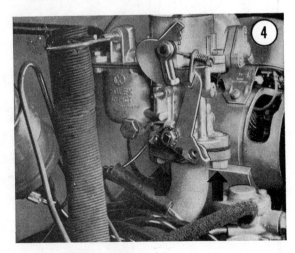

5. Installation is the reverse of these steps. Use a new gasket between the carburetor and intake manifold, tighten the nuts evenly and adjust the carburetors as described previously.

Carburetor Disassembly

Refer to **Figures 5, 6, 7, and 8** for the following procedure.

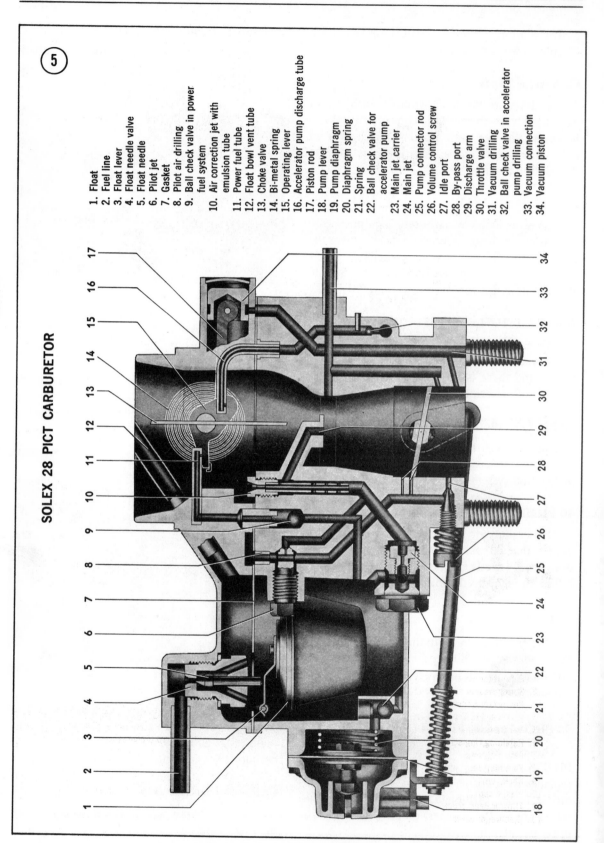

SOLEX 28 PICT CARBURETOR

1. Float
2. Fuel line
3. Float lever
4. Float needle valve
5. Float needle
6. Pilot jet
7. Gasket
8. Pilot air drilling
9. Ball check valve in power fuel system
10. Air correction jet with emulsion tube
11. Power fuel tube
12. Float bowl vent tube
13. Choke valve
14. Bi-metal spring
15. Operating lever
16. Accelerator pump discharge tube
17. Piston rod
18. Pump lever
19. Pump diaphragm
20. Diaphragm spring
21. Spring
22. Ball check valve for accelerator pump
23. Main jet carrier
24. Main jet
25. Pump connector rod
26. Volume control screw
27. Idle port
28. By-pass port
29. Discharge arm
30. Throttle valve
31. Vacuum drilling
32. Ball check valve in accelerator pump drilling
33. Vacuum connection
34. Vacuum piston

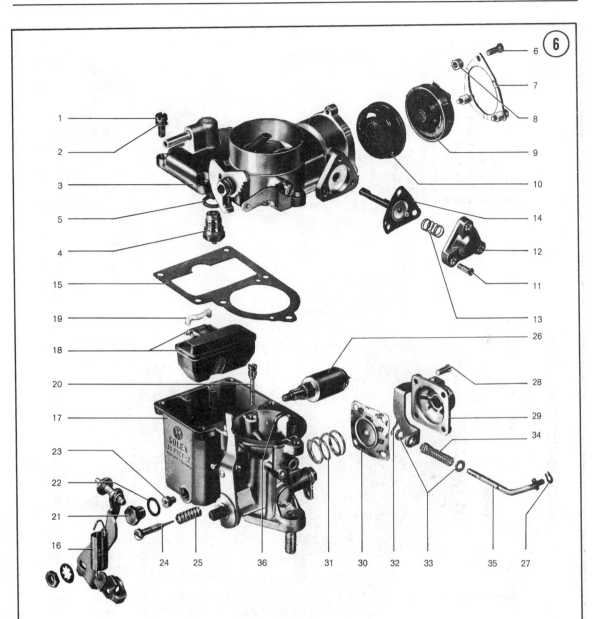

SOLEX 30 PICT-2 CARBURETOR

1. Carburetor upper half screw
2. Spring washer
3. Carburetor upper half
4. Float needle valve
5. Needle valve washer
6. Retaining ring screw
7. Retaining ring
8. Retaining ring spacer
9. Choke unit
10. Plastic cap
11. Fillister head screw
12. Diaphragm cover
13. Diaphragm spring
14. Diaphragm
15. Gasket
16. Accelerator cable return spring
17. Carburetor lower half
18. Float and pin
19. Float pin bracket
20. Air correction jet
21. Main jet plug
22. Plug seal
23. Main jet
24. Volume control screw
25. Spring
26. Pilot jet cutoff valve
27. Circlip
28. Fillister head screw
29. Pump cover
30. Pump diaphragm
31. Diaphragm spring
32. Cotter pin
33. Washer
34. Connecting rod spring
35. Connecting rod
36. Accelerator pump injector tube

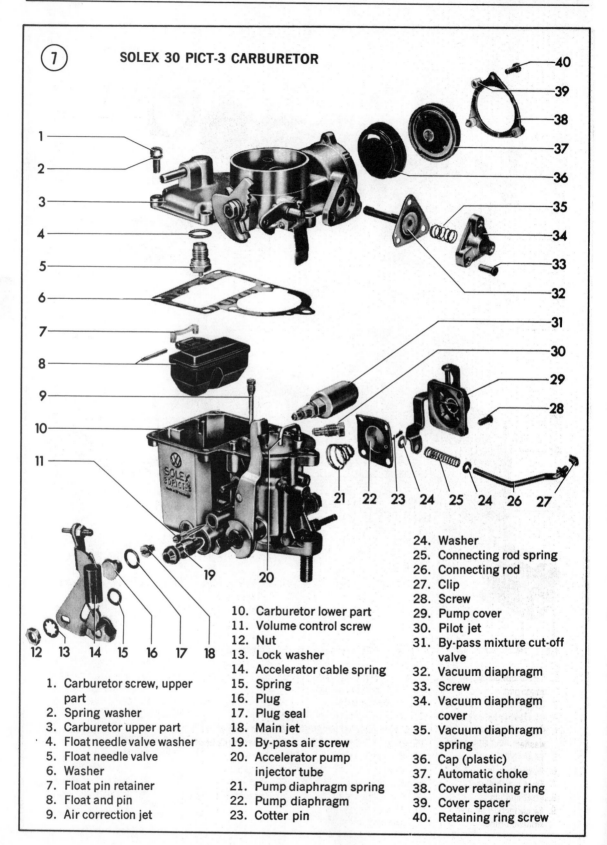

SOLEX 30 PICT-3 CARBURETOR

1. Carburetor screw, upper part
2. Spring washer
3. Carburetor upper part
4. Float needle valve washer
5. Float needle valve
6. Washer
7. Float pin retainer
8. Float and pin
9. Air correction jet
10. Carburetor lower part
11. Volume control screw
12. Nut
13. Lock washer
14. Accelerator cable spring
15. Spring
16. Plug
17. Plug seal
18. Main jet
19. By-pass air screw
20. Accelerator pump injector tube
21. Pump diaphragm spring
22. Pump diaphragm
23. Cotter pin
24. Washer
25. Connecting rod spring
26. Connecting rod
27. Clip
28. Screw
29. Pump cover
30. Pilot jet
31. By-pass mixture cut-off valve
32. Vacuum diaphragm
33. Screw
34. Vacuum diaphragm cover
35. Vacuum diaphragm spring
36. Cap (plastic)
37. Automatic choke
38. Cover retaining ring
39. Cover spacer
40. Retaining ring screw

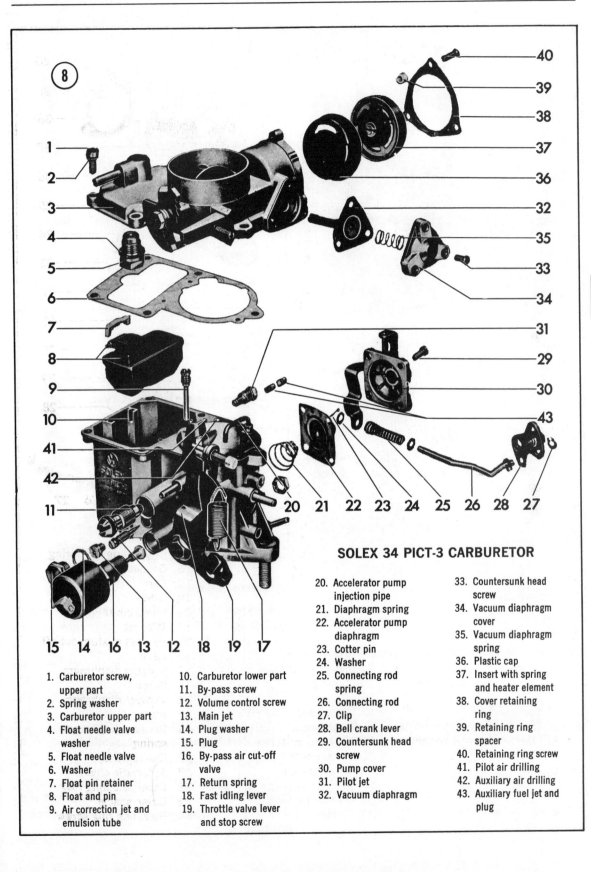

SOLEX 34 PICT-3 CARBURETOR

20. Accelerator pump injection pipe
21. Diaphragm spring
22. Accelerator pump diaphragm
23. Cotter pin
24. Washer
25. Connecting rod spring
26. Connecting rod
27. Clip
28. Bell crank lever
29. Countersunk head screw
30. Pump cover
31. Pilot jet
32. Vacuum diaphragm

33. Countersunk head screw
34. Vacuum diaphragm cover
35. Vacuum diaphragm spring
36. Plastic cap
37. Insert with spring and heater element
38. Cover retaining ring
39. Retaining ring spacer
40. Retaining ring screw
41. Pilot air drilling
42. Auxiliary air drilling
43. Auxiliary fuel jet and plug

1. Carburetor screw, upper part
2. Spring washer
3. Carburetor upper part
4. Float needle valve washer
5. Float needle valve
6. Washer
7. Float pin retainer
8. Float and pin
9. Air correction jet and emulsion tube

10. Carburetor lower part
11. By-pass screw
12. Volume control screw
13. Main jet
14. Plug washer
15. Plug
16. By-pass air cut-off valve
17. Return spring
18. Fast idling lever
19. Throttle valve lever and stop screw

1. Remove 5 screws securing the upper part of the carburetor to the body and lift it off. See **Figure 9**.

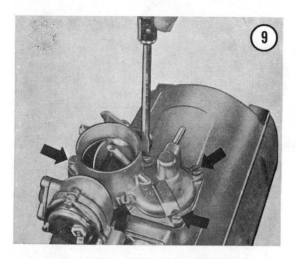

2. Pull out the float retainer and the float.

3. Unscrew the float needle valve from the upper part of the carburetor.

4. On 1964-1974 carburetors, remove **3** screws securing the vacuum diaphragm to the upper part. Remove the diaphragm and spring.

5. Remove 3 screws securing the automatic choke. Remove the retainer, spacers, choke, and plastic cap.

6. Unscrew the air correction jet.

7a. On 1961-1970 carburetors, unscrew the pilot jet cutoff valve.

7b. On 1971-1974 carburetors, unscrew the bypass mixture cutoff valve.

8. Remove the main jet plug, seal, and main jet.

9a. On 1961-1969 carburetors, remove the idle mixture screw and spring.

9b. On 1970-1974 carburetors, remove the air bypass screw shown in **Figure 10** or **Figure 11**.

> CAUTION
> *Do not remove volume control screw near the air bypass screws. This is factory preset and must not be removed or adjusted.*

10. Remove the cotter pin.

11. Remove 4 screws securing the accelerator pump cover. Remove the cover, diaphragm, and spring.

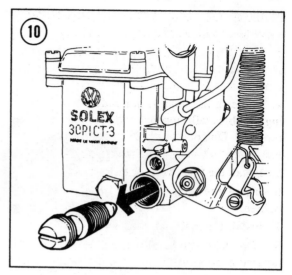

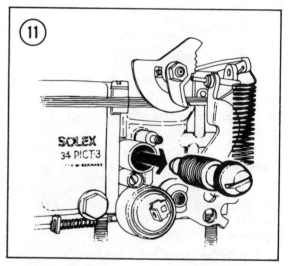

Carburetor Cleaning

1. Clean all parts except the automatic choke parts in solvent. Wipe the automatic choke parts with a clean cloth.

2. Clean jets and drillings in the carburetor body with compressed air. Do not clean them with pins or pieces of wire; you might enlarge the holes.

Lower Part Inspection and Assembly

1. Install the spring, new diaphragm, and cover. When tightening the cover screws, pull the pump lever back, away from the float chamber so the diaphragm is secured in the pressure stroke position.

2. Install the connecting rod on the butterfly valve lever with a snap ring, if removed.

3. Install the washers and spring in the order shown in the figure. Insert cotter pin in the innermost hole in the connecting rod.

4. Immerse the float in hot water. If it is leaking, bubbles will appear, and the float must be replaced. Do not attempt to solder the hole. This increases float weight and causes high fuel level.

5. Install the float with the float retainer.

6. Install the air correction jet. Do not overtighten.

7. Install the main jet, seal, and plug.

8a. On 1961-1969 carburetors, ensure that the tapered portion of the idle mixture screw is not grooved, bent, or marked. Replace if necessary. Install the idle mixture screw.

8b. On 1970-1974 carburetors, make sure that the tapered portion of the air bypass screw is not grooved, bent, or marked. Replace it if necessary. Install the air bypass screw.

9a. Install the 1961-1970 pilot jet cutoff valve.

9b. Install the bypass mixture cutoff valve on 1971-1974 carburetors.

Upper Part Inspection and Assembly

1. Check the float needle valve for leakage. To do this, install it in the upper body, hold the valve in lightly with your finger and blow in the fuel inlet. If it leaks, install a new needle valve.

2. Check the choke bimetal spring and heater element for obvious damage. Install it in the plastic cover with the lug on the ceramic element (a) in the notch in the plastic cover. Install the cover and element assembly in the upper part of the carburetor with the spacers and retainer ring. Turn the choke assembly so the index mark on the choke is on the center index mark on the carburetor. See **Figure 12**. Tighten the retaining ring screws.

> NOTE: *Due to improved preheating, beginning with 1972 models, the heater elements are different from those in earlier carburetors. Heater elements are not interchangeable between 1972-1974 carburetors and earlier versions. Elements for 1972-1974 are marked "60" on the cover (Figure 13).*

3. Install the vacuum diaphragm, spring, and cover.

4. Install the upper carburetor part on the lower part with a new gasket.

Accelerator Cable Replacement

The accelerator cable passes from the accelerator pedal, through the frame tunnel and fan housing in guide tubes to the carburetor linkage.

Removal

1. Loosen the screw on the throttle swivel pin securing the cable and pull the cable free. See **Figure 14**.

2. Pull the spring sleeve toward the fan housing to compress the return spring. Remove the small retainer.

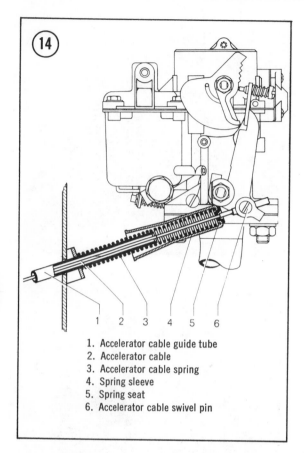

1. Accelerator cable guide tube
2. Accelerator cable
3. Accelerator cable spring
4. Spring sleeve
5. Spring seat
6. Accelerator cable swivel pin

5. Slide the spring and spring sleeve over the cable. Push the spring sleeve toward the fan housing to compress the spring and insert the spring retainer.

6. Insert cable end into throttle swivel pin.

7. Have an assistant depress the accelerator fully. Open the carburetor throttle valve until there is about 0.04 in. clearance between the throttle lever and carburetor stop. Tighten the screw on the swivel pin.

Throttle Positioner Removal/Installation

Two types of throttle positioners are used. A one-piece positioner mounted near the carburetor was used on 1966-1969 models, and a 2-piece positioner was used on 1970-1972 models. Neither type is repairable and both must be replaced as a unit if defective. Use of the positioner was discontinued on 1973 and later models (and 1972 models first sold in California).

1. Disconnect the vacuum line(s).

2. Remove 3 screws and retaining ring over the throttle positioner. See **Figure 15**. Remove the positioner.

3. Slide spring sleeve and spring off the cable.

4. Disconnect the rod from the accelerator pedal and disconnect the cable from the rod.

5. Raise the rear of the car on jackstands.

6. From underneath, pull the cable out the front of the fan housing.

7. Remove the plastic hose from the rear cable end, and remove the rubber boot from the rear of the guide tubes.

8. Pull the cable out the front.

Installation

1. Grease the accelerator cable with universal grease.

2. Install the cable through the frame tunnel. The accelerator cable must lay straight between the guide tubes with no kinks.

3. Install the rubber boot and plastic hose on the guide tubes.

4. From underneath, feed the cable through the fan housing guide tube.

3. On 2-piece units, remove the screws securing control portion to engine compartment.

4. Disconnect the positioner from the throttle linkage.

5. Installation is the reverse of these steps. Check the adjustment as described below.

Adjustment (One-piece Unit)

1. Connect a tachometer to the engine.

2. Loosen the set screw on the end of the throttle positioner and turn the adjusting screw (1, **Figure 16**) clockwise until the stop washer on the pull rod (arrow, Figure 16) contacts the throttle positioner housing. Idle speed should be 1,700-1,800 rpm.

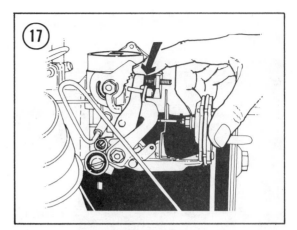

3. If the engine speed is not 1,700-1,800 rpm, loosen the locknuts at each end of the pull rod. Rotating the pull rod lengthens or shortens it, setting the engine speed. Tighten locknuts.

4. Readjust the throttle positioner adjusting screw (1, Figure 16) so engine speed is 850 rpm.

5. Increase engine speed to 3,000 rpm with the accelerator pedal, then release it quickly. Engine speed must drop from 3,000 rpm to 1,000 rpm within 3-4 seconds. If shortening the time is required, turn adjusting screw (1, Figure 16) clockwise and recheck. If a longer time is required, turn the screw counterclockwise and recheck.

6. Tighten the set screw for the adjusting screw, and recheck the rpm drop time.

Adjustment (Two-piece Unit)

1. Connect a tachometer to the engine. Check that engine idle speed is 850 rpm. Adjust if necessary.

2. Pull the lever connected to the throttle positioner back until it contacts the stop screw on the mounting bracket. See **Figure 17**. Engine speed should be 1,700-1,800 rpm.

3. If the engine speed is not 1,700-1,800 rpm, readjust the stop screw. See **Figure 18**.

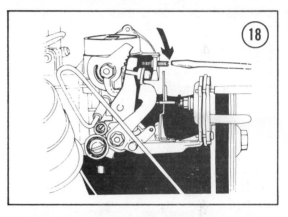

4. Loosen the set screw on the end of the control portion of the throttle positioner.

5. Increase engine speed to 3,000 rpm with the accelerator pedal, then release it quickly. Engine speed must drop from 3,000 to 1,000 rpm within 3-4 seconds. If a shorter time is required, turn the screw counterclockwise.

6. Tighten the set screw for the adjusting screw and recheck the rpm drop time.

INTAKE MANIFOLD

Removal

1. Remove the fan housing and rear cover plate as described in Chapter Five.

2. Remove nuts and bolts securing the manifold to the cylinder heads and exhaust flanges.

3. Remove the intake manifold with preheater pipe.

4. Remove the cylinder head sealing rings. See **Figure 19**.

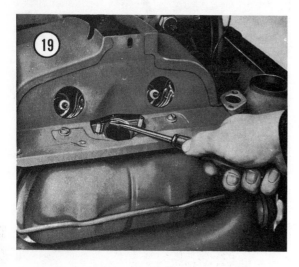

Inspection

1. Check the manifold and preheater pipe for leaks, and damaged flanges.

2. Check that the preheater pipe is not blocked. This can be a source of poor acceleration and eventual engine overheating.

3. Check the rubber sleeves on the 1971-1974 manifolds for cracks and other signs of deterioration. See **Figure 20**.

Installation

1. Install new gaskets in the cylinder head intake ports.

2. Install new gaskets in the preheater pipe flanges. The smallest diameter gasket goes in the left hand flange.

3. Place the intake manifold in position.

4. Install all nuts and bolts for the manifold and preheater pipe.

5. Install the fan housing and rear cover plate. See Chapter Five.

FUEL PUMP

Removal

1. Disconnect the fuel lines from the fuel pump. On 1961-1965 fuel pumps, the fuel inlet line must be unscrewed. The 1961-1965 fuel outlet and both lines on 1966 and later fuel pumps simply pull off.

2. Remove mounting nuts and lift pump off.

3. Remove the pushrod, intermediate flange, and gaskets.

Disassembly

Refer to **Figure 21 or 22** for the following procedure.

1a. On 1961-1965 fuel pumps, remove the top cover bolt and lift off the cover and filter.

1b. On 1966 and later fuel pumps, remove the plug and fuel filter. Remove 4 screws securing the top cover. Lift out the cutoff spring and diaphragm.

2. Remove 6 screws securing the top part of the pump to the main body.

3. Push down on the pump diaphragm to release it from the pump operating lever. Lift the diaphragm and spring out.

4. Carefully drive out the pin holding the operating lever.

5. Remove operating lever and spring.

Inspection

1. Examine diaphragm for cracks or hardening.

2. Blow gently on the delivery pipe to check the delivery valve. Suck gently on the intake pipe to check the suction valve. If either valve leaks,

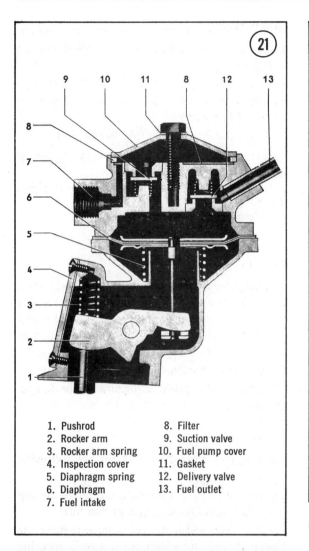

1. Pushrod
2. Rocker arm
3. Rocker arm spring
4. Inspection cover
5. Diaphragm spring
6. Diaphragm
7. Fuel intake
8. Filter
9. Suction valve
10. Fuel pump cover
11. Gasket
12. Delivery valve
13. Fuel outlet

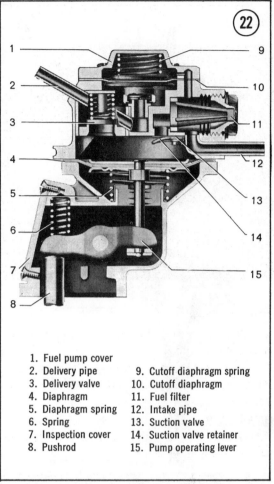

1. Fuel pump cover
2. Delivery pipe
3. Delivery valve
4. Diaphragm
5. Diaphragm spring
6. Spring
7. Inspection cover
8. Pushrod
9. Cutoff diaphragm spring
10. Cutoff diaphragm
11. Fuel filter
12. Intake pipe
13. Suction valve
14. Suction valve retainer
15. Pump operating lever

the entire top portion of the pump must be replaced. In this case, consider installing a rebuilt pump; it may be less expensive than salvaging the original.

Assembly

Assembly is the reverse of the disassembly procedure. Use new parts provided in a standard rebuild kit.

Adjustment

1. Install intermediate flange with 2 new gaskets underneath and one on top. See **Figure 23**.

2. Insert the pushrod with rounded end down.

3. Remove the center wire from the ignition coil so the engine will not accidentally start.

Turn the engine over by hand until the pushrod is as high as possible.

4. Measure the tip of the pushrod above the surface of the top gasket. This should be about 0.5 in. (13mm).

5. Turn the engine until the pushrod is at the bottom of its stroke.

6. Measure pushrod height as in Step 4. This should be about 0.3 in. (8mm). The difference, which is the stroke, should be about 0.16 in. (4mm). If not, add or remove a gasket under the intermediate flange.

Installation

1. Install and adjust the intermediate flange and pushrod as described above.

2. Pack the opening in the bottom of the fuel pump with universal grease.

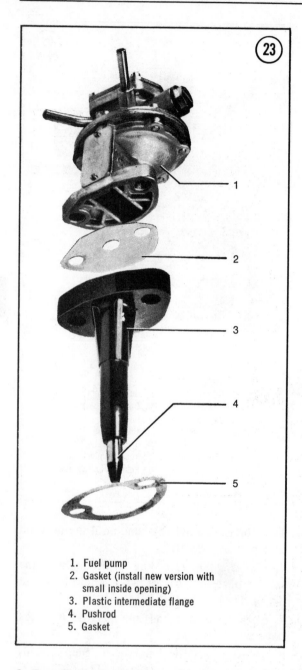

1. Fuel pump
2. Gasket (install new version with small inside opening)
3. Plastic intermediate flange
4. Pushrod
5. Gasket

3. Install the fuel pump with the inspection cover facing left. Install retaining nuts.

4. Connect the fuel lines.

FUEL INJECTION SYSTEM

Service information for the fuel injection system is beyond the scope of this manual. The owner/mechanic could replace most of the fuel injection components himself, but special knowledge and electronic test equipment is required to find the defective component. Substituting good components for suspected ones is not practical, since most of the components are very expensive.

The troubleshooting section in Chapter Two and the theory of operation in this chapter are intended primarily to help the owner talk intelligently about fuel injection troubles with the dealer's service manager and mechanics.

Basic Principles

The heart of the air flow controlled fuel injection system is the control unit, a small electronic computer. Various sensors transmit information concerning air temperature, engine temperature, engine speed, and engine load to the control unit. The control unit uses this information to determine the exact amount of fuel to be distributed to the cylinders. **Figure 24** is a simplified diagram of the entire fuel injection system; refer to it for the following descriptions. **Figure 25** is an electrical diagram which may be helpful when troubleshooting.

Air System

The air system consists of the intake air sensor, auxiliary air regulator, throttle valve housing, and intake air distributor.

Clean air from the air cleaner enters the intake air sensor, passes the throttle valve and enters the intake air distributor for distribution to the cylinders. The throttle valve, connected by a cable to the accelerator pedal, controls the flow of air into the engine. The intake air sensor measures the volume of the air flow and translates this into a proportional electrical signal. A temperature sensor in the intake air sensor produces an electrical signal proportional to incoming air temperature. The intake air sensor transmits the combined air volume/temperature signal to the control unit.

Incoming air volume is an accurate indication of engine load, since higher engine loads require larger amounts of air for combustion. When the intake air sensor detects a larger air flow, it signals the control unit to increase the amount of fuel injected.

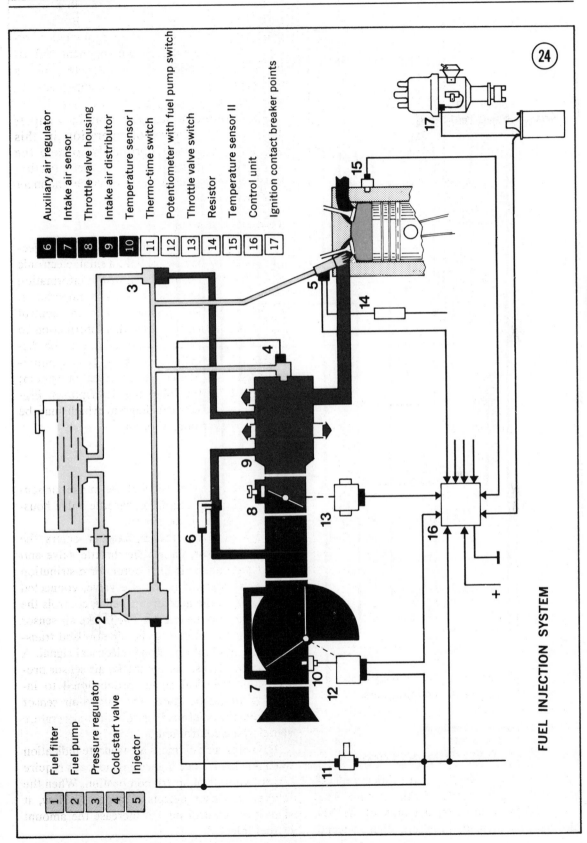

FUEL INJECTION SYSTEM

1 Fuel filter
2 Fuel pump
3 Pressure regulator
4 Cold-start valve
5 Injector

6 Auxiliary air regulator
7 Intake air sensor
8 Throttle valve housing
9 Intake air distributor
10 Temperature sensor I
11 Thermo-time switch
12 Potentiometer with fuel pump switch
13 Throttle valve switch
14 Resistor
15 Temperature sensor II
16 Control unit
17 Ignition contact breaker points

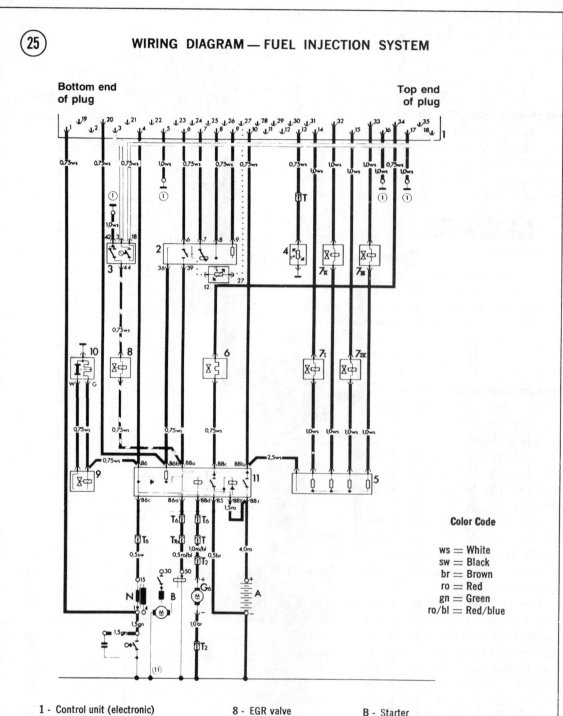

WIRING DIAGRAM — FUEL INJECTION SYSTEM

Bottom end of plug

Top end of plug

Color Code

ws = White
sw = Black
br = Brown
ro = Red
gn = Green
ro/bl = Red/blue

1 - Control unit (electronic)
2 - Intake air sensor
3 - Throttle valve switch
4 - Temperature sensor on cylinder head
5 - Series resistance
6 - Auxiliary air regulator
7 - Injectors

8 - EGR valve
9 - Cold starting valve
10 - Thermo switch
11 - Double relay
N - Ignition coil
G_6 - Fuel pump
A - Battery

B - Starter
T - Wire connector
T_1 - Wire connector
T_2 - Wire connector, double
T_6 - Wire connector, 6 point
① - Ground connector near alternator
⑪ - Ground connector, headlights

During idle, the throttle valve is completely closed. A bypass around the throttle valve permits a small amount of air, controlled by the idle speed screw, to pass.

When the engine is started, the auxiliary air regulator bypasses a larger amount of air around the throttle valve. The increased air flow causes the intake air sensor to request more fuel from the control unit. Increased air and fuel facilitate starting and running a cold engine. As soon as the engine is started, a heater in the auxiliary air regulator begins to warm up and eventually shuts the regulator and additional air off.

Fuel System

The fuel system consists of the fuel tank, fuel pump, filter, pressure regulator, and 4 injectors.

A contact in the intake air sensor operates the fuel pump any time the sensor flap opens, that is, anytime the engine is demanding air. The fuel pump draws fuel from the front-mounted tank through a filter and delivers it to 4 injectors mounted in the cylinder heads. A pressure regulator on the return line maintains fuel pressure at 28 psi. Excess fuel from the regulator returns to the fuel tank.

The control unit controls the electromagnetic fuel injectors. **Figure 26** shows a cutaway of an injector. The control unit sends an electrical pulse to the magnetic winding in the injector. The pulse causes the needle to move off its seat and inject fuel. A return spring reseats the needle at the end of the pulse. The time the injector is open varies from about 2-10 milliseconds (0.002-0.010 seconds).

The duration of the electrical pulses to the injectors depends primarily on engine speed and engine load. The ignition breaker points in the distributor connect to the control unit and indicate engine speed. The signals from the intake air sensor indicate engine load. The control unit processes the 2 signals, and opens all 4 injectors simultaneously every other crankshaft revolution for the computed duration.

During full load (full throttle) operation, additional fuel is required. The throttle switch, flanged to the throttle valve, indicates full throttle operation to the control unit to produce the necessary enrichment.

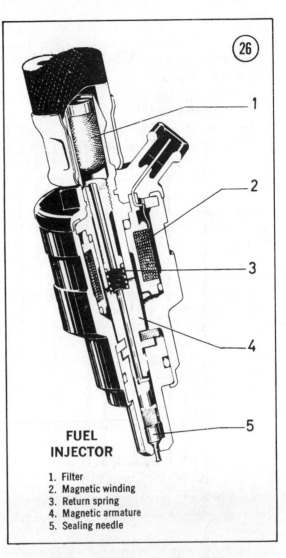

FUEL INJECTOR

1. Filter
2. Magnetic winding
3. Return spring
4. Magnetic armature
5. Sealing needle

In addition to engine speed and engine load signals, the control unit receives signals from temperature sensors. One sensor monitors temperature of incoming air (discussed under *Air System*) while another monitors cylinder head temperature. The control unit computes the effect these sensors should have on the injectors. When the sensors detect cold temperatures, the control unit increases injection.

Cold Start System

When the engine is cold, more fuel must be injected than when the engine is warm. A special cold start system provides this additional fuel.

When the ignition is switched on, the thermo-time switch turns the cold start valve on for about 11 seconds if the engine temperature is below 50°F (10°C). The cold start valve injects extra fuel through a jet fitted in the intake air distributor.

SERVICE PRECAUTIONS

The same precautions which apply to carburetor fuel systems apply to fuel injected systems, only more so. Before suspecting any trouble in the fuel system, thoroughly check out the ignition system, including spark plugs. Whenever disconnecting any fuel lines, clean away all traces of dirt from the end of the line before disconnecting it. When the line is reconnected, examine it for dirt. Even very small dust particles can jam the injectors.

There are a few more precautions which should be observed when working on the fuel injected engine. Never run the engine with the battery disconnected. And do not use a battery charger to start the car when the battery is dead. Furthermore, if you want to charge the dead battery, disconnect it first. If these precautions are ignored, the voltage to the control unit can rise high enough to cause expensive damage.

FUEL EVAPORATIVE CONTROL SYSTEM

All VW's sold in California beginning with 1970 are equipped with a fuel evaporative con-

trol system which prevents fuel vapor from being released into the atmosphere.

Regular Beetle and Karmann Ghia

Refer to **Figure 27**. Fuel vapor from the fuel tank passes through an expansion tank to the activated charcoal filter. When the engine runs, cool air from the fan housing forces the fuel vapor into the air cleaner. Instead of being released into the atmosphere, the fuel vapor takes part in the normal combustion process.

Super Beetle

The Super Beetle fuel tank has an integral expansion tank. Fuel vapor from the fuel tank passes through one or more of the 4 tubes to a separator located at the rear of the front luggage compartment. See Figure 27 and **Figure 28**. Condensed fuel from the separator returns directly to the fuel tank via the same 4 lines. Uncondensed fuel vapor passes to the activated charcoal filter and is treated in the same manner as in all other Beetles.

Maintenance

There is no preventive maintenance other than checking the tightness and condition of the lines linking parts of the system. The expansion tank is located on the right side of the front luggage compartment on regular Beetles (**Fig-**

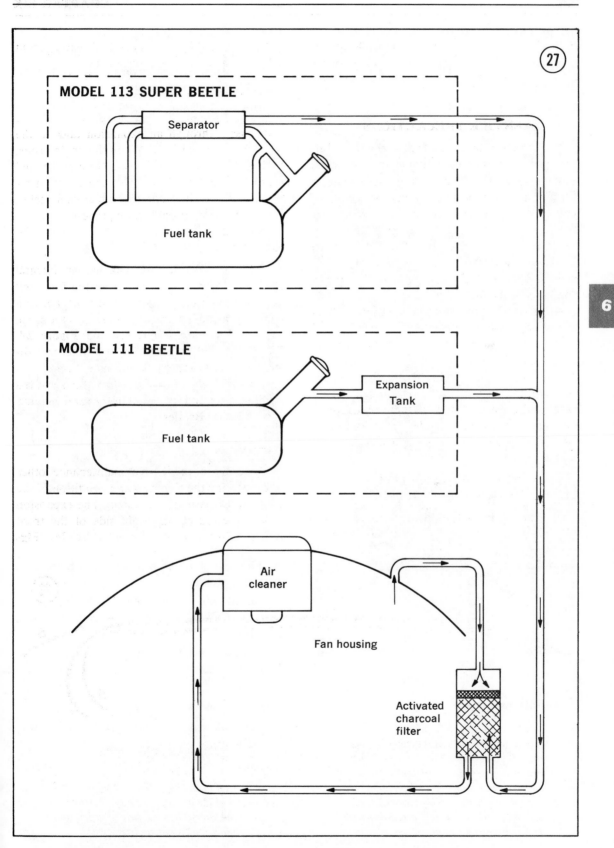

MODEL 113 SUPER BEETLE

Separator

Fuel tank

MODEL 111 BEETLE

Fuel tank

Expansion Tank

Air cleaner

Fan housing

Activated charcoal filter

ure 29); the Super Beetle expansion tank is built into the fuel tank. The activated charcoal filter is located under the right rear fender on all models. See **Figure 30**.

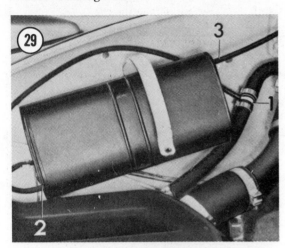

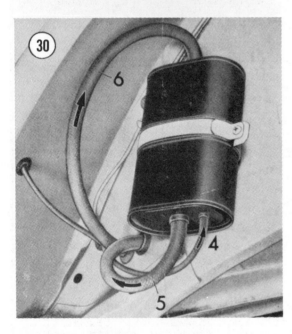

1. Empty the front luggage space.

2. Remove the luggage compartment liner.

3. Lift the sender unit cover off and disconnect the cable for the fuel gauge.

4. Pull the fuel outlet hose off the line in the frame and clamp or plug it so it does not leak.

5a. On 1961-1967 tanks, remove the fuel tank breather pipe.

5b. On 1968 and later tanks, remove the large clamp from the breather pipe boot. Remove the boot and breather pipe.

6. On Super Beetles (1971-1975), disconnect the 3 lines to separator. See Figure 28.

7. Remove the 4 retaining bolts (**Figure 31**) and lift the tank out.

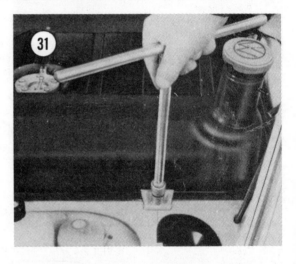

8. Flush the tank with solvent and blow it out with compressed air.

9. Installation is the reverse of these steps. Be sure the packing is around the tank to prevent squeaks.

10. Adjust the fuel gauge as described in Chapter Seven.

FUEL TANK

Removal/Installation

> WARNING
> *Always disconnect battery before starting tank removal. The tank can easily brush against the horn connection on the steering shaft housing during removal. With power connected, the resulting spark can cause a gasoline fire. It has happened many times.*

Repairing Leaks

Fuel tank leaks may be repaired by soldering or brazing.

> WARNING
> *A fuel tank is a potential bomb capable of killing anyone nearby. Always observe the following safety precautions when repairing a fuel tank.*

1. Have the tank steam cleaned *inside and outside*.

2. Fill the tank with inert gas such as carbon dioxide or nitrogen or fill the tank *completely* with water.

3. Set a fire extinguisher nearby.

After the repair is made, pour the water out, put about a quart of gasoline in the tank and slosh it around. Pour the gasoline out, blow the tank dry, and install it in the car.

Table 1   CARBURETTED FUEL SYSTEM SPECIFICATIONS

SPECIFICATIONS	1961-1963	1964 & 1965	1966 & 1967
CARBURETOR			
Type	28 PICT	28 PICT-1	30 PICT-1
Venturi	22.5mm	22.5mm	24mm
Main jet	122.5mm	122.5mm	0 125
Air correction jet	130Y, 145Y[3]	130Y, 145Y[3]	125Z, 135Z (1967)[3]
			170Z (1966)[3]
Pilot jet	55	55	g 55
Pilot jet air bleed	2.0mm	2.0mm	150
Accelerator pump jet	0.50	0.50	50
Power fuel jet	1.0mm	1.0mm	– – –
Float needle valve dia.	1.5mm	1.5mm	1.5mm
Float weight	5.7 grams	5.7 grams	5.7 grams
Accelerator pump feed	1.1-1.4cc/stroke	1.1-1.4cc/stroke	1.3-1.6cc/stroke
FUEL PUMP			
Delivery pressure (max)	2.8 psi	4 psi	4 psi
Delivery capacity (min)	400cc/min. @ 3400 rpm	400cc/min. @ 3800 rpm	400cc/min. @ 3800 rpm
AIR CLEANER			
Type	Oil bath	Oil bath	Oil bath
Oil capacity	0.53 pints (0.25 liters)	0.53 pints (0.25 liters)	0.53 pints (0.25 liters)[1]
			0.8 pints (0.4 liters)[2]

SPECIFICATIONS	1968 & 1969	1970	1971-1974	1974 (Calif.)
CARBURETOR				
Type	30 PICT-2	30 PICT-3	34 PICT-3	34 PICT-4
Venturi	24mm	24mm	26mm	26mm
Main jet	0 125	X 112	X 127.5	X 127.5
Air correction jet	125Z, 135Z[3]	125Z	75Z, 80Z[3]	75Z(M), 70Z(A)
Pilot jet	55	65	55	55
Pilot jet air bleed	130	135	147.5	147.5
Accelerator pump jet	50	42.5	42.5	42.5
Power fuel jet	60	100	100	100
Float needle valve dia.	1.5mm	1.5mm	1.5mm	1.5mm
Float weight	8.7 grams	8.5 grams	8.5 grams	8.5 grams
Accelerator pump feed	1.3-1.6cc/stroke	1.2-1.35cc/stroke	1.3-1.6cc/stroke	1.1-1.7cc/stroke
FUEL PUMP				
Delivery pressure (max.)	4 psi	4 psi	3-5 psi	3.5 psi
Delivery capacity (min.)	400cc/min. @ 3800 rpm	350cc/min. @ 3800 rpm	400cc/min. @ 4000 rpm	400cc/min. @ 4000 rpm
AIR CLEANER				
Type	Oil bath	Oil bath	Oil bath	Oil bath
Oil capacity	0.8 pints (0.4 liters)	0.8 pints (0.4 liters)	0.9 pints (0.45 liters)	0.9 pints (0.45 liters)

[1] 1300 engine   [2] 1500 engine   [3] Karmann Ghia

CHAPTER SEVEN

ELECTRICAL SYSTEM

Electrical systems since 1961 are very similar. Models from 1961 through 1966 have a 6-volt negative ground system; later models use a 12-volt system. Other differences occur mainly as small design changes in the generator/alternator, regulator, starter, distributor, fuse, and lighting arrangements.

This chapter includes service procedures for the battery, starter, charging system, lighting system, fuses, instruments, and windshield wipers. Wiring diagrams for all models are included at the end of this chapter.

BATTERY

Refer to **Table 1** for battery specifications.

Care & Inspection

1. Disconnect both battery cables and remove the battery.

2. Clean the top of the battery with baking soda solution. Scrub with a stiff bristle brush. Wipe battery clean with a cloth moistened in ammonia or baking soda solution.

CAUTION
Keep cleaning solution out of battery cells or the electrolyte will be seriously weakened.

Table 1   BATTERY SPECIFICATIONS

	1961-1966	1967-ON
Voltage	6V	12V
Capacity	66Ah	45Ah
Ground terminal	Negative	Negative

3. Clean battery terminals with a stiff wire brush or one of the many tools made for this purpose.

4. Examine entire battery case for cracks.

5. Install the battery and reconnect battery cables. Observe battery polarity.

6. Coat the battery connections with light mineral grease or Vaseline after tightening.

7. Check the electrolyte level and top up if necessary.

Testing

Hydrometer testing is the best way to check battery condition. Use a hydrometer with numbered graduations from 1.100 to 1.300 rather than one with color coded bands. To use the hydrometer, squeeze the rubber ball, insert the tip in the cell and release the ball (see **Figure 1**). Draw enough electrolyte to float the weighted float inside the hydrometer. Note the number in

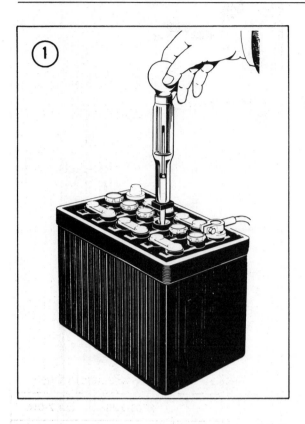

line with the surface of the electrolyte; this is the specific gravity for the cell. Return the electrolyte to the cell from which it came.

The specific gravity of the electrolyte in each battery cell is an excellent indication of that cell's condition. A fully charged cell will read 1.275-1.280, while a cell in good condition may read from 1.250-1.280. One in fair condition reads from 1.225-1.250 and anything below 1.225 is practically dead.

If the cells test in the poor range, the battery requires recharging. The hydrometer is also useful for checking the progress of the charging operation. A reading from 1.200 to about 1.225 indicates a half charge; 1.275-1.280 indicates full charge.

CAUTION
Always disconnect both battery connections before connecting charging equipment.

GENERATOR (1961-1972)

See **Table 2** for a list of generators used in 1961-1972 Beetles and Karmann Ghias.

Removal

1. Disconnect negative battery cable.

2a. On 1961-1966 voltage regulators mounted on the generator, disconnect the small wire and mark it 61. Disconnect the large wire(s) and mark it **B** (51).

2b. On 1967-1972 models, disconnect 3 wires from generator. Mark them in accord with the labels stamped on the generator.

3. Remove the fan housing. See Chapter Five.

Table 2 GENERATOR SPECIFICATIONS

Year	Chassis No.	Generator	Voltage Regulator	Mean Regulating Voltage (Volts)	Maximum Current (Amperes)	Output Power (Watts)	Nominal Output Speed (rpm)	Pulley Ratio
1961-1964	3 192 507 - 5 967 385	BOSCH 113 903 021C	113 903 801C	7V	30A	180W	2500	1.8:1
1964	5 967 386 - 6 502 399	VW 111 903 021F	113 903 801D	7V	30A	180W	2500	1.8:1
1965	115 000 001 - 115 979 202	VW 111 903 021G	113 903 801D	7V	30A	180W	2700	1.8:1
1966	116 000 001 - 116 1021 300	VW 111 903 021H 111 903 021J	Integrally Mounted	7V	30A	180W	2700	1.8:1
1967	117 000 001 - 117 999 000	211 903 031	211 903 803	14V	30A	360W	2000	1.8:1
1968	118 000 001 - 118 857 871	211 903 031A	211 903 803B	14V	30A	360W	2000	1.8:1
1968-1972	118 857 872 -	113 903 031G	113 903 803E	14V	30A	360W	2000	1.9:1

4. Make small marks on the fan housing and fan cover to aid in reassembly.

5. Remove 4 screws securing the fan cover to the fan housing.

6. Remove the generator and fan assembly.

7. Remove the fan nut.

8. Pull off the fan, thrust washers, shims, and hub.

9. Remove 2 nuts securing the fan cover to the generator.

Installation

1. Install the fan cover on the generator.

2. Place the fan hub on the generator shaft. Be sure the Woodruff key is seated properly.

3. Insert shims.

4. Place fan in position.

5. Install the nut and tighten to 40-47 ft.-lb. (5.5-6.5 mkg).

6. Check the distance from fan to cover (a, **Figure 2**). It should be 0.08 in. (2.0mm). If not, remove the nut, vary the number of shims under the thrust washer. Install the thrust washer, any unused shims, and then retorque the nut. Measure (a) again, and readjust it if necessary.

7. Reinstall the generator/fan cover assembly in the fan housing.

8. Install the fan housing. See Chapter Five.

9. Adjust the fan belt tension. See Chapter Two.

CAUTION

Polarize the generator as described below before connecting any wires. Otherwise the voltage regulator can be seriously damaged.

Polarizing

When either the generator or regulator has been disconnected, particularly if the generator has been rebuilt, it must be polarized. Polarizing ensures that residual magnetism in the pole shoes has correct polarity. Reversed polarity can burn out the regulator cutout relay contacts.

To polarize the generator, momentarily connect it to a battery of the proper voltage (6 or 12 volts) as shown in **Figure 3**. Note that the voltage regulator is completely disconnected. Install the generator as described earlier.

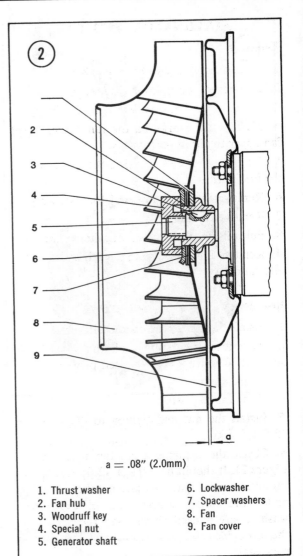

a = .08" (2.0mm)

1. Thrust washer
2. Fan hub
3. Woodruff key
4. Special nut
5. Generator shaft
6. Lockwasher
7. Spacer washers
8. Fan
9. Fan cover

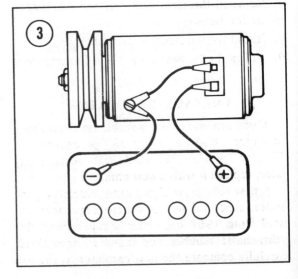

ALTERNATOR (1973 ON)

Removal

1. Disconnect negative battery cable.
2. Disconnect wires from alternator.
3. Remove fan housing. See Chapter Five.
4. Make small marks on the fan housing and fan cover to aid in reassembly.
5. Remove 4 screws securing the fan cover to the fan housing.
6. Remove the generator and fan assembly.
7. Remove the fan nut.
8. Pull off fan, thrust washers, shims, and hub.
9. Remove 2 nuts securing the fan cover to alternator.

Installation

1. Install the fan cover on the alternator.
2. Place the fan hub on the alternator shaft. Be sure the Woodruff key is seated properly.
3. Insert shims.
4. Place fan in position.
5. Install the nut and tighten to 40-47 ft.-lb. (5.5-6.5 mkg).
6. Check the distance from fan to cover (a, Figure 2). It should be 0.08 in. (2.0mm). If not, remove the nut and vary the number of shims under the thrust washer. Install the thrust washer, any unused shims, and then retorque the nut. Measure (a) again, and readjust if necessary.
7. Reinstall the alternator/fan cover assembly in the fan housing.
8. Install the fan housing. See Chapter Five.
9. Adjust the fan belt tension. See Chapter Two.

VOLTAGE REGULATOR

There are no repairs possible on the voltage regulator. If troubleshooting procedures in Chapter Three indicate a defective voltage regulator, replace it with a new one.

A new voltage regulator must match the generator. Since numerous voltage regulators are used from 1961 on, order a replacement by year, chassis number, and engine number. Then carefully compare the new regulator to the old to be sure they are exactly the same. This is important. The generator can be seriously damaged if the wrong regulator is installed.

Regulator Replacement (1961-1966)

1. Disconnect the battery ground cable.
2. Disconnect wires from terminals 51 and 61 at the regulator.
3. Remove screws securing the regulator to the generator. Lift the regulator up and disconnect wires from terminals D+ and DF.
4. Installation is the reverse of these steps. Note that the thicker wire goes to D+ and the thinner wire to DF.

Regulator Replacement (1967 on)

1. Lift up the rear seat cushion. Disconnect the battery ground cable.
2. Sketch terminals of voltage regulator. Mark wires with terminal numbers. Remove wires.
3. Remove screws securing voltage regulator and lift it out.
4. Installation is the reverse of these steps.

STARTER

See **Table 3** for a list of starters used since 1961 on Beetles and Karmann Ghias.

Removal/Installation

1. Disconnect the battery ground cable.
2. Disconnect battery cable from starter solenoid terminal 30, and the small wire from terminal 50.
3. Remove bolts securing the starter to the transmission case. Withdraw the starter.
4. Installation is the reverse of these steps. Before installing, apply universal grease to the starter shaft bushing. Use VW D1a Sealing Compound between the starter and transmission case.

Solenoid Replacement (Bosch)

1. Disconnect the large connecting wire between starter and solenoid. See **Figure 4**.
2. Remove 2 screws securing solenoid to the mounting bracket. See **Figure 5**.

7

Table 3   STARTER SPECIFICATIONS

Year	Starter	Voltage	Output (hp)	Minimum Commutator Diameter inch (mm)	Armature End-play inch (mm)	Solenoid Pull-in Voltage
1961-1965	VW 113 911 021 Bosch EEF 0.5/6 L1	6V	0.5	1.319 (33.5)	0.004-0.012 (0.1-0.3)	3.3V
1966	VW 113 911 021B Bosch 113 911 021A	6V	0.5	1.299 (33)	0.004-0.012 (0.1-0.3)	3.3V
1967	Bosch 211 911 023	12V	0.7	1.319 (33.5)	0.004-0.012 (0.1-0.3)	7V
1968	VW 111 911 023A Bosch 311 911 023B	12V 12V	0.7 0.7	1.299 (33) 1.358 (34.5)	0.004-0.012 (0.1-0.3)	7V
1969	VW 111 911 023 Bosch 311 911 023B	12V	0.7	1.358 (34.5)	0.004-0.012 (0.1-0.3)	7V
1970	Bosch 311 911 023B	12V	0.7	1.358 (34.5)	0.004-0.012 (0.1-0.3)	7V
1971 & later	Bosch 311 911 023 B/C/D	12V	0.7	1.358 (34.5)	0.004-0.012 (0.1-0.3)	7V
All Automatic Stick Shift Models	Bosch 003 911 023A	12V	0.8	1.350 (34.5)	0.004-0.006 (0.1-0.15)	8V

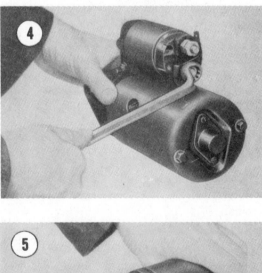

3. Lift solenoid pull rod free of the operating lever and remove solenoid (**Figure 6**).

4. Do not change pull rod adjustment if old solenoid is to be reinstalled. On new solenoids, loosen the locknut and adjust dimension (a) shown in **Figure 7** to 0.748 ± 0.004 in. (19 ± 0.1mm). Tighten locknut.

5. Place a strip of VW D14 Plastic Sealer on the outer edge of solenoid face.

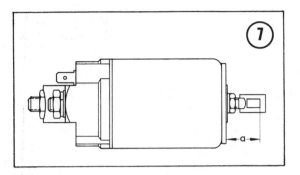

6. Pull the drive pinion to bring the operating lever back toward solenoid opening. Connect the pull rod to the operating lever.

7. Secure solenoid with mounting screws and reconnect large wire from starter.

Solenoid Replacement (VW)

1. Disconnect the connecting strap from the solenoid housing.

2. Remove mounting nuts securing the solenoid housing and then the solenoid itself.

3. Reassemble by reversing these steps.

LIGHTING SYSTEM

The following procedures describe replacement of lamps and relays associated with the lighting system. Refer to **Tables 4 and 5** for bulb type used for each function.

Headlight Replacement (1961-1966)
Beetle and Karmann Ghia

1. Loosen large screw at bottom of the trim ring. See **Figure 8**. Pull entire headlight assembly out as shown in **Figure 9**, and disconnect the cable.

2. Disconnect parking light cables.

3. Unscrew the parking light socket.

4. Remove the headlight retaining springs as shown in **Figure 10**.

7

Table 4   **BULBS, BEETLE**

Function	6V		12V	
	U.S. Replacement	VW Part No.	U.S. Replacement	VW Part No.
Headlights	6006	111 941 161A	6012	111 941 261A
Front turn signals	1129	N 17 731 1	1034	N 17 738 2
Front parking lights	81	N 17 719 1	1034	N 17 738 2
Side marker lights	– – –	– – –	57	N 17 717 2
Stop/tail lights	1154	N 17 737 1	1034	N 17 738 2
Rear turn signals	1129	N 17 731 1	1073	N 17 732 2
License plate light	81	N 17 719 1	89	N 17 719 2
Backup lights	– – –	– – –	1073	N 17 732 2
Interior light	– – –	N 17 723 1	– – –	N 17 723 2
Instrument lights	– – –	N 17 722 1	– – –	N 17 722 2
Warning lights	– – –	N 17 725 1	– – –	N 17 725 2

Table 5   BULBS, KARMANN GHIA

Function	6V		12V	
	U.S. Replacement	VW Part No.	U.S. Replacement	VW Part No.
Headlights	6006	111 941 161A	6012	111 941 261A
Front turn signals/ parking lights	1129	N 17 731 1	1073	N 17 732 2
Stop lights	1129	N 17 731 1	1073	N 17 732 2
Tail lights	81	N 17 719 1	67	N 17 718 2
Rear turn signals	1129	N 17 731 1	1073	N 17 732 2
License plate light	81	N 17 719 1	89	N 17 719 2
Backup lights	– – –	– – –	1073	N 17 732 2
Interior light	– – –	N 17 723 1	– – –	N 17 723 2
Instrument lights	– – –	N 17 722 1	– – –	N 17 722 2
Warning lights	– – –	N 17 725 1	– – –	N 17 725 2

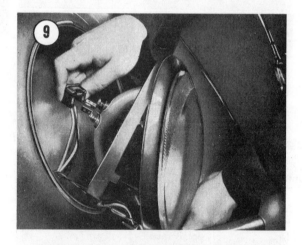

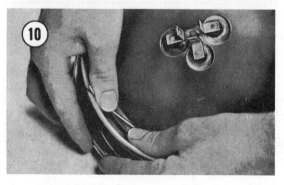

WARNING
Springs are under considerable tension. Hold spring with one hand while

unhooking it with the other to prevent springs from flying out.

5. Withdraw the retaining spring and remove the headlight.

6. Installation is the reverse of these steps. Adjust headlights according to local traffic regulations. Adjusting screws are shown in **Figure 11**.

Headlight Replacement (1967 on)
Beetle and Karmann Ghia

1. Remove the screw at the bottom of the trim ring and remove the ring. See **Figure 12**.

2. Remove 3 screws securing the retaining ring and remove the ring.

3. Withdraw the headlight and disconnect the cable.

4. Installation is the reverse of these steps. Adjust headlights according to local traffic regulations. Adjusting screws are shown in **Figure 13**.

Headlight Switch Replacement (1961-1972)

1. Disconnect the battery ground cable.

2. Open the front hood and remove the protective cover over the instrument panel.

3. Sketch the switch terminals indicating wire color. Mark wires with terminal number. Remove wires from the switch.

4. Unscrew the instrument panel knob. Unscrew the retaining ring with a special tool shown in **Figure 14**. Pull the switch out.

5. Installation is the reverse of these steps. Connect wires correctly according to your sketch.

Headlight Switch Replacement (1973 on)

1. Squeeze upper and lower lugs on switch.

2. Pull switch out the front of the instrument panel. See **Figure 15**.

3. Mark and disconnect the wires.

4. Installation is the reverse of these steps.

Headlight Dimmer Relay Replacement (Except Super Beetle)

The dimmer relay is mounted on the steering column support behind the instrument panel next to the directional signal flasher. The dimmer relay is usually round, while the flasher relay is usually square. Another means of identification is wire color; one wire to the dimmer relay is yellow.

1. Disconnect the battery ground cable.

2. Open the front hood and remove the instrument panel protective cover.

3. Sketch the relay terminals. Mark wires with terminal number. Remove wires.

4. Remove relay from bracket.

5. Installation is the reverse of these steps.

7

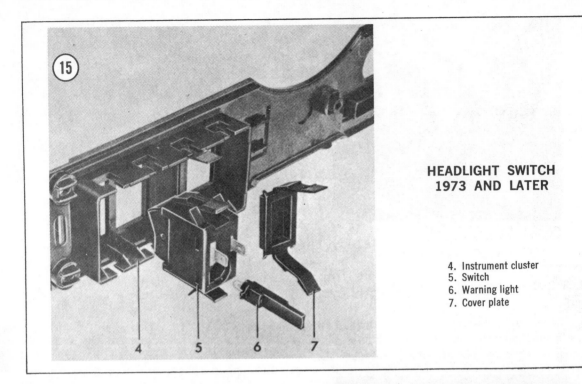

**HEADLIGHT SWITCH
1973 AND LATER**

4. Instrument cluster
5. Switch
6. Warning light
7. Cover plate

Headlight Dimmer Relay Replacement (Super Beetle)

The dimmer relay plugs into a special bracket behind the fuse box. The dimmer relay is mounted on the left edge of the bracket as viewed from the front of the car.

1. Open the front hood and remove the protective cover over the instrument panel.

2. Unplug the relay from the bracket.

3. Installation is the reverse of these steps.

Taillights

To replace the rear turn signal, brake, or back-up lamps (1968-1972 only), remove the screws securing the lens and remove the lens. The function of each bulb is shown in **Figure 16** (1961-1967 Beetle), **Figure 17** (1968-1972 Beetle), **Figure 18** (1973 and later Beetles), and **Figure 19** (Karmann Ghia). Replace the lens, but do not overtighten the screws or the lens may crack.

Front Parking, Turn and Side Marker Lights

Light placement differs with year. On 1961-1966 models, the front parking lights are located

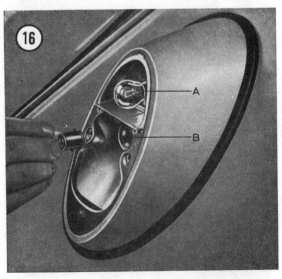

A. Turn indicator B. Stop/taillight

in the headlight assemblies and are accessible once the assembly is removed. See *Headlight Replacement*. Turn signal lights are located in a fender mounted assembly. To replace a lamp, remove the screw securing the lens and lift the lens off. See **Figure 20**. Replace the lamp and lens. There are no side marker lights on 1961 through 1966 cars.

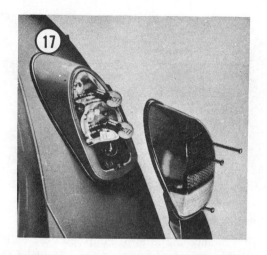

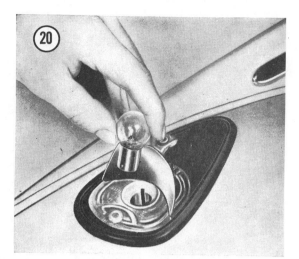

1. Turn signal   3. Stoplight
2. Taillight   4. Back-up light

Since 1967, front parking, turn and side marker lights are located in the same fender mounted assembly. To replace any of the lamps, remove 2 screws securing the lens and lift it off. Replace the lamp and secure the lens. See **Figure 21**.

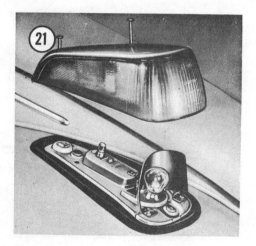

License Plate Light Replacement

Open the rear hood. Loosen screws securing lens and remove it. See **Figure 22**. Replace the bulb and reinstall the lens. Note Karmann Ghias have 2 license plate bulb holders.

Instrument Panel and Warning Lights

Instrument panel and warning lights are accessible at the rear of the panel through the front luggage compartment. All lamps except the lamp for the separate fuel gauge (1962-1967)

1. Turn indicator   2. Stoplight   3. Taillight

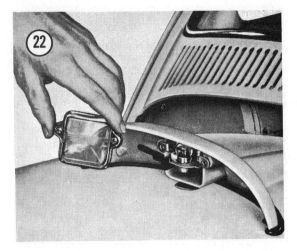

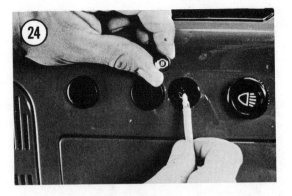

are on the rear of the speedometer. Pull the holder out and replace the lamp. Push the holder firmly back in. See **Figure 23**.

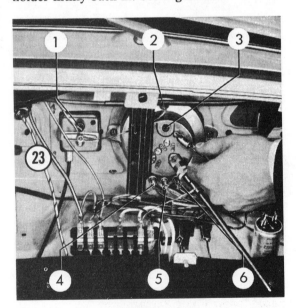

1. Fuel gauge light
2. Speedometer light
3. Headlights (high beam)
4. Oil pressure
5. Turn indicators
6. Generator

Brake Warning Light Replacement

This lamp is mounted on the dash. To replace it, remove the lens. Slip a piece of flexible rubber or plastic tubing over the lamp and pull it out. See **Figure 24**. The tubing must have an inside diameter of 5mm to firmly grip the lamp.

Interior Light Replacement

To replace the interior lamp, pull the entire assembly out of the roof member. Replace the lamp and install the holder back in the roof. Be careful not to damage the headliner.

INSTRUMENTS

Dash Panel Removal/Installation (1973 on)

1. Disconnect battery ground cable.

2. Remove steering wheel (Chapter Eleven) and directional signal switch.

3. Remove 5 screws—2 on each side and one in the center. See **Figures 25 and 26**.

4. Lift dash off its support bracket.

5. Installation is the reverse of these steps.

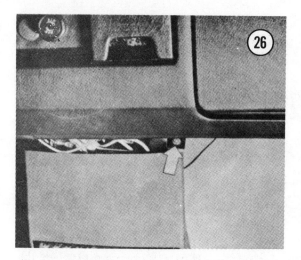

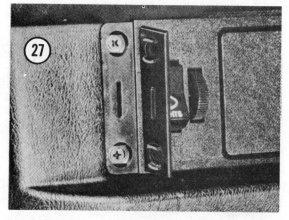

Speedometer Removal/Installation (1961-1972)

1. Disconnect the negative cable from the battery.

2. Open the front hood. Remove the protective cover over the instrument panel.

3. Pull out warning bulbs and instrument lamp from the speedometer case.

4. Unscrew the speedometer cable and remove it from the speedometer case.

5. Loosen the screws securing the speedometer case. Remove the case from the instrument panel.

CAUTION
On Karmann Ghias you must remove the steering wheel and turn signal switch before removing the speedometer case. See Chapter Eleven.

6. Installation is the reverse of these steps.

Speedometer Removal/Installation (1973 on)

1. Disconnect battery ground cable.

2. Pry off rectangular plastic cover to left of light switch. See **Figure 27**.

3. Pry off the left of 2 round buttons behind the steering wheel.

4. Remove rectangular cover to right of panel.

5. Remove 5 Phillips screws shown by arrows in **Figure 28**.

6. From behind dash, disconnect cable from speedometer cluster and push it out the front of the dash. See **Figure 29**.

NOTE: *The cluster is held in place by a rubber boot.*

7. Installation is the reverse of these steps.

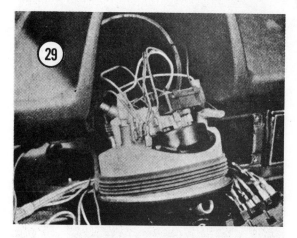

Speedometer Cable Replacement

1. On 1961-1972 models, open the front hood. Remove the protective cover over the instrument panel.

2. Unscrew the speedometer cable and remove it from the instrument cluster.

3. Remove the left front hub cap.

4. Remove the cotter pin securing the cable to the dust cap. See **Figure 30**.

5. Pull the cable out of the stub axle.

6. Pull the speedometer end of the cable out of the guide channel and grommet.

1. Safety belt warning system light
2. Trailer towing warning light
3. ATF temperature warning light
   (only for towing trailer)
4. Auxiliary heater switch
5. Fog light switch
6. Fresh air fan switch
7. Heater operating lever spotlight

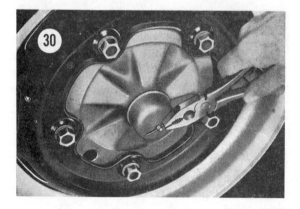

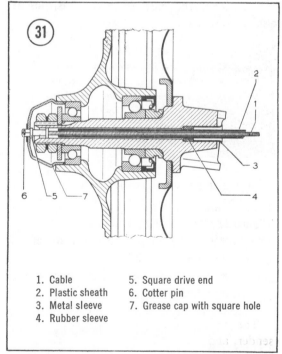

7. Push the new cable down into the guide channel through the grommet. Do not kink or strain the cable.

8. Slide a new rubber sleeve over the cable and insert the cable into the stub axle (**Figure 31**).

9. Secure the cable to the dust cap with a new cotter pin.

10. Screw the cable onto the speedometer case.

1. Cable
2. Plastic sheath
3. Metal sleeve
4. Rubber sleeve
5. Square drive end
6. Cotter pin
7. Grease cap with square hole

Fuel Gauge (1962-1967)

This gauge is mechanically operated by a cable from the sender. To replace the sender, remove the luggage compartment cover and remove the cap over the sender. Disconnect the cable from the sender lever and remove 5 screws securing the sender to the fuel tank.

WARNING
Fuel in the tank is exposed when the sender is removed. Avoid open flames or cigarettes until sender is replaced.

The sender is installed by securing it in place with the mounting screws. Before connecting the cable, the gauge must be adjusted.

To adjust the fuel gauge, press the sender lever to the rear to bring the float to its lowest position. While an assistant watches the gauge, adjust the potentiometer on the rear of the gauge until the gauge needle just rests on the stop below (R). See **Figure 32**.

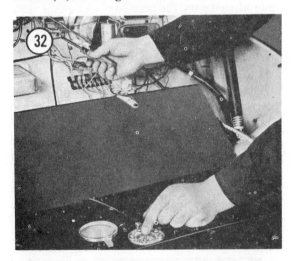

To remove the fuel gauge, unscrew the knurled nut and bracket over the gauge. See **Figure 33**. Pull the gauge out of the panel from the interior. Adjust the gauge when it is reinstalled.

Fuel Gauge (1968 on)

The newest fuel gauge has an electrical sender, and a fuel gauge which is in the speedometer case.

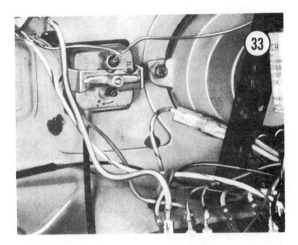

All components of the fuel gauge system can be checked without removal. To check the replaceable vibrator in the speedometer case, connect a voltmeter as shown in **Figure 34** and turn the ignition switch on. As long as the voltmeter reading pulsates, the vibrator is good; if it does not pulsate, replace it. If the vibrator is good, check the fuel gauge by disconnecting the wire from the sender at the gauge terminal. Momentarily connect this terminal to ground. If the gauge needle does not move, replace the gauge. If the gauge is good, reconnect the wire to the gauge. The trouble must be in the wire or the sender.

To replace the sender, disconnect the negative cable at the battery. Disconnect the wire to the sender. Remove screws securing the sender to the top of the fuel tank. Super Beetle senders are not secured by screws; twist the sender counterclockwise to remove.

WARNING
Fuel in the tank is exposed when the sender is removed. Avoid open flames or cigarettes until sender is replaced.

DIRECTIONAL SIGNALS

Directional Signal Switch
Removal/Installation

1. Disconnect the battery ground cable.
2. Remove the steering wheel as described in Chapter Eleven.
3. Remove 4 screws securing the switch.
4. Lift the switch out.

7

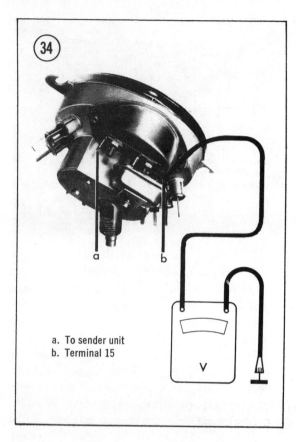

a. To sender unit
b. Terminal 15

5. Disconnect electrical connections.

6. On 1972 and later models, disconnect windshield washer hose from the combination directional signal/wiper switch.

7. Installation is the reverse of these steps.

Flasher Relay Replacement (Except Super Beetle)

The flasher relay is mounted on the steering column support behind the instrument panel next to the headlight dimmer relay. The flasher relay is usually square while the dimmer relay is usually round. Another means of identification is wire color; 2 wires to the flasher relay are red.

1. Disconnect the battery ground cable.

2. Open the front hood and remove the instrument panel protective cover.

3. Sketch the relay terminals, and mark the wires with terminal numbers. Remove wires.

4. Remove relay from bracket.

5. Installation is the reverse of these steps.

Flasher Relay Replacement (Super Beetle)

The flasher relay plugs into the center of a special bracket behind the fuse box.

1. Open the front hood and remove the protective cover over the instrument panel.

2. Unplug relay from the bracket.

3. Installation is the reverse of these steps.

Lamp Replacement

Front turn signal lamps are mounted on the front fenders. See *Front Parking, Turn and Side Marker Light* procedure given earlier.

Rear turn signal lamps are part of the brake lights. See *Taillight* procedure provided earlier.

FUSES

The main fuse box normally is located under the dash to the right of the steering column. It is mounted on the left on Super Beetles. On airconditioned cars, the fuse box is located behind the instrument panel, and is accessible behind the protective cover in the front luggage compartment. **Tables 6 through 9** show the function of each fuse in the main fuse box.

Cars with optional equipment have additional fuses. Two fuses in special holders near the ignition coil protect the backup lights (A) and Automatic Stick Shift control valve (B). See **Figure 35**. Both are 8 ampere fuses. Another special holder under the rear seat protects the rear window defogger (1969 on). See **Figure 36**. This fuse carries the main current for the window; a fuse in the main fuse box carries current for the window switch.

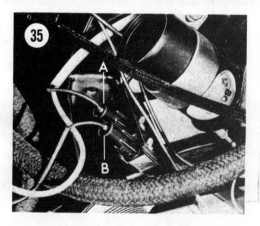

Table 6   FUSES — 1961-1966

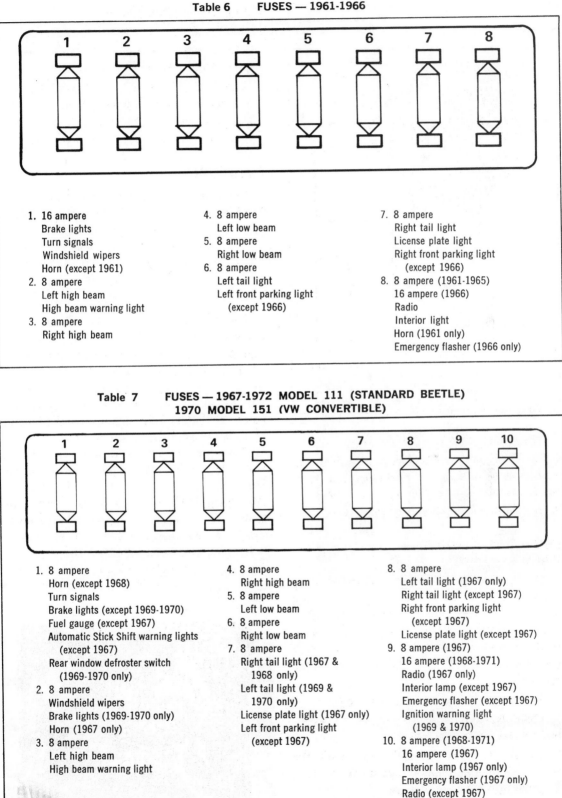

1. **16 ampere**
   Brake lights
   Turn signals
   Windshield wipers
   Horn (except 1961)
2. 8 ampere
   Left high beam
   High beam warning light
3. 8 ampere
   Right high beam

4. 8 ampere
   Left low beam
5. 8 ampere
   Right low beam
6. 8 ampere
   Left tail light
   Left front parking light
   (except 1966)

7. 8 ampere
   Right tail light
   License plate light
   Right front parking light
   (except 1966)
8. 8 ampere (1961-1965)
   16 ampere (1966)
   Radio
   Interior light
   Horn (1961 only)
   Emergency flasher (1966 only)

Table 7   FUSES — 1967-1972 MODEL 111 (STANDARD BEETLE)
1970 MODEL 151 (VW CONVERTIBLE)

1. 8 ampere
   Horn (except 1968)
   Turn signals
   Brake lights (except 1969-1970)
   Fuel gauge (except 1967)
   Automatic Stick Shift warning lights
   (except 1967)
   Rear window defroster switch
   (1969-1970 only)
2. 8 ampere
   Windshield wipers
   Brake lights (1969-1970 only)
   Horn (1967 only)
3. 8 ampere
   Left high beam
   High beam warning light

4. 8 ampere
   Right high beam
5. 8 ampere
   Left low beam
6. 8 ampere
   Right low beam
7. 8 ampere
   Right tail light (1967 &
   1968 only)
   Left tail light (1969 &
   1970 only)
   License plate light (1967 only)
   Left front parking light
   (except 1967)

8. 8 ampere
   Left tail light (1967 only)
   Right tail light (except 1967)
   Right front parking light
   (except 1967)
   License plate light (except 1967)
9. 8 ampere
   16 ampere (1968-1971)
   Radio (1967 only)
   Interior lamp (except 1967)
   Emergency flasher (except 1967)
   Ignition warning light
   (1969 & 1970)
10. 8 ampere (1968-1971)
   16 ampere (1967)
   Interior lamp (1967 only)
   Emergency flasher (1967 only)
   Radio (except 1967)

7

Table 8   FUSES — 1971-1972 MODEL 113 (SUPER BEETLE)
1971-1972 MODEL 151 (VW CONVERTIBLE)

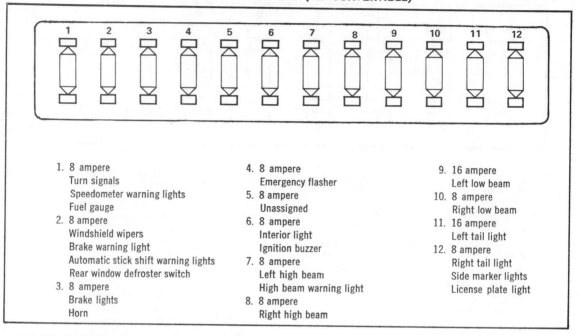

1. 8 ampere	4. 8 ampere	9. 16 ampere
Turn signals	Emergency flasher	Left low beam
Speedometer warning lights	5. 8 ampere	10. 8 ampere
Fuel gauge	Unassigned	Right low beam
2. 8 ampere	6. 8 ampere	11. 16 ampere
Windshield wipers	Interior light	Left tail light
Brake warning light	Ignition buzzer	12. 8 ampere
Automatic stick shift warning lights	7. 8 ampere	Right tail light
Rear window defroster switch	Left high beam	Side marker lights
3. 8 ampere	High beam warning light	License plate light
Brake lights	8. 8 ampere	
Horn	Right high beam	

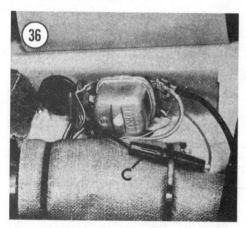

Whenever a fuse blows, ascertain the reason for the failure before replacing the fuse. Usually the trouble is a short circuit in the wiring. This may be caused by worn-through insulation or a wire which works its way loose and shorts to ground.

Carry several spare fuses in the glove compartment.

CAUTION
Never substitute tinfoil or wire for a fuse. An overload could result in fire and complete loss of the automobile.

HORN

If the horn works, but not loudly or not at the correct pitch, make sure it is not touching the body. Horn pitch and loudness can be adjusted by removing the seal on the rear of the horn and turning the adjusting screw underneath.

When the horn does not work at all, check the wiring to the horn and check the horn switch. To service the horn switch:

1. Disconnect the battery ground cable.

2. Carefully pry the horn ring cap off with a screwdriver.

3. Disconnect the cable (**Figure 37**).

Table 9　　FUSES — 1973 AND LATER

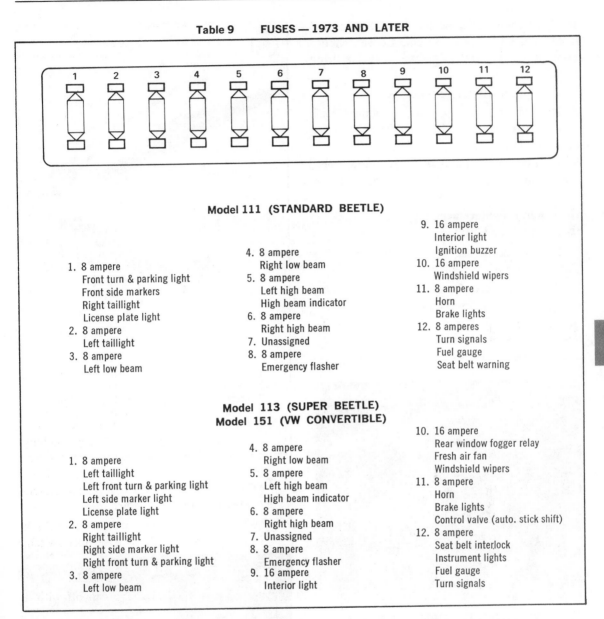

Model 111 (STANDARD BEETLE)

1. 8 ampere
   Front turn & parking light
   Front side markers
   Right taillight
   License plate light
2. 8 ampere
   Left taillight
3. 8 ampere
   Left low beam

4. 8 ampere
   Right low beam
5. 8 ampere
   Left high beam
   High beam indicator
6. 8 ampere
   Right high beam
7. Unassigned
8. 8 ampere
   Emergency flasher

9. 16 ampere
   Interior light
   Ignition buzzer
10. 16 ampere
    Windshield wipers
11. 8 ampere
    Horn
    Brake lights
12. 8 amperes
    Turn signals
    Fuel gauge
    Seat belt warning

Model 113 (SUPER BEETLE)
Model 151 (VW CONVERTIBLE)

1. 8 ampere
   Left taillight
   Left front turn & parking light
   Left side marker light
   License plate light
2. 8 ampere
   Right taillight
   Right side marker light
   Right front turn & parking light
3. 8 ampere
   Left low beam

4. 8 ampere
   Right low beam
5. 8 ampere
   Left high beam
   High beam indicator
6. 8 ampere
   Right high beam
7. Unassigned
8. 8 ampere
   Emergency flasher
9. 16 ampere
   Interior light

10. 16 ampere
    Rear window fogger relay
    Fresh air fan
    Windshield wipers
11. 8 ampere
    Horn
    Brake lights
    Control valve (auto. stick shift)
12. 8 ampere
    Seat belt interlock
    Instrument lights
    Fuel gauge
    Turn signals

4. Remove 3 screws securing the horn ring and remove it.

5. Inspect the 3 contact pins, and replace any that are badly burned (**Figure 38**). Others may be cleaned with fine crocus cloth.

6. Installation is the reverse of these steps.

Horn Replacement

1a. On Beetles, the horn is located under the left front fender. Remove the bolt securing the horn to its bracket.

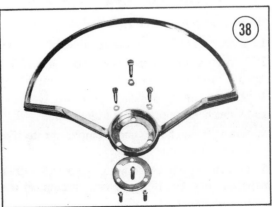

(38)

1b. On Karmann Ghias, dual horns are located in the spare tire compartment. Loosen rubber boot in front panel. Remove bolts securing horns.

2. Disconnect wire(s) from horn(s).

3. Remove the horn(s). On Karmann Ghias, remove defective horn from rubber boot after removing horns.

4. Installation is the reverse of these steps. Make sure that the horns do not touch the car.

Horn Relay Replacement (Karmann Ghia Only)

1. Remove horn fuse from the fuse box. See Tables 6 through 9 for location.

2. Disconnect wires from relay. Make a wiring sketch to simplify installation.

3. Pull the relay out of the side panel hole. See **Figure 39**.

4. Installation is the reverse of these steps.

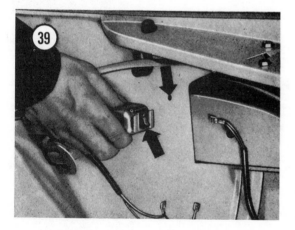

WINDSHIELD WIPER SYSTEM

Wiper Frame Removal/Installation

1. Disconnect battery ground cable.

2. Loosen clamp screws on wiper arms and remove the wiper arm and blade assembly.

3. Remove both wiper shaft seals, nuts, washers, and outer bearing seals. See **Figure 40**.

4. Open front hood and remove protective cover over instrument panel.

5. Disconnect and mark wires from 1961-1971 wiper motors. On 1972 motors, disconnect the motor connector.

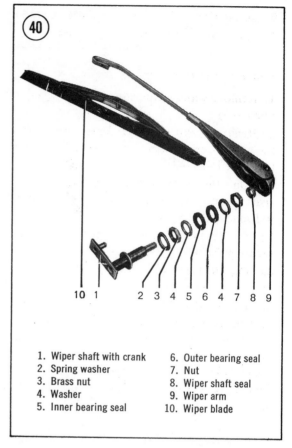

1. Wiper shaft with crank	6. Outer bearing seal
2. Spring washer	7. Nut
3. Brass nut	8. Wiper shaft seal
4. Washer	9. Wiper arm
5. Inner bearing seal	10. Wiper blade

6. Remove glove box.

7. Remove bolt securing wiper frame to body. See **Figure 41**.

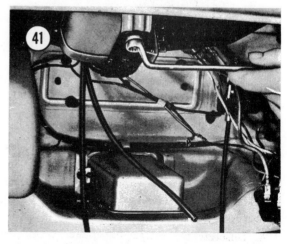

8. Remove frame complete with motor and linkage.

9. Installation is the reverse of these steps. Lubricate all bearing surfaces with oil.

Wiper Motor Removal/Installation

1. Remove wiper frame and motor as described previously.

2. Remove lockwasher and spring washer from the motor drive shaft crank and disconnect the drive link.

3a. On 1961-1969 systems, loosen the wiper shaft securing nut. Remove nut securing motor to frame and remove the motor.

3b. On 1970-1972 systems, remove 3 screws securing the motor to frame and remove motor.

4a. On 1961-1969 systems, installation is the reverse of these steps.

4b. On 1970-1972 systems, temporarily connect the wiper motor to the wiper switch. Run the motor a few minutes, and check that it stops at park position. The crank should be at a 15° angle from the pole housing centerline. See **Figure 42**. Installation is the reverse of these steps.

Wiper Switch Removal/Installation (1961-1971)

1. Disconnect battery ground cable.

2. Open the front hood and remove the protective cover over the instrument panel.

3. Sketch the switch terminals indicating wire color. Mark wires with terminal number. Remove wires from the switch.

4. Unscrew the instrument panel knob. Unscrew the retaining ring with a special tool. See Figure 14. Pull the switch out.

5. Installation is the reverse of these steps.

Wiper Switch Removal/Installation (1972)

1. Disconnect the battery ground cable.

2. Remove the steering wheel as described in Chapter Eleven.

3. Remove 4 screws securing the combination wiper and turn signal switch.

4. Lift the switch out as shown in **Figure 43**.

5. Disconnect the electrical connections and washer hose.

6. Installation is the reverse of these steps.

Wiper Switch Removal/Installation (1973 on)

1. Squeeze upper and lower lugs on switch.

2. Pull switch out the front of the instrument panel. See **Figure 44**.

3. Mark and disconnect wires.

4. Installation is the reverse of these steps.

IGNITION SYSTEM

The ignition system consists of the battery, ignition switch, ignition coil, distributor, spark plugs, and associated wiring. The following procedures describe replacement procedures. No ignition components except the distributor are repairable.

Ignition Switch Replacement (1961-1967)

1. Disconnect negative cable at battery.

2. Open the front hood and remove the protective cover for the instrument panel.

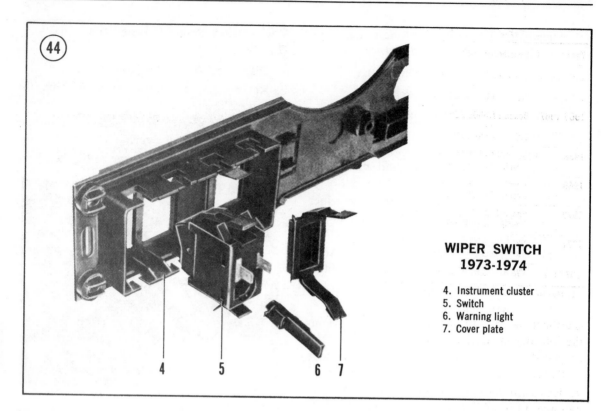

**WIPER SWITCH
1973-1974**

4. Instrument cluster
5. Switch
6. Warning light
7. Cover plate

4 5 6 7

3. Disconnect wires on the ignition switch terminals.

4. Remove screw securing switch bracket and remove the switch.

5. Installation is the reverse of these steps.

Ignition Switch Replacement (1968 on)

1. Remove the steering wheel as described in Chapter Eleven.

2. Loosen turn signal switch and remove 2 screws securing retaining plate (A, **Figure 45**).

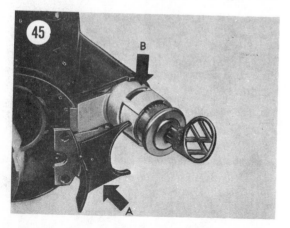

3. Insert key into lock cylinder, turn key slightly and pull cylinder out until the retaining spring is visible in opening (B, Figure 45).

4. Press on the retaining spring through the opening with a piece of stiff wire, while pulling lock cylinder out.

5. Installation is the reverse of these steps.

Ignition Coil

A defective ignition coil must be replaced. Disconnect the primary and secondary wires from the coil and remove the coil from its bracket. Install the new coil; connect the wires.

Distributor

Several different distributors are used from 1961 on, depending on year. In addition, within certain years either a VW or Bosch manufactured distributor may be found (**Table 10**).

Proper engine operation depends very heavily on the distributor ignition advance characteristics. On distributors prior to 1968, advance was controlled solely by engine vacuum. Later distributors employ centrifugal and vacuum advance. Adjustment of the advance mechanism

Table 6   DISTRIBUTORS

Year	Distributor	Advance Control
1961-1965	Bosch ZV PAU4 R2/R5 or VW 113 905 205 B	Vacuum only
1966-1967	Bosch 113 905 205 K or VW 113 905 205 L	Vacuum only
1968	Bosch 113 905 205 M[1] Bosch 113 905 205 P/AA[2]	Vacuum only Centrifugal & Vacuum
1969	Bosch 113 905 205 M/T[1] Bosch 113 905 205 AA[2]	Vacuum only Centrifugal & Vacuum
1970	Bosch 113 905 205 T[1] Bosch 113 905 205 AD[2]	Vacuum only Centrifugal & Vacuum
1971	VW 113 905 205 AJ[1] VW 113 905 205 AK[2]	Centrifugal & Vacuum
1972-ON	VW 113 905 205 AN[1] [2]	Centrifugal & Vacuum

1. Manual transaxle   2. Automatic Stick Shift

is critical and requires special test fixtures. Take the job to your dealer or a competent ignition specialist.

To remove the distributor:

1. Release hold-down clamps for the distributor cap and lift it off.

2. Disconnect the primary lead from ignition coil terminal No. 1.

3. Disconnect the vacuum lines to the vacuum advance unit.

4. Remove the distributor bracket screw.

5. Lift distributor out.

6. Look down the hole in the crankcase at the distributor drive shaft. The slot in the shaft should be at right angles to the crankcase seam and offset toward the *rear* of the engine. See **Figure 46**. This position indicates piston No. 1 is at TDC on its compression stroke. If necessary, crank the engine over.

7. Insert the distributor shaft in the hole and turn rotor until it points to the notch on the distributor housing. Ensure that the distributor shaft properly engages in the drive shaft slot.

8. Secure the distributor bracket with a screw.

9. Install the distributor cap and set ignition timing. See Chapter Two.

SEAT BELT
INTERLOCK SYSTEM (1974)

The seat belt interlock system prevents starting the engine unless the driver and front seat passenger fasten their safety belts. The system cannot be "cheated" by merely leaving the belts fastened. Special logic circuits require that a person sit in the seat first, then buckle the belt; the sequence is important.

The system has a number of features which make it convenient. Once the engine is started, both the driver and passenger can remove their belts without killing the engine. This permits you to get out of the car to open your garage, for example. Furthermore, you can restart the car within 3 minutes of shutting it off without buckling the belt(s). In both cases, the warning light and buzzer will operate.

For service purposes, you can reach in and start the car without buckling yourself in. The interlock does not operate unless the seat is actually occupied.

WIRING DIAGRAMS

Full color wiring diagrams are found at the end of the book. Reference to these diagrams will make electrical system troubleshooting easier.

CHAPTER EIGHT

CLUTCH

VW clutches are single, dry disc-types mounted on the flywheel. The 1961-1970 models have a coil spring pressure plate, while later models have a diaphragm spring type. From 1961-1965, Volkswagen used a carbon clutch release bearing, but changed in 1966 to a conventional ball bearing type. All models are mechanically operated through an adjustable wire cable. **Table 1** gives specifications.

This chapter includes adjustment and repair procedures for all clutch variations since 1961. **Figure 1** shows components of the clutch.

CLUTCH PEDAL ADJUSTMENT

Clutch adjustment involves taking up clutch cable slack caused by cable stretch and lining wear. To check clutch adjustment, depress the clutch pedal by hand. Free play should be ½-¾ in. See **Figure 2**. If it is more or less than this, adjust the cable as follows.

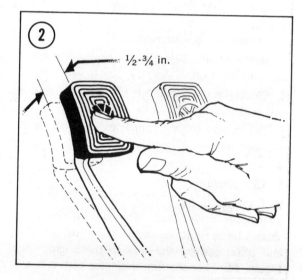

1. Jack up car and remove the left rear wheel.
2. Loosen the small locknut at the transmission end of the cable, and adjust free play with the large nut (it may be a wing nut). See **Figure 3**.

Table 1   CLUTCH SPECIFICATIONS

	1200 & 1300	1500 & 1600 (1970)	1600 (1971-ON)
Type	Single plate, dry disc	Single plate, dry disc	Single plate, dry disc
Spring type	Coil	Coil	Diaphragm
No. of spring	6	9	— — —
Diameter	7.1" (180mm)	7.8" (200mm)	
Friction area	41.6 in^2 (268 cm^2)	56.3 in^2 (363 cm^2)	7.8" (200mm)
Pedal free-play	0.4-0.8" (10-20mm)	0.4-0.8" (10-20mm)	56.3 in^2 (363 cm^2)
			0.4-0.8" (10-20mm)

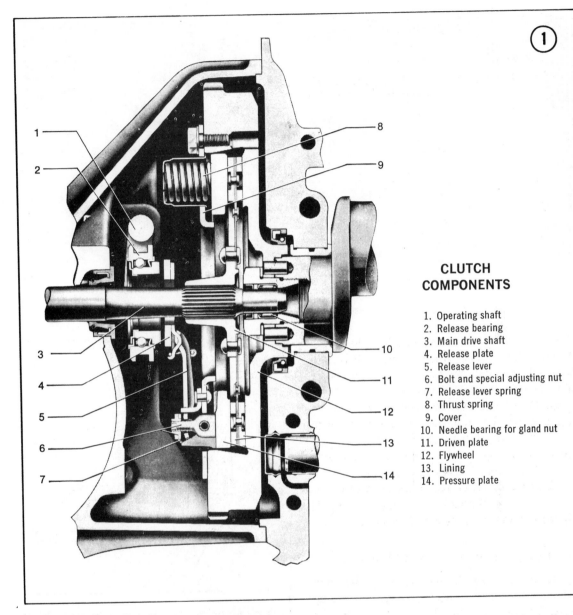

**CLUTCH
COMPONENTS**

1. Operating shaft
2. Release bearing
3. Main drive shaft
4. Release plate
5. Release lever
6. Bolt and special adjusting nut
7. Release lever spring
8. Thrust spring
9. Cover
10. Needle bearing for gland nut
11. Driven plate
12. Flywheel
13. Lining
14. Pressure plate

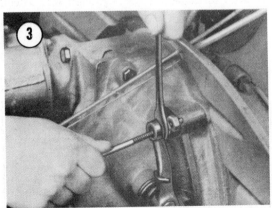

3. When free play is correct, retighten locknut.

4. Install the wheel and lower the car.

CLUTCH CABLE

Removal

1. Jack the car up and remove left rear wheel.

2. Remove both nuts from the cable end at the clutch lever. See **Figure 4**.

3. Pull the rubber boot located near the clutch lever off the guide tube and cable.

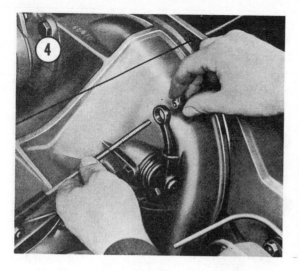

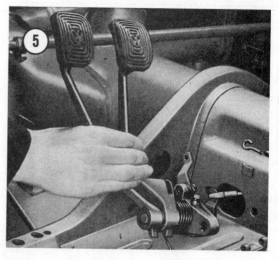

4. Remove the pin securing the accelerator pedal, disconnect the accelerator cable, and remove the pedal.

5. Remove 2 screws securing the clutch/brake pedal assembly to the tunnel. Disconnect the brake master cylinder pushrod from the pedal assembly and pull the assembly forward. See **Figure 5**.

6. Unhook the cable from the pedal assembly, and pull the cable out through the front.

Installation

1. Reach in the tunnel hole with your fingers and locate the end of the cable tube. Keep a finger on the tube, and insert the cable end. Guide the cable into the tube with your finger.

2. Once you are sure the cable is started in the tube, push the rest of the cable in fully to the rear, while lubricating it thoroughly with universal grease.

3. Check the cable tube sag (about ¾-1¼ in.) as shown in **Figure 6**. Install washers at (A) be-

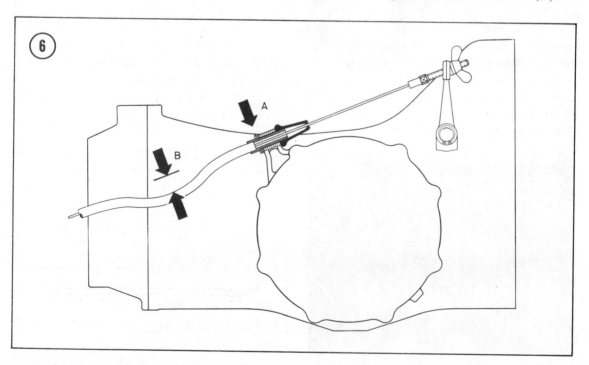

tween the holding bracket and cable tube end to vary the sag. Cable sag introduces a controlled amount of friction in the cable to minimize clutch chatter.

4. Grease the cable eye and hook it on the pedal assembly. Have an assistant pull on the rear end to maintain tension on the cable. Otherwise the cable eye will fall off the pedal assembly.

5. Install pedal assembly with 2 bolts. Reconnect the master cylinder pushrod and the accelerator pedal.

6. While maintaining tension on the cable, put the rear cable end into the clutch lever. Screw the large nut (sometimes a wing nut) on the cable end until there is about ½-¾ in. free play in the clutch pedal travel. Install the small locknut in place to hold the adjustment.

7. Install the wheel and lower the car.

CLUTCH MECHANISM

Removal

1. Remove engine, described in Chapter Four.

2. Using a sharp punch, mark the flywheel and the clutch cover for later reassembly.

3. Unscrew bolts securing the clutch cover, one turn at a time. Unscrew bolts diagonally opposite one another rather than working directly around the clutch cover. This ensures that heavy spring pressure will not warp the clutch cover.

4. Once spring pressure is relieved, unscrew each bolt entirely and remove the clutch. See **Figure 7** which shows the coil spring clutch (1961-1970). Remove diaphragm spring clutch (since 1971) in a similar manner.

Inspection

Never replace clutch parts without giving thought to the reason for failure. To do so only invites repeated troubles.

1. Clean the flywheel face and pressure plate assembly in a non-petroleum base cleaner such as trichloroethylene.

2. Check the friction surface of the flywheel for cracks and grooves. Attach a dial indicator and check runout. Compare with specifications for your engine. If necessary, have the flywheel reground; replace it in cases of severe damage.

3. Check the pressure plate for cracked or broken springs, evidence of heat, cracked or scored friction surface, and looseness. Check release lever ends for wear. On diaphragm spring clutches, check the spring fingers for wear. If there is any damage, replace with a professionally rebuilt pressure plate assembly.

CAUTION
Pressure plate adjustments and repairs require specialized tools and skills. Do not attempt repairs unless you are properly equipped for the job.

4. Check the clutch disc (drive plate) lining for wear, cracks, oil, and burns. The assembled thickness of the disc should be at least 0.36 in. (see **Figure 8**). Check for loose rivets and cracks in the spring leaves or carrier plate. Ensure that the disc slides freely on the transmission spline without excessive radial play. If the disc is defective, replace it with a new one.

5. Check the release bearing for wear to determine if it caused the original trouble. Never

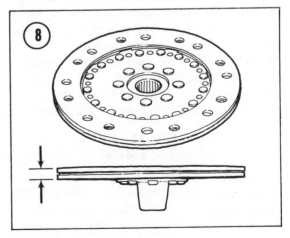

reuse a release bearing unless necessary. When other clutch parts are worn, the bearing is probably worn. If it is necessary to reinstall the old bearing, do not wash it in solvent; wipe it with a clean cloth.

Installation

1. Wash your hands *clean* before proceeding.

2. Sand the friction surface of the flywheel and pressure plate with a medium-fine emery cloth. Sand lightly across the surfaces (not around) until they are covered with fine scratches. This breaks the glaze and aids seating a new clutch disc.

3. Clean the flywheel and pressure plate with trichloroethylene or equivalent.

4. Insert the clutch disc. Place the pressure plate in position and line up the punch marks made when the clutch was removed. If installing a new or rebuilt pressure plate, align the clutch assembly with the balance marks 180° from each other. The balance marks, painted on the edge of the flywheel and clutch assembly, show the heaviest side of the part.

5. Center the clutch disc over the gland nut hole with a pilot. An excellent pilot is an old transmission main shaft available from a wrecking yard.

6. Start all pressure plate bolts. Tighten diagonally opposite bolts a few turns at a time until all are tight. Torque to 18 ft.-lb. (2.5 mkg).

7. Remove the centering pilot.

8. Measure the height of the release plate above the flywheel with a straightedge and depth gauge (**Figure 9**). This dimension should be 1.06-1.18 in. (26.7-30mm). Measure dimension at 6 (or more) points around the flywheel. If this is not correct, or if any 2 of the readings are more than 0.02 in. (0.5mm) apart, the clutch pressure plate fingers require adjustment. To adjust, remove the flywheel and take it with the clutch assembly to your VW dealer for adjustment.

RELEASE BEARING REPLACEMENT

The release bearing is mounted in the transmission case and is accessible after removing the engine. In addition to checking a suspect release bearing, always remove the clutch assembly

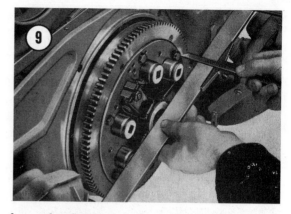

from the flywheel and check for damage as described earlier.

1. Unhook the retaining clips as shown in **Figure 10**. Slide the bearing off.

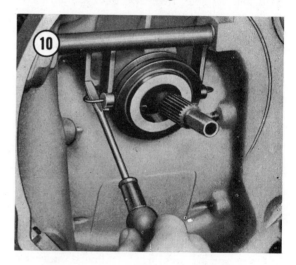

2a. Replace the carbon release bearing if the face is marked or cracked, or worn near the retaining cup. You may consider using one of the newer ball bearing types instead of another carbon block; see your VW dealer for the correct part.

2b. Hold the inner race of the ball bearing type. Lightly press the outer race against the inner race and rotate the outer race. If there is any noise or roughness, the bearing is defective and must be replaced.

> **CAUTION**
> *The release bearing is prelubricated and sealed. Do not wash in solvent or the bearing will be ruined. Wipe the bearing with a clean cloth.*

3. Before installing the release bearing, lightly sand the plastic ring with medium coarse emery cloth. Lubricate the sanded surface with molybdenum disulphate paste or powder.

4. Lubricate the contact points between the fork and bearing with lithium grease.

5. Install retaining clips as shown in **Figures 11 and 12**. The small bend in each clip must clip around the fork tightly.

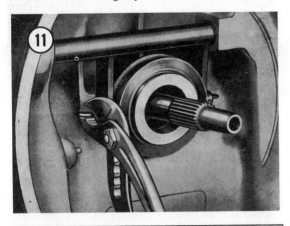

3. Remove the bushing lock screw (**Figure 14**).

4. Slide the operating shaft to the left to push the bushing out. Remove the bushing, washer, and spacer sleeve.

5. Slide the operating shaft to the right to remove it. See **Figure 15**.

6. Clean all parts in solvent. Check both bushings and the operating shaft for wear; replace if necessary. Lubricate shaft with lithium grease.

7. Installation is the reverse of these steps. Note that the lock screw must screw into bushing hole.

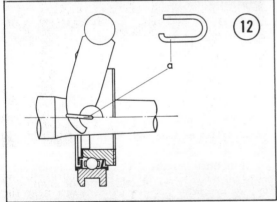

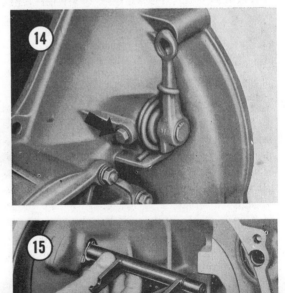

RELEASE LEVER MECHANISM

Whenever the engine is removed, it is a good idea to check the release lever.

Removal/Installation

1. Remove the clutch release bearing as described earlier.

2. On 1961-1964 models, loosen the clamp bolt on the lever. On 1965 and later models, remove the lock ring on the end of the lever shaft. Remove the lever, return spring and end cap. See **Figure 13**.

CHAPTER NINE

TRANSAXLES

Volkswagen transmissions mount in a yoke at the rear of the car. The engine bolts to the rear of the transmission. Manual and automatic transmissions are also transaxles, since the housing contains transmission and differential gears sharing a common oil supply. Each transmission is described in detail below.

Repairs requiring disassembly of either transaxle are not possible for home mechanics or garage mechanics without special skills and a large assortment of special VW tools. Most adjustments such as selector fork position and bearing preload are done at VW dealerships on special test jigs; these adjustments are impossible while the parts are installed in the case. The price of the test jigs and other tools necessary far exceeds the cost of a professionally rebuilt transaxle.

Considerable money can be saved by removing the old transmission and installing a new or rebuilt one yourself. This chapter includes removal and installation procedures, plus other simple repairs. Specifications are included at the rear of this chapter. See Chapter Two for lubrication and preventive maintenance.

MANUAL TRANSAXLE

The manual transaxle has 4 forward speeds and one reverse. The gears are in constant mesh and all forward speeds are fully synchronized. **Figure 1** shows a cutaway view of the entire transaxle.

As shown in Figures 2A to 2F, reverse, first, and second gears are fixed on the main shaft. In addition, the synchronizer hub for 3rd and 4th is fixed on the main shaft. Main shaft 3rd and 4th gears are free to rotate on needle bearings. On the drive pinion, the reverse is true. Gears for 3rd and 4th and the synchronizer hub for 1st and 2nd gears are fixed, while 1st and 2nd gears are free to rotate.

In neutral (**Figure 2A**), engine rotation transmitted through the clutch turns the main shaft. Main shaft gears for 1st and 2nd rotate since they are fixed to the shaft. Drive pinion gears for 1st and 2nd, however, are not engaged by the synchronizer and turn freely. No power is transmitted to the pinion gear.

When the gearshift lever is moved to 1st (**Figure 2B**), a fork slides the outer portion of the synchronizer toward 1st gear. Power is transmitted from the main shaft through both 1st gears to the pinion, which drives the differential.

In 2nd gear (**Figure 2C**), a fork moves the same synchronizer toward 2nd gear. Power is transmitted from the main shaft through both 2nd gears to the pinion.

Power transfer for 3rd and 4th gears is similar

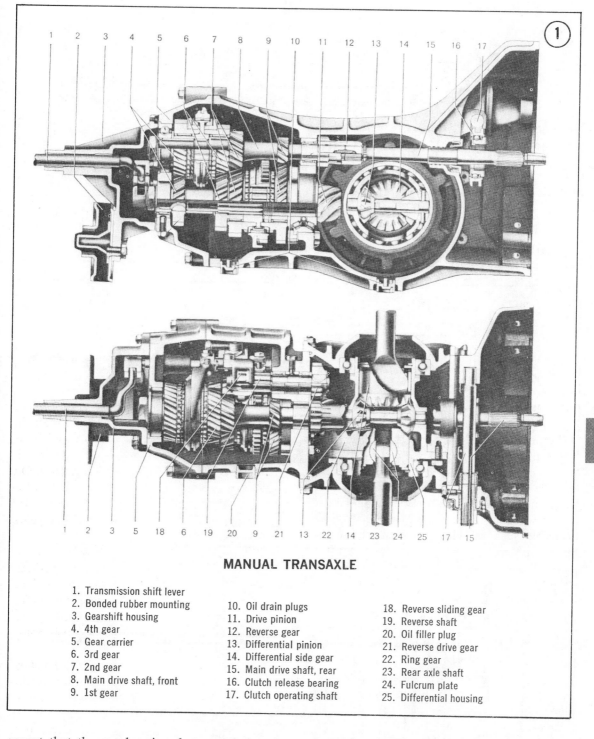

MANUAL TRANSAXLE

1. Transmission shift lever
2. Bonded rubber mounting
3. Gearshift housing
4. 4th gear
5. Gear carrier
6. 3rd gear
7. 2nd gear
8. Main drive shaft, front
9. 1st gear

10. Oil drain plugs
11. Drive pinion
12. Reverse gear
13. Differential pinion
14. Differential side gear
15. Main drive shaft, rear
16. Clutch release bearing
17. Clutch operating shaft

18. Reverse sliding gear
19. Reverse shaft
20. Oil filler plug
21. Reverse drive gear
22. Ring gear
23. Rear axle shaft
24. Fulcrum plate
25. Differential housing

except that the synchronizer between 3rd and 4th gears is used. See **Figures 2D and 2E**.

Reverse gear operates differently. See **Figure 2F**. A reverse gear on the main shaft drives a similar gear on the reverse shaft. When reverse is selected, a sliding gear on the reverse shaft meshes with teeth on the outer portion of the 1st/2nd gear synchronizer hub. The hub is fixed to the pinion shaft and therefore drives the pinion gear.

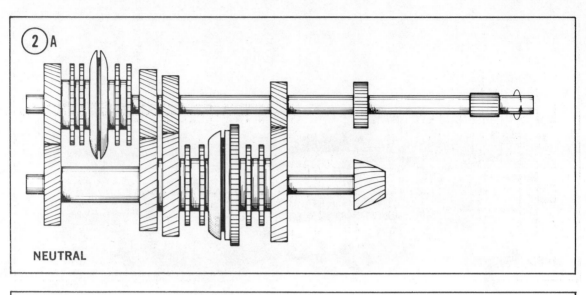

② A

NEUTRAL

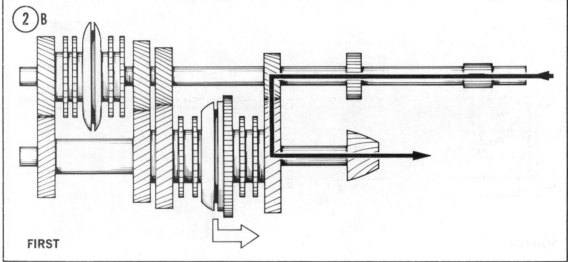

② B

FIRST

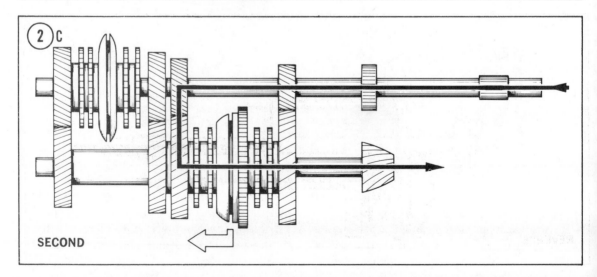

② C

SECOND

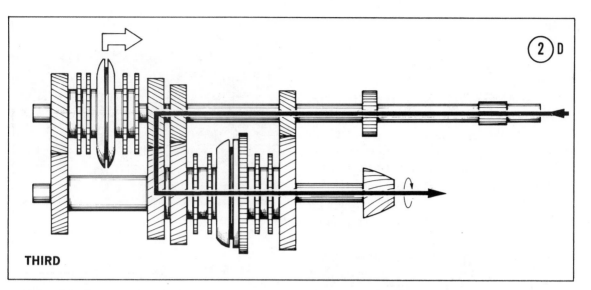

THIRD

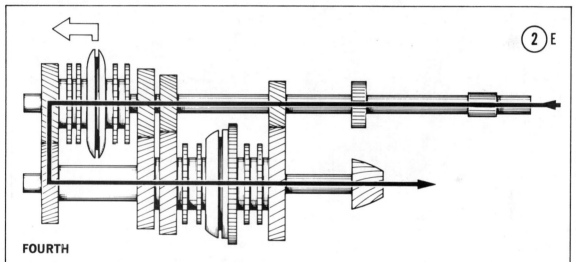

FOURTH

9

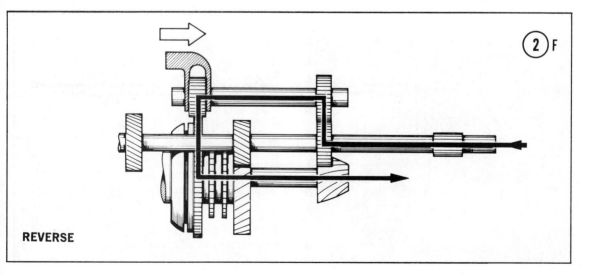

REVERSE

Removal

1. Remove engine as described in Chapter Four.

2. Jack the car up on jackstands and remove the rear wheels.

3. Disconnect the rear brake hoses from the backing plates.

4. Remove the handbrake lever and cable as described in Chapter Twelve, *Brakes*.

5. Loosen clamps around rubber axle boots.

6. Remove lower shock absorber bolts.

7a. On single joint axles, mark the spring plate in line with the groove on the axle bearing housing. See **Figure 3**.

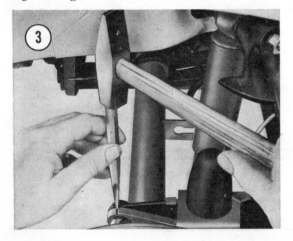

7b. On double joint axles, remove the drive shaft as described in Chapter Ten.

8. Disconnect the clutch cable from the transmission operating lever. See **Figure 4**. Withdraw the cable and sleeve.

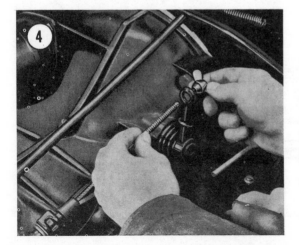

9. Disconnect the cables from starter terminals 30 and 50 (see **Figure 5**).

10. Remove bolts at rear axle bearing housing on single joint axles only. See **Figure 6**.

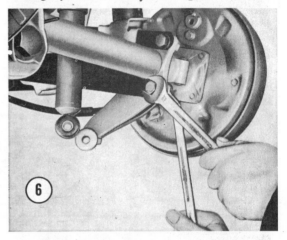

11. Remove the rear seat cushion, and inspection cover. Remove the shift rod coupling bolt. See **Figure 7**. Move the gearshift lever to withdraw the coupling from transmission shift rod.

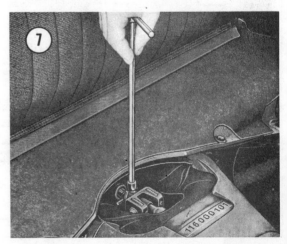

12. Remove the nuts on the front rubber mount as shown in **Figure 8**.

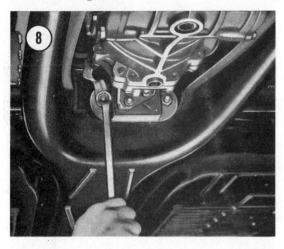

13. Place a garage-type floor jack under the transmission case, and raise it just enough to take the weight of the transmission.

14a. On 1961-1971 transaxles, remove carrier bolts under the transaxle. See **Figure 9**.

14b. On 1972 and later transaxles, remove carrier bolts at top of transaxle. See **Figure 10**.

15. Withdraw the transaxle toward the rear with the jack.

CAUTION
While the transaxle is out of the car, take special care not to damage or bend the splined main shaft. One method of protection is to drill a hole in a length of wood for the main shaft and bolt the wood across the transmission case.

Installation

1. Lift the transaxle into place. Grease the rear carrier bolts and install them. Tighten to 167 ft.-lb. (23 mkg).

2. Loosen the 4 nuts inside the bell housing which secure the transaxle to the rear rubber mount. Install the nuts on the front rubber mount and tighten them. Now tighten the rear rubber mount nuts.

3. Reconnect the shift rod coupling to the shift rod. Ensure that the pointed end of the securing bolt fits fully in the rod recess. Lock the bolt securely with wire. Install the inspection cover and seat cushion.

CAUTION
If the coupling is connected incorrectly, it is possible to select reverse when 2nd gear is engaged, causing considerable damage. In some cases it may be difficult or impossible to select 1st or 2nd. Connect the coupling carefully and check engagement of each gear.

4a. On single joint axles, install the bolts between the axle bearing housings and the spring plate. Line up the chisel mark on each spring plate with the groove in the housing. Tighten the bolts to 80 ft.-lb. (11 mkg).

4b. On double joint axles, install the drive shaft as described in Chapter Ten.

5. Install and tighten the lower shock absorber mounting bolt.

6. Reconnect the cables to terminals 30 and 50 of the starter.

7. Reinstall the clutch cable.

8. Reinstall the handbrake cable and lever. See Chapter Twelve.

9

9. Reconnect the rear brake hoses.

10. Install the rear wheels.

11. Install the engine. See Chapter Four.

12. Adjust the clutch cable (Chapter Eight), bleed the brakes and adjust the handbrake (Chapter Twelve).

Gearshift Lever Replacement

Since 1973, the lever is about 1½ in. (40mm) shorter than earlier levers. Keep this in mind if replacement is necessary.

1. Remove the front floor mat.

2. Remove bolts securing the boot and ball housing to the tunnel.

3. Remove the gearshift lever, ball housing, boot, and spring (see **Figure 11**). Remove the spring by twisting it counterclockwise.

4. Remove the stop plate. See **Figure 12**.

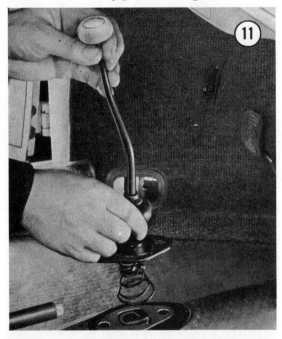

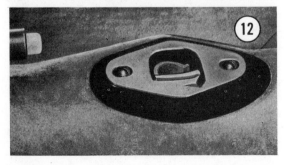

5. Clean all parts in solvent. Check for wear.

6. Grease all moving parts with universal grease.

7. Install the stop plate with the bent tab pointing up (see Figure 11).

8. Install the lever ball housing so the lever is vertical in neutral. The locating pin on the bottom of the lever fits in the slot in the ball socket.

9. Ensure that each gear engages properly.

Main Shaft Oil Seal Replacement

1. Remove engine. See Chapter Four.

2. Remove clutch release bearing. See Chapter Eight.

3. Clean exterior of old seal and surrounding area.

4. Pry oil seal out as shown in **Figure 13**. Do not nick any metal surface.

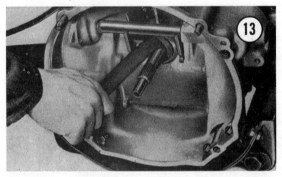

5. Clean the opening around the main shaft.

6. Coat exterior of the seal lightly with sealing compound. Oil the main shaft and seal lip.

7. Slide oil seal on the main shaft, and drive it into place. Use a special hollow drift or length of pipe as shown in **Figure 14**.

AUTOMATIC STICK SHIFT TROUBLESHOOTING

1. *Starter will not operate* — A starter inhibitor (neutral safety) switch permits the engine to be started in neutral only. If the switch becomes defective, replace it.

2. *Starter operates with transmission in gear* — See symptom 1.

3. *Clutch engages too slowly (slips) after gear change*—A control valve operates the clutch. Check the control valve adjustment and hose

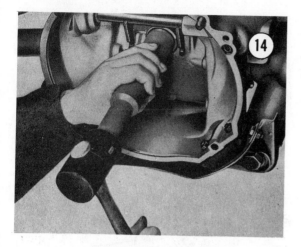

connections between control valve and carburetor. Check clutch linkage adjustment. Leaky control valve diaphragms may also cause this.

4. *Clutch engages too quickly (jerks) after gear change* — A control valve adjustment sets operating time of clutch.

5. *Clutch does not disengage (can't select drive range)* — First, check solenoid fuse near ignition coil (see Chapter Seven). Check electrical connections to control valve solenoid; you may even have a defective solenoid. Check all vacuum hoses associated with control valve. Check clutch linkage adjustment.

6. *Engine stalls when selecting gear* — Check vacuum hose between control valve and clutch servo. Check clutch servo for leaks. Replace both if necessary.

7. *Car jerks in idle when shifting into gear* — Readjust idle speed. Check control valve adjustment in this chapter.

8. *Converter continually overheats* — This trouble usually means low converter line oil pressure or defective oil temperature sensing components. Check automatic transmission fluid (ATF). Also check ATF oil pump on engine. Take the job to a dealer if the fluid level and pump are good, and the trouble persists.

9. *High pitched hissing from converter* — Check ATF level with dipstick. Check ATF pump on engine. Check torque converter stall speed as described below.

10. *Poor acceleration (engine output good)* —

Normally caused by defective torque converter. Check stall speed as described below.

11. *Temperature warning lamp does not work* — The only way to tell when this circuit is defective is to test it. As suggested in Chapter Two, this is done every **6,000** miles. If the lamp fails to light in either drive range, remove the wire from terminal K of the selector switch (see this chapter, Figure 12) and ground the wire. If the lamp lights, replace the selector switch. If the lamp doesn't light, replace the lamp.

Torque Converter Stall Speed

This test permits rapid evaluation of the torque converter.

1. Connect an accurate tachometer to the engine. Start the engine, set the handbrake, and warm up the engine.

2. Depress the foot brake firmly, shift the lever to Drive 2.

3. Depress accelerator briefly to full throttle while holding the car at a complete stop with the hand and foot brakes. Quickly read the engine speed reached on the tachometer.

CAUTION
This is a severe test, and ATF in the torque converter heats very rapidly. Do not run the engine under full load any longer than necessary to read the tachometer (5-10 seconds).

4. If the stall speed is more than 600 rpm below the specifications (2,000-2,250 rpm), the torque converter is defective and must be replaced. A stall speed only a few hundred rpm below specification indicates the engine is not delivering full power and probably needs a tune-up. A stall speed higher than specified indicates clutch slippage.

AUTOMATIC STICK SHIFT

The Automatic Stick Shift, introduced in 1968 models, consists of a torque converter, servo operated mechanical clutch, and 3-speed transmission. **Figure 15** is a detailed cutaway view of the transmission. **Figure 16** shows hydraulic and vacuum circuits in simplified form.

9

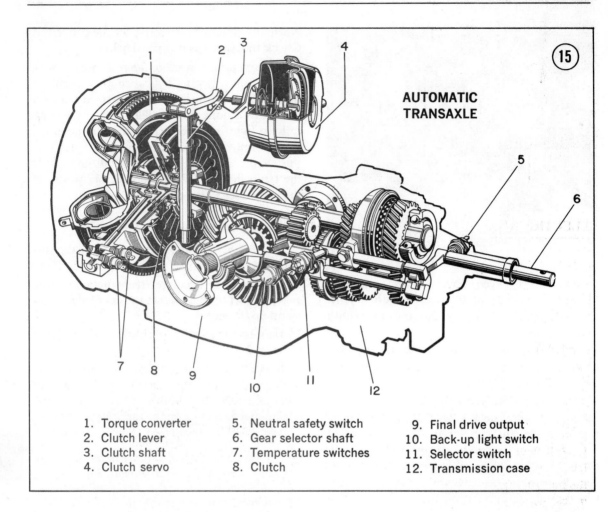

AUTOMATIC
TRANSAXLE

⑮

1. Torque converter
2. Clutch lever
3. Clutch shaft
4. Clutch servo
5. Neutral safety switch
6. Gear selector shaft
7. Temperature switches
8. Clutch
9. Final drive output
10. Back-up light switch
11. Selector switch
12. Transmission case

The Automatic Stick Shift has a conventional torque converter to provide smooth application of power over a wide range. But unlike full automatics, the Automatic Stick Shift requires a mechanical clutch to interrupt power flow for gear changes. Gear changes are entirely manual, not automatic.

The torque converter is capable of multiplying engine torque up to 2:1 when the car is moved from a complete stop. At this point, torque is maximum and slippage within the torque converter is also maximum. As slippage decreases, i.e., the speed difference between the turbine and impeller in the torque converter decreases, torque multiplication also decreases. When slippage decreases so that turbine speed is 84% of the impeller speed, there is no multiplication and coupling is direct. The turbine can reach 96% of the impeller speed — the maximum coupling efficiency possible.

The torque converter has its own oil supply independent of the rear axle and transmission. See Figure 16. An oil pump driven by the engine oil pump delivers automatic transmission fluid from a reservoir to the torque converter, and back through a return line to the reservoir. The fluid reservoir is located under the right rear fender.

The torque converter drives a conventional 3-speed transmission through a single dry disc clutch. A vacuum servo disengages and engages the clutch in response to the control valve.

When the driver moves the gearshift lever longitudinally, a contact in the lever operates the control valve solenoid. The control valve supplies engine vacuum from the intake manifold to the clutch servo, which disengages the clutch. Since power flow is interruped, the driver can continue to move the gearshift and manually select the desired gear.

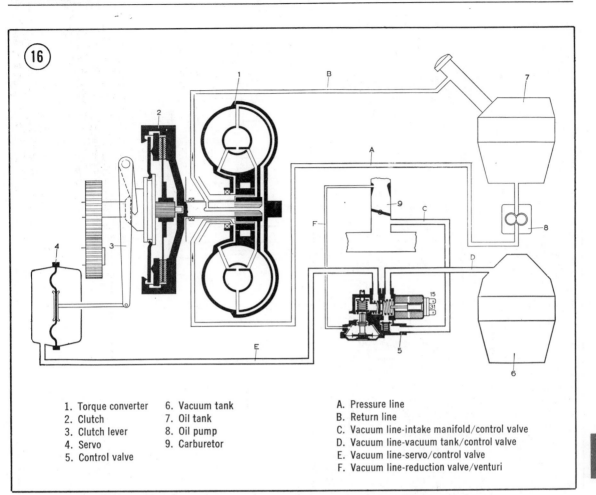

1. Torque converter
2. Clutch
3. Clutch lever
4. Servo
5. Control valve
6. Vacuum tank
7. Oil tank
8. Oil pump
9. Carburetor

A. Pressure line
B. Return line
C. Vacuum line-intake manifold/control valve
D. Vacuum line-vacuum tank/control valve
E. Vacuum line-servo/control valve
F. Vacuum line-reduction valve/venturi

The control valve engages the clutch automatically after an interval, determined by engine load. Vacuum line (F), between the carburetor and the control valve, senses variations in engine load. The control valve engages the clutch quickly during large engine loads (acceleration) and more slowly and smoothly for light loads (deceleration and downshifting).

The control valve is located on the left side of the engine compartment. A vacuum tank under the left rear fender connects to the control valve and stores sufficient vacuum to permit 5 or 6 gear changes regardless of engine vacuum.

Figure 17 shows the electrical circuits used for the Automatic Stick Shift. Two temperature senders (D & E) monitor torque converter fluid temperature. Temperature selector switch (K) connects sender (D) to a warning lamp on the speedometer face when drive range 2 is selected, and connects sender (E) to the lamp when drive range 1 is selected. Switch (D) lights the lamp at 257°F (125°C); switch (E) lights the lamp at 284°F (140°C). Whenever the lamp comes on, the driver must select the next lower range until the lamp extinguishes.

A simplified circuit introduced on Automatic Stick Shifts in late 1971 uses only one temperature sender. The warning light goes on when fluid temperature exceeds 284°F and remains on until fluid cools regardless of drive range.

Neutral safety switch (B) prevents the engine starter from operating unless the gear selector is in N (neutral). Any other gear opens the connection within switch (B) between the ignition switch (H) and the starter solenoid (J). In addition, switch (B) grounds the clutch control valve solenoid, preventing the gearshift lever switch from affecting the clutch when in neutral.

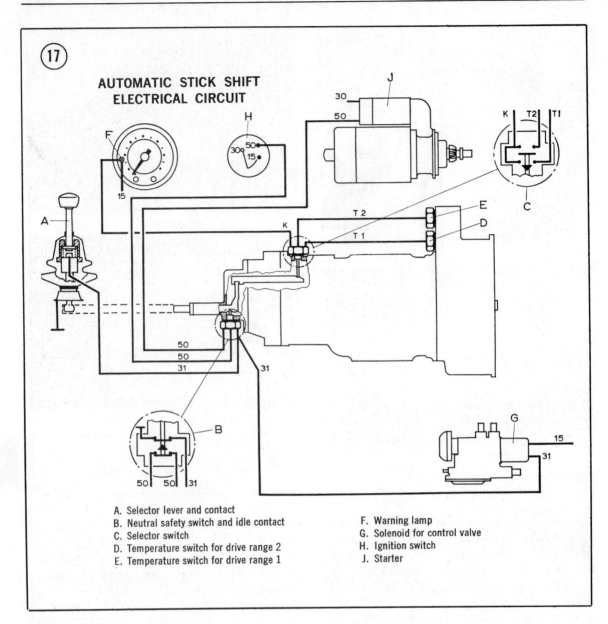

⑰

**AUTOMATIC STICK SHIFT
ELECTRICAL CIRCUIT**

A. Selector lever and contact
B. Neutral safety switch and idle contact
C. Selector switch
D. Temperature switch for drive range 2
E. Temperature switch for drive range 1
F. Warning lamp
G. Solenoid for control valve
H. Ignition switch
J. Starter

Removal

1. Remove the engine as described in Chapter Four. A retainer must be in place or the torque converter may fall out. See **Figure 18**.

2. Jack the car up on jackstands and remove the rear wheels.

3. Remove the rear seat cushion and inspection cover. Remove the shift rod coupling bolt. See Figure 7. Move the gearshift lever to withdraw the coupling from the transmission shift rod.

4. Remove the drive shaft screws as shown in **Figure 19** and remove the drive shaft com-

pletely. See Chapter Ten. Cover the joints with plastic caps to prevent entry of dirt.

5. Disconnect banjo connections (top arrow, **Figure 20**). Pull off the electrical connections (bottom arrow).

6. Disconnect starter cable connections shown in Figure 5.

7. Slide back the rubber cover and pull off 3-pin temperature selector switch plug. See **Figure 21**.

8. Disconnect vacuum hose clip on the clutch servo and pull the hose off.

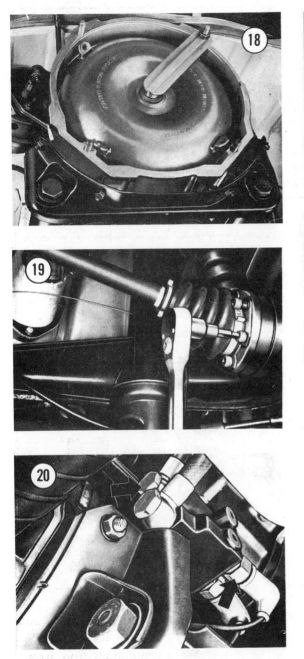

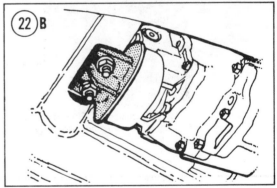

9. Pull back the rubber cover and pull off the 3-pin neutral safety switch plug (top arrow, **Figure 22A**).

10a. On 1972 and earlier models, remove nuts on front transmission mount (bottom arrows, Figure 22A).

10b. On 1973 and later models, remove nuts from 2 studs holding transmission mount (**Figure 22B**).

11. Loosen the rear transmission mounting bolts. Place a garage-type floor jack under the transmission. Raise the jack far enough to take the weight of the transmission.

12. Remove the rear mounting bolts, lower the transmission, and withdraw it completely.

Installation

1. Raise the transmission into place and tighten the front mounting nuts.

2. Grease the rear mounting bolts. Install and tighten them.

3. Connect clutch servo vacuum hose and tighten the clip.

4. Connect the banjo fittings. Use washers on each side of the banjo.

5. Connect the 3-pin neutral safety switch plug (Figure 22A).

6. Connect the 3-pin temperature selector switch plug (Figure 21).

7. Connect starter cables (Figure 5).

8. Remove protective covers from joints and install the drive shafts.

9. Connect the gearshift coupling. Ensure that the pointed end of the securing bolt fits fully in the rod recess. Lock the bolt securely with wire.

10. Check engagement of each gear.

Clutch Removal

Refer to **Figure 23** for this procedure.

1. Remove the transaxle as described earlier.

2. Remove the torque converter and close off the shaft opening to keep out dirt.

3. Loosen the clamp bolt on the clutch operating lever (Figure 15) and disconnect the lever from the transmission.

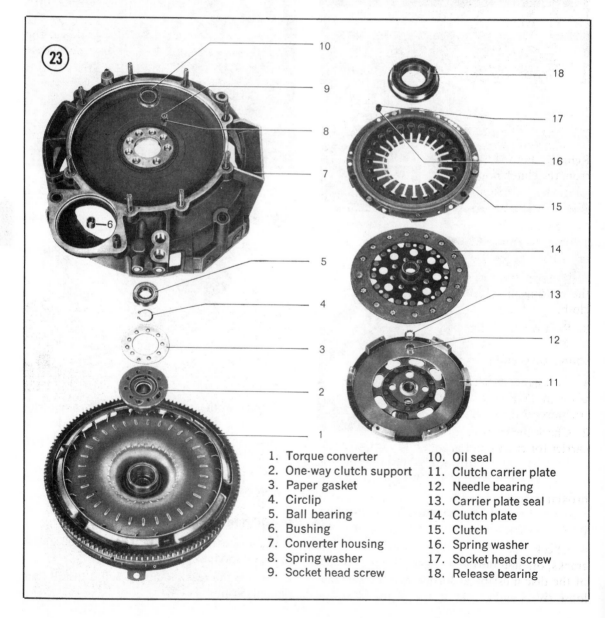

1. Torque converter
2. One-way clutch support
3. Paper gasket
4. Circlip
5. Ball bearing
6. Bushing
7. Converter housing
8. Spring washer
9. Socket head screw
10. Oil seal
11. Clutch carrier plate
12. Needle bearing
13. Carrier plate seal
14. Clutch plate
15. Clutch
16. Spring washer
17. Socket head screw
18. Release bearing

4. Remove 8 nuts securing the clutch housing to the transmission case. Two nuts are accessible only after removing the bottom cover. See **Figure 24**.

5. Separate the clutch housing and transmission case. Turn the clutch operating lever shaft so the jaws disengage from the release bearing. Remove both lower engine mounting bolts from the clutch housing.

6. Remove all 12 point 8mm bolts securing the clutch pressure plate to the clutch housing. Loosen diagonally opposite bolts a few turns at a time to prevent warpage due to spring pressure.

7. Remove the release bearing. Do not wash the bearing in solvent. Wipe with a clean dry cloth.

8. Remove the clutch disc.

Clutch Inspection

1. Clean the clutch plate carrier and pressure plate in non-petroleum base cleaner such as trichloroethylene.

2. Check the friction surface of the clutch plate carrier for cracks and grooves. If worn, replace as described in a later procedure.

3. Check the pressure plate for cracked or broken spring fingers, cracked or scored friction surface, and evidence of heat (bluish tint). Replace if necessary.

4. Check the clutch disc lining for wear, cracks, oil, and burns. The assembled thickness of the disc must be at least 0.36 in. Check for loose rivets and cracks in the spring leaves or

carrier plate. Ensure that the disc slides freely on the transmission main shaft spline without excessive radial play. Replace the disc if necessary.

5. Check the release bearing for noise or excessive wear. It is good practice to replace an inexpensive part like this, regardless of condition, to prevent having to tear the transmission down again. If other clutch parts are worn, it's very likely the release bearing is also worn.

Clutch Installation

Refer to Figure 23 for the following procedure.

1. Lubricate the release bearing guide on the transmission case and both lugs of the release bearing (see **Figure 25**) with lithium grease. Insert the bearing into the clutch pressure plate.

2. Apply lithium grease to the needle bearing in the clutch carrier plate.

3. Install the clutch disc, and pressure plate with release bearing, into the clutch housing. Center the clutch disc with a pilot cut from a scrap main shaft. See **Figure 26**. Ensure that the release bearing is properly centered in the diaphragm spring. Tighten diagonally opposite

9

pressure plate bolts a few turns at a time until all are tight. Torque to 7 ft.-lb. (0.97 mkg).

4. Install the lower engine mount bolts with new seals. See **Figure 27**.

5. Assemble the transmission and clutch housing. Ensure that the clutch lever shaft engages behind the release bearing lugs. Tighten all nuts evenly, a few turns at a time, then torque to 14 ft.-lb. (2 mkg).

6. Reconnect clutch operating lever to its shaft. Adjust the clutch as described later in this chapter.

7. Install the torque converter. Rotate until the converter seats fully into the turbine shaft.

Clutch Carrier Plate Replacement

Refer to Figure 23 for the following procedure.

1. Remove the clutch as described previously.

2. Remove 8 Allen screws securing the one-way clutch support through any of 4 holes in the carrier plate. See **Figure 28**.

3. Tap the one-way clutch support with a small drift to remove it. See **Figure 29**. Remove the paper gasket.

4. Remove the C-ring on the clutch carrier plate turbine shaft. Knock the carrier plate out with a rubber hammer as shown in **Figure 30**.

5. Pull the seal and needle bearing out of the carrier plate with a puller. See **Figure 31**. If a puller cannot be substituted, take the carrier plate to the dealer.

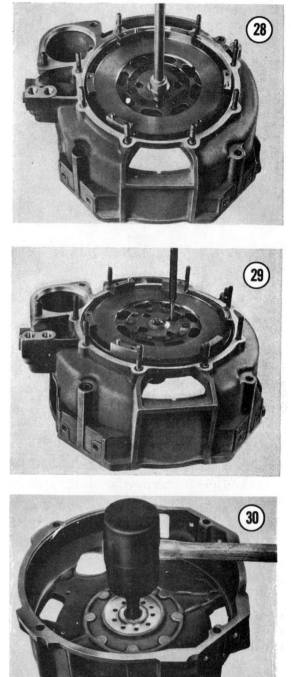

6. Knock the ball bearing and seal out of the clutch housing with suitable drifts (**Figure 32**).

7. Insert the new ball bearing in the clutch housing with a drift as far as the stop on the housing. See **Figure 33**. Support the bottom of the housing near the bearing on a small sleeve

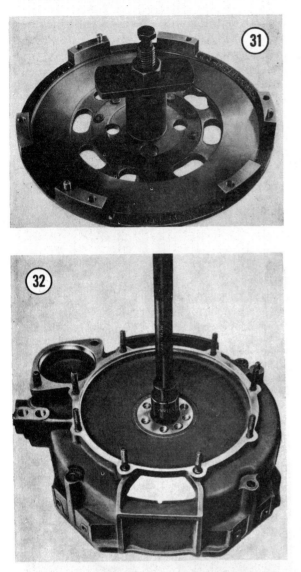

11. Lubricate the needle bearing with lithium grease and install needle bearing and seal in the carrier plate as shown in **Figure 34**.

12. Reinstall clutch as described earlier.

so the studs and housing are not damaged by the pounding.

8. Drive the seal in with the sealing lip toward the torque converter.

9. Drive the turbine shaft of the carrier plate into the ball bearing and install the C-ring.

10. Using a new paper gasket and O-ring, install the one-way clutch support into the clutch housing. Install the Allen screws through holes in the carrier plate.

CAUTION
The paper gasket goes on only one way. The large oil drillings in the one-way clutch support must be clean and not blocked by the gasket.

Basic Clutch Adjustment

These adjustments are performed whenever the clutch or servo are disassembled. See the next procedure for clutch free play adjustment.

1. Install the clutch servo on the mounting bracket.

2. Connect the clutch operating lever to the clutch operating shaft so that the lever touches

the clutch housing. See **Figure 35**. Tighten the clamp bolt slightly.

3. Adjust dimension (a) to 0.335 in. (8.5mm) and (b) to 3.03 in. (77mm) in **Figure 36**, with the clutch lever disconnected.

4. Push the servo rod in fully. Turn the operating lever freely on the shaft until dimension (c) in Figure 36 is reached. This dimension

is 1.54 in. (40mm). VW uses a special tool shown in **Figure 37**. You can use a steel ruler, measuring between eye centers on the servo rod and operating lever. Tighten the lever in this position with the clamp bolt.

5. Connect the operating lever to the servo rod (see **Figure 38**). Ensure that the plastic sleeves are in place on the lever. Insert the bolt from the top and secure with a new cotter pin.

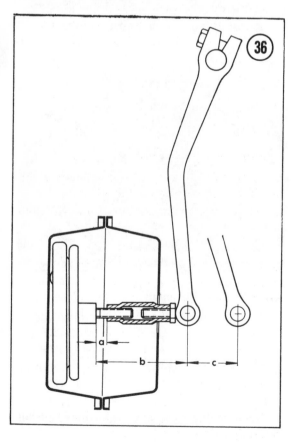

Clutch Play Adjustment

As a result of normal clutch lining wear, clutch play will increase. At intervals specified in Chapter Two, the play should be checked and adjusted if necessary.

The small tool shown in **Figure 39** is easily made and simplifies both checking and adjusting. Cut from a piece of sheet metal about 0.040 in. (1mm) thick.

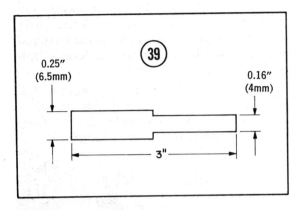

1. Disconnect the vacuum line to the clutch servo.

2. Measure the clearance between the upper edge of the servo bracket and the adjusting nut with the 0.16 in. (4mm) end of the tool. See **Figure 40**. If this dimension is greater than 0.16 in. (4mm), the clutch requires adjustment.

3. To adjust the clutch, loosen the locknut on the servo rod slightly. Leave the nut in this position.

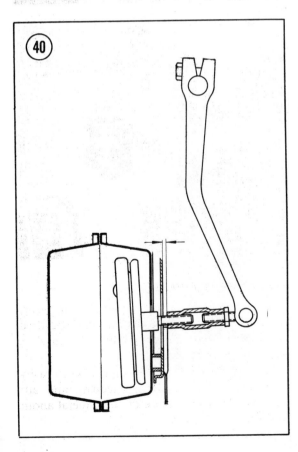

4. Turn the adjusting nut *away* from the locknut about 5 or 5½ turns. Measure dimension (b) with the 0.25 in. (6.5mm) end of tool. See **Figure 41**.

5. Tighten the locknut against the adjusting nut.

6. Reconnect the vacuum line to clutch servo.

7. Road test. If reverse engages silently and the clutch does not slip in 3rd gear, the clutch is properly adjusted.

> NOTE: *If the clutch has been adjusted previously, and the clutch lever is touching the clutch housing, the clutch disc is worn and requires replacement.*

Control Valve Replacement

1. Disconnect the black wire (terminal 15) and brown wire (ground) from the solenoid.

2. Loosen hose clamps and disconnect vacuum lines.

3. Remove 3 screws securing the control valve bracket and remove the valve with bracket.

4. Installation is the reverse of these steps. Road test car to check control valve adjustment. See adjustment procedure later in this chapter.

Control Valve Disassembly

Refer to **Figure 42** for the following procedure.

1. Remove bracket. Pry lock ring (13) out carefully with a screwdriver.

9

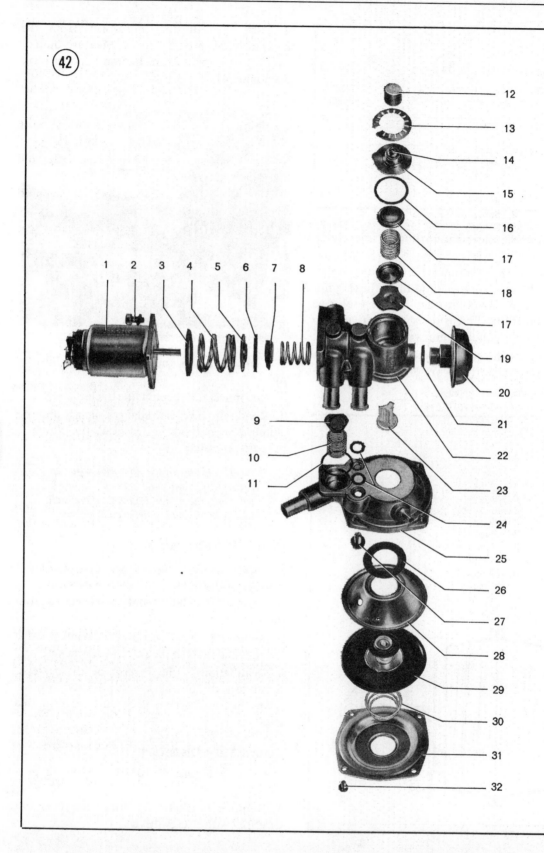

CONTROL VALVE

1. Solenoid
2. Screw and washer
3. O-ring
4. Solenoid spring
5. Main valve seat
6. Sealing ring
7. Main valve
8. Main valve spring
9. Check valve
10. Check valve spring
11. Sealing ring
12. Protective cap
13. Concave washer
14. Stud
15. Cover
16. Sealing ring
17. Valve spring retaining plate
18. Reducing valve spring
19. Reducing valve
20. Air filter
21. Washer
22. Housing
23. Spacer
24. Sealing ring
25. Diaphragm housing
26. Seal
27. Screw and washer
28. Support
29. Diaphragm
30. Spring
31. Cover
32. Screw and washer

2. Remove cover (15) and seal (16). Remove spring (18), retaining plates (17) and reduction valve (19).

3. Remove screws (32) and cover (31). Remove spring (30), diaphragm (29), support washer (28), rubber washer (26), and spacer (23).

4. Remove 2 screws (27) securing the diaphragm cover (25) to the housing (22).

5. Remove check valve (9), spring (10), and seal (11) from diaphragm housing (25).

6. Remove 4 screws (2) securing the solenoid (1) to the housing (22).

7. Remove the seal (3), spring (4), valve seat (5), seal (6), main valve and spring (8).

8. Unscrew air filter and remove washer (21).

Control Valve Assembly

1. Clean all non-rubber parts in solvent.

2. Check solenoid, valve seats, valves, springs, diaphragms, and seals for wear and deterioration. Regardless of condition, replace all parts included in the standard VW repair kit.

3. Install check valve (9), spring (10) and seal (11) in the diaphragm housing (25). Install seals (24) for mounting screws.

4. Attach the diaphragm housing (25) to housing (22) with 2 screws.

5. Insert spacer (23), rubber washer (26), support washer (28), diaphragm (29), and spring (30). Install cover (31).

> NOTE: *If a new diaphragm is installed, adjust reducing valve clearance as described in the following step.*

6. Press the center of the diaphragm towards the reducing valve seat. Screw the stud in the diaphragm in or out until the difference (X) between dimension (a) and (b) in **Figure 43** is 0.012-0.016 in. (0.3-0.4mm).

7. Install reducing valve (19), spring (18), retaining plates (17), seal (16), and cover (15). Insert the lock ring. Ensure the ring seats firmly in the groove.

8. Install items (3-8) in the order shown in Figure 42.

9. Install the solenoid with 4 screws.

9

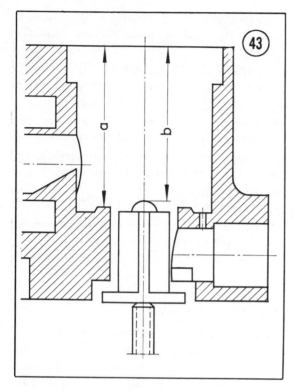

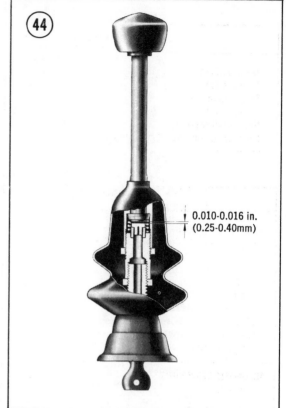

0.010-0.016 in.
(0.25-0.40mm)

10. Screw the air filter (20) on, using a new washer (21).

Control Valve Adjustment

The control valve is adjusted so that the clutch engages smoothly after a gear selection. To check the adjustment, accelerate to about 44 mph, take your foot off the accelerator and shift from drive 2 to drive 1. The clutch should engage fully within 1 second after releasing the gearshift lever. Adjust as follows.

1. If the clutch engages too quickly, turn adjusting screw on top of control valve ¼ to ½ turn clockwise.

2. If the clutch engages too slowly, turn adjusting screw ¼ to ½ turn counterclockwise.

Gearshift Lever Contact Adjustment

1. Slide the rubber boot up to expose the upper locknut.

2. Bend up the lock plate securing the upper locknut in place. See **Figure 44**. Loosen the upper locknut.

3. Unscrew the top sleeve and remove the upper portion of the gearshift lever.

4. Examine the electrical contacts in the upper and lower portions. If they are burned, polish lightly with fine crocus cloth or a relay burnishing tool. If badly damaged, replace the contacts.

5. Check the rubber boot. If cracked or deteriorating, replace it.

6. Screw the top sleeve back on the lower portion. Screw it down lightly as far as it goes. Back it off ½ turn; this is equivalent to a 0.010-0.016 in. (0.25-0.40mm) contact gap.

7. Tighten the locknut and lock plate. Refit the rubber boot.

Switch and Temperature Sender Replacement

The location of the neutral safety switch, selector switch, and temperature senders is clearly shown in Figure 15. To replace any of these switches or senders, disconnect the wires and unscrew the part. Screw the new switch or sender in and reconnect the wires.

Table 1   TIGHTENING TORQUES

	foot-pounds	mkg		foot-pounds	mkg
Transmission to frame bolts	167	23.0	Pressure plate bolts	11	1.5
Transmission mounting nuts (front)	14	2.0	Clutch housing nuts	11	1.5
Temperature senders	18	2.5	One-way clutch bolts	11	1.5
Selector switch	18	2.5	Oil filler plug	14	2.0
Neutral safety switch	18	2.5	Oil drain plug	14	2.0
Converter-to-drive plate bolts	18	2.5			

Table 2   SPECIFICATIONS, TRANSAXLES

	1200 & 1300	1500	1600
MANUAL TRANSAXLE			
Gear ratios			
1st	3.80:1	3.80:1	3.80:1
2nd	2.06:1	2.06:1	2.06:1
3rd	1.32:1	1.32:1	1.26:1
4th	0.89:1	0.89:1	0.88:1
Reverse	3.88:1	3.88:1	3.61:1
Oil Capacity	5.3 pints (2.5 liters)	5.3 pints (2.5 liters)	5.3 pints (2.5 liters)
Lubricant	See Table 3, Ch. 2	See Table 3, Ch. 2	See Table 3, Ch. 2
Final drive ratio	4.375:1	4.125:1	4.125:1
AUTOMATIC STICK SHIFT			
Gear ratios			
L	— — —	2.06:1	2.06:1
D1	— — —	1.26:1	1.26:1
D2	— — —	0.89:1	0.89:1
Reverse	— — —	3.07:1	3.07:1
Oil capacity	— — —		
(except torque converter)	— — —	6.3 pints (3 liters)	6.3 pints (3 liters)
Lubricant		See Table 3, Ch. 2	See Table 3, Ch. 2
Converter			
Torque ratio	— — —	2:1 to 1:1	2:1 to 1:1
Stall speed	— — —	2000-2250 rpm	2000-2250 rpm
Fluid type	— — —	ATF (DEXRON)	ATF (DEXRON)
Capacity	— — —	7.6 pints (3.6 liters)	7.6 pints (3.6 liters)
Final drive ratio	— — —	4.375:1	4.125:1

9

CHAPTER TEN

REAR AXLE AND SUSPENSION

The VW Beetle and Karmann Ghia rear suspension changed for the first time with the introduction of the Automatic Stick Shift in 1968. Prior to this, rear suspensions consisted of swing axles which pivoted only at their inner end, i.e., the rear wheels swung vertically in an arc with the transaxle at the center. See **Figure 1A**. The rear wheels connect through spring plates to torsion bars. Conventional shocks dampen wheel movement.

Automatic Stick Shift VW's in 1968, and all 1969 and later VW's have had double-jointed axles. Instead of swinging in an arc, the rear wheels have slight negative camber which increases with load or during cornering. See **Figure 1B**. Lateral forces are taken by diagonal trailing arms which connect to the rear wheels and transfer lateral forces directly to the frame. Rear wheels connect to torsion bars through spring plates as on earlier suspensions.

This chapter includes repair or replacement of all rear suspension and rear axle components, except the transaxle which is covered in Chapter Nine. Specifications are at end of chapter.

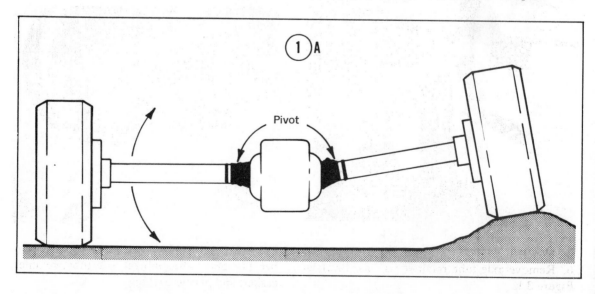

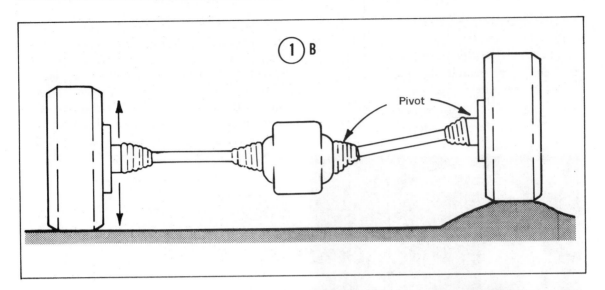

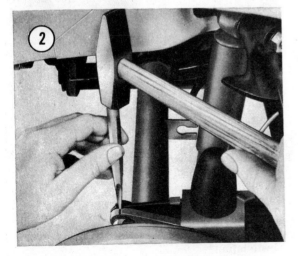

DRIVE SHAFT (SWING AXLE)

Removal

1. Remove brake drums as described in Chapter Twelve.

2. Disconnect handbrake cable and brake hose from backing plate.

3. Remove bearing cover, backing plate and wheel bearing as described under *Wheel Bearing Replacement (Swing Axles)*.

4. Mark spring plate position in relation to the rear axle bearing housing groove. Use a chisel. See **Figure 2**.

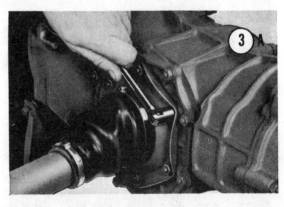

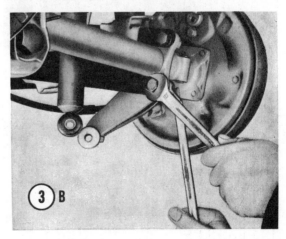

7. Remove bolts securing axle bearing housing to spring plate. See **Figure 3B**.

5. Disconnect lower end of shock absorber.

6. Remove axle tube retainer nuts as shown in **Figure 3A**.

8a. On 1961-1967 axles (up to chassis number 117 580 249), pull off axle tube, retainer, gasket, and plastic packing.

8b. On all axles from chassis No. 117 580 250, pull off axle tube, hard paper shims, and O-ring. Count number of shims removed.

9. Remove differential side gear lock ring and thrust washer shown in **Figure 4**.

10. Remove drive shaft. See **Figure 5**.

11. Remove differential side gear.

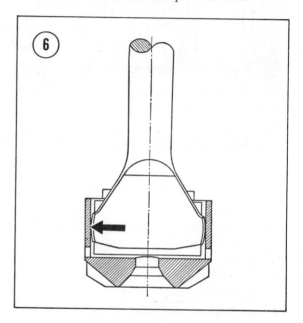

3. Check drive shaft, side gear and thrust washer for damage or wear. Clearance between rounded end of shaft and the side gear should be 0.001-0.004 in. (0.03-0.1mm). See **Figure 6**. Clearance between flat portions (see **Figure 7**) should be 0.001-0.010 in. (0.025-0.25mm). Oversize fulcrum plates for the side gears are available if clearance is excessive. In such cases, consider new standard size parts as well.

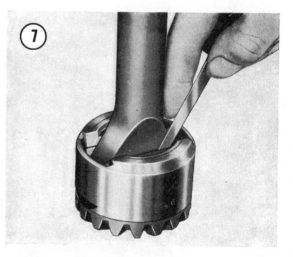

Inspection

1. Clean all parts in solvent. Clean the retainer seat on the final drive cover.

2. Check rubber boot for cuts or deterioration. Replace it if necessary with split-type replacement boot.

CAUTION

To install original unsplit type, the axle tube and bearing housing must be separated. Do not attempt this as there is considerable chance of damage to the housing.

Installation

1. Install differential side gear, drive shaft and thrust washer as shown in **Figure 8**. Secure with lock ring.

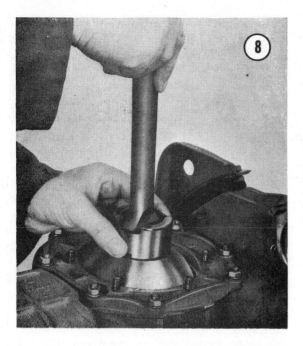

5. Check parts for obvious damage. Constant velocity joints at either end of shaft are described in the following procedures.

6. Installation is the reverse of these steps.

2. Install axle tube over drive shaft with paper gasket (or new shims) and plastic packing (or O-ring). Tighten the retainer nuts to 14 ft.-lb. (2 mkg).

3. Tighten rubber boot clamps.

4. Bolt bearing housing to spring plate. Align chisel mark with groove and tighten the bolts to 80 ft.-lb. (11 mkg).

5. Connect lower end of shock absorber.

6. Install wheel bearing as described under *Wheel Bearing Replacement*.

7. Install backing plate and bearing cover.

8. Connect the handbrake cable. Connect the brake hose.

9. Install brake drum as described in Chapter Twelve. Bleed and adjust footbrake and the handbrake.

DRIVE SHAFTS
(DOUBLE JOINT AXLE)

Removal/Installation

1. Raise the car on jackstands.

2. Remove Allen bolts at both ends of the drive shaft. See **Figure 9**.

3. Tilt the shaft and remove it.

4. Cover all exposed openings to prevent entry of dirt.

CONSTANT VELOCITY JOINTS
(DOUBLE JOINT AXLES)

Removal

1. Remove drive shaft as described previously.

2. Loosen rubber boot clamps and slide the boot back. See **Figure 10**.

3. Drive metal cap off joint with a drift as shown in **Figure 11**.

NOTE: *Do not tilt the ball hub more than 20° after removing the cap or the balls will fall out.*

4. Remove circlip from ball hub.

5. Slide outer part with balls onto the ball hub.

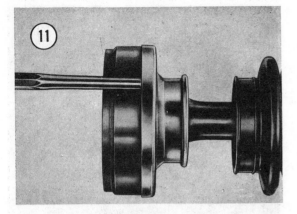

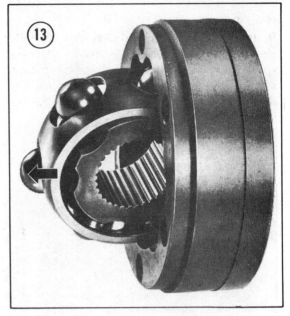

6. Press the drive shaft out of the ball hub as shown in **Figure 12**. Support the hub from underneath when doing this.

7. Remove the dished washer from the joint.

8. Slide the rubber boot off drive shaft.

Disassembly/Assembly

1. Remove constant velocity joint as described previously.

2. Press ball hub and cage out of the outer ring as shown in **Figure 13**.

3. Press the balls out of the cage.

4. Tip the ball hub out of the ball cage using the grooves shown in **Figure 14**.

5. Clean all parts in solvent. Check each part for signs of wear or scoring.

6. Install the ball hub in the cage using the grooves in the hub.

7. Press the balls into the cage as shown in **Figure 15**.

8. Hold the outer ring so the large diameter end faces up. Look at the ball groove spacing. Note

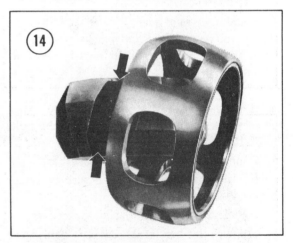

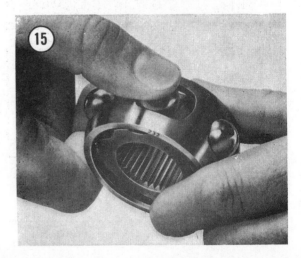

that the spacing at (a) is wider than at (b), directly opposite. See **Figure 16**.

9. Insert the ball hub and cage into the outer ring as shown in **Figure 17**. Ensure that wide spaced balls line up with wide spaced grooves, and that the chamferred end of the hub will face toward the large diameter end of the outer ring when the hub is pivoted.

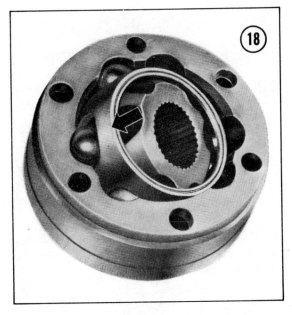

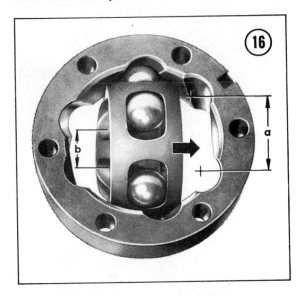

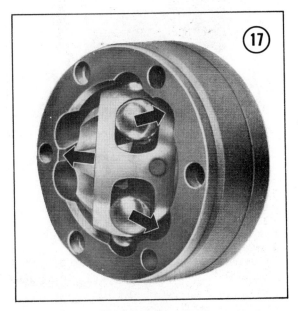

10. Pivot the ball hub in the hub until the balls fit into their grooves.

11. Press the cage firmly where indicated in **Figure 18** until the hub swings into position.

12. Check the joint before installing. It should be possible to move the hub by hand through its full range.

Installation

1. Inspect all parts for damage and replace if necessary.

2. Install rubber boot over drive shaft. Make sure that boot is not damaged by the splined end.

3. Slide the metal cap, then the dish washer, over the drive shaft.

4. With a hydraulic press, press the joint onto the drive shaft. See **Figure 19**.

> NOTE: *The large diameter end (see arrow,* **Figure 20**) *faces the metal cap.*

5. Install a new circlip on the drive shaft and press it tightly into its groove with water pump pliers. See **Figure 21**.

6. Pack about 2 ounces (60 grams) of lithium grease (with molybdenum disulphite additive) between outer part of joint and metal cap. Do not get any grease on contact surfaces between the cap, joint, or rubber boot. Pack another ounce (30 grams) into the end of the joint which faces the wheel.

7. Tap the metal cap into place over the joint.

8. Slide the rubber boot over the metal cap. Tighten both clamps securing the boot.

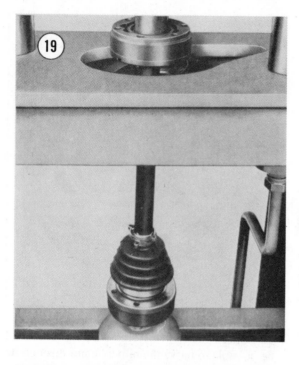

5. Install the boot with the split toward the rear. Tighten the boot screws (see **Figure 22**), and install new clamps with a full load on the rear axle. Do not overtighten screws or clamps.

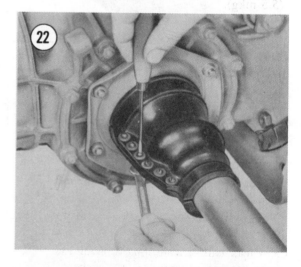

9. Squeeze the rubber boot by hand to force grease into the rear of the joint.

10. Install drive shaft as described previously.

REAR AXLE BOOTS

To permit boot replacement without removing drive shafts, a split boot is available.

1. Remove retaining clamps on boot.

2. Cut the old boot off.

3. Clean areas the boot had covered.

4. Coat joining faces of the split boot lightly with sealing compound.

OIL SEAL REPLACEMENT

1. Remove brake drum as described in Chapter Twelve.

2. Clean bearing cover and backing plate carefully with solvent. Do not get grease, oil, or solvent on brake shoes. If necessary, remove them to prevent damage.

3. Remove bolts securing bearing cover and remove the cover.

4a. On swing axles only, remove spacer, all rubber O-rings, and washer.

4b. On double joint axles, remove spacer and rubber O-ring.

5. Pry the oil seal out of the bearing cover. Do not try to pound it out from the outer end or the oil slinger will be damaged. Remove the oil slinger.

6. Fit the oil slinger into the bearing cover.

7. Install the oil seal with the open end (spring visible) toward the transmission. Tap it in evenly until it fits against the shoulder near the bottom of the cover.

8. Slide a new large rubber O-ring over the outer bearing race.

9. On swing axles only, slide the washer and a new small rubber O-ring on the shaft next to the inner bearing race.

10. Slide the spacer onto the shaft.

11. Install the bearing cover with a new paper gasket. Tighten the cover bolts to 40 ft.-lb. (5.5 mkg).

WHEEL BEARINGS

Replacement (Swing Axles)

This procedure requires a special bearing puller which grips between the inner and outer bearing races. If this type puller is not available and cannot be improvised, take the job to a VW dealer for replacement.

1. Perform Steps 1-4 of the *Oil Seal Replacement* procedure.

2. Remove bearing with the special puller. See **Figure 23**.

3. Clean ball bearing in solvent and check for wear, scoring, or signs of excessive heat. Replace the bearing if necessary.

4. Slide spacer on the drive shaft.

5. Slide the bearing into place with the nylon cover toward the transmission and the numbers facing out. Tap the inner race, working around the drive shaft evenly, to seat the bearing. When the outer race contacts the backing plate, tap around the outer race as well. Continue working around both races until the bearing is firmly seated.

6. Perform Steps 8-11 of the *Oil Seal Replacement* procedure.

Replacement (Double Joint Axles)

Wheel bearings are located in the diagonal trailing arms. For replacement, see disassembly and assembly procedure for the trailing arms.

DIAGONAL TRAILING ARMS

Removal

1. Remove the brake drum as described in Chapter Twelve.

2. Remove drive shaft and cover exposed constant velocity joint to prevent entry of dirt.

3. Disconnect brake hose and handbrake cable from the brake backing plate.

4. Remove bolts securing bearing cover. Remove the bearing cover and backing plate.

5. Mark position of spring plate in relation to diagonal arm with a chisel. See **Figure 24**.

6. Disconnect lower end of shock absorber.

7. Remove bolts securing spring plate to diagonal arm.

8. Remove Allen bolt securing diagonal arm to bracket (**Figure 25**) and remove diagonal arm.

Disassembly

1. Hold the diagonal arm in a vise and knock the shaft out with a rubber mallet.

10

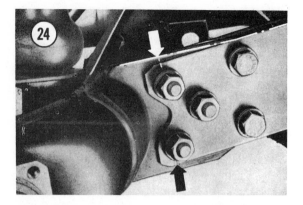

2. Remove the spacer ring, bearing inner ring and spacer from the opening facing the wheel.

3. Knock the outer ring out with a drift, and pry the oil seal out. See **Figures 26**.

4. Remove the large circlip (see **Figure 27**) and pull the bearing out.

5. Press the rubber bushing out of the diagonal arm. See **Figure 28**.

6. Pry the oil seal out of the bearing cover.

Assembly

1. Press new rubber bushing into the diagonal arm as shown in **Figure 29**.

2. Press ball bearing in as far as it will go, and install the circlip. See **Figure 30**.

3. Press oil seal in diagonal arm.

4. Pack the bearing housing in arm with lithium grease until the spacer sleeve will just fit. Usually about 2 ounces (60 grams) are required.

5. Press the outer roller bearing ring in.

6. Press shaft with inner spacer ring into the bearing.

7. Press inner roller bearing ring in. Support the shaft flange during this step.

8. Press the oil seal into the bearing cover.

Installation

1. Secure diagonal arm to frame bracket with Allen bolt. Lock the bolt by peening the bracket collar into a bolt head groove with a dull chisel.

2. Connect diagonal arm to spring plate. Align chisel marks and tighten to 87 ft.-lb. (12 mkg). If a new diagonal arm or spring plate is installed, align as close as possible by eye, then take the car to a VW dealer for final adjustment on special alignment equipment.

3. Connect lower end of shock absorber.

4. Grease bearing cover O-ring lightly and install it with the backing plate and bearing cover. Tighten the bolts to 36 ft.-lb. (5 mkg).

5. Connect brake hose and handbrake cable. Adjust the handbrake. See Chapter Twelve.

6. Install drive shaft as described previously.

7. Install brake drums as described in Chapter Twelve.

TORSION BARS

Removal

1. Raise the car on jackstands and remove the rear wheels.

2. On double joint axles, remove the drive shaft.

3. Disconnect handbrake cable at the handbrake operating lever and pull them toward the rear slightly.

4a. On swing axles, mark the spring plate position in relation to the rear axle bearing housing groove with a chisel, as shown in **Figure 2**.

4b. On double jointed axles, mark the spring plate and trailing arm with a chisel as shown in Figure 24.

5. Disconnect lower end of shock absorber.

6. Remove bolts securing spring plate to axle shaft housing (swing axles) or trailing arm (double joint axles). Tie housing or arm up.

7. Remove bolts securing spring plate hub cover and remove the cover.

8. Pull spring plate off lower stop as shown in **Figure 31**. Pull spring plate off torsion bar.

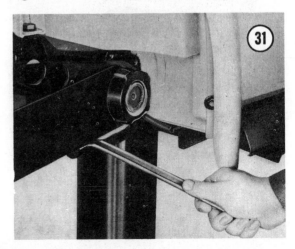

9. Remove 5 or 6 bolts from front edge of fender. Pull fender *carefully* aside and withdraw the torsion bar. See **Figure 32**.

> CAUTION
> *A protective paint covers the torsion bars. Do not nick or scratch this paint. Even slight damage leads to corrosion and eventual fatigue fractures. Touch up with paint, if necessary.*

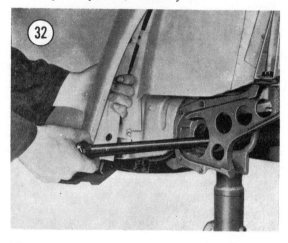

Installation

1. Grease splines on torsion bar and insert it.

> CAUTION
> *Torsion bars are marked left (L) and right (R) and must not be interchanged.*

2. On double joint axles, coat the inner rubber bushing with talcum and fit it over the torsion bar with the word "oben" at the top (**Figure 33**).

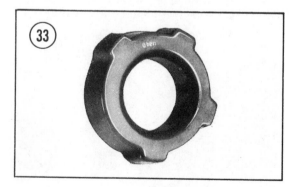

3. Install the spring plate and adjust it as described later.

4. Coat outer rubber bushing with talcum and install it with the word "oben" at the top.

5. Install the spring plate hub cover, but do not tighten the bolts.

6. Lift the spring plate as shown in **Figure 34** until its lower edge fits above the lower stop.

7. Tighten the spring plate hub cover bolts.

8. Clean mating surfaces between spring plate and axle bearing housing or trailing arm.

9. Bolt the spring plate to the bearing housing or trailing arm. Ensure that the chisel marks on the spring plate and bearing house or trailing arm line up. Tighten bolts to 80 ft.-lb. (11 mkg).

10. Connect and adjust handbrake cable. See Chapter Twelve.

Spring Plate Adjustment

In order to obtain proper wheel alignment and adequate spring travel under all load conditions, the spring plate angle must be adjusted on the torsion bar. There are 40 splines on the inner end of the torsion bar and 44 splines on the outer end. Turning the inner end of the bar one spline alters the spring plate angle 9° 0′; turning the spring plate one spline on the bar alters the angle by 8° 10′. Therefore, it is possible to set the spring plate angle at any multiple of 50′ by turning the splines in opposite directions.

Measurement of this angle is most easily done with a special VW tool made for this purpose. See **Figure 35**. Since this tool is expensive and not easily available, the following procedure allows adjustment with simple tools. No doubt other tools on hand can be used.

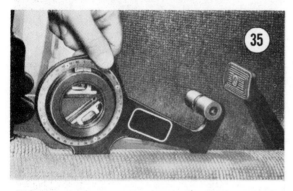

Always adjust both spring plates, even if only one was disassembled, especially if the car has high mileage.

1. Spring plate angle is measured in relation to the bottom of the door opening or frame tunnel. See Figure 35. Since it is doubtful if either surface is level with the car jacked up, first determine the angle the car slants. **Figure 36** shows one method. Place a protractor on the frame tunnel. Hold a spirit level against the protractor as shown in the figure; the bottom right corner of the level must touch the exact center of the protractor. Prop up the opposite end of the level until the spirit bubble is centered. Record the angle made by the level and the frame tunnel measured on the protractor.

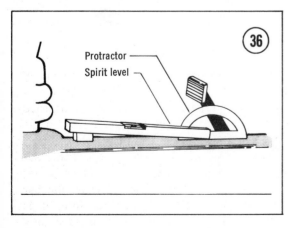

2. Measure the spring plate angle as shown in **Figure 37**. Lift the plate lightly to remove any play. Record this angle.

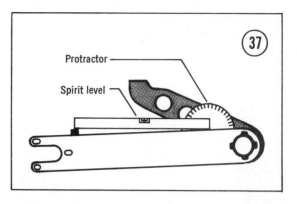

3. Subtract the angle measured in Step 1 from the angle in Step 2. The resulting angle should be the spring plate angle shown in the specifications for your model and year.

4. Move the torsion bar in its spline or move the spring plate on the torsion bar spline to correct the angle if necessary.

SHOCK ABSORBERS

1. Raise rear of car on jackstands.

2. Remove bolts securing top and bottom of shock absorber and then the shock absorber itself. See **Figure 38**.

3. Installation is the reverse of these steps. If old shock absorbers are reinstalled, check the rubber bushings and replace them if necessary. Tighten nuts to 43 ft.-lb. (6 mkg).

EQUALIZER SPRING (1967-1968)

Removal

1. Raise rear of car on jackstands and remove rear wheels.

2. Remove nuts on operating rod shown in **Figure 39**.

3. Remove rubber caps over top of operating rods and remove the nuts. See **Figure 40**.

4. Remove operating rods and rubber damper rings.

5. Remove nuts securing inner and outer supports (1 & 3, **Figure 41**). Remove supports and bushing.

6. Loosen the locknut and Allen screw securing the left spring lever (5, Figure 41) and remove the lever.

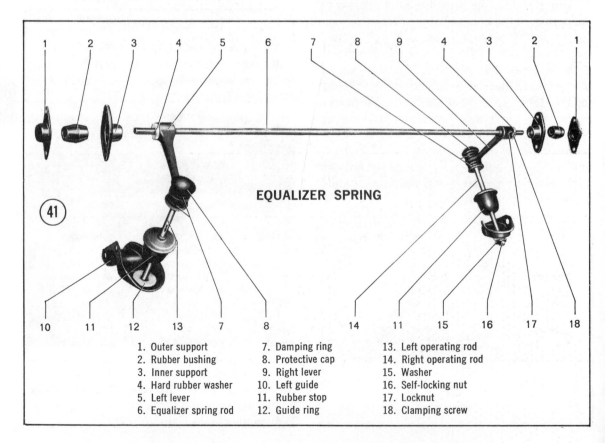

EQUALIZER SPRING

1. Outer support	7. Damping ring
2. Rubber bushing	8. Protective cap
3. Inner support	9. Right lever
4. Hard rubber washer	10. Left guide
5. Left lever	11. Rubber stop
6. Equalizer spring rod	12. Guide ring

13. Left operating rod	
14. Right operating rod	
15. Washer	
16. Self-locking nut	
17. Locknut	
18. Clamping screw	

7. Pull right spring lever and equalizer spring out together.

Inspection

1. Check operating rod guide rings and replace if necessary. They are easily pried out with a screwdriver as shown in **Figure 42**.

2. Check the equalizer spring, bushings, and rubber stops for wear or deterioration.

Installation

Refer to Figure 41 for the following procedure.

1. Install the right spring lever on the equalizer spring. Tighten the Allen screw and locknut.

2. Install the spring in the car from the right, and install the left spring lever.

CAUTION
The left spring lever is marked with an "L"; the right spring lever is unmarked. The right spring lever must point down and toward the FRONT when installed.

3. Install the hard rubber washers (4) and supports (1 and 3) and the rubber bushings (2).

4. Install operating rods. The longest operating rod fits on the right side. Use damping ring (7) above and below the spring levers. Tighten the nuts and install rubber caps.

5. Insert operating rods into the guides and tighten the nuts.

6. Install wheels and lower the car.

Table 1   TIGHTENING TORQUES

	foot-pounds	mkg
Axle tube retainer nuts	14	2.0
Bearing housing to spring plate	80	11.0
Drive shaft allen bolts	25	3.5
Wheel bearing cover bolts	43	6.0
Shock absorber nuts	50	7.0

10

Table 2   SPECIFICATIONS

	1200 & 1300	1500 (1967 & 1968) (with Manual Transaxle)	1500 & 1600 (except 1968) (with Manual Transaxle)	Super Beetle
Type	Independent swinging half axles	Independent swinging half axles	Independent double-jointed half axles	Independent double-jointed half axles
Springing	Torsion bars	Torsion bars	Torsion bars	Torsion bars
Spring plate inclination	17° 30′ +50′	20° +50′	20° 30′ +50′	20° 30′ +50′
Wheel alignment				
Toe-out	5′ ±10′	5′ ±10′	0° ±15′	0° ± 15′
Camber	2° 30′ ±1°	1° ±1°	50′ ± 40′	50′ ± 40′
Rear track	51.2″ (1300mm)	53.2″ (1350mm)	53.1″ (1350mm)	53.1″ (1352mm)

CHAPTER ELEVEN

FRONT SUSPENSION AND STEERING

VW Beetle and Karmann Ghia front suspensions changed very little until the introduction of the Super Beetle. Front wheels on 1961-1965 models were independently sprung with torsion bars running across the front in large tubes. Steering knuckles are attached with kingpins. Models since 1966, except the Super Beetle, use the same torsion bar suspension except that balljoints connect the steering knuckles.

The Super Beetle front suspension and steering are completely different from those of other Beetles. VW's version of the popular McPherson strut suspension replaces the torsion bar suspension providing more luggage space and better interior arrangement. The 1974 Super Beetle suspension is further refined with a negative steering roll radius to improve steering stability. In 1975, Volkswagen added rack-and-pinion steering to the Super Beetle.

All 3 suspensions are discussed in this chapter. Tightening torques (**Table 1**) and specifications (**Table 2**) are at the rear of the chapter.

WHEEL ALIGNMENT

Several front suspension angles affect running and steering of the front wheels. These angles must be properly aligned to maintain directional stability, ease of steering, and proper tire wear.

The angles involved define:

a. Caster
b. Camber
c. Toe-in
d. Steering axis or kingpin inclination
e. Toe-out on turns

Only camber and toe-in are adjustable. Camber should not be adjusted without a front-end rack. Toe-in, however, is easily measured on a level surface with a good steel tape measure or calibrated rod. Other suspension angles, though not adjustable, should be measured on a front-end rack to check for bent suspension parts.

Pre-alignment Check

Several factors influence suspension angles, or steering. Before attempting any adjustments, perform the following checks.

1. Check tire pressure and wear.
2. Check play in front wheel bearings. Adjust if necessary.
3. Check play in ball-joints or kingpins.
4. Check for broken springs or torsion bars.
5. Remove any excessive load.
6. Check shock absorbers.
7. Check steering gear adjustments.

8. Check play in pitman arm and tie rod parts.

9. Check wheel balance.

10. Check *rear* suspension for looseness.

A proper inspection of front tire wear can point to several alignment problems. Tires worn primarily on one side show problems with toe-in. If toe-in is incorrect on one wheel, the car probably pulls to one side or the other. If toe-in is incorrect on both wheels, the car is probably hard to steer in either direction. Incorrect camber may also cause wear on one side. Tire cupping (scalloped wear pattern) can result from worn shock absorbers, one wheel out of alignment, a bent spindle, or a combination of all. Tires which are worn in the middle, but not the edges, or worn nearly even on both edges, but not in the middle are probably overinflated or underinflated, respectively. These conditions are not caused by suspension misalignment.

Toe-in

Camber and rolling resistance tend to force the front wheels outward at their forward edge. To compensate for this tendency, the front edges are turned slightly inward when the car is at rest—this is toe-in. See **Figure 1**. Unlike other suspension angles, toe-in is easily adjusted.

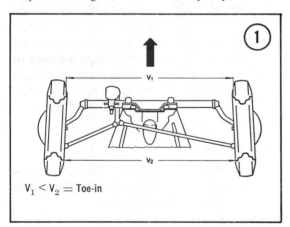

$V_1 < V_2 =$ Toe-in

To check toe-in, proceed as follows.

1. Drive the car onto any level smooth surface such as a driveway or parking lot. The front wheels must point straight ahead. One method of ensuring this is to take advantage of wheel caster. Drive the car straight forward without touching the steering wheel. Stop the car with the handbrake. The wheels should stop straight ahead.

2. Mark the inside wheel rim at 3 o'clock and at 9 o'clock using chalk.

3. Measure the distance between forward chalk marks. Two pieces of telescoping aluminum tubing spanning the distance makes an accurate tool. Place this tool between the forward edges of the wheel rims, and telescope the tubing so each end contacts the chalk marks. Mark the small diameter tubing exactly where it enters the large tube with a sharp scribe. See **Figure 2**.

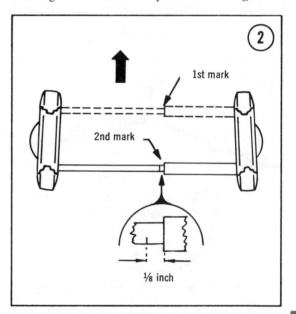

4. Measure between the rear chalk marks with the telescoping tubes. Make another mark on the small tube where it enters the large tube. There should be 2 scribe marks which are exactly ⅛ in. (3.2mm) apart, i.e., the front measurement is ⅛ in. less than the rear. If toe-in is not correct, adjust as described below.

To adjust toe-in, proceed as follows.

1. Turn the front wheels straight ahead as described in Step 1 of the checking procedure.

2. If the steering wheel spokes are *not* horizontal when the wheels are straight ahead, this must be corrected before adjusting toe-in. If the steering wheel is turned to the left, adjust tie rods in the direction shown in **Figure 3**. If the steering wheel is turned to the right, adjust tie rods as shown in **Figure 4**.

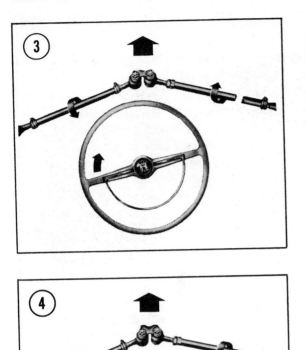

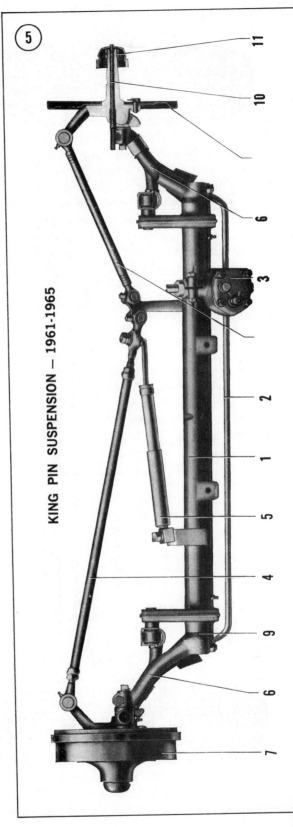

KING PIN SUSPENSION – 1961-1965

NOTE: *Never correct steering wheel position by repositioning the steering wheel on the column.*

KINGPIN SUSPENSION

The kingpin suspension consists of upper and lower laminated torsion bars running parallel across the car, supporting 2 trailing arms per wheel. See **Figure 5**. Large axle tubes contain torsion bars and bolt to the floor pan. Torsion bars are rigidly secured at the center forming, in effect, 4 separate torsion bars. Torsion arms (trailing arms) fit over the ends of the torsion bars, and extend partially inside the axle tube. The inner end is supported by a replaceable bushing; the outer end by a needle bearing.

Torsion arms connect at one end to a torsion arm link via link pins. Link pins are adjustable

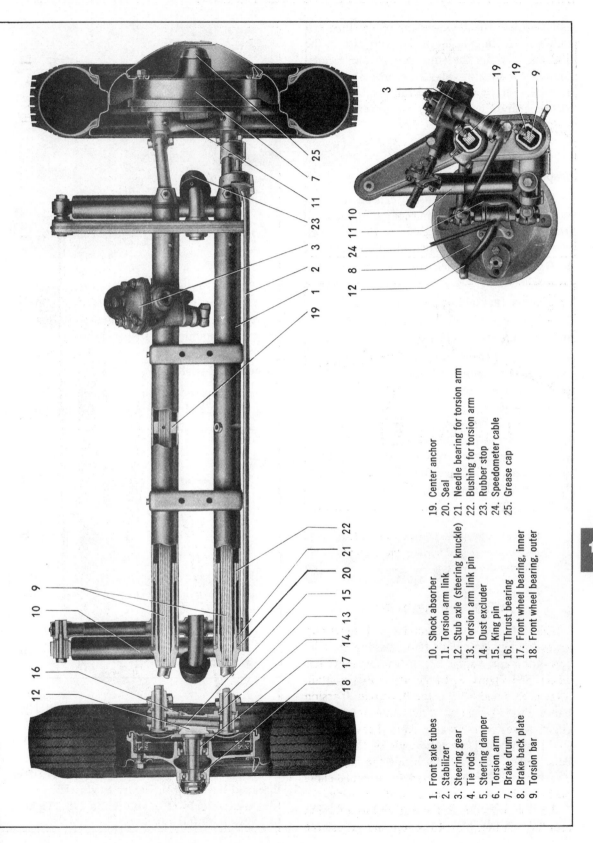

1. Front axle tubes
2. Stabilizer
3. Steering gear
4. Tie rods
5. Steering damper
6. Torsion arm
7. Brake drum
8. Brake back plate
9. Torsion bar
10. Shock absorber
11. Torsion arm link
12. Stub axle (steering knuckle)
13. Torsion arm link pin
14. Dust excluder
15. King pin
16. Thrust bearing
17. Front wheel bearing, inner
18. Front wheel bearing, outer
19. Center anchor
20. Seal
21. Needle bearing for torsion arm
22. Bushing for torsion arm
23. Rubber stop
24. Speedometer cable
25. Grease cap

11

and permit vertical movement of the link and stub axle. A kingpin holds the stub axle in the link and permits the stub axle to move horizontally for steering. Shock absorbers attach to a bracket on the upper axle tube and the lower torsion arm to dampen vertical movement.

Suspension Removal

The entire front suspension can be removed as a unit to facilitate certain repairs. In addition, front suspensions damaged beyond repair, e.g., in an accident, can be replaced completely.

1. Raise the car on jackstands and remove the front wheels.

2. Remove fuel tank as in Chapter Six.

3. Disconnect speedometer from left dust cap and pull the cable out of the steering knuckle.

4. Disconnect the steering column as described later under *Steering Column Removal*.

5. Disconnect brake hoses at brackets. See Chapter Twelve.

6. Disconnect steering damper at bracket.

7. Remove the tie rod end nuts on the long tie rod. Press both ends out with a special tool. Remove with steering damper attached.

8. Remove 2 bolts at upper edge of top axle tube. See **Figure 6**.

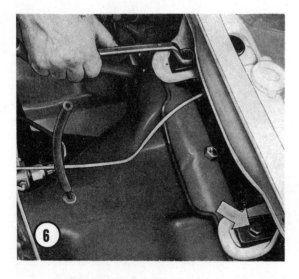

9. Loosen 4 screws securing front axle to front floor pan. See **Figure 7**.

10. Place a garage-type floor jack under the front suspension assembly. Have 2 helpers steady the suspension on the floor jack. Remove the 4 bolts holding the suspension and lower it.

Suspension Installation

1. Install new rubber pads on threaded bushings on upper edge of top axle tube (4, **Figure 8**).

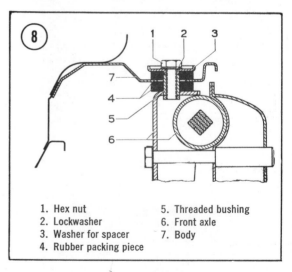

1. Hex nut	5. Threaded bushing
2. Lockwasher	6. Front axle
3. Washer for spacer	7. Body
4. Rubber packing piece	

2. Place suspension on garage-type floor jack. While 2 helpers steady the suspension, raise it into position and secure to the floor pan with 4 bolts. Tighten to 36 ft.-lb. (5.0 mkg).

3. Install new rubber pads on body over threaded bushings (4, Figure 8). Install spacers (3), lockwashers (2), and bolts (1). Tighten to 14 ft.-lb. (2.0 mkg).

4. Install the long tie rod with steering damper. Tighten tie rod nuts to 22 ft.-lb. (3.0 mkg) and tighten the steering damper bolts to 18 ft.-lb. (2.5 mkg). Turn tie rod nut additionally if necessary to install the cotter pin.

5. Connect the steering column as described under *Steering Column Installation* later in this chapter. Ensure that the wheels point straight ahead and the steering wheel spokes are horizontal.

6. Connect brake hoses. Bleed and adjust the brakes. See Chapter Twelve.

7. Connect speedometer cable.

8. Install fuel tank. See Chapter Six.

9. Check and adjust toe-in.

Steering Knuckle Removal

1. Raise front of car on jackstands and remove the wheel.

2. Disconnect speedometer cable from left dust cover and pull the cable out of the steering knuckle.

3. Disconnect the brake hose at the bracket. Cover the ends to prevent entry of dirt and water vapor.

4. Disconnect the tie rod end from the steering knuckle as described later in this chapter.

5. Remove the brake drum as described in Chapter Twelve. Remove the backing plate from the steering knuckle. It is unnecessary to remove brake shoes from backing plate.

6. Remove the clamp bolts securing the steering knuckle to the torsion arms. Count the number of wheel camber shims at the point indicated in **Figure 9** and record each number on the figure for future reference. There should be 8 shims total on each link pin.

7. Tap steering knuckle off with a rubber hammer as shown in **Figure 10**.

Steering Knuckle Installation

1. Measure the offset in millimeters between the torsion arm ends as shown in **Figure 11**. This measurement must be between 5mm and 9mm. If not, look for bent torsion arms or defective axle tube needle bearings. If the measurement is

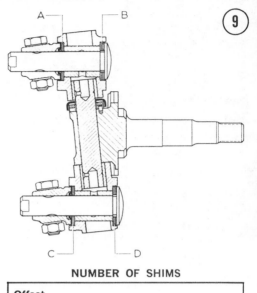

NUMBER OF SHIMS

Offset (mm)	A	B	C	D
5.5	2	6	5	3
6	2	6	4	4
6.5	3	5	4	4
7	3	5	3	5
7.5	4	4	3	5
8	4	4	2	6
8.5	5	3	2	6

from 5-9mm, record the exact figure. This is the offset.

2. See Figure 9. Compare the number of shims required for the offset measured in Step 1 to the number removed. If the numbers do not agree, use the numbers in the figure.

3. Install the shims and link pins on the steering knuckle.

4. Install steering knuckle on torsion arms.

5. Insert the link pin clamp bolts. Turn the link pins until the bolts go through.

6. To adjust and tighten the link pins, first tighten the link pin, then loosen it about ⅛ turn. See **Figure 12**. Retighten the pin just to the point when resistance is felt. Tap the ends of the pins lightly. See **Figure 13**. Tighten the clamp bolt. Do this for all 4 link pins.

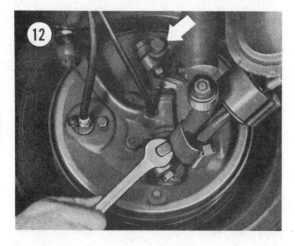

7. Connect the tie rod end to the steering knuckle.

8. Install the backing plate with brake shoes. Connect the brake hose.

9. Install the brake drum. Adjust the front wheel bearings. Bleed and adjust the brakes.

10. Connect the speedometer.

11. Install the wheels and lower the car.

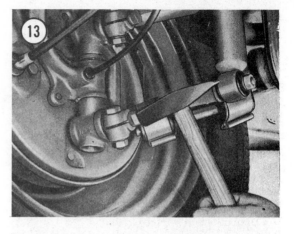

Kingpin and Bushing Replacement

Kingpin and bushing replacement requires several special tools including a hydraulic press. Remove the steering knuckle as described previously. Take the steering knuckle, kingpin repair kit, and link pin repair kit to a VW dealer or front-end shop.

Torsion Arm Removal/Installation

1. Remove steering knuckle complete with backing plate and brake drum as described earlier.

2. Remove stabilizer and shock absorber if lower torsion arm is to be removed.

3. Loosen the locknuts on torsion arm pins and screw the pins out. See **Figure 14**.

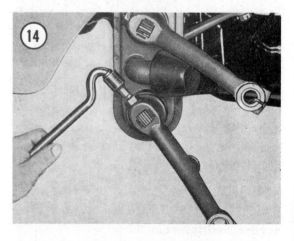

4. Pull torsion arm off.

5. Installation is the reverse of these steps. Check wheel alignment.

Torsion Bar Removal

1. Remove steering knuckles complete with backing plates and brake drums as described earlier.

2. Remove torsion arm on one side of torsion bar. See previous procedure.

3. Loosen torsion bar retaining bolt locknut. Remove retaining bolt. See **Figure 15**.

4. Pull torsion arm out with torsion bar attached. See **Figure 16**.

Torsion Bar Inspection

1. Clean torsion bars with solvent. Check for cracks or breaks. Install new bars if necessary.

2. Check torsion arms, needle bearings, and bushings in axle tubes. Bearing and bushing

replacement must be done by a VW dealer. Remove entire front suspension and take it to the dealer.

Torsion Bar Installation

1. Liberally coat bars with universal grease.

2. Insert the torsion bar in the axle tube. Position the countersunk recess in the bar so it points forward at about a 45° angle. See **Figure 17**.

3. Align the recess in the center of the bar with the retaining bolt hole. Install the bolt, tighten to 29-36 ft.-lb. (4.0-4.5 mkg), and tighten locknut to the same torque.

4. Install the torsion arms as described earlier.

BALL-JOINT SUSPENSION

The ball-joint suspension is similar to the kingpin suspension except torsion arms connect to the steering knuckle via ball-joints instead of link pins and kingpins. See **Figure 18**. Upper ball-joints fit in eccentric bushings by which wheel camber can be adjusted. See Chapter Two for lubrication and maintenance.

Suspension Removal/Installation

The entire front suspension can be removed as a unit to facilitate certain repairs. In addition, front suspension damaged beyond repair, e.g., in an accident, can be replaced completely. Remove and install ball-joint suspension in the same manner as kingpin suspensions described earlier.

11

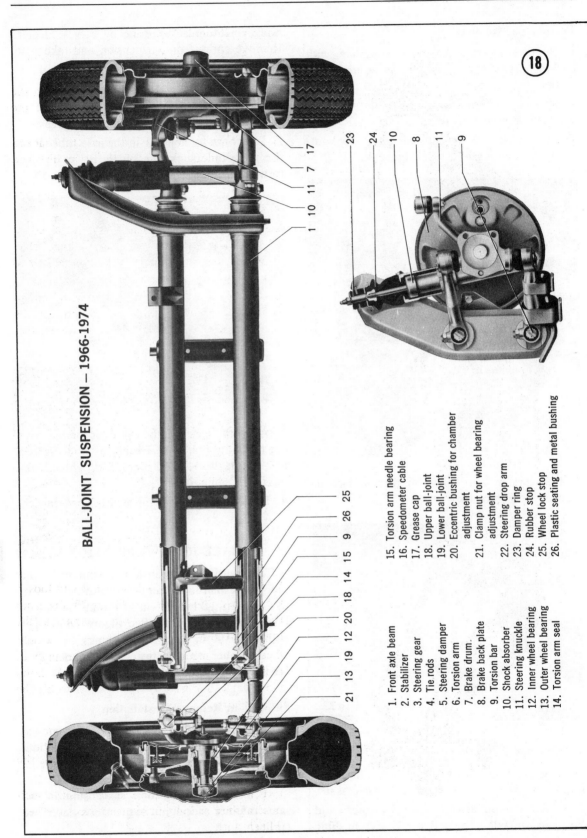

BALL-JOINT SUSPENSION — 1966-1974

1. Front axle beam
2. Stabilizer
3. Steering gear
4. Tie rods
5. Steering damper
6. Torsion arm
7. Brake drum.
8. Brake back plate
9. Torsion bar
10. Shock absorber
11. Steering knuckle
12. Inner wheel bearing
13. Outer wheel bearing
14. Torsion arm seal
15. Torsion arm needle bearing
16. Speedometer cable
17. Grease cap
18. Upper ball-joint
19. Lower ball-joint
20. Eccentric bushing for chamber adjustment
21. Clamp nut for wheel bearing adjustment
22. Steering drop arm
23. Damper ring
24. Rubber stop
25. Wheel lock stop
26. Plastic seating and metal bushing

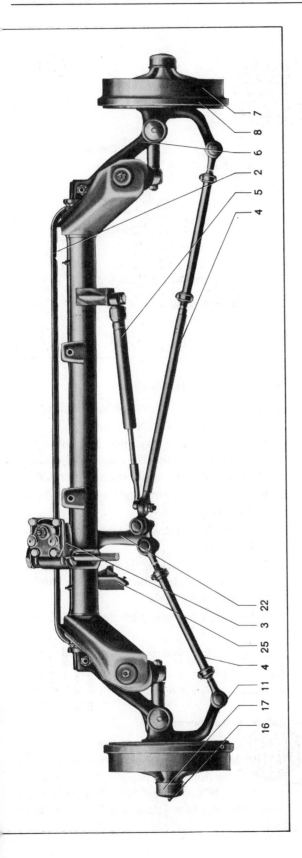

Steering Knuckle Removal

1. Raise front of car on jackstands and remove the wheel.

2. Disconnect the speedometer cable from the left dust cover and pull the cable out of the steering knuckle.

3. Disconnect the brake hose at the bracket. Cover the ends to prevent entry of dirt and water vapor.

4. Disconnect the tie rod end from the steering knuckle as described later.

5. Remove the brake drum as described in Chapter Twelve. Remove the backing plate from the steering knuckle. It is unnecessary to remove brake shoes from backing plate.

6. Remove the lower ball-joint nut. Screw an acorn nut onto the ball-joint to protect the threads and press the ball-joint out with a special tool as shown in **Figure 19**.

7. Remove the upper ball-joint nut and loosen the camber adjustment. See **Figure 20**. Press out the upper ball-joint in the same manner as the lower ball-joint.

8. Lift the upper torsion arm far enough to remove the steering knuckle. **Figure 21** shows the special tool used by Volkswagen to lift the torsion arm.

Steering Knuckle Inspection

This procedure can be performed with the steering knuckle installed.

1. Check the bearing surfaces for damage such as scratches, scoring, or signs of excessive heat (bluish tint).

11

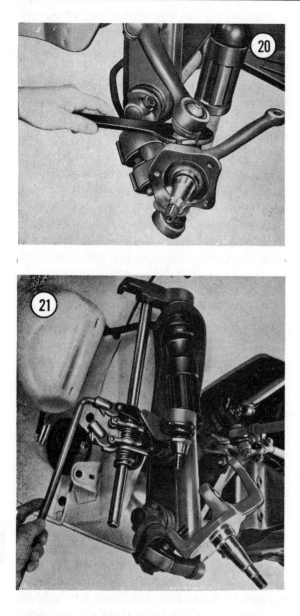

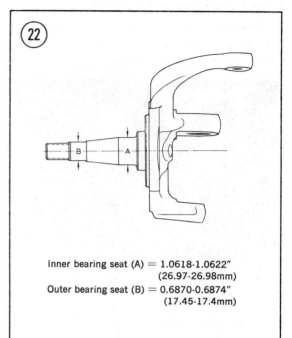

Inner bearing seat (A) = 1.0618-1.0622"
(26.97-26.98mm)
Outer bearing seat (B) = 0.6870-0.6874"
(17.45-17.4mm)

2. Measure bearing surfaces and compare to **Figure 22**.

3. Visually examine the steering knuckle for bends, cracks, or other damage. A steering knuckle suspected of bends should be taken to a VW dealer for testing. A large variety of special test fixtures is required.

> WARNING
> *Never attempt to straighten or reuse bent front end components. They have been structurally weakened and may fail in use.*

Steering Knuckle Installation

1. Lift the upper torsion arm as described in Step 8 of the removal procedure.

2. Install the steering knuckle and lower the torsion arm. Ensure that the camber adjustment notch points forward as shown in Figure 20.

3. Install ball-joint nuts and tighten to 36-51 ft.-lb. (5-7 mkg).

4. Connect tie rod end to steering knuckle as described later.

5. Install brake backing plate, brake drums, and brake shoes as described in Chapter Twelve. Connect the brake hose.

6. Adjust the front wheel bearings as described later.

7. Connect speedometer cable (left side only).

8. Bleed brakes.

9. Adjust toe-in and camber.

Ball-joint Replacement

Ball-joints are pressed into the torsion arms. If they are worn, remove the torsion arms as described on following page. Take the torsion arms to a VW dealer and have him replace the ball-joints. Replace joints which exceed wear limits.

Torsion Arm Removal/Installation

1. Remove the steering knuckle complete with backing plate and brake drum as described earlier. See **Figure 23**.

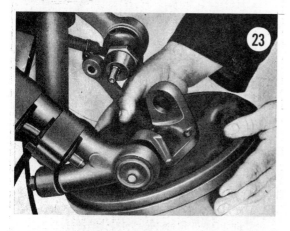

2. Remove stabilizer and shock absorber if lower torsion arm is to be removed.

3. Loosen locknuts on torsion arm pins, and screw the pins out. See **Figure 24**.

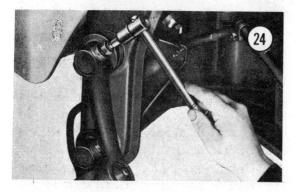

4. Pull torsion arm off.

5. Check the ball-joint for excessive play as described in Chapter Three. Check the axle tube seal; replace, if necessary. Check the torsion arm for bends and cracks. If suspect, take it to a VW dealer for testing.

6. Installation is the reverse of these steps. Check wheel alignment.

Torsion Bar Removal

1. Remove steering knuckles complete with backing plates and brake drums as described earlier. See Figure 23.

2. Remove torsion arm on one side of torsion bar. See previous procedure.

3. Loosen torsion bar retaining bolt locknut. Remove retaining bolt. See Figure 15.

4. Pull torsion arm out with torsion bar attached. See Figure 16.

Torsion Bar Inspection

1. Clean torsion bars with solvent. Check for cracks or breaks. Install new bars if necessary.

2. Check torsion arms, needle bearings, and bushings in axle tubes. Bearing and bushing replacement must be done by a VW dealer. Remove entire front suspension and take it to the dealer.

Torsion Bar Installation

1. Liberally coat bars with universal grease.

2. Insert the torsion bar in the axle tube. Position the countersunk recess in the bar so it points forward at about a 45° angle. See Figure 17.

3. Align the recess in the center of the bar with the retaining bolt hole. Install the bolt, tighten to 29-36 ft.-lb. (4.0-4.5 mkg), and tighten locknut to the same torque.

4. Install the torsion arms as described earlier.

SUPER BEETLE
STRUT SUSPENSION

The Super Beetle front suspension represents a significant deviation from the traditional torsion bar suspension used on other Beetles. This suspension, a version of the McPherson strut suspension, is used on most other VW models. This suspension requires a slightly longer front end, but it permits a much larger luggage compartment and better interior arrangement.

The complete 1971-1973 front suspension including steering is shown in **Figure 25**. The front wheels are independently suspended on struts each consisting of a large shock absorber and progressive coil spring. The top of each strut is attached to the body through a ball bearing and rubber mount. The bottom of each strut bolts to a steering knuckle and ball-joint and is held in position by a track control arm. Track control arms attach to the frame with

11

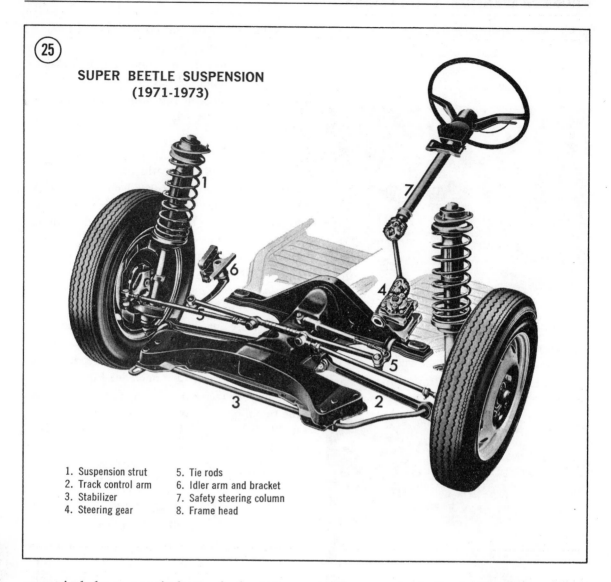

(25)

SUPER BEETLE SUSPENSION
(1971-1973)

1. Suspension strut   5. Tie rods
2. Track control arm   6. Idler arm and bracket
3. Stabilizer   7. Safety steering column
4. Steering gear   8. Frame head

eccentric bolts to permit front wheel camber adjustment.

The suspension on 1974 and later models is similar. The steering knuckle bolts to a bracket on the strut. The ball-joint is pressed into the track control arm, and the ball stud clamps to the steering knuckle. **Figure 26** shows the arrangement.

Steering Knuckle Removal/Installation

1. Raise front of car on jackstands and remove front wheels.

2. Remove stabilizer as described later.

3. Disconnect tie rod from steering knuckle as described later.

4. Disconnect brake line from bracket on shock absorber. Plug the line to prevent entry of dirt and water vapor.

5. Disconnect speedometer cable from steering knuckle (left side only) and pull it free. See Chapter Seven.

6. Remove the brake drum and brake shoes as described in Chapter Twelve. Remove the backing plate from the steering knuckle.

7a. On 1971-1973 models, remove 3 bolts connecting the shock absorber, steering knuckle, and ball-joint. See **Figure 27**. Push track control arm down and remove steering knuckle.

7b. On 1974 and later models, loosen ball-joint clamp bolt and disconnect ball-joint from

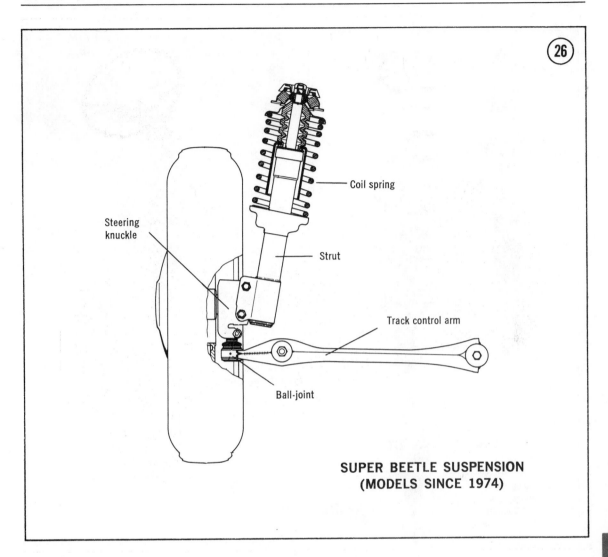

Coil spring

Steering
knuckle

Strut

Track control arm

Ball-joint

**SUPER BEETLE SUSPENSION
(MODELS SINCE 1974)**

steering knuckle. Remove 2 bolts securing steering knuckle to strut. See Figure 26.

8. Installation is the reverse of these steps. Adjust the wheel bearings as described later and bleed the brakes.

Steering Knuckle Inspection

This procedure can be performed with the steering knuckle installed.

1. Check the bearing surfaces for damage such as scratches, scoring, or signs of excessive heat (bluish tint).

2. Measure bearing surfaces and compare to **Figure 28**.

3. Visually examine the entire steering knuckle for bends, cracks, or other damage. If a steering

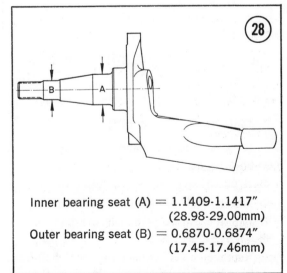

Inner bearing seat (A) = 1.1409-1.1417″
(28.98-29.00mm)
Outer bearing seat (B) = 0.6870-0.6874″
(17.45-17.46mm)

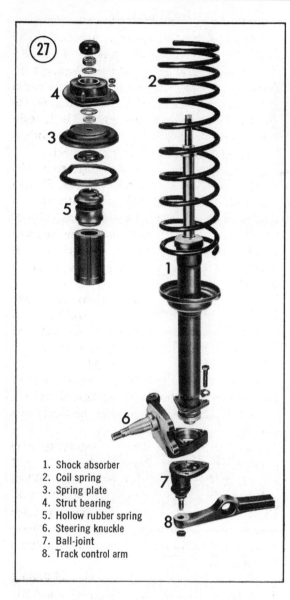

1. Shock absorber
2. Coil spring
3. Spring plate
4. Strut bearing
5. Hollow rubber spring
6. Steering knuckle
7. Ball-joint
8. Track control arm

the ball-joint, and tie up the steering knuckle to relieve tension on the brake line.

6. Installation is the reverse of these steps. Wipe all grease away from ball-joint stud before installing it. Tighten 3 bolts and the ball-joint nut to 29-32.5 ft.-lb. (4.0-4.5 mkg).

Ball-joint Replacement (1974 on)

1. Remove track control arm as described below.

2. Press ball-joint out as shown in **Figure 30**.

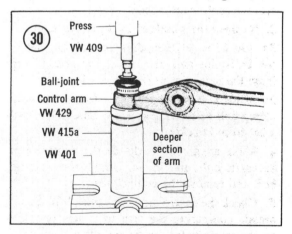

3. Press new ball-joint in from the deeper section of the track control arm. See **Figures 31 and 32**.

knuckle is suspect, take it to a VW dealer for testing. A large variety of special test fixtures is required.

Ball-joint Replacement (1971-1973)

1. Raise car on jackstands and remove front wheels.

2. Remove stabilizer as described later.

3. Remove nut on bottom of ball-joint.

4. Pull the control arm off the ball-joint as shown in **Figure 29**.

5. Remove bolts connecting the ball-joint, steering knuckle, and shock absorber. Remove

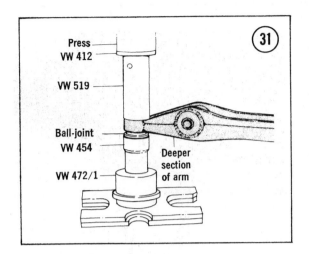

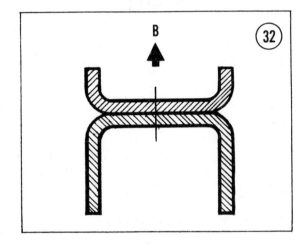

STEERING

Three steering arrangements are used on all Beetles from 1961 to the present. Figures 5 and 18 show steering for all Beetles except the Super Beetle. The steering gear is of the worm and roller type. Motion of the pitman arm moves the steering knuckle through adjustable tie rods. A steering damper, similar to a shock absorber, lessens road shock to the steering wheel.

Figure 25 shows Super Beetle steering. The steering gear is also worm and roller. Pitman arm motion is transmitted to a center tie rod supported at one end by an idler arm. Center tie rod movement, in turn, moves the steering knuckles through 2 adjustable outer tie rods. A steering damper lessens road shock as in all other Beetles.

Three steering column designs are used. Beetles from 1961-1965 have a solid column with the steering wheel bolted on one end. The other end connects to the steering gear through a flexible coupling. See **Figure 33**.

Beetles and Karmann Ghias from 1966-1971 (except Super Beetles) have a collapsible section in the steering column to protect the driver in a collision. See **Figure 34**.

Super Beetles also have a safety steering column design. The steering column is in 2 pieces connected by universal joints. When either the steering gear or steering wheel is subjected to an impact force, the small steering column shaft deflects. The impact energy, therefore, cannot be transmitted through the column to injure the driver.

All VW's since 1972 provide additional driver protection. The safety steering wheel has a collapsible section which absorbs impact energy. See **Figure 35**.

Track Control Arm Removal/Installation

1. Raise the front of the car on jackstands and remove both front wheels.

2. Remove the stabilizer as described later.

3a. On 1971-1973 models, remove the nut on the ball-joint and disconnect the control arm from the ball-joint as shown in Figure 29.

3b. On 1974 and later models, loosen ball-joint clamp bolt on steering knuckle. Disconnect ball-joint from knuckle.

4. Make alignment marks on the control arm, eccentric bolt, and frame. Unbolt the eccentric bolt and remove the control arm.

5. Check the control arm for bends. VW recommends comparing the arm to a new one. Examine carefully for cracks and other damage.

6. Installation is the reverse of these steps.

7. Check and adjust wheel camber.

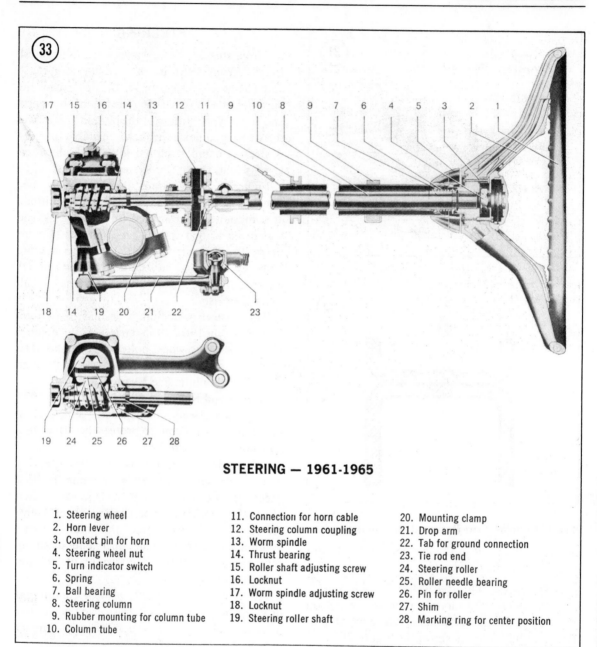

STEERING — 1961-1965

1. Steering wheel	11. Connection for horn cable	20. Mounting clamp
2. Horn lever	12. Steering column coupling	21. Drop arm
3. Contact pin for horn	13. Worm spindle	22. Tab for ground connection
4. Steering wheel nut	14. Thrust bearing	23. Tie rod end
5. Turn indicator switch	15. Roller shaft adjusting screw	24. Steering roller
6. Spring	16. Locknut	25. Roller needle bearing
7. Ball bearing	17. Worm spindle adjusting screw	26. Pin for roller
8. Steering column	18. Locknut	27. Shim
9. Rubber mounting for column tube	19. Steering roller shaft	28. Marking ring for center position
10. Column tube		

Steering Gear Adjustment (Except 1975 Super Beetle)

With both wheels on the ground and pointing straight ahead, move the steering wheel gently from side to side until resistance is felt. The amount of free play at the outer rim of the steering wheel should be one inch or less. If free play is more than this, the steering gear may need adjustment. First ensure that free play is not caused by loose tie rods or ball-joints.

1. Raise the front of the car on jackstands.

2. Turn the steering wheel to one lock or the other.

3. Loosen the large locknut on the worm shaft end play adjustment located at the lower end of the steering gear. See Figure 33.

4. Tighten the worm shaft adjustment until no play is felt when moving the worm back and forth at the coupling. Hold the adjustment and tighten the locknut.

5. Turn the steering wheel from lock-to-lock. If any binding is felt, loosen the worm shaft adjustment slightly until the binding disappears.

6. Lower the car. Turn the wheels straight ahead and test free play in steering again. If free play still exceeds one inch (25mm), complete the following steps.

7. Turn steering wheel 90° to the left or right.

8. Loosen the roller shaft adjusting screw locknut. See Figure 33.

9. Loosen the adjusting screw one complete turn. Then tighten the adjusting screw until you feel the roller contact the steering worm. Hold adjusting screw and tighten locknut to 16-18 ft.-lb. (2.2-2.5 mkg).

10. Check free play with steering turned 90° to the left, then 90° to the right. Free play should not exceed one inch. If free play is greater on one side than the other, readjust as in Steps 8 and 9 on the side with the greatest free play.

11. If free play with wheels straight ahead still exceeds one inch, internal parts are badly worn. The steering gear must be repaired by a VW dealer.

Steering Gear Adjustment (1975 Super Beetle)

1. Park car on a level surface with the front wheels pointed straight ahead.

2. Open luggage compartment and remove spare tire.

3. Remove plug over access hole in floor of compartment.

4. Loosen locknut on adjustment.

5. Turn Allen screw in until you feel it just makes contact internally.

6. Hold the adjuster with the Allen wrench and tighten the locknut.

7. Install the access hole plug and spare tire.

Steering Gear Removal/Installation (1961-1967)

1. Raise car on jackstands and remove front wheels.

2. Disconnect the tie rod ends from the pitman arm on the steering gear with a special tool.

3. Disconnect the horn ground wire from the steering column coupling.

11

4. Loosen the clamp bolt at the bottom of the steering column.

5. Pull the steering column upward until it clears the coupling.

6. Mark the position of the steering gear on the upper axle tube.

7. Remove bolts clamping the steering gear to the axle tube and remove the steering gear.

8. Installation is the reverse of these steps. Use new lock plates under the mounting clamp screws.

9. Check and adjust toe-in.

Steering Gear Removal/Installation (1968 on, Except Super Beetle)

1. Remove steering column as described in a later procedure.

2. Mark the position of the steering gear on the upper axle tube.

3. Remove bolts clamping the steering gear to the axle tube and remove the steering gear.

4. Installation is the reverse of these steps.

5. Check and adjust toe-in.

Steering Gear Removal/Installation (1971-1975 Super Beetle)

1. Raise the left side of the car on jackstands and remove the left front wheel.

2. Disconnect the steering damper from the pitman arm on the steering gear.

3. Disconnect the center tie rod end from the pitman arm.

4. Slide the rubber boot off the bottom steering column universal joint. Loosen the clamp bolt and pull the universal joint off the steering gear.

5. Remove bolts securing the steering gear to the body. All bolts are accessible through the left wheel well.

6. Installation is the reverse of these steps.

7. Check and adjust toe-in.

Steering Gear Cover Gasket Replacement

1. Remove steering gear, described previously.

2. Remove steering gear cover.

3. On 1966 and later models, top up steering housing with liquid transmission grease available from VW dealer.

4. Install cover with new gasket.

5. Install steering gear as described previously.

6. On 1961-1965 models, remove old filler plug from cover. Bring level to the bottom of the filler hole threads with SAE 90 transmission oil.

Idler Arm Removal/Installation (1971-1973 Super Beetle Only)

1. Raise the right side of the car on jackstands and remove the right front wheel.

2. Disconnect the center tie rod end from the idler arm.

3. Remove bolts securing idler arm bracket to the body. These bolts are accessible through the right wheel well.

Steering Wheel Removal

1. Disconnect battery ground cable.

2a. On 1961-1971 models, carefully pry the horn cap off with a screwdriver.

2b. On 1972 and later models, pry the horn cover off at one of the spokes. See **Figure 36**.

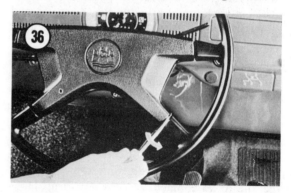

3. Disconnect the horn ground cable.

4. Remove steering wheel nut and lockwasher. See **Figure 37**.

5. Remove steering wheel.

Steering Wheel Installation

1. Ensure that the brass washer for the self-canceling turn switch is positioned with the cutaway portion to the right and the front wheels straight ahead. See **Figure 38**.

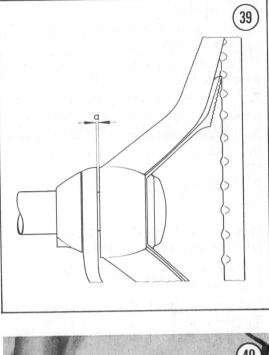

2. Install the steering wheel with the spokes horizontal. The tab on the steering wheel must engage in the cutaway portion of the brass washer.

> NOTE: *The safety steering wheel used since 1972 may be installed on earlier models with no modifications.*

3. Install the lockwasher and nut. Tighten the nut to 36 ft.-lb. (5.0 mkg).

4. Check the gap at (a) in **Figure 39**. This gap should be 0.04-0.08 in. (1-2mm). Adjust as described in *Steering Column Installation*.

5. Connect horn cable, and install horn cap.

6. Connect the battery ground cable.

Steering Column Removal/Installation (1961-1967)

1. Remove clamp bolt and clamp on steering column. See **Figure 40**.

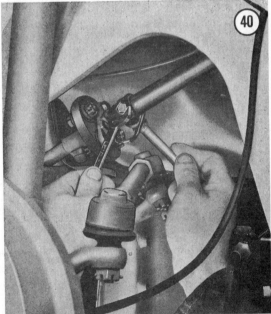

2. Disconnect the horn ground wire from the steering column coupling.

3. Loosen the steering wheel nut. Pull the steering wheel complete with steering column out of the tube. Remove steering wheel from column.

4. Check the ball bearing in the top portion of the tube. This bearing is packed with special grease and requires no periodic maintenance.

5. Install the steering column in the tube.

6. Install the support ring (2, **Figure 41**) on the steering column with the shoulder up. Install the spring (3) and brass washer. Secure with circlip.

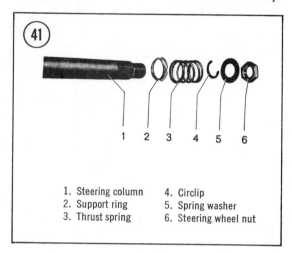

1. Steering column   4. Circlip
2. Support ring   5. Spring washer
3. Thrust spring   6. Steering wheel nut

7. Install the steering wheel as described in previous procedure.

8. Set the gap shown in Figure 39 to 0.04-0.08 in. (1-2mm) by moving the steering column in the coupling.

9. Install the lower clamp and tighten the clamp bolt. Use a new lock plate on the bolt.

Steering Column Removal
(1968 on, Except Super Beetle)

1. Disconnect battery ground cable.

2. Remove fuel tank. See Chapter Six.

3. Disconnect ground cable from steering column coupling (A, **Figure 42**).

4. Remove clamp nut (B, Figure 42).

5. Bend up support ring tabs and remove the support ring (C, Figure 42, or 5, **Figure 43**).

6. Remove steering wheel as described in an earlier procedure.

7. Remove the steering column circlip (6, Figure 43).

8. Turn ignition key to unlock steering column.

9. Remove 3 Allen screws securing steering column tube and steering column switch. See **Figure 44**. Take switch off column and hang it so there is no tension on wires.

10. Pull steering column and tube upward and then out.

Steering Column Installation
(1968 on, Except Super Beetle)

1. Ensure that the Allen screws securing the mounting bracket are tight and that the open ends of the slots holding the threaded aluminum inserts faces toward the front. See arrows in **Figure 45**.

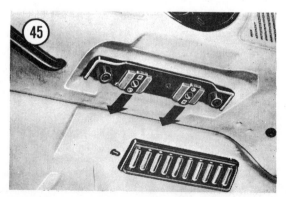

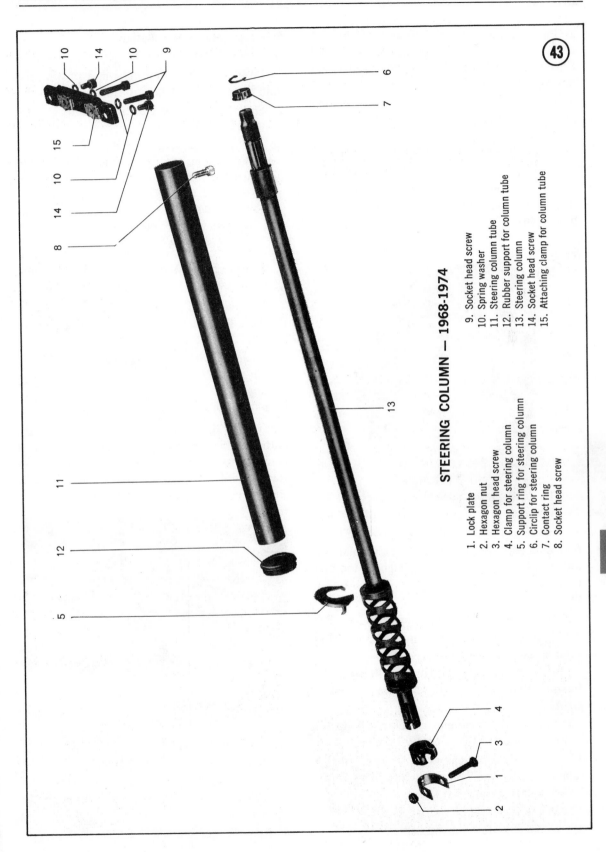

STEERING COLUMN – 1968-1974

1. Lock plate
2. Hexagon nut
3. Hexagon head screw
4. Clamp for steering column
5. Support ring for steering column
6. Circlip for steering column
7. Contact ring
8. Socket head screw
9. Socket head screw
10. Spring washer
11. Steering column tube
12. Rubber support for column tube
13. Steering column
14. Socket head screw
15. Attaching clamp for column tube

2. Push steering column tube and steering column through the rubber bushings in the firewall. Fit column over the flexible coupling, but do not tighten clamp.

3. Install Allen screws securing steering column tube and switch to the dash bracket. Tighten finger-tight.

4. Install circlip (6, Figure 43).

5. Check that front wheels point straight ahead and that the mark on the steering gear worm shaft aligns with the cast housing seam. See **Figure 46**.

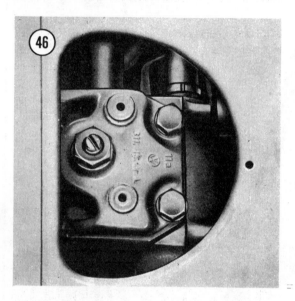

6. Install clamp bolt with new locking plate on lower end of steering column. Tighten the bolt to 11 ft.-lb. (1.5 mkg) and bend the tab up on the lock plate.

7. Connect horn ground to coupling.

8. Install steering support ring and secure by bending the tabs over.

9. Install the steering wheel as described earlier. Ensure that turn signal lever is in its center position.

10. Move steering column switch until gap (a) in Figure 39 is 0.08-0.12 in. (2-3mm).

11. Tighten 3 Allen screws on steering column tube and steering column switch to 3.5-7 ft.-lb. (0.5-1 mkg).

12. Install fuel tank. See Chapter Six.

13. Connect battery ground cable.

**Steering Column Installation
(1971-1975 Super Beetle)**

1. Push steering column tube and steering column through the opening in the body.

2. Slide the lower end of the column into the universal joint.

3a. On 1971 models, slide the column switch over the column tube and secure both to the dash panel bracket. Install the circlip at the top of the column.

> NOTE: *Steps 5 through 9 apply to 1971 models only.*

5. Remove circlip at top end of steering column.

6. Turn ignition key to unlock steering column.

7. Remove bolts securing the column tube to the dash. Remove Allen screws securing column switch.

8. Remove switch from column tube and hang it with wire so there is no tension on the connecting wires.

9. Pull steering column and tube up and out.

10. On 1972-1975 models, remove bolts securing the column tube to the dash. Disconnect connectors and windshield washer hose from steering column housing. See **Figure 47**. Lift steering column assembly out.

**Steering Column Removal
(1971-1975 Super Beetle)**

1. Disconnect the battery ground cable.

2. Remove fuel tank. See Chapter Six.

3. Slide rubber boot off upper universal joint. Remove bolt securing steering column to the universal joint.

4. Remove steering wheel as described earlier.

3b. On 1972-1975 models, secure the column to the dash panel with 2 bolts. Reconnect the connectors and windshield wiper hose.

4. Ensure that the wheels point straight ahead, and tighten the bolt in the universal joint to 14 ft.-lb. (2 mkg). Slide rubber boot over universal joint.

5. Install steering wheel as described earlier.

6. Install fuel tank.

7. Connect battery ground cable.

Steering Damper Replacement

1. Raise car on jackstands and remove wheels.

2a. On all except Super Beetles, remove bolt securing the damper to axle tube. See **Figure 48**.

2b. On Super Beetles, remove bolt securing steering damper to the floor pan.

3a. On all except Super Beetles, remove nuts securing the damper to the tie rod (**Figure 49**). Remove damper.

3b. On Super Beetles, remove bolt securing steering damper to drop arm on steering gear.

4. Installation is the reverse of these steps. Tighten nut on tie rod to 18-22 ft.-lb. (2.5-3.5 mkg) and secure with locknut. Install the bracket bolt with a new lock plate. Tighten the bolt to 18-21 ft.-lb. (2.5-3.0 mkg).

Tie Rod Replacement
(Except Super Beetle)

1. Raise car on jackstands and remove front wheels.

2. Bend up lock plates on tie rod nuts. Remove the nuts.

3. Disconnect steering damper from right side tie rod.

4. Press tie rod end out with special tool as shown in **Figure 50**.

CAUTION
Do not damage rubber seals when removing tie rods.

5. Check tie rods for bends and other damage. Bent tie rods must be replaced, not straightened.

6. Check tie rod pin. If there is any play or the pin is frozen, the tie rod end must be replaced.

7. Check rubber seals. Damaged seals must be replaced.

8. Check steering damper bushing for wear. Replace if necessary.

9. Install all tie rods so the end with left-hand threads is toward the left side of the car.

11

10. Connect steering damper to tie rod.

11. Adjust toe-in.

Tie Rod Replacement (Super Beetle)

Outer tie rod replacement on the Super Beetles is identical to that described for other Beetles, except that the steering damper need not be disconnected.

Center tie rod replacement is the same as for any other tie rod. However, the outer tie rods should first be disconnected from center tie rod.

STABILIZER

Removal/Installation
(Except Super Beetle)

1. Raise the car on jackstands and remove both front wheels.

2. Bend the lugs up on the clips and tap the clips off the damper as shown in **Figure 51**.

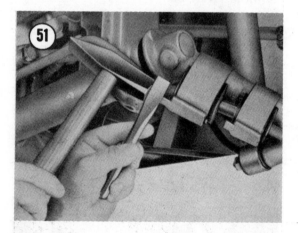

3. Remove the clamps. See **Figure 52**.

4. Pull the stabilizer out.

5. Inspect all parts for damage.

6. Reinsert stabilizer into rubber bushings.

7. Install the clamps with the slot tapering toward the steering knuckle.

8. Compress the clamps with water pump pliers and slide the clips on. See **Figure 53**. Bend the lugs to secure them.

Removal/Installation (Super Beetle)

Refer to **Figure 54** for following procedure.

1. Raise front of car on jackstands.

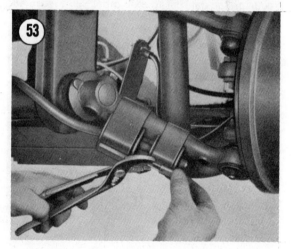

2. Remove nuts and washers securing the stabilizer to the track control arms.

3. Remove screws securing the front clamps and remove clamps.

4. Pull stabilizer out of track control arms.

5. Installation is the reverse of these steps.

SHOCK ABSORBERS

Replacement (Except Super Beetle)

1. Raise the front of the car on jackstands and remove both front wheels.

2. Remove upper nut while holding the bottom of the stud as shown in **Figure 55**.

3. Remove the bottom nut securing the shock absorber.

4. Remove the shock absorber.

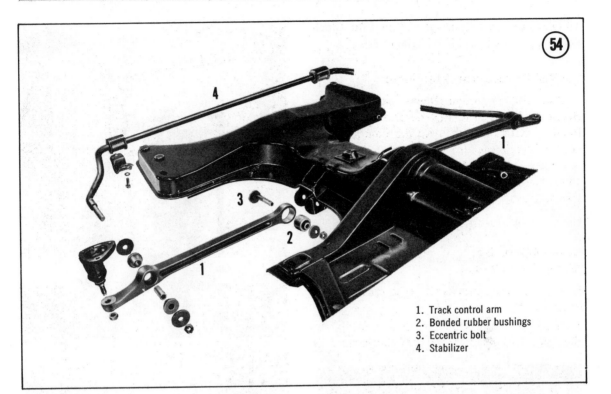

1. Track control arm
2. Bonded rubber bushings
3. Eccentric bolt
4. Stabilizer

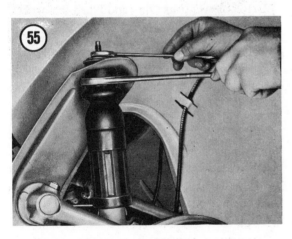

5. Grease the lower mounting pin lightly.

6. Install the shock absorber and nut on the lower pin.

7. Slide a rubber bushing on the top stud with the shoulder facing up. See **Figure 56**.

8. Pull the top stud up until it passes through the upper mounting hole.

9. Install another rubber bushing with the shoulder facing down.

10. Install the washer. Install the nut and tighten down as far as it goes.

11. Tighten the lower nut to about 22-25 ft.-lb. (3.0-3.5 mkg).

Replacement (Super Beetle)

1. Remove stabilizer bar as described earlier.

2. Disconnect tie rods from steering knuckle as described later. Only one end of each rod must be disconnected.

3. Disconnect the brake line from its bracket on the shock absorber. Plug the line to prevent entry of dirt and water vapor.

4. Remove 3 nuts securing the top of the shock absorber to the body. See **Figure 57**.

> **WARNING**
> Do not *remove the large nut in the center. This would relieve tension on the coil spring which could fly out and cause serious injury when the shock absorber is removed.*

5a. On 1971-1973 models, remove 3 bolts securing the bottom of the shock absorber to the steering knuckle and ball-joint. See Figure 31. Push the track control arm down and lift the shock absorber out.

5b. On 1974 and later models, remove 2 bolts securing bottom of shock absorber (strut) to steering knuckle.

> NOTE: *The following 2 steps are impossible without a spring compressor. Let a VW dealer transfer the coil spring from the old to the new shock absorbers.*

6. Compress the spring with a special tool as shown in **Figure 58**. Remove the center nut on top of the shock absorber. Release spring tension slowly and disassemble the shock absorber.

7. Reassemble the spring and rubber parts on the shock absorber. Compress the spring, install the top plate, and secure with the large nut. Release spring tension.

8. Connect ball-joint, steering knuckle, and shock absorber together with 3 bolts.

9. Lift the upper part of the shock into the upper mounting holes. Install 3 nuts.

10. Reconnect tie rod ends.

11. Install stabilizer bar.

12. Reconnect brake line and bleed the brakes.

COIL SPRING REPLACEMENT

The coil spring is part of the shock absorber assembly. To replace the spring, follow the shock absorber procedure. Since the procedure requires a special tool, it is best to remove the shock absorber assembly following the procedure, and let a VW dealer replace the spring. Then install the assembly following the same procedure.

WHEEL BEARINGS

Two types of wheel bearings are used from 1961 on. Ball bearings are used in kingpin suspension cars (1961-1965), while tapered roller bearings are used in later cars (1966 on). The adjustment procedures vary slightly for each type.

Wheel Bearing Replacement

1. Remove brake drums and wheel bearings as described in Chapter Twelve.

2. Clean the wheel bearings thoroughly in solvent and blow dry. Check balls or rollers for

scores, wear, and evidence of overheating (bluish tint). Check bearing races on the axle stub and brake drum. Do not mix the bearings up if they are good; they must be replaced on the same race.

3. If a bearing or a bearing race is damaged, the bearing and both bearing races must be replaced. Bearing race replacement requires special equipment and must be done by a VW dealer or front end repair shop.

4. If necessary to drive the car to a repair shop, repack the bearings and adjust them as well as possible. See *Front Brake Drum Installation* for steps describing wheel bearing packing.

Wheel Bearing Adjustment (1961-1965)

VW attaches a dial indicator to the wheel as shown in **Figure 59**, then rocks the wheel to determine axial play. Axial play should be 0.001-0.005 in. (0.03-0.12mm). The following procedure does not require a dial indicator and works equally as well if you are careful.

1. Remove the outer hub nut and lock plate.

2. Now tighten the inner nut to about 15 ft.-lb. (2 mkg) while rotating the wheel. This takes all slack out of the bearings.

3. Loosen the inner nut just to the point where the thrust washer can be moved when pried with a large screwdriver. This represents about 0.001 in. (0.03mm) of end play.

4. Install a new lock plate and outer hub nut. Hold the inner nut with a thin wrench while tightening the outer nut or the adjustment will change.

5. Bend the lock plate tabs to secure the nuts.

Wheel Bearing Adjustment (1966 on)

VW attaches a dial indicator on the wheel as shown in Figure 59, then rocks the wheel to determine axial play. Axial play should be

0.001-0.005 in. (0.03-0.12mm). The following procedure does not require a dial indicator and works equally as well for wheels with drum or disc brakes.

1. Loosen screw in clamp nut.

2. Tighten the clamp nut to about 15 ft.-lb. (2 mkg) while rotating the wheel. This takes all slack out of the bearing.

3. Loosen the clamp nut just to the point where the thrust washer can be moved when pried with a screwdriver. Loosen nut an additional 1/12 turn (½ flat on the hex).

4. Tighten the clamp screw 7-9 ft.-lb. (1-1.3 mkg) and check the thrust washer with a screwdriver. If it is very loose, repeat entire procedure.

> NOTE: *When the axial play is near 0.005 in. (0.12mm), very slight axial play can be felt when rocking the wheel by hand. This is permissible as long as the bearings are not noisy.*

Table 1   TIGHTENING TORQUES

	foot-pounds	mkg		foot-pounds	mkg
All except Super Beetle			Stabilizer to track control arm	22	3.0
Front axle to frame	36	5.0	Stabilizer clamp to frame	14	2.0
Shock absorber (upper)	14	2.0	Strut to body nuts	14	2.0
Shock absorber (lower)	22-25	3.0-3.5	Strut to shock absorber	50-61	7.0-8.5
Ball-joint nuts (M10x1)	29-36	4.0-5.0	Steering knuckle to ball-joints bolts	29	4.0
Ball-joint nuts (M12x1.5)	36-50	5.0-7.0	Idler arm bracket to body	22	3.0
Tie rod nuts	22	3.0	Idler arm to bracket	29	4.0
Steering damper nut	18	2.5	Steering gear to axle	18-22	2.5-3.0
Steering damper bolt	29-32	4.0-4.5	Roller shaft adj. locknut	18	2.5
Torsion bar setscrew	29-36	4.0-5.0	Steering worm adj. locknut	36-43	5.0-6.0
Torsion bar locknut	29-36	4.0-5.0	Steering gear cover bolts	14-18	2.0-2.5
Pitman arm nut	50	7.0	Pitman arm nut	72	10.0
			Steering wheel nut	36	5.0
Super Beetle			Steering coupling	14-18	2.0-2.5
Track control arm nut	29	4.0	Steering column mounting bolts	11	1.5
Ball-joint nut	29	4.0	Steering U-joint bolts	18	2.5

Table 2   SPECIFICATIONS

	1961-1965	1968-ON (except Super Beetle)	1971-ON Super Beetle
WHEEL ALIGNMENT			
Toe-in (no pressure on wheels)	$+30' \pm 15'$	$+30' \pm 15'$	$+30' \pm 10'$
Toe-in (with pressure on wheels)	$+5' \pm 15'$	$+5' \pm 15'$	$+10' \pm 10'$
Pressure applied for above spec.	22±4 lbs (10±2 kg)	22±4 lbs (10±2 kg)	22±4 lbs (10±2 kg)
Max. permissible difference in			
toe-in specs. above	25'	25'	25'
Castor	$3° 20' \pm 1°$	$3° 20' \pm 1°$	$2° \pm 35'$
Camber	$+30' \pm 20'$	$0° 30' \pm 20'$	$1° 20' \pm 20'$
Steering axis inclination	5°	5°	8° 15'
Toe-out on turns (at full left			
or right lock)			
inner wheel	$34° \pm 2°$	$34° \pm 2°$	40°
outer wheel	$28° \pm 1°$	$28° \pm 1°$	35°
STEERING GEAR			
Turns lock-to-lock	2½	2½	2¾
Steering ratio	14.34, 14.14[1]	14.34, 14.14[1]	16.5
Free-play (measured at outer			
edge of steering wheel)	1" (25mm)	1" (25mm)	1" (25mm)

1. Karmann Ghia

CHAPTER TWELVE

BRAKES

Volkswagen uses conventional hydraulically operated brakes on all 4 wheels. Beetles and Karmann Ghias from 1961-1966 use a single circuit hydraulic system which operates both front and rear brakes. Both models since 1967 use a dual circuit hydraulic system. One circuit operates front brakes, while the other circuit operates the rear brakes. In addition, Karmann Ghias and some European Beetles from 1967 have front disc brakes. All systems operate in a similar manner. Tightening torques (**Table 1**) and specifications (**Tables 2 and 3**) are found at the end of the chapter.

The driver depresses the brake pedal which operates a master cylinder piston through a pushrod. See **Figure 1**. Hydraulic pressure developed in the master cylinder expands the wheel cylinders in each wheel, forcing the brake shoes to contact the brake drums. Hydraulic pressure also closes the brake light switch mounted in the end of the master cylinder.

The dual circuit brakes shown in **Figure 2** work similarly. The master cylinder has 2 independent pressure circuits. When the pedal is depressed, pressure in the front half of the master cylinder operates both front wheel brakes; pressure from the rear half operates both rear wheel brakes. If one circuit should fail, the other circuit remains intact permitting a safe stop with 2 wheels.

A warning circuit incorporated in master cylinders since 1968 tells the driver that pressure in one circuit is defective. Increased pedal travel and decreased braking also indicate trouble.

Two brake light switches are required with the dual circuit system. Otherwise a pressure failure in one circuit could disable the brake lights. Since 1968, these switches operate the warning light also.

A cable-operated mechanical handbrake acts on the rear wheels. When the hand lever is drawn up, the rear brake shoes expand to provide emergency or parking brakes.

This chapter describes repair procedures for all parts of the brake system. A variety of master cylinders, wheel cylinders, brake shoes, and drums are used. Where differences exist, they are pointed out. Because of these differences, *always* order brake parts by chassis number and compare the new parts to the old parts before installation.

MASTER CYLINDER

Several master cylinders are used from 1961 on. All 1961-1966 models use a single circuit master cylinder. In 1967, VW introduced a dual circuit master cylinder. In 1968 and 1969 they incorporated a warning circuit with a shuttle piston to sense when pressure in one circuit

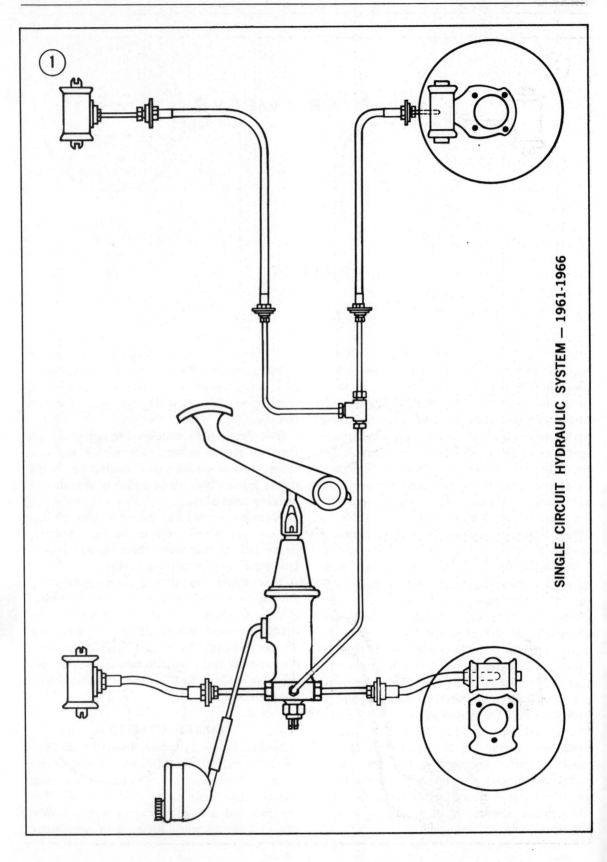

SINGLE CIRCUIT HYDRAULIC SYSTEM — 1961-1966

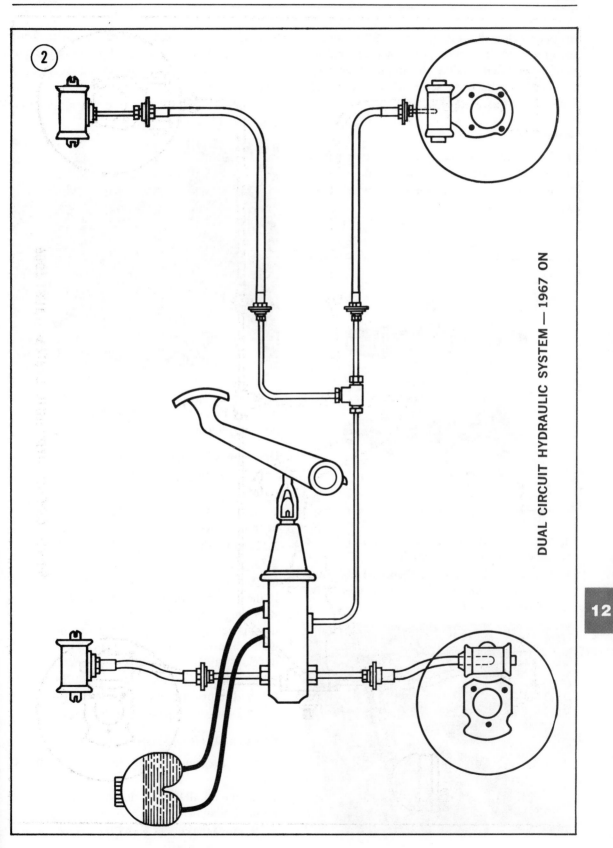

DUAL CIRCUIT HYDRAULIC SYSTEM — 1967 ON

12

dropped below the other. Since 1970 models, they replaced the shuttle piston warning circuit with a simplified version; the stoplight switches have extra contacts to sense when one switch doesn't operate.

Removal

1. Suck brake fluid out of the reservoir with a pump used exclusively for brake fluid.

2. Jack up the car and remove the left front wheel.

3. Pull out the rubber plug and line(s) leading to the brake fluid reservoir. See **Figure 3**.

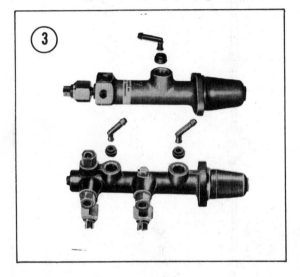

4. Disconnect the stop light wire(s) from the master cylinder stop light switches.

5. Remove brake lines (see **Figure 4**) and cover the ends to prevent entry of dirt. Bleeder valve caps work well for this.

6. Bend the lock plate up on the pin securing the pushrod to the brake pedal. Remove the pin.

7. Loosen the brake pedal stop bracket, and take the pushrod out.

8. Remove the bolts securing the master cylinder. See **Figure 5**.

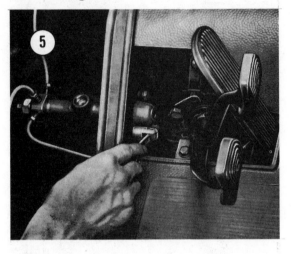

9. Pull the master cylinder free towards the front. Remove the spacers in the cross member holes so they don't get lost.

Disassembly (Single Master Cylinder)

Refer to **Figure 6** for the following procedure.

1. Scrape off all outside dirt, and wash with denatured alcohol.

2. Remove the rubber boot (2).

3. Remove the lock ring (3).

4. Remove the stop washer (4) and piston (6). If the piston is stuck, seal the brake line holes with plugs, insert the rubber plug in the top of the master cylinder, and force the piston out with compressed air. Even a bicycle tire pump develops sufficient pressure.

5. Remove the piston washer (7), primary cup (8), and return spring (9) with check valve (10).

6. Unscrew the stop light switch.

Disassembly (Dual Master Cylinder)

Refer to **Figure 7** for the following procedure.

1. Scrape off all outside dirt, and wash with denatured alcohol.

2. Remove the rubber boot (2).

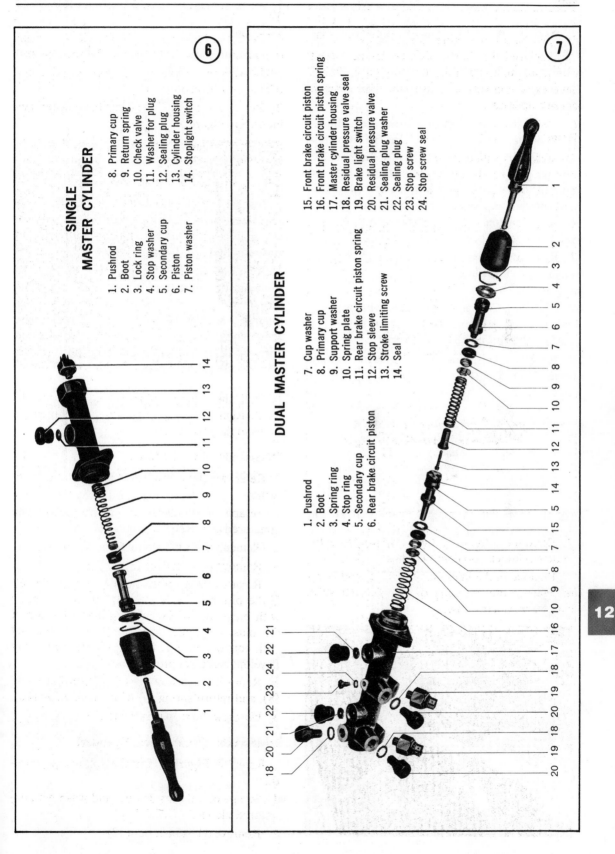

SINGLE MASTER CYLINDER

1. Pushrod
2. Boot
3. Lock ring
4. Stop washer
5. Secondary cup
6. Piston
7. Piston washer
8. Primary cup
9. Return spring
10. Check valve
11. Washer for plug
12. Sealing plug
13. Cylinder housing
14. Stoplight switch

DUAL MASTER CYLINDER

1. Pushrod
2. Boot
3. Spring ring
4. Stop ring
5. Secondary cup
6. Rear brake circuit piston
7. Cup washer
8. Primary cup
9. Support washer
10. Spring plate
11. Rear brake circuit piston spring
12. Stop sleeve
13. Stroke limiting screw
14. Seal
15. Front brake circuit piston
16. Front brake circuit piston spring
17. Master cylinder housing
18. Residual pressure valve seal
19. Brake light switch
20. Residual pressure valve
21. Sealing plug washer
22. Sealing plug
23. Stop screw
24. Stop screw seal

12

3. Remove the lock ring (3) and the stop washer (4).

4. Remove stop screw and seal (23 and 24).

5. Remove rear piston and stroke limiter parts (items 5-13).

6. Tamp the open end of the master cylinder on a wooden bench or block, and the front piston (15) will slide out. If it sticks in the bore, remove the residual pressure valves (20) and plug the holes. Insert the front rubber plug (22) and inject compressed air through this plug to force the piston out. A bicycle tire pump develops sufficient pressure to do this.

7. Remove cup washer, primary cup, support washer, spring plate, and spring (items 7-10 and 16).

8. On 1968-69 master cylinders with warning switch, refer to **Figure 8**. Remove the plug (1), washer (2), springs (3), and piston (5).

9. Remove all residual pressure valves and seals (items 18 and 20).

> NOTE: *Since no residual pressure must remain when disc brakes are off, master cylinders for these systems do not have residual pressure valves. These cylinders are identified by a blue vinyl band as noted in Figure 3.*

10. Remove both stoplight switches (19). On the 1968-69 master cylinders, remove warning switch (see Figure 8).

Inspection

1. Clean all parts in denatured alcohol or clean brake fluid.

CAUTION
Never use gasoline, kerosene, or any solvent other than alcohol for rubber brake parts. You may wash metal parts in other solvents if you blow them dry, rinse several times in clean alcohol and blow dry again.

2. Inspect cylinder bore for scoring, pitting, or heavy corrosion. Very light scratches and corrosion may be removed with *crocus cloth*. Discard master cylinder if damage is more severe.

3. Run a small, smooth copper wire through the compensating ports and intake ports. Note that dual master cylinders have 4 ports in all. See **Figures 9 and 10**. Don't use steel or rough wire which may damage the port. Ensure that no burrs exist at the bottom of these ports which may cut the primary cup.

> NOTE: *Both ATE and Schaefer manufacture brake parts for VW. While complete cylinders can be exchanged, internal parts for one make cannot be used with the other.*

Assembly (Single Master Cylinder)

When assembling the master cylinder, use parts from a standard VW repair kit. Never reuse old parts. Refer to Figure 6.

1. Clean all parts in alcohol or brake fluid. Blow

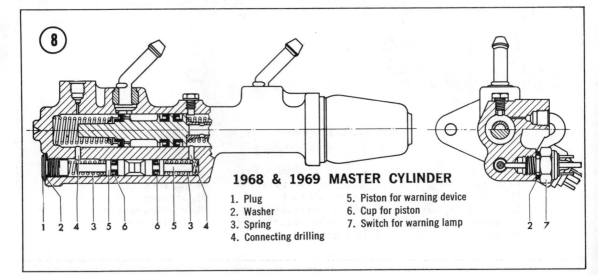

1968 & 1969 MASTER CYLINDER

1. Plug
2. Washer
3. Spring
4. Connecting drilling
5. Piston for warning device
6. Cup for piston
7. Switch for warning lamp

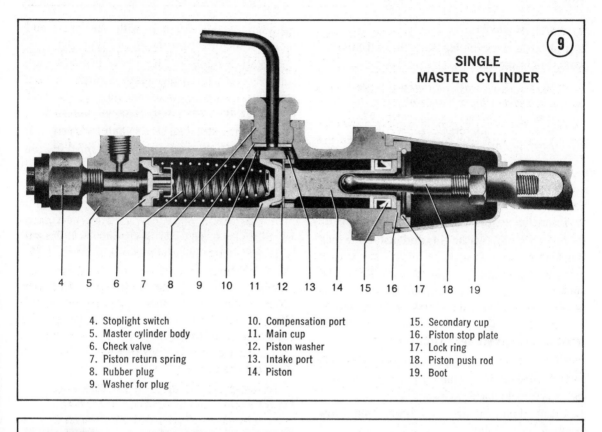

SINGLE
MASTER CYLINDER

4. Stoplight switch
5. Master cylinder body
6. Check valve
7. Piston return spring
8. Rubber plug
9. Washer for plug

10. Compensation port
11. Main cup
12. Piston washer
13. Intake port
14. Piston

15. Secondary cup
16. Piston stop plate
17. Lock ring
18. Piston push rod
19. Boot

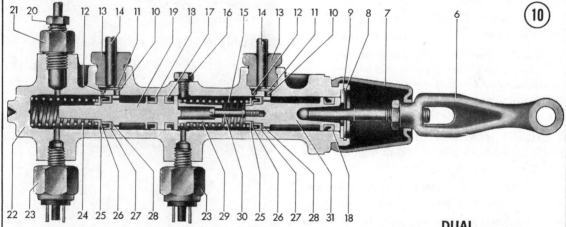

DUAL
MASTER CYLINDER

6. Pushrod
7. Boot
8. Spring ring
9. Stop ring
10. Feed port
11. Sealing plug washer
12. Compensating port
13. Sealing plug
14. Feed line

15. Rear brake circuit piston spring
16. Stop screw and seal
17. Seal
18. Secondary cup
19. Front brake circuit piston
20. Brake line union nut
21. Residual pressure valve
22. Master cylinder housing
23. Brake light switch

24. Front brake circuit piston spring
25. Spring plate
26. Support ring
27. Primary cup
28. Cup washer
29. Stop sleeve
30. Stroke limiting screw
31. Rear brake circuit piston

12

dry if you use alcohol.

2. Lubricate the cylinder walls and all internal parts with brake fluid.

> NOTE: *Volkswagen developed a special brake cylinder paste which may be used to lubricate brake parts. This paste does not attack rubber brake parts, but mineral oil and grease will.*

3. Insert check valve (10) and return spring (9).

4. Insert the primary cup (8) in the direction shown.

5. Insert the piston washer (7) and piston (6).

6. Insert the stop washer (4) and install the lock ring (3).

7. Install the rubber boot (2) and insert the pushrod (1). Lubricate the rounded end of the pushrod with brake fluid or VW brake paste.

Assembly (Dual Master Cylinder)

When assembling the master cylinder, use all parts furnished in a standard VW repair kit. Never reuse old parts. Refer to Figure 7.

1. Clean all parts in alcohol or brake fluid. Blow dry if you use alcohol.

2. Lubricate the cylinder walls and all internal parts with brake fluid.

> NOTE: *Volkswagen developed a special brake cylinder paste which may be used to lubricate brake parts. This paste does not attack rubber brake parts, but mineral oil or grease will.*

3. Install a new seal (14) and secondary cup (5) on the front piston. Install with the open end as shown in Figure 10.

4. Assembly the cup washer, new primary cup, support washer, spring plate, and tapered spring (items 7-10 and 16) on the front piston. Install the open end of the primary cup as shown in Figure 10.

5. Hold the master cylinder vertically with the open end down. Insert the front piston assembly up into the cylinder bore. If you try to install these parts horizontally, they will fall off the piston.

6. Install a new secondary cup (5) on the rear piston (6). Note that the secondary cup has thicker lips than all the other cups in the master

cylinder. Install the cup with the open end facing in the direction shown in Figure 10.

7. Install the cup washer, new primary cup, support washer, spring plate, straight spring, stop sleeve, and screw (items 7-13) on the rear piston (6). Insert assembly into cylinder bore.

8. Install the stop washer (4) and lock ring (3).

9. Check that the rear piston is not blocking the stop screw hole, and insert the stop screw and seal (23 and 24). If the hole is blocked, push the rear piston toward the front with the pushrod until the hole is clear.

10. Install residual pressure valves and stop light switches and tighten to 11-14 ft.-lb. (1.5-2.0 mkg).

11. On 1968-1971 master cylinders, install springs, piston (with new cups), washer, and plug for the warning switch circuit (Figure 8). Install the warning switch.

Installation

1. Insert spacers in the front crossmember. See **Figure 11**.

2. Install the master cylinder from the front with 2 mounting bolts. Ensure that the boot remains in place.

3. Connect the pushrod to the brake pedal with the pin. Use a new lock plate.

4. Adjust pedal stop plate until there is 0.04 in. (1mm) clearance between the tip of the pushrod and the recess in the piston. See **Figure 12**.

5. Connect brake lines and stoplight wire.

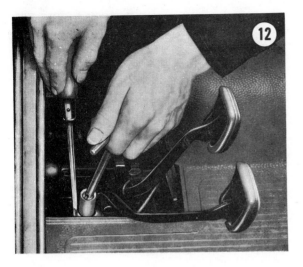

6. Ensure that the vent in the reservoir cap is open.

7. Bleed the brakes as described later in this chapter.

BRAKE HOSES

Hoses vary in length for different years. You must order new hoses by chassis number to ensure getting the right length. Do not use a hose unless it is exactly the same length as the original.

Removal

1. Remove the wheel associated with the defective brake hose.

2. Loosen the union nut and remove the hose clip from the bracket. See **Figure 13**.

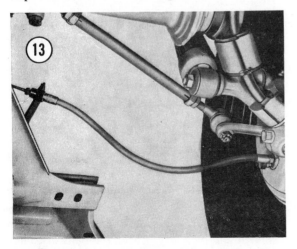

3. Pull the hose from the bracket.

4. Disconnect the hose from the wheel cylinder.

Installation

1. Connect the new brake hose to the wheel cylinder.

2. Install the hose in the bracket, and tighten the union nut. Do not allow the hose to twist.

3. Turn the wheels from one lock to the other and ensure that the hose is not twisted or strained.

4. Bleed the brakes.

BRAKE LINES

The brake lines are steel with 0.028 in. (0.72mm) walls. The ends are double-lap flared to prevent splitting and leaking.

To replace a brake line, disconnect the union nuts at both ends. Unclip the line from the chassis and pull it out. Install the new line in the chassis clips. Moisten the ends in brake fluid, then tighten the union nuts. To ensure brake line of suitable strength and length, purchase new lines from your VW dealer.

BRAKE DRUMS

Front Drum Removal

1. Jack the front of the car up on jackstands.

2. Remove the front wheels.

3. Remove the cotter pin securing the speedometer cable to the left dust cap. See **Figure 14**.

4. Remove the dust caps. See **Figure 15**.

5a. On 1961-1965 wheels, bend up the tabs on the locking plate and remove the outer nut, locking plate, and inner nut.

12

5b. On 1966 and later wheels, loosen the adjusting nut clamp bolt with a 6mm Allen wrench. See **Figure 16**. Screw the nut off; the left nut has a left-hand thread.

6. Pull the brake drum out as far as it goes, then push it back in (see **Figure 17**). This leaves the thrust washer and outer bearing where they may be easily removed.

7. Pull the brake drum off. If necessary, back off the brake adjustment. See brake adjustment procedures later in this chapter.

8. Lay the drum over a clean rag with the outside up. Insert a piece of wood through the hub opening and pound around the inner bearing in a circle until the bearing and oil seal drop out.

Rear Drum Removal

1. Put the transmission in gear and pull up the handbrake.

2. Loosen the wheel lug bolts.

3. Remove cotter key in castellated hub nut and loosen nut with a 36mm socket and a long breaker bar. The nut is torqued to 217 ft.-lb.

> **CAUTION**
> *Never loosen the nut unless all 4 wheels are firmly on the ground. The force required to loosen the nut is sufficient to knock the car off the jackstand.*

4. Raise the rear of the car on jackstands.

5. Remove the hub nut.

6. Pull the wheel with brake drum off after backing off the brake adjustment. Separate the wheel and drum to permit a thorough inspection.

Inspection

1. Blow brake dust and dirt from the brake drum. Remove grease and oil with cleaning solvent. Blow dry.

2. Clean the drum braking surface with alcohol.

3. Inspect brake drums for scoring, cracking, taper, out-of-roundness, heat evidence, etc. Drums which are scored or worn should be turned by a VW dealer, and brake shoes replaced by oversize shoes. Cracked drums cannot be turned; replace them.

4. Remove glaze on serviceable drums with fine emery cloth.

5. Clean the front wheel bearings thoroughly in solvent and blow dry. Check the balls or rollers for scores, wear, and evidence of overheating (blue tint). Check the bearing races on the axle

stub and brake drum also. Do not mix the bearings up if they are good; they must be replaced on the same wheel. If bearings or races are damaged, refer to the wheel bearing replacement procedure in Chapter Twelve.

6. Clean all traces of grease and dirt from the front axle stubs.

Front Drum Installation

1. Pack both wheel bearings with wheel bearing (lithium) grease. Press grease thoroughly into the cage and balls or rollers.

2. Grease the race on the stub axle lightly.

3. Install the inner bearing and oil seal in the brake drum. The seal should be flush with or slightly below the hub.

4. Pack the hub of the brake drum full of wheel bearing grease. Hold your hand over the inner hole to keep grease from coming out.

5. Install the brake drum, and push any grease that tries to come out of the hub back in. Don't force grease out the back, though.

6. Install the outer bearing (packed in Step 1) and thrust washer.

7. Install the hub nut finger-tight, then adjust wheel bearings exactly as described in Chapter Twelve.

8. Adjust the brakes.

Rear Drum Installation

1. Install the rear brake drum on the axle, and tighten the nut to about 100 ft.-lb.

2. Install the rear wheel and lower the car.

3. With a large torque wrench, or small one with range extender, tighten the hub nut to 217 ft.-lb.

> CAUTION
> *Never tighten the nut unless all 4 wheels are firmly on the ground. The force required to tighten the nut is sufficient to knock the car off the jackstands.*

4. Install the cotter key through the nut castellations. If the hole in the hub does not line up, tighten the nut additionally until the cotter key fits. Spread the ends of the cotter key.

5. Adjust the brakes.

FRONT BRAKE SHOES

Brake shoes require relining or replacement when linings are soaked with oil, grease, or brake fluid. In addition, replace linings worn to less than 1/16 in. Check by looking through the brake drum inspection/adjustment holes. If brake drums have been turned, use oversize linings. Always replace linings on both front wheels to ensure uniform braking. Refer to **Figure 18** for the following procedures.

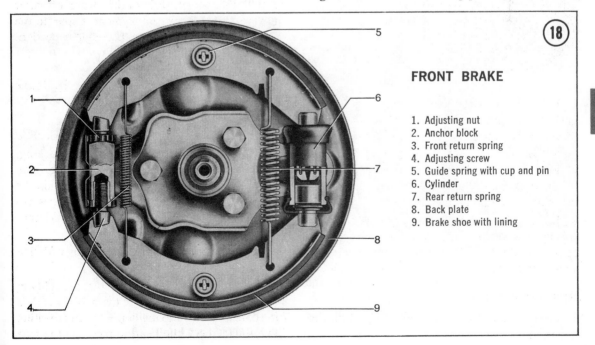

FRONT BRAKE

1. Adjusting nut
2. Anchor block
3. Front return spring
4. Adjusting screw
5. Guide spring with cup and pin
6. Cylinder
7. Rear return spring
8. Back plate
9. Brake shoe with lining

12

Removal

1. Remove the brake drum as described earlier.

2. Remove shoe retainer spring cups, springs, and pins. See **Figure 19**.

3. Disconnect the front (small) return spring.

4. Pull one shoe out of the slot in the adjuster.

5. Lift both shoes out.

Installation

1. Note that the bottom of the adjuster slots are angled. Turn the adjusters so the deepest part of the slot is toward the rear of the car. See **Figure 20**.

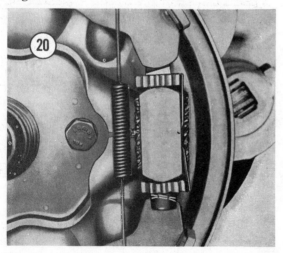

2. Hook the 2 brake shoes together with the large return spring. This spring fits the holes nearest the slots in the brake shoe web. See Figure 18.

3. Hold the shoes slightly apart to keep the spring in place. Insert the ends nearest the spring into the slots in the wheel cylinder pushrods.

4. Pull the other ends in and fit them in the adjuster slots. Ensure that the angled slots are still in the position shown in Figure 20.

5. Install the brake shoe pins, retainer springs, and spring cups.

6. Install the small retainer spring.

REAR BRAKE SHOES

Brake shoes require relining or replacement when linings are soaked with oil, grease, or brake fluid. In addition, replace linings worn to less than 1/16 in.; check by looking through the brake drum inspection/adjustment holes. If brake drums have been turned, use oversize linings. Always replace linings on both rear wheels to ensure uniform braking. Refer to **Figure 21** for the following procedures.

Removal

1. Remove the brake drum as described earlier.

2. Remove the brake shoe retainer spring cups, springs and pins.

3. Unhook the lower return spring (Figure 21).

4. Disconnect the brake cable (**Figure 22**).

5. Remove the brake shoes with lever connecting link and upper return spring. See **Figure 23**.

6. Remove the C-ring and take the lever off the brake shoes. See **Figure 24**.

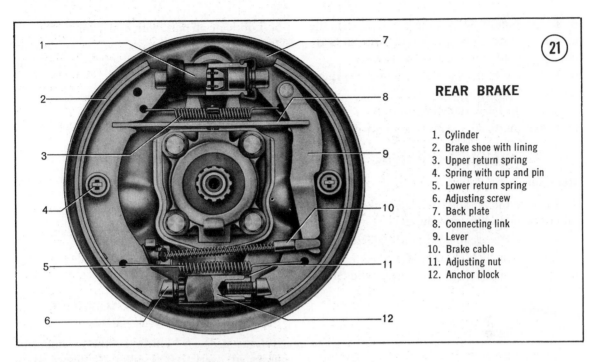

REAR BRAKE

1. Cylinder
2. Brake shoe with lining
3. Upper return spring
4. Spring with cup and pin
5. Lower return spring
6. Adjusting screw
7. Back plate
8. Connecting link
9. Lever
10. Brake cable
11. Adjusting nut
12. Anchor block

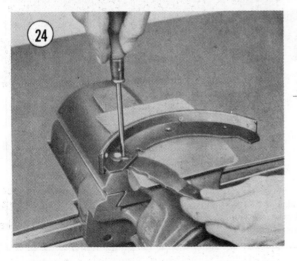

Installation

1. Note that the adjusting screw slots are angled. Turn the adjuster until the deepest part of the slot faces up. See **Figure 25**.

2. Install handbrake lever on rear brake shoe.

3. Connect the upper return spring between the brake shoes. Use the holes nearest the slots in the shoe webs. Slip the connecting link into the slots.

4. Lift both shoes into position. Engage the top ends in the wheel cylinder pushrod slots as shown in Figure 23.

12

5. Fit the bottom ends of the brake shoes in the adjusting screw slots. Ensure that the slots remain positioned as shown in Figure 25.

6. Install the brake shoe pins, retainer springs, and spring clips.

7. Install the lower retaining spring.

8. Install the brake drums as described earlier.

WHEEL CYLINDERS

Removal

1. Remove the brake drum and brake shoes as described in earlier procedures.

2. Remove the brake hose as described earlier.

3. Remove the bolt securing the wheel cylinder to the backing plate and take wheel cylinder off.

Rebuilding

Refer to **Figure 26**.

1. Remove both rubber boots.

2. Remove pistons, cups, cup expanders, and spring.

3. Remove bleeder valve.

4. Clean all parts in alcohol or brake fluid.

5. Examine the cylinder bore for scoring, pitting, or heavy corrosion. Very light scratches may be removed with *crocus cloth*. Flush out with alcohol and blow dry. Replace wheel cylinders which show more extensive damage.

6. Lubricate all parts with brake fluid.

7. Install new cups, cup expanders, and springs provided in the repair kit. Do not reuse old parts.

8. Install pistons and new rubber boots.

9. Install bleeder valve.

Installation

1. Install the wheel cylinder with the mounting bolt.

2. Install the brake hose as described earlier.

3. Install brake shoes as described earlier.

4. Bleed the brakes.

BRAKE PAD REPLACEMENT (KARMANN GHIA)

Brake pads on both front wheels should be inspected every 6,000 miles as described in Chapter Two. Replace brake pads on both front wheels if pad thickness is 0.08 in. (2mm), or less. It is rarely necessary to bleed the brake system after a single brake pad replacement.

Three types of front disc brakes have been used on Karmann Ghias: early ATE, late ATE, and Girling. See **Figure 27**. Pad replacement for both ATE models is similar, but a different procedure is required for Girling brakes (1973 on).

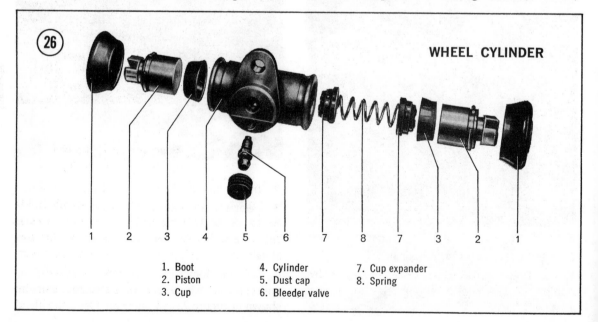

WHEEL CYLINDER

26

1. Boot	4. Cylinder	7. Cup expander
2. Piston	5. Dust cap	8. Spring
3. Cup	6. Bleeder valve	

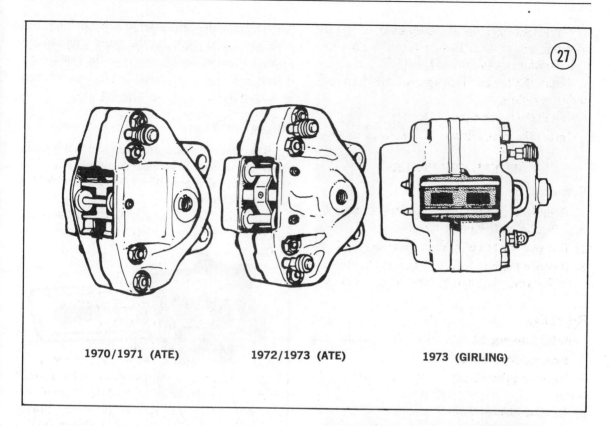

| 1970/1971 (ATE) | 1972/1973 (ATE) | 1973 (GIRLING) |

ATE Brakes (1970-1973)

1. Jack up the car on jackstands and remove the wheels.

2. With a punch, drive out retaining pin as shown in **Figure 28**.

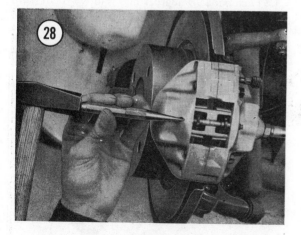

3. Remove brake pad spreader spring.

4. Pull brake pads out as shown in **Figure 29**. A piece of wire with a hook at one end makes a suitable tool.

CAUTION
If brake pads are to be reinstalled, mark them so they are installed in the same position.

5. Carefully clean out the cavity which holds the brake pads. Inspect the rubber dust covers; if they are damaged, replace them. If dirt has penetrated the cylinders due to a damaged cover, recondition the brake unit as described later.

6. Before installing new brake pads, push the pistons in as shown in **Figure 30**. Open the bleed

12

valve to make this easier. The master cylinder may overflow when the pistons are pressed in. Draw some fluid out first to prevent this, and discard the fluid. Also place rags under the master cylinder to protect the paint.

> CAUTION
> *Do not let brake fluid spill on the brake pads or discs.*

7. Install new brake pads, and ensure that they slide in and out of caliper assembly smoothly. See **Figure 31**.

8. Install a *new* brake spreader spring.

9. Insert the pad retaining pin into the brake caliper. Drive the pin in with a hammer only, not a punch, so that the pin is not inadvertently driven too far.

10. Depress the brake pedal several times before driving the car so the pads can assume correct alignment with respect to the brake disc.

11. Bleed brakes if bleed valve was opened in Step 6.

Girling (1973 on)

1. Raise car on jackstands. Remove locking clip from one leg of U-shaped retaining pin, then remove retaining pin and pad spreader spring as shown in **Figure 32**.

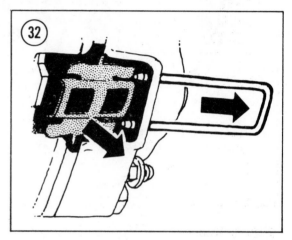

2. Bend tabs on caliper lock mounting bolts, remove bolts, and remove caliper. Hang caliper from tie rod with wire hook.

3. Turn pads 90 degrees and remove them from caliper, one at a time. See **Figure 33**. If pads are to be reused, mark their positions.

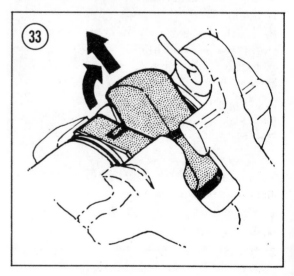

4. Remove noise-damping shims located between pads and pistons.

> NOTE: *Always replace all 4 pads even if only one is bad.*

5. Install noise-damping shims in calipers with arrows pointing in direction of wheel rotation. See **Figure 34**.

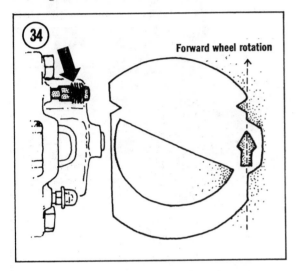

Forward wheel rotation

6. Push pistons back into caliper for clearance and install pads, turning them 90 degrees from correct position while inserting them into calipers. If old pads are being reinstalled, make sure they go into their original positions.

7. Install caliper on steering knuckle, using a new lockplate. Make sure long bleeder valve is at top. Torque mounting bolts to 29 ft.-lb. (4.0 mkg).

8. Install pad retaining pin, using new spreader spring and new locking clip. Bend straight side of locking clip about 45 degrees as shown in **Figure 35**.

9. Pump brake pedal a few times to seat pads against disc. Check fluid level in master cylinder reservoir and add brake fluid if required.

BRAKE CALIPERS

Removal/Installation

1. Jack up front of car on jackstands. Remove front wheel(s).

2. Remove brake hose and cover the end to prevent entry of dirt and moisture.

3. Bend lock plates up on mounting bolts and remove the bolts. See **Figure 36**.

4. Remove the brake caliper.

5. Installation is the reverse of these steps.

Reconditioning

The following procedure describes replacement of all parts included in the VW caliper repair kit. Use all parts included in the kit. Refer to **Figure 37** for an exploded view of the caliper assembly.

1. Remove brake pads as described earlier.

2. Clamp the caliper in a vise and remove piston retaining plates.

3. Pry out the rubber boot retaining ring as shown in **Figure 38**. Do not damage rubber boot.

4. Remove rubber boot, using a plastic or rubber rod. See **Figure 39**.

12

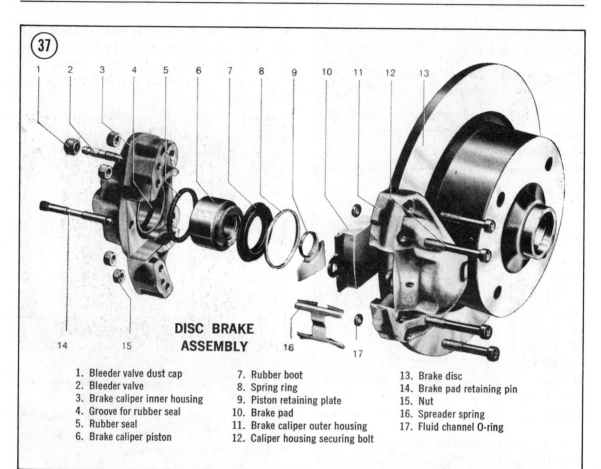

DISC BRAKE
ASSEMBLY

1. Bleeder valve dust cap
2. Bleeder valve
3. Brake caliper inner housing
4. Groove for rubber seal
5. Rubber seal
6. Brake caliper piston
7. Rubber boot
8. Spring ring
9. Piston retaining plate
10. Brake pad
11. Brake caliper outer housing
12. Caliper housing securing bolt
13. Brake disc
14. Brake pad retaining pin
15. Nut
16. Spreader spring
17. Fluid channel O-ring

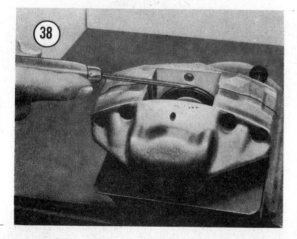

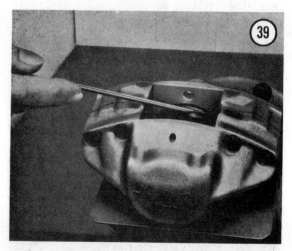

5. Clamp one piston in place as shown in **Figure 40**. Hold a piece of ¼ in. thick wood in the housing and force the other piston against it with compressed air.

NOTE: *Once one piston is removed, pressure cannot be built up to force*

the other out. Therefore, completely rebuild one side before working on the other.

6. Remove the rubber seal with a plastic or rubber rod to prevent damage to housing.

7. Clean all parts in alcohol or clean brake fluid.

8. Check parts for wear. If a cylinder is worn or damaged, the complete caliper must be replaced.

9. Coat the rubber seal and piston with special VW brake cylinder paste. Install the seal and piston.

CAUTION
VW uses a special installation tool to ensure that the piston does not tilt when pressed in. Consider taking the caliper to VW for this operation.

10. Install new rubber boot and retaining ring.

11. Insert the special gauge shown in **Figure 41** to ensure that the piston recess is inclined 20° from the lower guide area of the caliper.

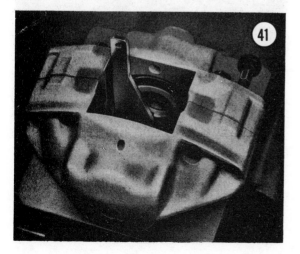

12. Install piston retaining plate (**Figure 42**). Note that the circular part of the plate (a) must be firmly pressed into the piston crown. The plate must lie below the recessed part of the piston (b).

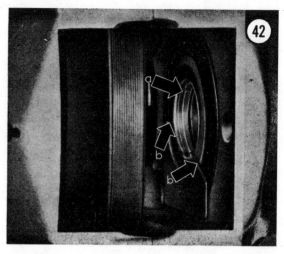

13. Repeat Steps 5-12 for the other piston/cylinder.

14. Do not disassemble the caliper assembly any further. If the caliper assembly leaks, take it to a VW dealer for repair.

BRAKE DISC

Inspection

Check the brake disc for deep scratches, excessive runout, and uneven thickness.

Small marks on the disc are not important, but deep radial scratches reduce braking effectivness and increase pad wear.

To check disc runout, use a dial indicator and rotate the disc; runout should not exceed 0.008 in. (0.2mm). This procedure assumes that the wheel bearings are properly adjusted. Check them if in doubt.

Check the thickness of the disc with a micrometer. Make about 12 measurements around the disc about one inch from outer edge. Measurements should not vary more than 0.0008 in. (0.02mm).

If the disc has excessively deep scratches, excessive runout, or variation in thickness, renew or replace the disc. If the disc is renewed, minimum thickness must be at least 0.335 in.

12

(8.5mm), and an equal amount must be removed from each side.

1. Remove caliper as described earlier, except leave brake hose attached and brake pads installed. Hang the assembly up with a piece of wire. See **Figure 43**.

2. Remove dust cap over bearing clamp nut. The C-ring must be removed from the left dust cover before cap can be removed.

3. Loosen the clamp nut Allen screw and unscrew the nut.

4. Pull the disc out about one inch and push it back in. This leaves the thrust washer and outer bearing where they may be easily removed.

5. Pull the brake disc off.

6. Install the brake disc, bearing, thrust washer, and clamp nut. Tighten the nut finger-tight, then adjust wheel bearings exactly as described in Chapter Eleven.

7. Install caliper and wheel.

BRAKE BLEEDING

Brakes require bleeding whenever air enters the system, lowering the effective braking pressure. Air can enter when the master cylinder or wheel cylinders are serviced, or if the fluid in the reservoir runs dry. Air can also enter through a leaky brake line or hose. Find the leaky line and replace it before bleeding.

Whenever handling brake fluid, do not get any on the brake shoes or body paint. Brake shoes will be permanently damaged, requiring replacement. Body paint can be damaged also unless you wipe the area with a clean cloth, then wash it with a soapy solution immediately.

1. Ensure that the brake fluid reservoir is full, and that the vent in the cap is open.

2. Connect a plastic or rubber tube to the bleeder valve on the right rear wheel. Suspend the other end of the tube in a jar or bottle filled with a few inches of clean brake fluid. See **Figure 44**. During the remaining steps, keep this end submerged at all times and never let the level in the brake fluid reservoir drop below about ½ full.

3. Open the bleeder valve on the right rear wheel about one turn. Have an assistant depress the brake pedal slowly to the floor. As soon as the pedal is all the way down, close the bleeder valve and let the pedal up. Repeat this step as many times as necessary, i.e., until fluid with no air bubbles issues from the tube.

4. Bleed the remaining valves in the same manner described in the steps above. Follow the sequence shown in **Figure 45**. Keep checking

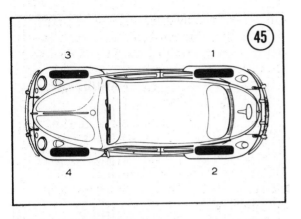

the brake fluid reservoir to be sure it does not run out of fluid.

5. When all wheels are bled, discard the brake fluid in the jar or bottle; never reuse such fluid. Top up the brake fluid reservoir with clean brake fluid.

HANDBRAKE

Cable Replacement

1. Remove the lock and adjusting nut from the threaded cable ends at the handbrake lever. These nuts are accessible through slots in the lever cover. See **Figure 46**.

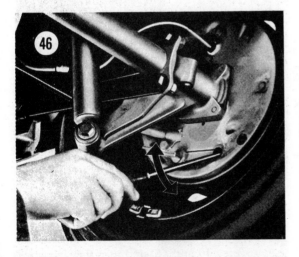

2. Raise the rear of the car on jackstands and remove the rear wheels.

3. Remove the rear brake drums and brake shoes as described in earlier procedures.

4. Detach the cable clip from the backing plate at each wheel.

5. Pull the cable ends with guide tubes out of the backing plate.

6. Pull the cable out of the guide tubes from the front.

7. Compare the length of new cables to old cables. Cables used from 1961-1965 are shorter than in later years.

8. Grease the cables with universal grease and push them into the guide tubes from the front.

9. Reconnect the guide tubes to the backing plate.

10. Install the brake shoes and brake drums as described in earlier procedures.

11. Connect the front cable ends to the handbrake lever using the adjusting nuts and locknuts.

12. Adjust the rear footbrakes, then the handbrake as described in a later procedure.

Lever Removal

Refer to **Figure 47** for this procedure.

1. Remove the front seats and front floor covering.

2. Pull the brake lever cover off.

3. Remove the nuts on the cable ends and lift off the compensating lever.

4. Remove the lock ring securing the lever pin and pull the pin out. See **Figure 48**.

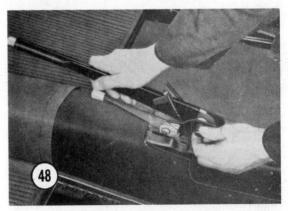

5. Without pressing the release button, push the lever rearward and lift it out complete with ratchet segment.

6. Press the release button and take the ratchet segment out.

12

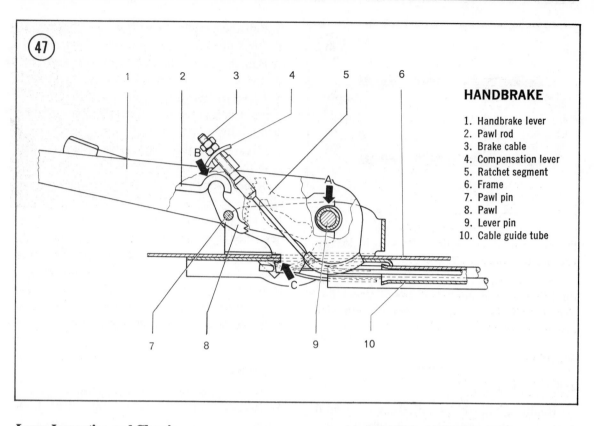

HANDBRAKE

1. Handbrake lever
2. Pawl rod
3. Brake cable
4. Compensation lever
5. Ratchet segment
6. Frame
7. Pawl pin
8. Pawl
9. Lever pin
10. Cable guide tube

Lever Inspection and Cleaning

1. Disassemble the lever and clean the pawl rod, release button, pawl spring, and ratchet segment in solvent.

2. Grease all parts and reassemble.

Lever Installation

1. Insert the ratchet segment so the half round hole in the segment fits over the lever pin tube, and the teeth engage in the pawl. See Figure 47.

2. Insert the lever without pressing the release button. Guide the threaded ends of the cable into the side holes provided.

3. Grease the lever pin and insert it. Install the lock ring.

4. Install the compensating lever.

5. Connect the cables with the adjusting nuts and locknuts.

6. Install the lever cover.

7. Replace the floor covering and install the front seats.

8. Adjust the handbrake as described later and road test the car.

BRAKE ADJUSTMENT

Footbrake

1. Raise the car on jackstands and release the handbrake.

2. Depress the brake pedal fully several times to centralize the shoes in the drums.

3. On 1961-1967 models, turn the wheel to be adjusted until the hole in the brake drum lines up with one of the adjuster star wheels. There is no hole in the brake drums from 1968 on.

> NOTE: *On 1961-1967 models, the adjuster hole is in the brake drum; see* **Figure 49**. *On 1968 and later models, the adjuster hole is in the brake backing plate; see* Figure 46.

4. Insert a screwdriver through the adjuster hole (see Figures 49 and 46) and turn the star wheel until there is a slight drag on the wheel when turned by hand. Then back the star wheel off 3 or 4 teeth.

5. Repeat Steps 3 and 4 for the other star wheel on this brake.

6. Repeat Steps 3-5 on the other 3 wheels.

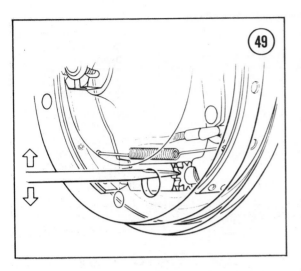

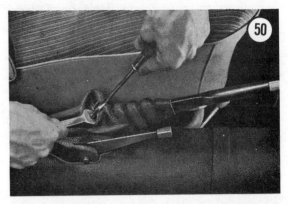

7. Road test the car. Check pedal free play and ensure that the car does not swerve to one side. If it does, recheck the adjustments.

Handbrake

1. Raise the rear of the car on jackstands, and release the handbrake.

2. Loosen the locknuts on the adjusting screws which are accessible through slots in the lever boot. See **Figure 50**.

3. Tighten the adjusting screws evenly so the rear wheels turn by hand with only slight drag. Loosen the screws until the drag disappears.

4. Pull the handbrake lever up 2 notches. Turn the wheels by hand and ensure that the same effort is required for each wheel.

5. Pull the handbrake lever tup an additional 2 notches. It should not be possible to turn either wheel by hand.

6. Tighten the locknuts and slip them back in the boot.

7. Road test the car to ensure that the brakes hold the car properly.

Table 1   TIGHTENING TORQUES

	foot-pounds	mkg		foot-pounds	mkg
Master cylinder			Rear brakes		
Mounting bolts	18	2.5	Wheel cylinder mounting bolts	14-22	2.0-3.0
Stop screw	3.6-7.0	0.5-1.0	Brake drum nut	253	35
Residual pressure valve	14	2.0	Bearing cover bolts	4.4	6.0
Brake lines	11-15	1.5-2.0	Pedal cluster		
Front brakes (drum)			Mounting bolt	29-33	4.0-4.5
Backing plate bolts	36	5.0	Stop plate bolt	14-18	2.0-2.5
Wheel cylinder mounting bolt	18	2.5	Front brakes (disc)		
Bleeder valve	3.6	0.5	Caliper mounting bolt	29	4.0
Brake hose	11-15	1.5-2.0			

12

Table 2 DRUM BRAKE SPECIFICATIONS

	1961-1967	1968-ON (except Super Beetle)	1971-ON Super Beetle
SINGLE MASTER CYLINDER			
Bore inch (mm)	0.687 (17.46)	— — —	— — —
Stroke inch (mm)	1.299 (33)	— — —	— — —
DUAL MASTER CYLINDER			
Bore inch (mm)	— — —	0.750 (19.05)	0.750 (19.05)
Front circuit stroke inch (mm)	— — —	0.556 (15.5)	0.689 (17.5)
Rear circuit stroke inch (mm)	— — —	0.493 (12.5)	0.453 (11.5)
FRONT BRAKE DRUMS			
Diameter (new) inch (mm)	9.059 + 0.008 (230.1 + 0.2)	9.059 + 0.008 (230.1 + 0.2)	9.768 + 0.008 (248.1 + 0.2)
Max. diameter (turned) inch (mm)	9.102 + 0.008 (231.2 + 0.2)	9.102 + 0.008 (231.2 + 0.2)	9.811 + 0.008 (249.2 + 0.2)
Taper inch (mm)	0.004 (0.1)	0.004 (0.1)	0.004 (0.1)
Out-of-roundness inch (mm)	0.004 (0.1)	0.004 (0.1)	0.004 (0.1)
REAR BRAKE DRUMS			
Diameter (new) inch (mm)	9.055 + 0.008 (230 + 0.2)	9.055 + 0.008 (230 + 0.2)	9.055 + 0.008 (230 + 0.2)
Max. diameter (turned) inch (mm)	9.098 + 0.008 (230.1 + 0.2)	9.098 + 0.008 (230.1 + 0.2)	9.098 + 0.008 (230.1 + 0.2)
Taper inch (mm)	0.004 (0.1)	0.004 (0.1)	0.004 (0.1)
Out-of-roundness inch (mm)	0.004 (0.1)	0.004 (0.1)	0.004 (0.1)
WHEEL CYLINDER DIAMETER			
Front inch (mm)	0.875 (22.2)	0.875 (22.2)	1.13 (23.81)
Rear inch (mm)	0.750 (19.05)	0.687 (17.46)	0.687 (17.46)
FRONT LININGS			
Width inch (mm)	1.57 (40)	1.57 (40)	1.57 (40)
Area (2 wheels) inch² (cm²)	55.5 (358)	55.5 (358)	55.5 (358)
Thickness (new) inch (mm)	0.15-0.16 (3.8-4.0)	0.15-0.16 (3.8-4.0)	0.15-0.16 (3.8-4.0)
Oversize available	0.17-0.18 (4.3-4.5)	0.17-0.18 (4.3-4.5)	0.17-0.18 (4.3-4.5)
REAR LININGS			
Width inch (mm)	1.18 (30)	1.57 (40)	1.77 (45)
Area (2 wheels) inch² (cm²)	40.5 (262)	55.5 (358)	69.75 (450)
Thickness (new)	0.15-0.16 (3.8-4.0)	0.15-0.16 (3.8-4.0)	0.15-0.16 (3.8-4.0)
Oversize available	0.17-0.18 (4.3-4.5)	0.17-0.18 (4.3-4.5)	0.17-0.18 (4.3-4.5)
PEDAL FREE-PLAY inch (mm)	0.2-0.28 (5-7)	0.2-0.28 (5-7)	0.2-0.28 (5-7)

Table 3 DISC BRAKE SPECIFICATIONS

Brake Disc		Brake Caliper	
Diameter	10.9" (277mm)	Piston diameter	1.5748" (40mm)
Thickness (new)	0.374-0.004" (9.5-0.1mm)	**Brake Pads**	
Min. thickness	0.335" (8.5mm)	Thickness (new)	0.394" (10mm)
Thickness variation	0.0008" (0.02mm)	Min. thickness	0.08" (2mm)
Lateral run-out (max.)	0.008" (0.2mm)	Area (4 pads)	12.2 in.² (72cm²)

CHAPTER THIRTEEN

BODY

This chapter includes replacement or repair procedures for the seats, doors, hoods, fenders, and bumpers. In addition, a procedure for door window replacement is included. Other body repairs require special knowledge and/or tools and should be done by your dealer or local body repair shop.

SEATS

Front Seat Removal (1961-1972)

1. Lift adjustment lever, and move seat forward until the rear edge contacts the leaf spring. See **Figure 1**.

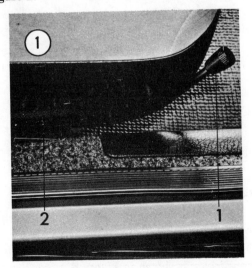

2. Depress the leaf spring with a screwdriver, lift the adjustment lever and slide the seat forward about 1½″.

3. Disconnect the tension spring as shown in **Figure 2**.

4. Slide the seat forward and remove it.

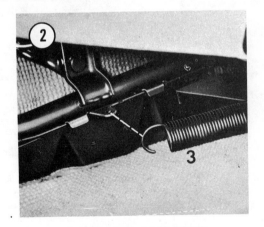

Front Seat Installation (1961-1972)

1. Position the seat in front of the runners.

2. Lift the seat slightly and guide it onto the runner on the tunnel side.

3. Pull the seat slightly toward the door, and guide it into the runner on the door side.

4. Lift adjustment lever and slide seat back.

5. Connect the tension spring.

Front Seat Removal/Installation (1973 on)

1. Remove plastic covers from rear end of seat runners. See **Figure 3**.

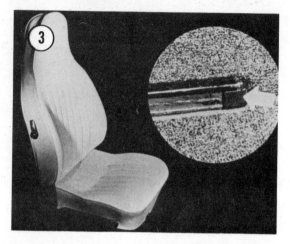

2. Move the seat backward into its next-to-last position.

3. Release lock plate under front bracket by pressing plate down with screwdriver. See **Figure 4**.

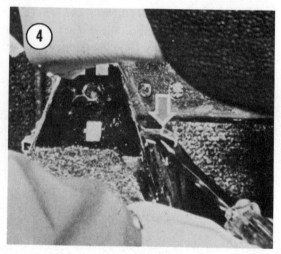

4. Pull seat adjusting lever and slide seat out to the rear.

5. When installing seat, be sure that 4 friction pads (2 on each side) are in place and anti-rattle springs are pressed into upper clips. See **Figure 5**.

6. Slide seat onto rear runners.

7. Pull seat adjusting lever and slide seat forward on runners.

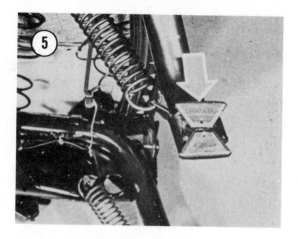

Rear Seat Removal/Installation

1. Raise the front edge of the bottom cushion and pull the seat forward.

2. Tilt one side up and remove the cushion.

3. Installation is the reverse. Ensure that the seat belts are not stuffed behind the cushion. In addition, make sure that they are not twisted.

DOORS

Doors for 1973 and later have reinforced side-guards. These doors can be installed on earlier models. However, a special bracket for the earlier armrest must be used. See **Figure 6**.

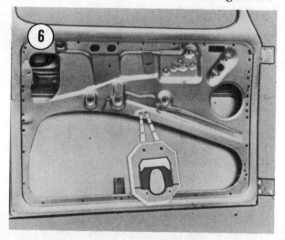

Removal

1. Open the door and remove the door stop pin. See **Figure 7**.

2. Loosen the hinge screws with an impact screwdriver as shown in **Figure 8**.

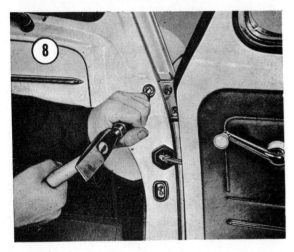

over the hinge pin and fill the chamber with oil. Install the plug.

7. Lubricate the contact surfaces of the striker plate and door wedge lightly with Vaseline or molybdenum disulphide paste.

Striker Plate Inspection (1961-1966)

1. Push the door handle button and watch the latch bolt under the latch housing. The latch bolt should retract fully. See **Figure 10**. If it doesn't, the door may be difficult to open and close.

3. With a helper supporting the door, remove the hinge screws. Pull the door sideways out of the door pillar with hinges attached.

Installation

1. Check the door weather stripping. Replace if damaged.

2. Remove the door striker plate.

3. Install the door and secure the hinges to the door post.

4. Ensure that the door can open and close without jamming and check alignment at the points shown in **Figure 9**. Loosen the door hinge screws and align the door if necessary.

5. Install the strike plate and adjust as described later in this section.

6. Oil the hinge pins. From late 1967 on (chassis No. 117 496 043), remove the plastic plug

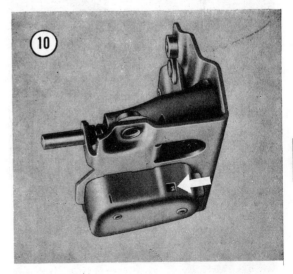

2. Examine the bearing surfaces and notches in the striker plate. See **Figure 11**. If badly worn, replace the striker plate.

13

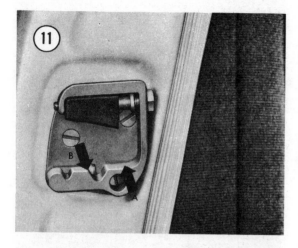

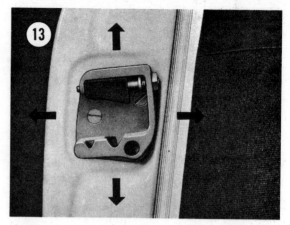

3. Examine the plastic wedge for wear and scoring. Replace if damaged.

Striker Plate Adjustment (1961-1966)

1. Remove the striker plate and check door alignment. If necessary, adjust the door. See *Door Installation.*

2. Install the striker plate. Slightly tighten the mounting screws.

3. Loosen the plastic wedge locknut. Turn the adjusting screw (see **Figure 12**) clockwise until the stop is against the striker housing.

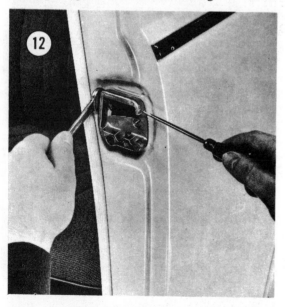

4. Close the door. If the door edge is not flush with the rear quarter panel, move the striker plate in or out to correct this. See **Figure 13**.

5. Adjust the striker plate vertically so that the gap at (X) is slightly greater than at (Y). See **Figure 14**. When vertical alignment is proper, the latch housing (and door) will be lifted approximately 0.08″ (2mm) when the door is closed.

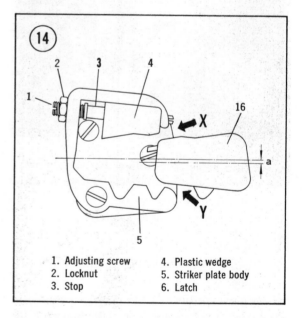

1. Adjusting screw	4. Plastic wedge
2. Locknut	5. Striker plate body
3. Stop	6. Latch

6. Open and close the door several times. Ensure that the bearing surfaces of the striker plate and latch contact each other evenly. Tilt the striker plate slightly if necessary to correct uneven contact.

7. Tighten the striker plate screws.

8. Loosen the locknut on the plastic wedge. While holding the locknut with a wrench, adjust the screw counterclockwise to move the

stop away from the striker plate housing. The adjustment is excessive if undue pressure is required to open the door, or if the door springs open when trying to close it. Tighten the locknut when the adjustment is correct.

9. Lubricate bearing surfaces of the door latch and striker plate with Vaseline or molybdenum disulphide paste.

Striker Plate Adjustment (1967 and Later)

1. Remove the striker plate.

2. Insert the striker plate pin into the lock latch on the door and press the lock latch down into locking position.

3. Twist the striker plate upward as shown in **Figure 15**.

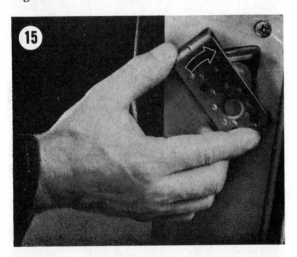

4. Try to move the striker plate up and down (see **Figure 16**). If there is any play on 1967-1971 models, remove screws securing the wedge (see **Figure 17**), and insert a shim between the wedge and the striker plate. On 1972 and later models, replace the wedge if there is any play. To do this, pull the worn wedge out and press in a new one as shown in **Figure 18**.

5. With the striker plate removed, close the door and check alignment. Adjust the door if necessary.

6. Install the striker plate and tighten the screws slightly.

7. Close the door. If the door edge is not flush with the rear quarter panel, move the striker plate in or out.

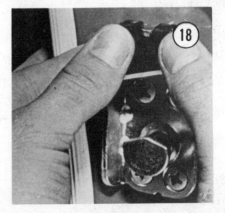

13

8. If the door is difficult to close, and the pushbutton is hard to operate, the top of the striker plate may be inclined too far inward. Loosen the screws and properly align the plate.

9. If the door springs back to the safety position when slammed, the top of the striker plate may be inclined too far outward. It is also possible the striker plate is too low. Realign the striker plate.

10. If the door is difficult to open and drops noticeably when opened, the striker plate is too high. Realign the striker plate.

Door Panel Removal/Installation

1a. On 1961-1966 doors, press window crank escutcheon against the upholstered panel. Drive the retaining pin out with a punch (**Figure 19**). Remove the crank and escutcheon.

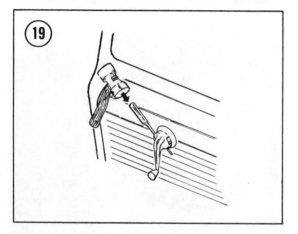

1b. On 1967 and later doors, pry the plastic trim away from window crank as shown in **Figure 20**. Note the scrap wood used to protect the upholstery. Remove the Phillips screw securing the window crank and remove the crank.

2a. On 1961-1966 doors, remove the inner door handle in the same manner as the window crank.

2b. On doors from 1967 on, pry the recessed trim plate out as shown in **Figure 21**. Remove the Phillips screw and escutcheon (**Figure 22**).

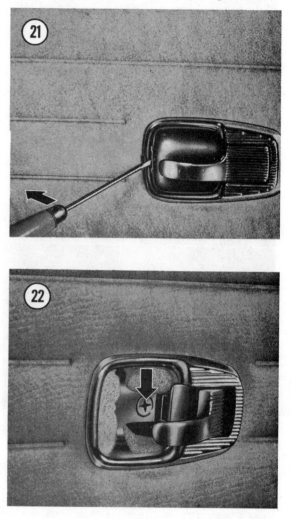

3. To remove the door panel upholstery, insert a wide blade screwdriver or similar object under the edge of the panel and very carefully pry the panel away. Work slowly all around the panel.

4. Installation is the reverse of these steps.

WINDOWS

Window replacement is limited to door windows. Other windows require special skills and equipment. Take these jobs to your dealer or local glass shop.

Door Window Removal/Installation

1. Remove the door panel as described previously.

2. Remove the door stop pin so the door can be opened fully. See Figure 1.

3. Remove the bolts securing the window lifter channel and glass to the window lifter mechanism. See **Figure 23**. Push the glass upward.

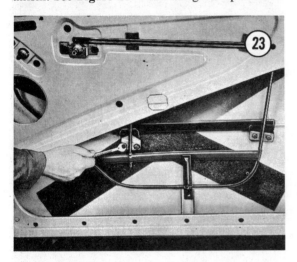

4. Remove 5 bolts securing the window lifter mechanism to the door. See **Figure 24**.

5. Pull the lifter mechanism out and down as shown in **Figure 25** to remove it.

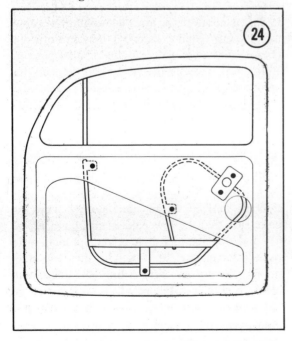

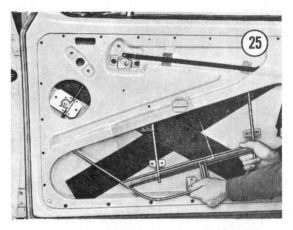

6. Pull the window glass down and out, as shown in **Figure 26**.

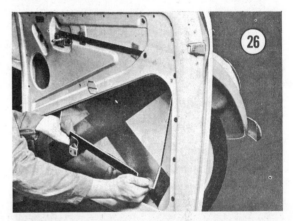

7. Installation is the reverse of these steps. Ensure that the glass is installed in the channel with dimension (a) shown in **Figure 27** equal to 3.15 in. (80mm).

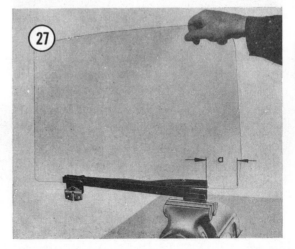

13

HOODS AND LOCKS

Front Hood Removal/Installation

1. Open the hood.

2. Scribe marks on the hood around the hinges to aid in reassembly.

3. Remove the bolts while an assistant supports the hood.

4. Lift the hood off.

5. Installation is the reverse of these steps. Line up scribe marks for proper hood alignment.

Rear Hood Removal/Installation

1. Open the hood.

2. Scribe marks on the hood around the hinges.

3. Disconnect the wires for the license plate light.

4. Remove the bolts while an assistant supports the hood.

5. Lift the hood off.

6. Installation is the reverse of these steps. Line up the scribe marks for proper alignment.

Front Hood Lock Replacement (1961-1967)

1. Open the hood.

2. Remove bolts securing upper part of lock. See **Figure 28**. Remove handle and lock bolt.

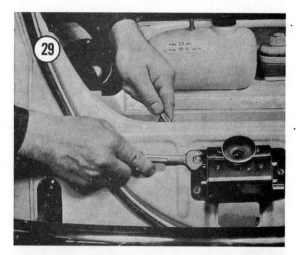

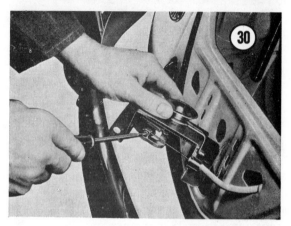

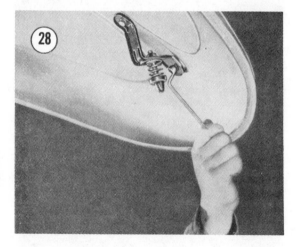

3. Remove bolts securing the lower part of the lock. See **Figure 29**.

4. Remove the cover plate on the lower part, and loosen the cable clamp screw (**Figure 30**). Remove the lock.

5. To install, push the lever containing the cable clamp screw counter to spring tension until the lever is directly under the lock bolt opening. Insert the cable in the lever and tighten the clamp screw. If the cable should break, the spring tension will automatically open the hood, ensuring easy repairs.

6. Install the cover plate on the lower part of the lock and install the lower part on the body.

7. Install the hood handle and upper part of the lock.

8. Open and close the hood several times to make sure that the lower part is centered properly and that the lock bolt is long enough. Adjust the lower part by loosening the bolts and moving the lower part. Adjust the lock bolt length as shown in **Figure 31**.

9. Check that the cable locks and unlocks the hood properly. If necessary, remove the cover

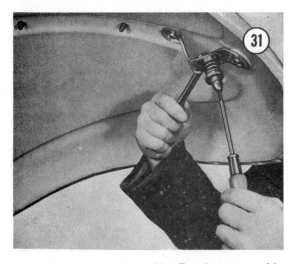

plate and readjust the cable. Bend excess cable back so the cable can't slip out.

Front Hood Lock Replacement (1968 on)

1. Open the hood.

2. Remove bolts securing upper part of lock to hood. See **Figure 32**. Remove handle and lock bolt.

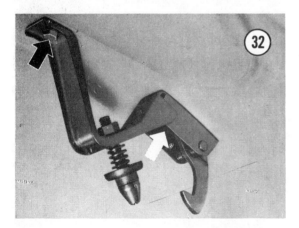

3. Loosen the cable clamp screw (**Figure 33**).

4. Cut off the pop rivets on the lower part with a chisel or drill them out. See **Figure 34**. In either case, take care you don't damage the body.

5. Remove the lower part of the lock from below.

6. Lightly lubricate the lock parts.

7. Push the lock cable into the guide on the lower part and temporarily secure it with the clamp screw.

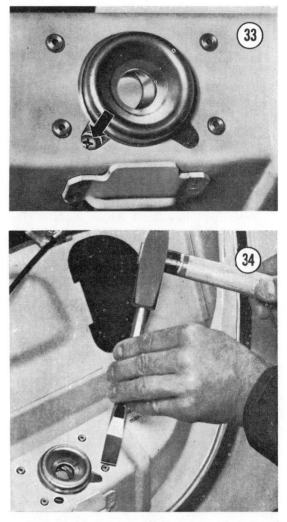

8. Attach the lower part to the body with pop rivets (see **Figure 35**) or nuts and bolts. Use lockwashers on the bolts.

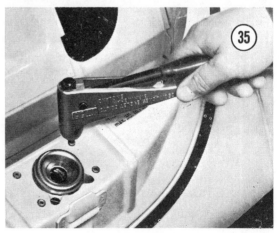

13

9. Loosen the clamp screw and pull the cable taut. Retighten the clamp screw.

10. Install the hood handle and upper part of the lock with plastic packing under the handle.

11. Open and close the hood several times to ensure it works properly. Adjust the length of the lock bolt if necessary by loosening the lock-nut and screwing the bolt in or out. Tighten the locknut.

Rear Hood Lock Replacement

1. Open the rear hood.

2. Remove Phillips head screws securing the lock and handle to the hood. Remove the lock and handle.

3. Install by reversing these steps. Use a new plastic packing if necessary.

4. Open and close the hood several times to ensure that the lock is positioned properly. If necessary, move the striker plate position (1961-1967). See **Figure 36**. On 1968 and later models, adjust the upper lock position.

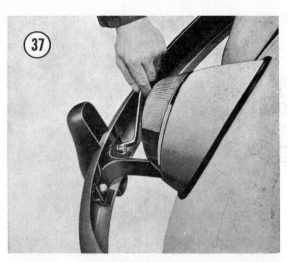

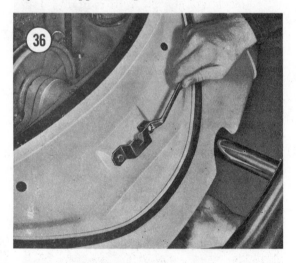

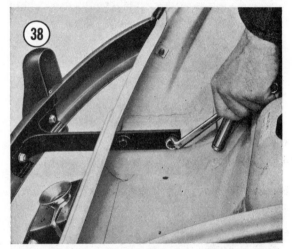

BUMPERS

Bumper Replacement (1961-1967)

1. Remove bolts securing the bumper to the bracket. See **Figure 37**.

2. Open front hood and remove spare wheel.

3. Remove bolts securing brackets to the body. See **Figure 38** for front bumper and **Figure 39** for the rear bumper. Pull the bracket out through the fender.

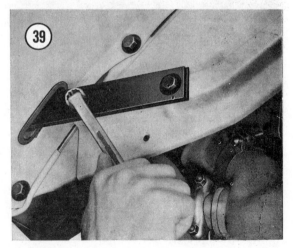

4. When installing, check bracket seals. Replace if necessary. Then reverse these steps to install.

Bumper Replacement (1968-1973)

1. Remove 2 bolts securing the horn and bumper bracket on the left front side. See **Figure 40**.

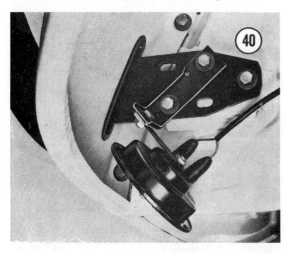

2. Remove the remaining bumper bracket bolts. All bolts are accessible from under the fenders. Pull the bumper out of the fender.

3. Check the rubber grommets in the fenders. If damaged, replace them.

4. Install the bumper by reversing these steps.

Bumper Replacement (1974 and Later)

1. Remove bolts securing bumper to energy absorbers. See **Figure 41**.

2. Remove bolts securing energy absorbers to body. See **Figure 42**.

3. Installation is the reverse of these steps.

FENDER AND RUNNING BOARDS

Front Fender Replacement

1. Lift car.

2. On 1968 and later cars, disconnect horn cables. Remove the horn and bumper bracket. See Figure 40.

3. Remove headlight and turn indicator. Pull cables and protective sleeves from fender. See Chapter Seven.

4. Remove bolt between fender and running board. See **Figure 43**. Remove remaining fender bolts. See **Figure 44**.

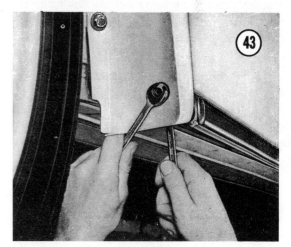

5. Remove fender and beading.

6. Install the fender with beading. Use new beading if necessary.

7. Install the bolt between the fender and running board with a new rubber washer.

13

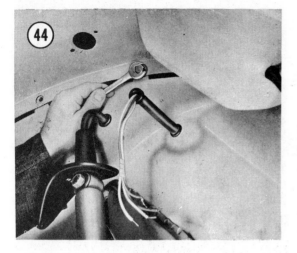

8. Install the turn indicator and headlight. Aim the headlights as described in Chapter Seven.

9. Install the horn and bumper bracket on all cars from 1968 on.

Rear Fender Replacement

1. Raise the car.

2. Remove rear lamp assembly. Pull cables out of the fender. See Chapter Seven.

3. Remove bumper and brackets. Take bracket seal out of fender.

4. Remove nut and bolt between fender and running board. Remove remaining fender bolts.

5. Remove fender and beading.

6. Install the fender with beading. Use new beading if necessary.

7. Install the bolt and nut between the fender and running board. Use a new rubber washer.

8. Install the rear lamp assembly, and connect the cables. Use a new gasket if necessary.

9. Install the bumper bracket seals, brackets, and rear bumper.

Running Board Replacement

1. Remove bolts securing each end of the running board to the fenders.

2. Loosen the bolts securing the running board to the body. See **Figure 45**.

3. Lift the running board up and remove it.

4. Install the new running board on the body bolts.

5. Install the bolts at each end loosely. Use new rubber washers.

6. Tighten the bolts securing the running board to the body. Then tighten the end bolts.

SUN ROOF AND CONVERTIBLE TOP

Adjustments and repairs to these tops are difficult without considerable experience. Minor leaks can quickly become major leaks after incorrect adjustments. If leaks or drafts develop, take the job to your dealer or local shop specializing in these repairs.

CHAPTER FOURTEEN

PERFORMANCE IMPROVEMENT

To most auto enthusiasts, performance modifying means increasing engine power. The engine is bored, stroked, cammed, balanced, and more. The rest of the car gets a few pin stripes, tinted windows, scoops, and tires with raised letters. Very seldom does the modifier pay proper attention to the entire car.

VW engineers design each model as a complete package. Engine performance is tailored for good low speed power, economy, reliability, and long life. The suspension is designed at minimum cost to yield reasonable comfort and safety when driven moderately and unenthusiastically. Tires are chosen for long wear and passenger comfort. The complete package provides dependable, low cost transportation when driven as the VW engineers intended.

As performance modifiers, we try to improve on the original to get a level of performance VW engineers did not intend. But to be successful, we must approach the job exactly like the engineers. Each modification must be judged according to its effect on the entire car. Engine modifications which overpower an inadequate suspension, or poor tires which nullify suspension improvements, must be avoided. The automobile is a system; each component must be compatible with every other component in the system.

Modifications must be carefully planned and applied in the proper order. Some modifications work only when done in conjunction with certain others. Other modifications must be done to the *exclusion* of others. This chapter points out the best modifications in the order they should be installed.

For more extensive information on modifying your VW, see Clymer's *VW Performance Tuning*. This comprehensive book explains the theory behind the modifications, as well as providing detailed modification procedures.

STOCK ENGINES

A great many different VW engines were made. They may be similar in appearance, but vary widely in performance and reliability. Some respond well to performance modifications, while others become far too unreliable. The only sure way to identify a VW engine is by serial number. You cannot go by the year and model of the car, because VW makes engine changes in mid-year. In addition, engine rebuilders may slip a different engine into a car, with or without the owner's knowledge and permission.

VW 1200 (36 hp)

This engine is used on all 1954-1960 VW's. Serial numbers run up to 5,000,000 on these A series engines. Not too many of them are left.

14

As far as performance is concerned, it is just as well—these engines are very unreliable when modified. If you have a 36 horsepower engine, trade it for a 1300/1500/1600 engine or leave it stock. This book does not cover the 36 hp engine at all.

VW 1200 (40 hp)

This engine is used on most 1960-1963 Type I's. Engine serial numbers begin at 5,000,001 and they are D series engines. These engines were the first to be extensively modified. Some speed equipment is available, but not much can really be done with bolt-ons. If possible, invest your money in a 1300, 1500, or 1600 engine instead of expensive 40 hp speed equipment.

VW 1300

Used on the 1966 Type I only, this F series engine is very strong and forms the basis for later 1500/1600 engines. In fact, it is easily converted to a 1500 or 1600 with stock pistons and cylinders; the heads need only slight machine work to accomplish this. An excellent engine to replace any of the earlier engines and well suited for any amount of performance modification.

VW 1500

The H series 1500 engine was used on the 1967-1969 Type I and is a very good candidate for high performance modifying.

VW 1600

There are several different versions of the 1600 engine. The B series was used on the 1970 Type I. This engine has single port cylinder heads. The AE series began with the 1971 Type I. It has dual port heads and is probably the best VW engine available for any use, stock or modified. Considerable speed equipment is available. The AK series (AH and AM California cars and The Thing) were used on 1973 and 1974 models, while the fuel injected AJ

engine was introduced in 1975 and continued to the end of production.

BOLT-ON PERFORMANCE

The term "bolt-on" is often misleading. To several people it means something you can add in 10 minutes with ordinary hand tools. In this chapter, it means a component which can be added by any VW enthusiast who can do similar work on a stock engine. Very little, if any, machine work is necessary. The fact that a component is a bolt-on does not relieve you of the tedious checking and double checking required when assembling even stock parts. **Table 1**, at the end of this chapter, lists the suppliers of all the bolt-on equipment discussed.

PERFORMANCE STAGES

It is rarely practical to go "all out" on performance modifications in one large step. Not all of us desire or can afford the same level of performance. And some of us like to perform one or two simple changes, evaluate them fully, then go on to a few more changes. The stages of modification described here let you go as far as you want and still have a balanced machine.

One of the first "bolt-ons" you should consider has been around a long time and is available for all VW's. This "bolt-on" may add up to 7 horsepower to a stock engine, improve gas mileage, make the engine run smoother, and quieter, and costs less than $15. It is called a tune-up. Of course, "tune-up" sounds very mundane—not nearly as exciting as "big bore kit," "turbocharger," etc. But a proper tune-up is very important for achieving best engine performance. Think of it as Performance Stage Zero if it will give you more incentive to do it.

Each step is spelled out in Chapter Two.

a. Valve adjustment

b. Ignition adjustment

c. Carburetor adjustment

Once your engine is running properly in its stock form, you will be better able to evaluate other changes which claim to improve performance.

NORMALLY ASPIRATED ENGINE

Each of the following stages add several horsepower and/or increased reliability.

Stage I:

a. Extractor exhaust

b. Handling package

c. Instrumentation

d. Power pulley (upright engine)

This stage can add 5-10 horsepower to your engine and greatly improve handling if you make all changes listed under *Handling* in this chapter. The extractor exhaust is essential to take advantage of breathing improvements in later stages. The power pulley is difficult to recommend; at this early stage, however, the cooling system has enough reserve to handle the reduced cooling, but keep an eye on oil temperatures.

Stage II:

a. Stage I, plus

b. 2-barrel carburetor

c. Centrifugal advance distributor

d. Competition valve job

e. Raise compression ratio to 9:1

f. Colder plugs, if necessary

If you added a power pulley for Stage I, take it off now; you will probably need the extra cooling afforded by the stock pulley.

Stage III:

a. Stage II, plus

b. High capacity oil pump

c. Oil cooler

d. Oil filter (full flow)

e. 200mm clutch

f. High lift rocker arms

g. 8-dowel crankshaft/flywheel

This stage may add a few horsepower due to higher valve lift. The engine needs the extra carburetor from Stage II to fully benefit from higher lift, though. The heavier clutch is needed to take the extra power from the engine. If you do not "hot rod" the engine while driving, the stock clutch may still be adequate. Items b-d keep this more powerful engine cool.

Stage IV:

a. Stage III, plus

b. Big bore kit

The amount of extra power produced is directly related to engine displacement. Generally, the bigger, the better; but taking everying into account, 88mm seems to be ideal. This is undoubtedly the most trouble-free way to add extra power.

Stage V:

a. Stage IV, plus

b. Counterbalanced or roller crankshaft

This stage generally does not add horsepower unless you get a stroker crankshaft (longer than stock stroke). In any event, a balanced crankshaft will permit higher engine speeds and more reliable operation throughout the engine speed range.

Stage VI:

a. Stage V, plus

b. Camshaft, 270-290° duration

This is the last modification to consider. To benefit from a "wilder" than stock camshaft, intake and exhaust breathing modifications, as outlined in earlier stages, are essential. The wrong camshaft or careless installation of any camshaft can make a totally inflexible engine which is useless for the street.

TURBOCHARGED ENGINE

These stages describe a logical progression for adding a turbocharger. Turbocharged Stage II is equivalent to Stage V or VI for a normally aspirated engine as far as power is concerned. Most stages beyond Stage II add reliability more than horsepower.

Stage I:

a. Handling package

b. Instrumentation

14

These items are basic to any VW performance modifications.

Stage II:

a. Turbocharger kit

Order single or dual port version, depending on your engine. This stage nearly doubles stock horsepower.

Stage III:

a. Big bore kit to 1650cc *maximum*

VW 1500 engines can benefit from any bore increase up to 85mm. VW 1200 engines should be limited to 82mm (1351cc). Compression ratio must be kept at or near stock.

Stage IV:

a. 8-dowel crankshaft

b. Competition valve job

c. Oil cooler

d. 200mm clutch

This stage is mainly to beef up the engine for added reliability. With these additions, you can safely use all the potential offered by turbocharging. The crankshaft must have a stock (69mm) stroke, but it may be counterweighted or it may be a roller crankshaft.

HANDLING

Though methods of achieving good handling may seem complex, the result is easily explained. Handling is control, *period*. The more control you have of your automobile under varying conditions, particularly adverse ones, the better your car handles.

The main shortcomings of the VW suspension are:

a. Considerable body roll

b. Inadequate shock absorbers

c. Narrow tires and rims

d. Flexible suspension parts

The best solution to these problems, using available bolt-ons, is:

a. 5½-6 in. wide wheels

b. Radial or belted tires

c. Heavy duty shock absorbers

d. Heavier front anti-roll bar

e. Rear anti-roll bar (double joint), control bars, or camber compensator (swing axle)

Addition of these components can improve VW handling so dramatically that some authors have referred to similarly equipped VW's as mini-Porsches.

Modifications recommended here will be more impressive and useful than any others you can make to your VW. In fact, no engine modications *at all* should be made until your suspension is adequate to handle the increased horsepower.

Tires

Ultimately, the tires must sustain any cornering or acceleration forces. In fact, most handling difficulties and peculiarities can be traced to the characteristics of tires. If the tires are inadequate, you cannot possibly benefit fully from other suspension or engine improvements.

Stock rubber is usually 6.00 x 15 bias tires on 4 or 4½ in. rims. They are inexpensive and are designed for a "smooth" ride. Unfortunately, they have very flexible sidewalls which lose shape during hard cornering and operate at very large slip angles.

Whether a particular tire will fit on your VW is a question only experience can answer. Wheel rim width, wheel offset, and model year must be considered. The best way to determine if a tire will fit is to check with other VW owners who have tried the tire or ask at the local VW speed shop. Another way is to have the dealer mount the tires and check clearance before you buy them.

Here are a few combinations that have been tried and work well. Several VW owners have used 165HR14's on 5½ in. rims at the front and 185HR14's on 6 in. rims at the rear. The slightly smaller than stock tire diameter gives slightly better acceleration. Most important, though, larger tires on the rear than on the front help reduce oversteer.

Other VW owners have used D70 x 14's on 6 in. rims all the way around. You may have to get special 14 in. rims on VW centers with stock offset; never use American car rims with adapters. Still others use E70 x 14 tires all around on 14 x 6 in. rims with no offset. This particular setup has a larger diameter than stock and reduces acceleration below stock. Finally, we have seen several E60 x 15 tires on 5½ or 6 in. rims all around.

Wheels

Installing wider rims is one of the easiest and least expensive ways to noticeably improve your VW's handling. Stock rims are 4 or 4½ in. wide. Several "wide" wheels offered especially for the VW are 5 in. wide. You will need at least 5½ in. rims, preferably 6 in. This gives the tire a wider base and increases its resistance to distortion during cornering.

Wheels can be aluminum or magnesium castings, or steel stampings. See **Figure 1**. If you can afford it, go for the aluminum wheels. However, be prepared to pay extra for tire mounting. These wheels are relatively brittle and chip easily if not handled properly.

Steel wheels are definitely worth considering, especially if money is tight. They do not look as good as "mag" type wheels, but if wide enough, they are great. No worries about chips during tire replacement, either.

Wheels have varying amounts of offset. See **Figure 2**. If the mounting surface of the wheel is at its centerline, it has no offset. If the rim is moved out (positive offset), the track is wider; if the rim is moved in (negative offset), the track is narrower. Too much offset, particularly positive offset, can cause interference between tire and fender.

Anti-roll Bars

These bars are known by a variety of names: sway bars, anti-sway bars, stabilizer bars, and anti-roll bars. See **Figures 3 and 4**. All have the same basic function: they permit the wheel assemblies to move up and down simultaneously, but twist the bar if one wheel goes up alone. During hard cornering, the body leans, raising the outer wheel and lowering the inner wheel. A front anti-roll bar resists these wheel movements

transfers additional weight to the outer wheel, which washes out as its slip angle increases. The effect is increased understeer. A rear anti-roll bar balances the front bar and eliminates most of the body roll. Never increase roll resistance at the rear, particularly on swing axle models, without also increasing it at the front.

Anti-roll bars are available from several manufacturers. Some builders recommend ⅝ in. bars front and rear. Addco recommends ¾ in. bars front and rear. For about $80, in either case, handling is improved so dramatically you will not believe it is the same car. There probably is not a better performance buy for your money.

Shock Absorbers

Shock absorbers are relatively simple, but frequently misunderstood components. Basic-

14

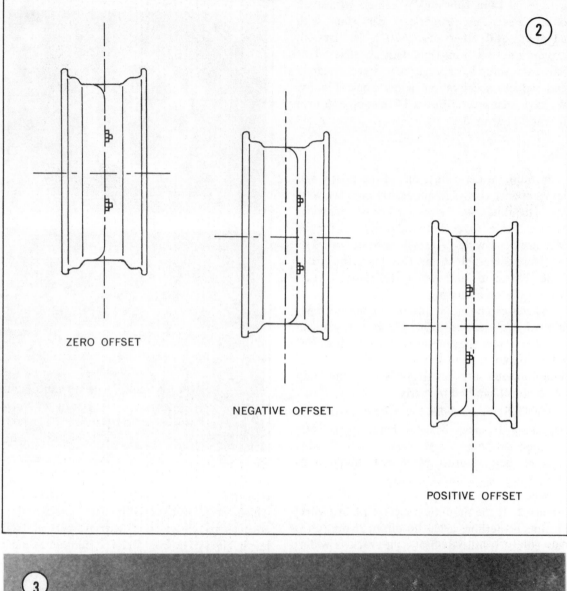

ZERO OFFSET

NEGATIVE OFFSET

POSITIVE OFFSET

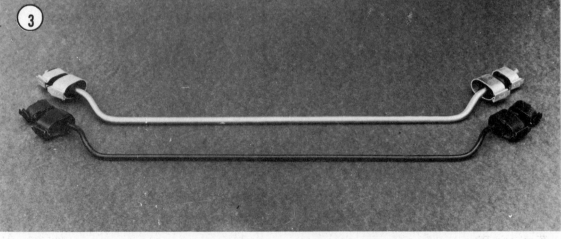

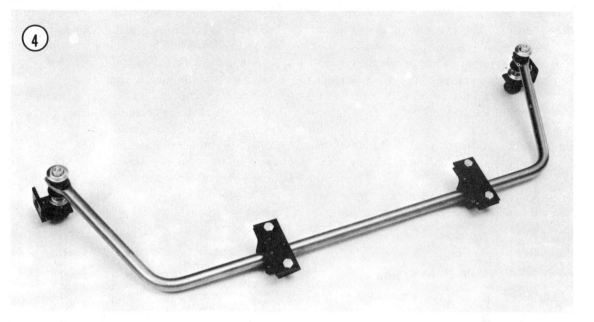

ally, they slow down the reaction time of the wheels. Contrary to what many believe, shocks do not minimize body roll or affect spring rates (stiffness) of the suspension.

The main purposes of shock absorbers are to:

a. Prevent suspension bottoming from high speed bumps

b. Force the tire to absorb small bumps rather than the suspension

c. Dampen wheel rebound after a large bump

The stock shock absorbers are designed for ride comfort, not handling, and should be replaced. A number of heavy shocks are available for the VW. Some are non-adjustable gas pressure shocks; others are adjustable.

Adjustable shocks have two advantages. First, they allow you to set the damping action to suit your own preferences. Second, you can progressively increase firmness as the shocks wear, and thereby maintain the same damping as new shocks. This feature justifies the higher price of adjustables. Ordinary shocks are rarely adequate after 20,000-30,000 miles, and should be replaced. With adjustables, you simply take up another notch every 20,000-30,000 miles. Eighty-thousand miles and more is not uncommon.

Koni and Bilstein are among the more popular performance shock absorbers today. Bilsteins are not adjustable, but are available for many applications. A relative newcomer, KYB "Gas-a-just," is gaining in popularity and should be considered, especially if cost is a factor (they are priced lower than either Konis or Bilsteins). Many other brands are available, including Armstrong, Maverick, Rough Country, and Gabriel. All of these brands have users that swear by them. Cost is usually (but not always) a fair indicator of quality.

Decambering

Introducing negative camber at the front and rear wheels, called decambering, can improve handling on any VW. Decambering has two primary benefits. First, it improves the tire contact patch because the tire fits flatter against the road. Secondly, it lowers the vehicle's roll center, which reduces weight transfer to the outside wheels during cornering, and minimizes jacking effect on swing axles. Benefits are more noticeable on swing axle VW's than on later models with double joint axles.

The amount of negative camber needed is strictly a matter for experimentation. VW enthusiasts have set in as much as 2-5° negative camber at the rear end and 0-2° at the front. As

14

a starting point, try 0-½ ° negative front and rear. Individual VW's require different amounts of decambering.

Accurate wheel alignment is hopeless without an optical alignment rack. Trying to decamber a VW in your driveway will lead to extremely rapid tire wear and possibly dangerous handling. Talk to other VW enthusiasts running similar tires and wheels. Get the benefit of their experimentation, then take your VW to a properly equipped suspension specialist. Have him set in the desired negative camber. Also have him readjust rear wheel toe-in, as decambering increases toe-in.

EXHAUST SYSTEMS

The stock exhaust system is designed to attenuate engine noise over a wide range of speeds without seriously decreasing engine performance. Considering the modest increases in horsepower achieved with "performance" exhaust systems, the stock muffler does a good job.

All of the more popular extractor exhaust systems perform about equally well. Horsepower increases average 5%. Noise levels are slightly higher, but usually not enough to attract the police. Is this increase worth the $50 it costs for an extractor exhaust? Yes, it definitely is.

First of all, the more efficiently your engine can get rid of burned gases, the more efficiently it can breathe fresh air/fuel mixture. You must have an efficient exhaust to realize the full potential of carburetion changes, for example. Secondly, these systems really sound great on a VW engine. While not a rational justification for spending $50, exhaust notes do add some excitement to automobile engines.

There are several different construction methods in extractor exhaust systems. The best system is a 4-in-1 arrangement, which practically all modern units use. See **Figure 5**. The 4-in-1 system has proven itself quieter and more powerful than others.

The conclusion is, by all means add an extractor exhaust to your VW. Since they all perform about the same, consider:

a. Price

b. Workmanship

c. Availablity of replacement muffler

d. Appearance

IGNITION SYSTEM

The modern VW coil ignition system has two important things going for it: it is inexpensive and it works. With so many other areas of the VW screaming for attention, why waste time or money on the fantastic variety of special VW ignition components available?

There are some inexpensive and worthwhile changes you can make to improve the stock system. These include selection of a better distributor (still VW) and selection of spark plugs in the correct heat range. This section explains the necessary changes.

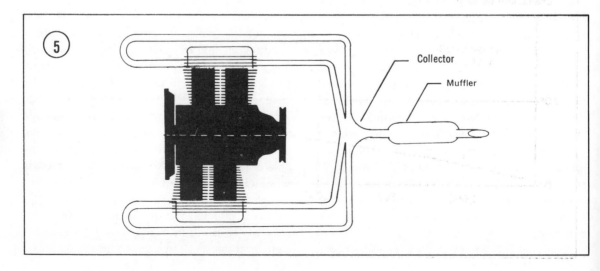

Collector

Muffler

Distributor

If you are maintaining stock carburetion, there is no need to change the distributor. Use the one you have.

If you change carburetion, it is doubtful the new carburetor will have provisions to operate the vacuum advance at the right rate. In this case, you must convert to one of the centrifugal-advance-only distributors.

Two centrifugal-advance-only distributors are used most by VW performance modifiers: the Bosch 231 129 019 originally used on 1959 and earlier Transporters, and the Bosch 231 129 010 used on 1960 Transporters. Advance characteristics of both distributors are shown in **Figure 6**.

NOTE: *The Bosch 010 distributor is no longer available. It has been replaced by the 009, which has similar characteristics.*

Note that the 010 has a total advance of 20° at the crankshaft (10° at distributor) which is all in by 2,500 crankshaft rpm. The 019 has 17° total advance (8.5° at distributor) which is all in by 3,500 crankshaft rpm. Both distributors perform perfectly at engine speeds over 8,000 rpm. You will not be demanding anywhere near that much performance even in a highly modified, hard-raced engine.

The sooner maximum advance is produced, the better acceleration in most cases. The 010

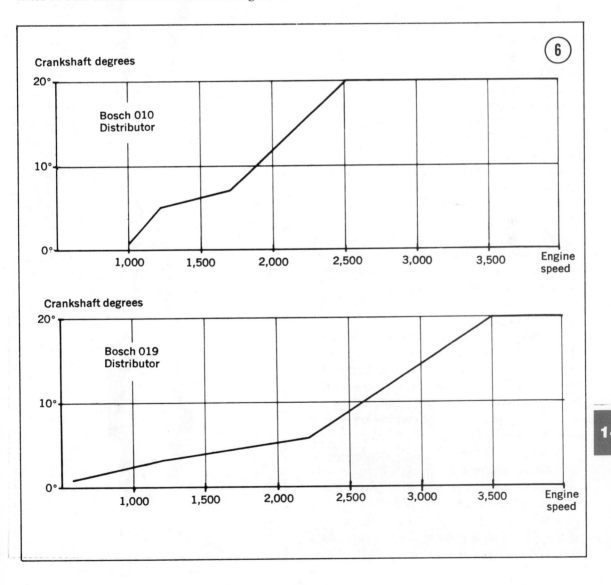

produces maximum advance at 2,500 rpm, the 019 at 3,500 rpm. Therefore, the 010 (and 009) is better for acceleration needed in racing. The 019 is better for a pure street machine.

Ignition Coil

There is absolutely nothing wrong with the stock coil, even for all-out racing. The Bosch Blue Coil used in the Bosch Screamer Kit looks much faster, but adds nothing to performance at all.

Spark Plugs

There is nothing wrong with stock plugs for a stock engine, but these plugs may run too hot if the engine has been modified.

Spark plugs are designed to work within a specific heat range. Below 1,000°F (550°C), carbon deposits do not burn off the tip and may form a conducting track which short circuits the plug. Above 1,550°F (850°C), the plug tip gets so hot it can pre-ignite the mixture like a glow plug. The spark plug operates best when the center electrode is 1,300-1,400°F (700-750°C).

Modified engines usually run hotter and require a "cold" plug that can dissipate heat rapidly. This prevents the center electrode from running hotter than desired. The center electrode and insulating core are made short so that there is a short heat conduction path to the metal body and the comparatively cool cylinder head. See **Figure 7A**.

A cold-running engine requires a hot plug that does not quickly dissipate the heat. Thus, the central electrode stays hotter. Otherwise, the central electrode temperature would drop below the desired range. The central electrode is made long so that th heat conduction path is long. See **Figure 7B**.

A modified VW engine usually requires plugs just slightly colder than stock. Champion has developed spark plugs with a projected core-nose. See **Figure 8**. This plug acts like a "warm" plug at low rpm's and like a cold plug at high rpm's. The result is a variable heat range plug. Two that work well in the VW are the UL-82Y

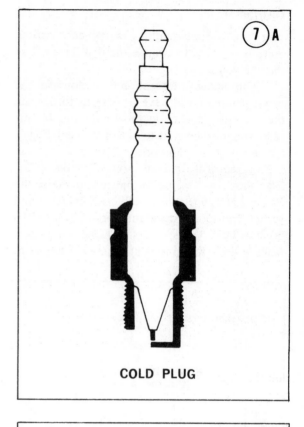

COLD PLUG

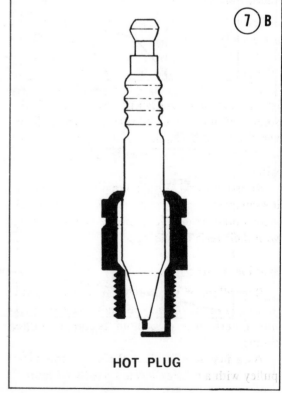

HOT PLUG

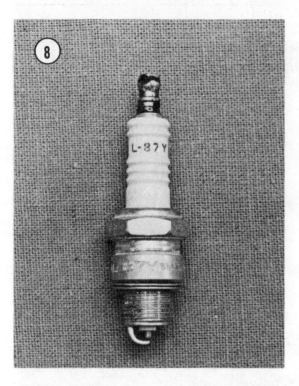

and the slightly warmer L-87Y. Full race VW's will require a colder plug.

Spark Plug Wires

Several special ignition wires are marketed for the VW. If your stock wires are in good condition, keep them even if they are of the resistance type. If the wires show obvious deterioration, or you have 40,000 or more miles on them, install new ones. Old ignition wires are often a source of mysterious misfire problems. Stock wires are best if you have a radio; you may end up with considerable interference with other wires.

Resistive wires in good condition do not rob horsepower. Volkswagen engineers have designed other components in the system to work with their resistive wiring.

Ignition Timing

Regardless of the condition of your engine and its ignition system, you cannot achieve maximum performance without accurate ignition timing.

As a first step, replace the stock crankshaft pulley with a fully calibrated one. See **Figure 9**.

If you have a 010, 009, or 019 Bosch distributor, set ignition timing as follows:

1. Connect accurate tachometer to engine. Range should cover up to about 4,000 rpm.

2. Connect stroboscopic timing light to cylinder No. 1 following manufacturer's instructions.

3. Run engine at 2,500 rpm (010 distributor) or 3,500 rpm (019 distributor).

4. Loosen the distributor housing and turn it until the 30° BTDC mark, illuminated by the timing light, aligns with TDC. Tighten the distributor in this position.

The static or idle ignition timing recommended by VW may or may not be correct after performing these steps. Do not change it; let it fall where necessary to get full advance timing correct.

Electronic Ignition Systems

The number of special electronic ignition systems available as aftermarket equipment has proliferated greatly in the last 10 years. So has the fancy jargon used to describe them. Only two types are discussed here:

   a. Transistorized

   b. Capacitive-discharge

Electronic ignitions have not replaced conventional breaker point/coil ignitions except in a few production cars. The reasons are obvious. They are far more expensive and do not perform any better than a conventional system *in good condition.*

No electronic ignition system sold today can increase horsepower, acceleration, gas mileage, or any other measurement of performance over a conventional VW ignition in proper working order. This is not to say electronic ignitions have no value. They can:

   a. Make cold/damp weather starting easier

   b. Increase point life

   c. Increase spark plug life

Plug life on a performance modified VW can be very short. For this reason, a capacitive-discharge (CD) ignition, which can increase plug life several times, is justified. In fact, some new Porsche 911's have a CD ignition as standard equipment to overcome short plug life.

14

FUEL SYSTEM

The stock fuel system is designed to give reasonable fuel economy, good low end torque, and fair performance over a very wide range. A number of things can be done to vastly improve performance, but you are going to pay a price. Fuel economy and engine flexibility will suffer.

You cannot possibly evaluate any fuel system changes until you have the stock system working right. The first place to start is a good engine tune-up as described in Chapter Two. Do not touch the fuel system until the ignition system works *perfectly*. Next, remove the air cleaner, have an assistant floor the accelerator pedal (engine off), and look into the carburetor throat with a flashlight. Be sure that the throttle valve opens fully; adjust the linkage if necessary. If your engine has more than 40,000 miles on it, disassemble and clean the carburetor. Few engines fail to benefit from these steps.

Air Cleaners

A special air cleaner is usually the first "speed equipment" a VW enthusiast adds. This is OK if he adds the right air cleaner. The kind you want is often called a "hi-rise" or "ram" air cleaner. These incorporate a 4 in. velocity stack which catches the fuel spray. See **Figure 10**. Low profile air cleaners are not tall enough to contain the fuel fog. If you already have one, mount a 4 in. piece of metal or plastic tubing between the air cleaner and carburetor. See **Figure 11**.

Of course, it is not necessary to mention that you should *never* operate your engine without an air cleaner. A clean air cleaner does not rob your engine of enough power to offset its advantages, namely:

a. Contains fuel fog

b. Reduces intake noise

c. Reduces engine wear

d. Supresses flames from backfires

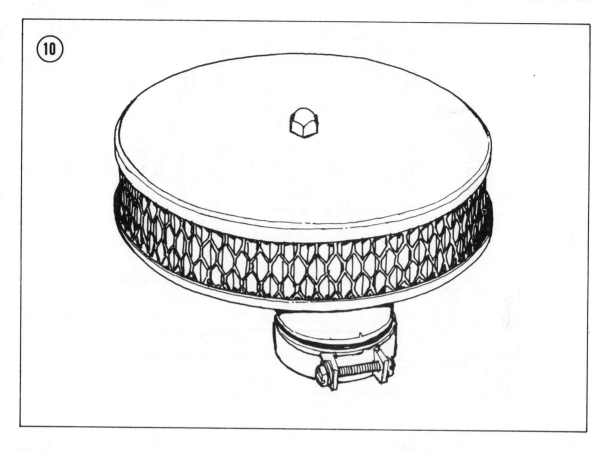

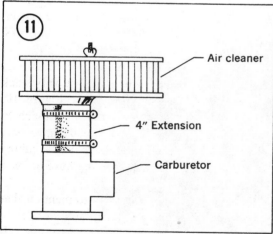

Air cleaner

4" Extension

Carburetor

Intake Manifolds

The small size of the stock manifold seriously limits VW perfomance, particularly at high engine speeds.

Adding a large carburetor to a stock manifold will not work. Whether you use an adapter or buy one of the modified stock manifolds, you will be lucky to get stock horsepower. When considering a larger carburetor, add the price of a new intake manifold.

Two major types of intake manifolds are sold for the VW.

a. Isolated tube type

b. Plenum chamber type

The isolated tube type is shown in **Figure 12** and is exactly what it says. The tube for each barrel is completely isolated from the other. This type manifold should be used with carburetors like the Holley Bug Spray and Zenith 32NDIX with a slot cut in the base. See **Figure 13**.

A plenum chamber in the manifold under the carburetor dampens the intake pulsations. See **Figure 14**. This reduces the fuel fog at the carburetor inlet and reduces the tendency for over-enrichment at high rpm, which a pulsating air flow creates.

Intake manifolds are available for nearly every VW model and year. Construction of

14

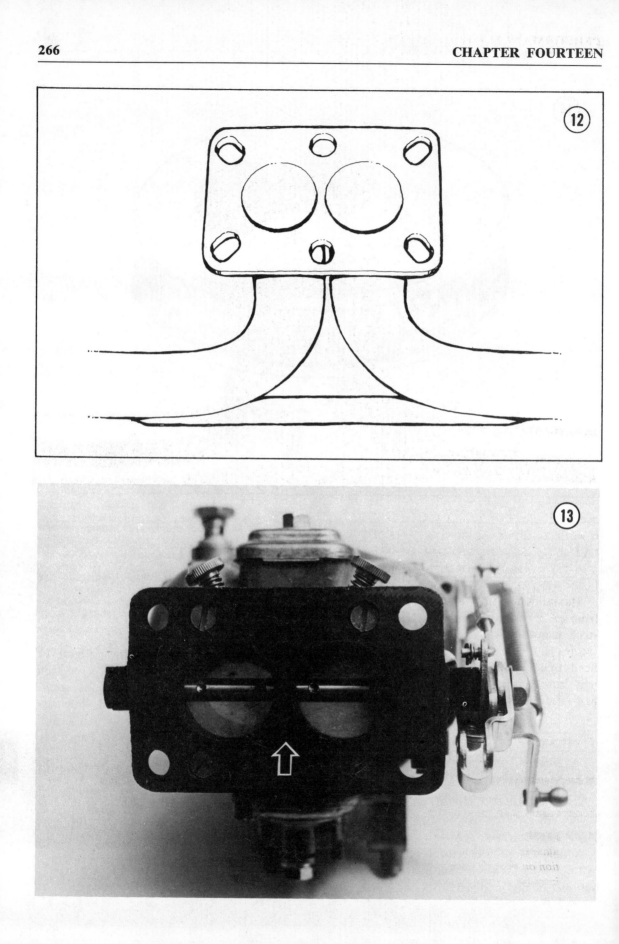

nearly all of them, regardless of manufacturer, is virtually identical. Most offer both isolated tube and plenum chamber types. They also use a manifold heater, like the stock manifold, for faster warm-up.

Manifolds for 1971 and later engines differ from earlier manifolds in that they mate to the stock manifold castings instead of directly to the heads. If you are converting from single port heads to dual port heads, get a set of stock castings from your VW dealer and use the 1971 and later manifold design.

Carburetors

A 2-barrel carburetor can add considerable horsepower to your VW, particularly if you have installed an extractor exhaust system, high lift rocker arms, and/or a hotter cam.

> NOTE: *Check local air pollution regulations before changing the carburetion on any car, especially late models, intended for use on public streets.*

Three carburetors are popular for street VW's:

a. Holley Bug Spray (R-6244)

b. Carter WGD

c. Zenith 32NDIX

Several Solex and Weber carburetors are packaged for the VW, but they are very expensive and do not perform well enough on the street, even though they are the ultimate for racing VW's.

Holley Bug Spray

The Holley Bug Spray is specifically designed for the VW. See **Figure 15**. The automatic choke is electric and uses the wire originally connected to the stock carburetor. The throttle is actuated by the stock cable; a small extension piece is included with the carburetor. There is no vacuum take-off for the distributor, so you must use a centrifugal-advance-only distributor. The Holley Bug Spray performs nearly as well

as far more expensive carburetors. At about half the price ($55-75), it is an excellent value.

Actually, there are two versions of the Bug Spray. The R-6244 has a 200CFM (cubic feet/minute) flow capacity and may be used singly on 1800cc or smaller engines. The R-4691 has a 300CFM capacity and may be used singly on engines over 1800cc. Of course, these carburetors may also be used in pairs, but you will have to go to a hotter cam.

The carburetor must be used with an isolated tube manifold. Do not use adapters to the stock manifold, and do not use a plenum chamber type manifold.

Carter WGD

This 2-barrel carburetor, like the Holley, is specifically designed for the VW. It is equipped with two 27mm venturis and an electric choke which uses the stock VW wiring. There is no vacuum advance connection, so you must use a centrifugal-advance-only distributor. The Carter is a fine performer for the price ($35-50).

This carburetor must be used with an isolated tube manifold, like the Holley. Do not use an adapter for stock manifold and do not use plenum chamber manifolds.

Zenith 32NDIX

This unit has been a favorite with VW performance enthusiasts for many years. See **Figure 16**. The main reason is that the Zenith offers fully adjustable circuits which allow it to be more finely tuned to a particular engine for a specific purpose. For this convenience, you pay a premium price: the Zenith 32NDIX carburetor costs around $145.

The carburetor comes in several configurations. The P010 is for single carburetor installations. It has a balancing slot between the throttle bores and must be used on isolated tube (not plenum chamber) manifolds. The P019L and P019R are left and right carburetors for dual installation. There is no balancing slot.

The Zenith 32NDIX has been used on many production automobiles. Buy one that has been specifically set up for the VW. These have a VW throttle arm, 23mm venturis, 135 main jets, and 180 air correction jets. None of the Zeniths for the VW have a vacuum advance connection.

Solex 40 P11

This carburetor was used on early 4-cylinder Porsches as standard equipment. A number of companies market dual carburetor setups with 2 Solex carburetors, manifolds, and linkage. These kits are expensive and from reports by local VW enthusiasts perform no better than dual Holley's at twice the Holley price.

Fuel Pumps

The stock fuel pump is adequate even for full race VW's. There is no need for a "high performance" mechanical fuel pump and no need for an electric fuel pump. Put the money into something that does some good.

Fuel Injection

Many production automobiles are switching to fuel injection. The reasons are:

a. Higher horsepower with given displacement

b. Lower fuel consumption

c. Better low-end torque

d. Better air/fuel distribution

e. Lower harmful exhaust emission

Volkswagen has used Bosch electronic fuel injection in all Type II's since 1975. The system has proven itself a strong, reliable performer.

Many VW enthusiasts have toyed with the idea of adding the Bosch system to other VW's. Some have actually done it. The conversion is not as difficult as it may seem, but it is not a job for a novice. The problems and combinations possible are too varied to permit describing a step-by-step conversion. Instead, here are a few guidelines.

1. Do your homework. Buy every service manual and article written on the Bosch fuel injection system.

2. When you buy the system, be sure you get all of it, including the wiring harnesses. Service manuals will help identify parts. Consider buying the whole engine.

3. Prepare to do some air intake fabricating.

COOLING AND LUBRICATION

Any modification which increases engine power also increases the amount of heat pro-duced. Such heat seriously taxes the stock cooling systems (air and oil). Consequently, the oil cooler can no longer cool the oil adequately, and temperatures soar. Spark plugs run too hot and pre-ignite. Engine bearings run hotter and wear faster. This condition cannot be tolerated for long before it leads to engine failure.

Stock Air Cooling System

The stock air cooling system is completely adequate for high performance use if in proper condition. Always assemble the engine with all cover plates; never run the engine with any missing cover plates. Ensure that the rubber spark plug seals are in good condition and securely in place so that no air can escape. Furthermore, never disable the thermostatic control system whether it is the older air ring type or the newer air flaps. No horsepower or cooling will be gained. Adjust the control system exactly as described in Chapter Five. The only "modification" to the air cooling system might be to move the stock oil cooler as described in the oil cooler section to improve air flow to the left cylinder bank.

14

Power Pulley

Power pulleys (**Figure 17**) are some of the most insidious accessories designed for the up-right engine. While increasing useable horse-power and engine heat production, they lower the cooling fan speed and air cooling.

A power (crankshaft) pulley increases useable engine horsepower by reducing the speed of the cooling fan and thus the horsepower required to drive it. This can save up to 4 horsepower at 5,000 rpm, but seriously decreases the cooling fan air output. There are better ways to gain 4 horsepower and at a lower cost in terms of engine life.

High-capacity Oil Pumps

Increasing engine oil flow with a larger capacity oil pump provides better cooling and lower bearing temperatures. Actually, there are two ways to achieve a larger pump capacity:

  a. Install a high-capacity pump
  b. "Blueprinting" the stock pump

All oil pumps offered for the VW replace the stock pump without any modifications. You do not even have to remove the engine.

"Blueprinting" Stock Pump

1. Measure the outside diameter of the oil pump body with a micrometer. This should be 2.7560 ± 0.005 in.

2. Check clearance between gear teeth and pump body with a feeler gauge. Maximum clearance should be 0.003 in. (0.08mm).

3. Measure the shaft hole diameter in the pump body with a small hole gauge and micrometer. Measure the drive shaft diameter with a micrometer. Clearance should be 0.0005-0.0015 in. (0.013-0.038mm).

4. If measurements in Steps 1-3 are not as specified, get another pump.

5. Install gears in pump body. Check backlash by inserting a feeler gauge between gear teeth as shown in **Figure 18**. Backlash should be 0.0012-0.0031 in. (0.03-0.08mm).

6. Reduce gear end play from specified 0.004 in. (0.1mm) to zero. To do this, lay a piece of Wet-or-Dry sandpaper on a flat piece of plate glass. Flood the paper with solvent. Install the gears in the pump body. Invert the pump on the sandpaper and sand back and forth while continually turning the body. When you begin sanding the gears, stop. The gear faces are now flush with the pump body. The only gear end play will be the space provided by the paper gasket.

7. Clean the gears and pump body very thoroughly. Lightly deburr the gears with a fine file.

Several high-capacity oil pumps are offered for the VW. The production tolerances are no better than the stock pump tolerances, so check the high-capacity pump out as described in Steps 1-5 for a stock pump before you buy it. Or make arrangements to return a pump which is not "tight" enough. Do not buy a pump by mail-order or in a sealed package. Regardless of the past reputation of the oil pump supplier or manufacturer, check the actual pump you plan to buy thoroughly.

Auxiliary Oil Coolers

The stock oil cooler is inadequate in a modified VW engine for two reasons:

 a. Poor mounting position

 b. Small cooling capacity

The stock cooler on most upright engines is right in the way of the cooling air stream for cylinders No. 3 and 4, which therefore tend to run hotter than the others. In 1971, VW bulged

the fan housing outward to permit mounting the cooler out of the way of cylinders No. 3 and 4. This modification can be made to earlier VW's by installing the new oil cooler adapter, a Type 3 oil cooler, and a 1971 or later fan housing. See **Figure 19**.

Auxiliary oil coolers are available to greatly decrease engine oil temperatures. There are two main types of oil coolers: bypass and full-flow. Bypass oil coolers tap off a portion of the oil for cooling, then return it to the crankcase; the stock oil cooler is retained. These are characterized by very small oil lines (1/16 in. ID). If large lines are used, oil pressure drops dangerously. Full-flow oil coolers pass all the engine oil. The stock cooler is removed on most installations. These coolers must have very large lines (½ in. ID or more) to pass oil when it is cold and thick. Full-flow installations are generally more expensive than bypass coolers, but are far more efficient.

Careful attention to mounting position can greatly affect the cooler's performance. Most coolers offered for the VW mount ahead of the cooling air inlet; the stock cooler is removed. This position preheats the cooling air and may result in the same oil temperatures as the stock

14

cooler; however, the restriction to the left bank will be gone. Better cooling would result by fashioning brackets to get the cooler in the air stream or duct cold air to it with a scoop.

Oil Filters

Several methods have been devised to add a full-flow filter to the VW engine. By far the easiest are offered by Claude's Buggies, Bug Pack, and others. The stock oil pump is replaced by a high-capacity oil pump with integral oil filter. See **Figure 20**. This type uses a cartridge filter available in any parts supply house. Another easy solution is to buy one of the many oil coolers on the market which incorporate an oil filter adapter. Claude's Buggies 1720, 1721 and 1722 coolers and Motion Minicar's 31-015 cooler offer this feature.

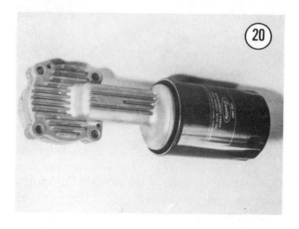

Other solutions require tapping into the main oil gallery. This requires complete disassembly of the engine to drill and flush the crankcase. In addition, the stock pump must be modified and fitted with a special tapped cover. Oil from the pump cover connection passes to the full-flow oil filter, then returns via the tap in the main gallery. Many VW performance shops can do the work if you choose this method.

Oil Sumps

Oil sumps for the VW add 1½ quarts to the oil capacity. See **Figure 21**. This added margin prevents oil starvation during hard cornering or acceleration, which forces oil into the heads or in any event away from the oil pump pickup.

Extra capacity is vital for any VW driven "enthusiastically" as oil starvation can occur even while quickly negotiating a freeway on-ramp.

Contrary to what many say, added oil capacity will not reduce oil temperatures. It may take longer to heat the larger quantity of oil, but eventually it will get just as hot.

Finned oil sumps do not significantly reduce oil temperatures. The oil at the bottom of the sump is cooled, but this increases its viscosity and it remains there instead of circulating through the engine. In addition, the cooler oil in the bottom insulates the oil above it so that no further cooling occurs.

Finned oil sumps are even less effective in lowering oil temperatures if they are polished or chromed. Sandblasting, black anodizing, or painting with flat black paint will improve their heat radiating capability.

Engine Oil Temperatures

Engine oil temperatures will increase more and more as you increase power output. Since the oil is used for engine cooling, it is important to limit oil temperature.

As a rule, 230°F should be a safe *maximum* with 30 weight oil. Some modifiers permit up to 280°F with a 40-50 weight racing oil, but this is far too high for reliable day-to-day driving. If your engine runs hotter than 230°F, you should install an oil cooler, preferably a full-flow type. If your oil pressure is less than about 30 psi at this temperature, change to a good quality 40 weight oil.

CYLINDER HEADS

Cylinder heads, like so many other parts of the VW, are fine for what they were designed to provide—economical, low speed operation. Stock heads greatly limit the power capabilities of the engine, but fortunately, they respond very nicely to performance modifications.

Stock Heads

Before getting into what can be done to improve your cylinder heads, let us try to identify what you have.

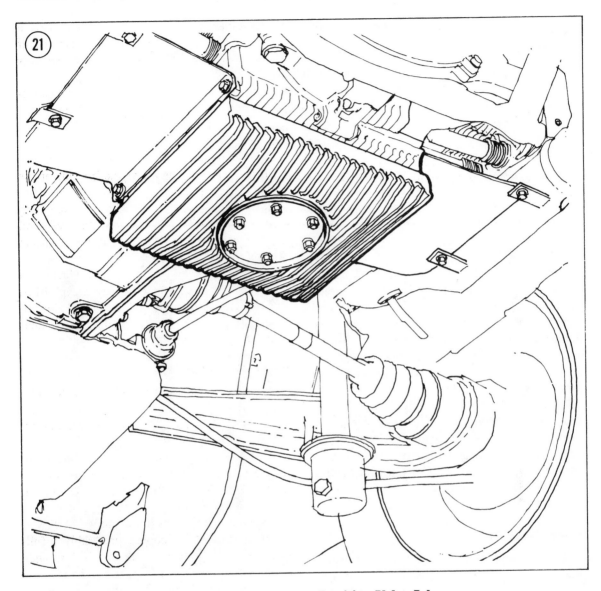

Possible modifications depend on which heads you have. The latest dual port heads are the best ones for a modified VW. If you have 1200 heads, there is little that can be done to improve them; exchange them for the 1500/1600 single port or dual port heads. **Table 2** summarizes all VW heads of any interest; this table will help you identify those which are separate from the engine.

Cleaning and Inspection

Before any modification can begin, the heads must be thoroughly cleaned and inspected as described in Chapter Four.

Precision Valve Job

A good competition valve job is overlooked by far too many VW enthusiasts. VW valves begin to seat poorly after 10,000-15,000 miles. By 40,000-50,000 miles, compression losses are so great, loss in performance is very significant.

Get a precision valve grind at a performance shop experienced in VW's, regardless of how many miles on your engine. Do not take the job to your dealer or a local service station. A precision competition valve job could mean extra horsepower. Expect it to cost up to $50 plus parts, and go back for the same treatment every 30,000 miles for peak performance.

Table 2   STOCK CYLINDER HEADS

Part No.	Used on		Description
113 101 351A	Type I	1961-1965	Single port, "right angle" intake
	Type II	1959-1962	
211 101 351A	Type II	1962-1970	Single port, slanted intake
113 101 353B	Type I	1966-1970	
311 101 353,	Type III	1965-1966	
311 101 353A			
311 101 353D	Type I	1971-present	Dual port, slanted intake
	Type II	1971 only	
	Type III	1967-present	

Special Valves

Special valves are definitely a good invest-
ment for a VW engine. Special alloy and forged
stainless steel valves are available from a number of sources in stock sizes and larger. See
Figure 22. Stock size valves are worth considering because of their added reliability over stock
VW valves. Large size valves are worth the
trouble and expense due to superior breathing
afforded. Some stock size valves fit right into
place with no modifications. Larger size valves
require machining the heads for larger valve
seats and some porting to improve air flow
through the larger valves. Consider exchanging
your stock heads for dual port heads with larger
valves installed.

Compression Ratio

Compression ratio is one of the major factors
determining the amount of work which can be
produced by a given amount of fuel. Stock compression ratios (around 7-7.5:1) are not high
enough to extract the maximum efficiency from
the fuel. Raising the compression ratio, when
done in conjunction with other cylinder head
modifications, increases horsepower, but requires that you burn premium fuel.

There are three ways to change compression
ratio:

  a. Change bore

  b. Change stroke

  c. Flycut heads

Most people only think about flycutting the
heads when they decide to change compression

ratio. This procedure is equivalent to milling the
heads on a water-cooled engine. It decreases the
volume of the combustion chamber. But keep
in mind that installing a big bore kit or "stroker"
crankshaft will also increase compression ratio.
If you flycut the heads to raise the compression
ratio, then later decide to add a big bore kit,
you may raise the compression ratio far beyond
the desired limit (about 9-9.5:1).

Measuring Combustion Chamber Volume

This process, often called "cc'ing the head,"
is important for two reasons. First, it is the only

way to accurately determine actual compression ratio. Second, it permits comparing the volume of all 4 combustion chambers so that they can be matched. Matching permits the cylinders to produce equal power.

Ideally, all combustion chamber volumes should be within one cubic centimeter of each other. There are two major ways to match them:

a. Recess valves into the head in the smallest chambers

b. Remove metal from smallest chambers

Give your cylinder heads to an *experienced VW performance shop*, and let them match the combustion chambers.

Changing Compression Ratio

Although some VW drag machines run compression ratios of 11:1 and up, a street or off-road VW should not exceed a 9-9.5:1 compression ratio, even if it sees occasional competition use.

Normally, deliberate compression ratio changes are made by flycutting the area around the combustion chambers. This recesses the cylinder into the head and reduces the combustion chamber volume. Changing bore or stroke also affects compression ratio, but such changes are normally made to increase displacement, not raise or lower the compression ratio.

Porting and Polishing

This is not an area in the bolt-on category, but it is such a generally accepted "performance trick" a few words about it are necessary.

Porting and polishing usually means enlarging the intake ports and the area behind the valves, followed by careful polishing. Many hours of work are required to do the job, but more importantly, you must know what you are doing. Unless you are very experienced with modifying VW heads, leave the ports alone. Take your heads to a professional or trade them for ported and polished dual port heads from a reliable supplier.

Commercially Available Modified Heads

Several suppliers, including Claude's Buggies and Gene Berg, carry dual port heads in differ-

ent stages of modification. Usually they are available for 85.5, 88, and 92mm bores. They are ported and polished, cc'd, and flycut for higher compression ratio. Larger intake valves (39-42mm) and exhaust valves (35.5-37.5mm) are fit in special aluminum-silicone-bronze guides with dual springs and heavy retainers. Naturally, a competition valve job is included.

The heads bolt right on with no difficulty, but expect to pay $300 and up for a set.

INCREASING DISPLACEMENT

Increasing displacement is one of the least complicated and most reliable methods of adding power to your VW.

Displacement can be increased by enlarging the bore or the stroke. Bore increases involve swapping the stock cylinders and pistons for larger ones. Increasing the stroke means adding a new crankshaft as well.

Big Bore Piston/Cylinder Kits

Table 3 summarizes the displacement provided by currently available big bore kits. These are computed on the basis of a stock stroke and stock heads (no modifications which affect compression ratio). **Figure 23** shows the components normally provided.

Table 3   AVAILABLE BIG BORE KITS

Engine	Bores Available	Equivalent Displacement
40 hp[1]	82mm, 83mm	1352cc, 1385cc
1200		
1300[2]	85.5mm, 87mm	1585cc, 1640cc
1500	88mm, 92mm	1679cc, 1835cc
1600	87mm, 88mm 92mm	1640cc, 1679cc 1835cc
1. 64mm stroke	2. 69mm stroke	

Stock Parts as Big Bore Kits

If you have a 1300 or 1500 VW engine, "big bore" kits are available at your local VW dealer as stock equipment. For example, a 1300 engine can be upgraded to a 1500 or 1600cc engine simply by adding stock 1500 or 1600 pistons

and cylinders. VW 1300 heads must be flycut to fit the larger cylinders; the crankcase does not require flycutting. VW 1500 engines require no machine work.

VW 1200 engines will not accept larger stock piston/cylinder sets. Later cylinders are longer than 1200 cylinders. To use them would mean using longer connecting rods, studs, sheet metal cover plates, etc. It is simply not worth it.

Installing a Big Bore Kit

Installing a big bore kit is no different from installing stock cylinders and pistons, except when machine work is required for large kits. Follow the cylinder and piston removal and installation procedures in your service manual.

Machine work is often required on the crankcase and cylinder heads to accommodate larger diameter cylinders. See **Figures 24 and 25**. A number of VW performance shops can do this for you in about 2 hours.

Take the completely disassembled crankcase and cylinder heads with your new cylinder barrels. The machinist mikes the cylinder barrels and cuts the case and heads just large enough to provide 0.010 in. clearance. He must have the

actual cylinder barrels to do this. Prices vary from $25-50 for the crankcase and 2 heads.

In most cases, you must change to a better exhaust system and 2-barrel carburetor to get full benefit from a displacement increase.

STOCK CRANKSHAFT

The stock steel forged crankshaft is one of the major engine components limiting high speed performance. Four main bearings support the crankshaft, but the crankshaft is not adequately counterbalanced for high rev's. At much over 5,500 rpm, the crankshaft begins to pound out the crankcase at the No. 2 bearing. See **Figure 26**.

The stock crankshaft is very sturdy, but needs care to give good service in a high performance engine. Start with a thorough cleaning and inspection as described in Chapter Four.

Even new VW crankshafts straight from the dealer may have excessive runout. Be sure that you have the new one checked; return it to the dealer if it is out of specifications.

Crank Dowels

The stock crankshaft and flywheel are located by 4 metal 8mm dowels and held together by a

large gland nut. The nut is tightened to over 217 ft.-lb., but high performance VW engines easily twist the flywheel on the crank and wear the flywheel dowel holes into ovals. This is one of the most serious hazards in adding horsepower to the VW.

Fortunately, the problem can be cured. Add 4 more dowels to the end of the crankshaft and

14

flywheel. See **Figure 27**. If you are running less than 80-90 hp, add 4 more 8mm x 20mm dowels. If you run more power than this, install eight 11/32 x 3/4 in. dowels. Most VW performance shops can do the necessary drilling for $35-40. That is inexpensive insurance.

Gland Nut and Washer

Another way to keep the flywheel and crankshaft together is a modified gland nut and larger washer. See **Figure 28**. Motion Minicar and others supply a high grade steel gland nut with longer threads; about 0.040 in. is machined off the head to provide clutch clearance. A large washer, supplied by the same companies, distributes the gland nut pressure over a wider area. Although offered separately, you should use the larger washer and modified gland nut together.

While the stock gland nut is torqued to 217+ ft.-lb., high performance engines require more than this. Clean the threads of the crankshaft

and modified gland nut very thoroughly. Clean the flywheel surface which meets the washer. Install the large washer and gland nut with Loctite, following the manufacturer's directions. Torque the gland nut to 400 ft.-lb. **Figure 29** shows one method of creating this much force. Do not start the engine for a couple of days to be sure that the Loctite sets up properly.

STROKER CRANKSHAFTS

Added displacement is one of the surest and most reliable methods of increasing power. Increasing stroke has another benefit. Longer strokes broaden the effective power at the lower end of the rpm range.

Table 4 shows displacement increases possible with available stroker crankshafts and bore kits.

Installing a Stroker Crankshaft

There are a few problems in adding a stroker crankshaft. First, the longest stroke that will fit

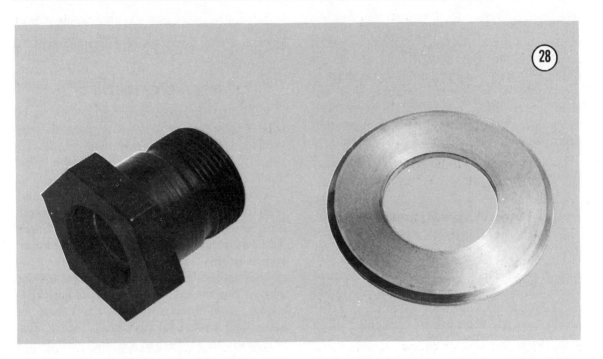

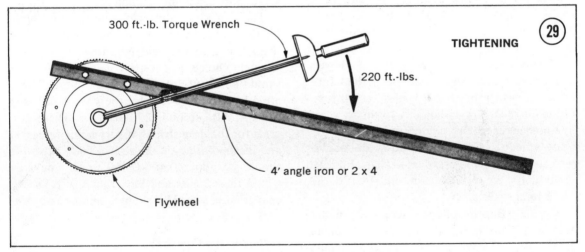

Table 4   DISPLACEMENT CHART

		Displacement							
Stroke	**Bore**	**83**	**85.5**	**87**	**88**	**90**	**92**	**94**	**100**
64		1385	1470	1522	1557	1629	1702	1777	2011
66		1428	1516	1569	1606	1679	1755	1832	2073
69		1493	1585	1641	1679	1756	1835	1915	2168
71		1537	1631	1688	1727	1807	1888	1971	2231
74		1602	1699	1760	1800	1883	1968	2054	2325
78		1688	1791	1855	1897	1985	2074	2165	2450
80		1721	1837	1902	1946	2035	2127	2221	2576
82		1775	1883	1950	1995	2087	2180	2276	2576
84		1818	1929	1997	2044	2138	2234	2332	2639

14

easily in the case is 82mm; but even shorter strokes can cause clearance problems at BDC. In addition, the piston tops will come right out of the cylinders at TDC, eliminating the mandatory 0.040 in. minimum clearance. You will need spacers under the barrels to re-establish the proper deck height. Finally, compression ratio is raised with a longer stroke; you may have to modify the cylinder heads to keep it below 9:1.

COUNTERWEIGHTED CRANKSHAFTS

Up to 5,000 rpm, the stock crank does well enough. Above this speed, it begins to pound the bearings into the bearing saddles. A roller crankshaft helps some, but as good or better results can be achieved by switching to a counterweighted crankshaft.

One of the oldest counterweighted crankshafts available is the Okrasa made in Germany. This crankshaft is forged from chrome-moly steel with integral weights. It is available in 74mm and 78mm strokes with 8 dowels. While more expensive ($300-450) than most available now, it has had a well-deserved reputation for reliability and quality for many years.

Another excellent counterweighted crankshaft is made by Gene Berg, who welds counterweights on the stock forged crankshaft. Finished crankshafts are available in 69, 74, 78, 82, and 84mm strokes.

Claude's Buggies offers a series of counterweighted crankshafts, that they say are manufactured by a VW original equipment manufacturer. These are available in 69, 74, 76, 78, and 82mm strokes.

Pauter Machine Company has a complete line of counterweighted crankshafts fabricated from genuine VW stock cranks. They have separate lines to use with stock VW rods, Chevrolet 350 (2.165 in. journal) rods, modified Chevrolet 327 rods, and modified Pinto rods.

Many counterweighted crankshafts are available through mail order. In some cases the quality is excellent, in other cases it is not too good. An item this important and expensive to return should probably be purchased from a local, trusted VW performance shop. It may cost more, but may save a lot of disappointment.

SPECIAL CAMSHAFTS

Replacing the stock camshaft is not to be taken lightly. It is too expensive and time consuming. Unless you consider your needs realistically, and prepare the engine with other modifications, you will end up with an engine you cannot live with.

Before even thinking about a camshaft replacement, get the engine breathing better. Add an extractor exhaust, 2-barrel carburetor, and matching intake manifold. Early 1200 engines should be increased to at least 1500cc with a big bore kit (82mm or larger). Exchange 1200 heads for 1500 single port, or better yet, 1600 dual port heads. Stock dual port heads are better than any stock or modified single port head you can find.

The number of different camshafts available for the VW is staggering. Rather than list all of them, here are some guidelines to help you make the right choice. For a street machine, duration should be about 260-280° and no more. These are often called ¾ race for the VW. A full race camshaft is around 290-300°+. These are great for the drag strip, but very temperamental and disappointing on the street. Total valve lift should be about 0.400-0.450 in. If you stay within these limits and buy from a well-known cam grinder, your VW should remain streetable.

Installing the Camshaft

Reputable cam suppliers like Iskenderian, Sig Erson, Racer Brown, and others provide a very high quality product. Their cams fit in the engine like a stock cam, using the same timing marks.

Cam grinding tolerances are fairly tight, and so are the tolerances of your VW engine. But individual camshafts and engines are different. Through no fault of the cam grinder, cam and engine tolerances can stack up to produce significant valve timing errors. To be safe, you must check actual valve timing with the cam installed in your engine. You have spent many hours tearing your engine down to get to the camshaft.

Now spend an extra couple hours checking the timing to prevent tearing it all down again.

Basically, the valve timing check ensures that the camshaft is installed in the correct relation to the crankshaft. The instructions with the cam explain how for that particular cam.

ROCKER ARM COVERS

Stock rocker arm covers can be a source of many annoying problems. Most of them leak, especially at high engine speeds. They may interfere with rocker arms if a high lift cam or rocker arm assembly is installed. If you do not have any of these problems, use the stock covers and save your money.

Valve interference is easily cured. If you have installed a high lift camshaft and/or a high lift rocker arm assembly, paint the inside of the rocker arm covers with Prussian (machinist's) blue, and install them on the engine. Turn the crankshaft several revolutions, but do not start the engine. Remove the covers and inspect the inside surface. If there are scratches or nicks in the blue dye, the cover interferes with the rocker arms. Try dimpling stock covers as shown in **Figure 30**. Use a rotary file to gain added clearance on cast covers. Do not take off any more metal than necessary.

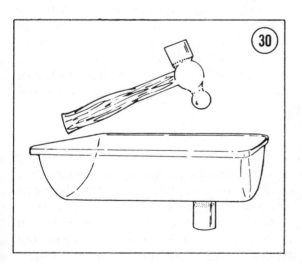

Several cast covers on the market are designed with extra clearance to prevent rocker arm interference. They also provide some cooling due to integral fins.

Chrome plated or polished metal rocker arm covers of any kind are to be avoided. Several advertise that they "improve cooling." In fact, they do just the opposite. The stock VW covers are painted black for a reason; black radiates heat better than polished metal. Better radiation means better cooling. Chrome plated surfaces are great for retaining heat; for example, turbocharger exhaust stacks. If you already have polished metal or chrome plated covers, sandblast them, then spray with a thin coat of flat black paint. Aluminum parts can be black anodized at many plating shops.

ROCKER ARMS

Stock rocker arms have a 1:1 ratio on 1200 engines and 1.1:1 on 1300-1600 engines. See **Figure 31**. The adjustable screw is at the valve end of the stock rocker arm. This is designed to contact the valve tip slightly off center (see **Figure 32**). The purpose is to rotate the valve slightly each time it is operated and improve valve face and seat life. Unfortunately, the resulting side force on the valve stem wears the valve guide prematurely and increases both heat and friction.

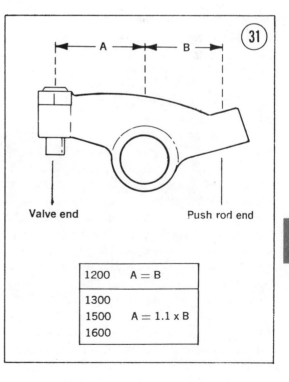

Valve end   Push rod end

1200	A = B
1300 1500 1600	A = 1.1 x B

14

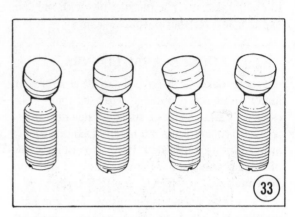

RIGHT

One solution to these problems is to install swivel-foot adjustable screws in the stock rocker arms. See **Figure 33**. These contact the valve tip squarely at all rocker arm angles.

Alignment between rocker arms and valve tips is disturbed by the following modifications:

a. Flycutting cylinder heads
b. Cylinder length
c. Pushrod length
d. Different camshaft
e. Different rocker arms

High Performance Rocker Arms

A number of high performance rocker arms are available for the VW. Most of these have the adjustable screw at the pushrod end of the arm. This permits the manufacturer to design a better rocker tip. Some manufacturers use a hardened radiused steel button at the valve end. Others harden the rocker tip and radius it (**Figure 34**).

Scat offers a high lift (1.4:1), wide roller lifter which contacts the valve tip. See **Figure 35A**. All of these designs reduce side loads on the valve stems, improve overall rocker geometry, and reduce friction.

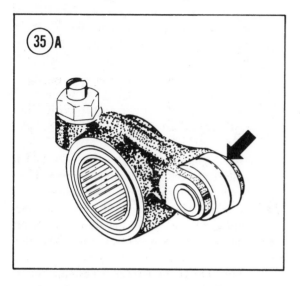

Some high performance rocker arms also contain roller bearings which ride on the rocker shaft. See **Figure 35B**. Stock rockers do not even have bushings and gall fairly quickly. Bearings reduce friction on the shaft to a minimum.

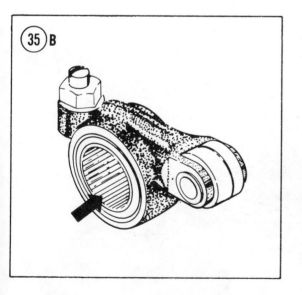

Several manufacturers offer high-lift rocker arms which incorporate the relocated adjustment screw and roller bearings discussed above.

In addition, they have either a 1.3, 1.4, 1.5, or 1.6 to 1 lift ratio compared to stock 1:1 (1.1:1 on the 1300/1500/1600 engine) and generate more valve lift with a given camshaft. For example, the intake valve lift on a stock 1600 engine is 0.322 in. By adding 1.4:1 rocker arms, lift is increased to 0.410 in. **Table 5**, below, shows how to estimate the final valve lift when installing high-lift rocker arms in place of stock 1.1:1 rocker arms.

Table 5   VALVE LIFT

Rocker Arm Ratio	Multiply Valve Lift[1] by
1.3	1.182
1.4	1.273
1.5	1.364
1. Valve lift produced with stock 1.1 rocker arms	

High-lift rocker arms are a simple way to add a few horsepower, provided you have made the same engine modifications suggested for a camshaft to improve breathing. Basically, these include extractor exhaust, 2-barrel carburetor with intake manifold and cylinder head improvements (if you have single port heads).

Nearly all high-lift rocker arms require shorter pushrods. These are available from the same source as the rocker arms. Besides being shorter, they are usually chrome-moly steel which is far more resistant to flexing than the aluminum used for stock pushrods.

VALVE SPRINGS

Changing the stock springs is not going to increase the performance of your engine. The stock springs are good for at least 5,000 rpm. The stock crankshaft is limited to 5,000-5,500 rpm anyway, so unless you have a better crankshaft, you have no business running above 5,000 rpm. If a better crankshaft permits operation over 5,000 rpm, then by all means get new springs rated for 6,000 rpm. Valve springs are available for use up to 6,000 rpm. Since these can only be used in a highly modified drag machine, their use on the street is a waste of horsepower, engine parts, and money.

14

VALVE SPRING RETAINERS

Practically everyone selling VW performance parts carries lightweight aluminum valve spring retainers. See **Figure 36**. They claim to be strong enough for high performance racing engines. However strong they claim to be, they shed aluminum flakes as they wear. These flakes are carried to all parts of the engine by the oil. The slight weight reduction over stock retainers is not justified in anything less than an all-out drag machine. Use stock late-model steel retainers. They are plenty strong and will not fill your valuable engine with metal flakes.

OVERSIZE AND SPECIAL VALVES

Bigger valves mean better breathing. Better breathing usually means more power. A number of VW enthusiasts have verified this by installing oversize valves. The benefits are even greater if a special camshaft is also installed. Bigger valves, a "mild" cam, and 2-barrel carburetion can add up to 30 horsepower.

We can only recommend bigger valves on dual port heads. If you have single port heads, spend the money on dual ports rather than bigger valves. The improvement in performance will be at least as great.

FLYWHEEL

The stock 18 pound flywheel robs the engine of power and responsiveness. Lightening the flywheel reduces its inertia and improves engine response. See **Figure 37**. Replacement flywheels are available from 5 to 12 pounds. The lightest flywheels are for racing and do not work well on the street. The best street flywheels are 10½ pounds or more. The 10½ pound flywheel is popular for off-road use also.

Lightened flywheels are drilled for 4 or 8 crankshaft dowels. Get the 8 dowel flywheel for reasons discussed earlier in this chapter under *Crank Dowels*.

Flywheel ring gears match either a 6-volt or a 12-volt starter. Replacement flywheels must be selected to fit the appropriate clutch disc diameter and starter voltage. This becomes particularly important when installing a 12-volt engine in a 6-volt car.

CLUTCH MODIFICATIONS

VW 1200 (40 hp)

The stock 180mm clutch is the weakest of all VW clutch systems.

To improve this clutch system, first replace the carbon release bearing with ball or roller

(36)

release bearing (VW 1200). For engine power up to 70-80 horsepower, install a 1961-1966 Transporter (Type II), 200mm flywheel and clutch assembly. To handle more than 80 horsepower, install a 180mm diaphragm clutch assembly and stock or lightened 10½-12 pound flywheel.

VW 1500/1600

The stock clutch assembly on these engines is fairly good up to 70-80 horsepower. For best performance in this range, install the latest stock 200mm diaphragm spring clutch assembly and a stock or lightened flywheel. To handle more than 80 horsepower, install a Crown, Claude's, or Gene Berg 200mm clutch assembly with a lightened flywheel. See **Figure 38**.

Quite often these 12-volt engines are installed in early 6-volt cars. This always means deciding whether to convert the car to 12 volts to match the engine or convert the engine to 6 volts to match the car. Keep in mind here that if you convert the engine to 6 volts, you must install a flywheel with a 6-volt ring gear.

TRANSAXLE

VW-based high performance vehicles, especially those used off-road, require some degree of strengthening of the transaxle. The exact degree depends on how the car is to be used. For severe street usage and light off-road driving, adding 2 more spider gears to the differential will probably do the job. This is a simple bolt-on modification, and kits (**Figure 39**) containing all necessary parts are available from many sources, including Crown Manufacturing Co., Inc., Gene Berg, and Claude's Buggies, Inc. For more severe usage, heavy duty replacement differentials, with 4 spider gears, and beefed up side covers, as well as solid transmission mounts, are available from the same sources. All of these kits come with fairly complete instructions, and can be installed by the amateur mechanic with a reasonable amount of skill.

TURBOCHARGING

Turbocharging has long been associated with high-altitude aircraft and industrial engines. Its use in passenger automobiles has been very limited; and application by hot rodders has been only slightly more frequent. The fact remains, though, that turbocharging is the most effective and easiest way to significantly increase output from an internal combustion engine.

Special high-lift cams, multiple carburetors, high compression heads, and tuned exhaust systems cannot compare to simply forcing more

14

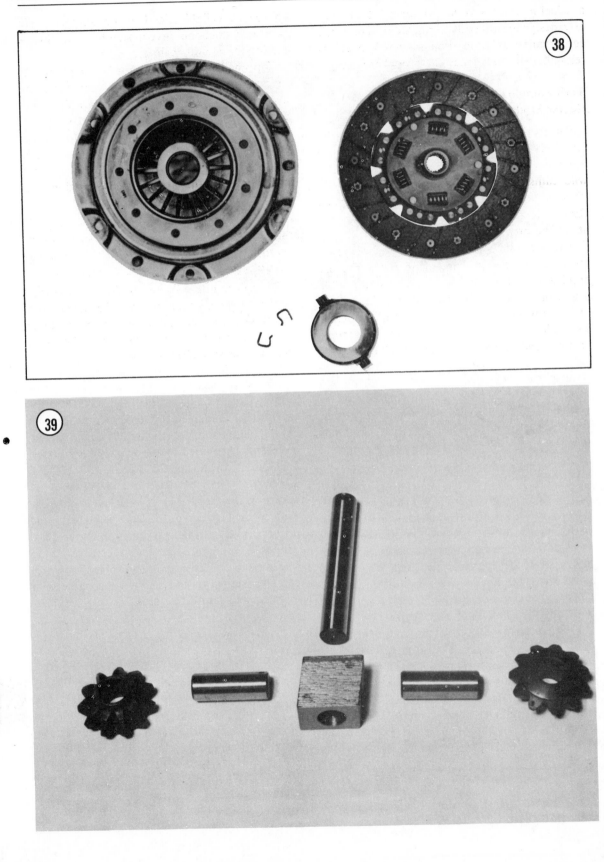

air/fuel mixture into the cylinders with a properly designed supercharger system. The ultra-conservative aviation industry has proven the reliability and efficiency of turbocharging.

Turbocharging Versus Conventional Engine Modifications

Turbocharging has not had the popularity among hot rodders that "conventional" engine modifications, such as increased displacement, wild cams, and big carburetors have enjoyed. This is not an indictment of turbocharging. Rather it reflects the widespread ignorance about the process.

The ignorance is justified. A turbocharger must be matched to an engine for a specific application. This matching requires selection of a specific size turbocharger and selection of the proper turbine housing for the turbocharger. Turbocharger selection requires detailed specifications and compressor maps for all the turbo-chargers available; and manufacturers have been very uncooperative in supplying this information for one-off engines.

Turbine housing selection is "cut-and-try." It involves trying several housings until the compressor performs properly in the operating range desired. Not many people would be willing to invest in a large inventory of housings to hot rod the family car. Turbocharging thus has not been popular simply because hot rodders have not had access to the necessary information and equipment to properly install a unit.

The BAE kits change all this for the VW owner. Now the question is, is turbocharging an acceptable and possibly more desirable alternative to conventional performance modifying?

Turbocharging will nearly double performance of a stock engine for 8 to 16 hours work and less than $1,000. As a comparison, building a 100 horsepower engine will take a week or two and about $1,500 or more.

14

Table 1   PERFORMANCE EQUIPMENT SUPPLIERS

Addco Industries, 151 Watertown Road, Lake Park, Florida 33403

Gene Berg, 1725 North Lime Street, Orange, California 92665

Bosch Products (Most VW and performance equipment dealers)

Bugpack (Products available only through authorized dealers)

Centerline, 13521 Freeway Drive, Santa Fe Springs, California 90280

Dick Cepek, 9201 California Avenue, South Gate, California 90280

Chenowth Racing Products, Inc., 943 Vernon Way, El Cajon, California 92020

Claude's Buggies, Inc., 28813 Farmersville Boulevard, Farmersville, California 93223

Crown Manufacturing Company, 858 Production Place, Newport Beach, California 92663

Elite Enterprises, Inc., 690 East Third Street, Cokato, Minnesota 55321

Fiber-Tech Engineering, Inc., 10809 Prospect Avenue, Santee, California 92071

Fourtuned Exhaust Company, 5953 Ordway, Riverside, California 92504

Iskenderian Racing Cams, 16020 South Broadway, Gardena, California 90248

IECO, 1431-D Broadway, Santa Monica, California 90404

Jackman Wheels, 1000 North Johnson Avenue, El Cajon, California 92020
  or 3221 Woodson Road, St. Louis, Missouri 63114

Motion Minicar Corporation, 594 Sunrise Highway, Baldwin, New York 11510

Pauter Machine Company, 367 Zenith Street, Chula Vista, California 92011

Racer Brown, Inc., 9270 Borden Avenue, Sun Valley, California 91352

RAC Instruments, 3485 South La Cienega Boulevard, Los Angeles, California 90016

Rayjay Turbochargers, BAE (a division of Turdyne Corporation)
  3032 Kashiwa Street, Torrance, California 90505

S&S Headers, Inc., 3430 West Carriage Drive, Santa Ana, California 92704

Scat Enterprises, P.O. Box 4096, Inglewood, California 90302

Sig Erson Racing Cams, Inc., 20925-27 Brant Avenue, Long Beach, California 90810

Stuska Engineering Company, 1900 West Colfax Avenue, Denver, Colorado 80204

Sway-A-Way Company, 7840 Burnett Avenue, Van Nuys, California 91405

VDO Instruments, 116 Victor Avenue, Detroit, Michigan 48203

APPENDIX

MODEL IDENTIFICATION

This appendix includes general specifications for all models since 1961. These specifications are given in **Table 1. Table 2** matches chassis numbers to engine numbers.

WHAT YEAR IS IT?

It's not easy to tell one year from another. External changes throughout the years have been relatively minor. The only *positive* way to tell the year is by chassis number. Volkswagen began a chassis numbering sequence that ran consecutively from the 1940's through 1964. To determine the year, refer to **Figures 1A through 1E** or Table 2 and find the range in which your chassis number fits.

Beginning in 1965, VW incorporated the year and model in the chassis number. The first 2 digits identify the modeal as a Beetle (11) or a Karmann Ghia (14). The 3rd digit is the last digit of the year, e.g., 5 would indicate 1965 and 2 would indicate 1972. The last 6 to 7 digits are the chassis serial number.

Figure 2 shows the chassis number and engine number location. Note the chassis number:

a. Stamped on the frame tunnel under the rear seat.

b. On the ID plate behind the spare tire on all except Super Beetles.

c. On the ID plate next to the front hood lock on Super Beetles.

On all cars since January 1, 1969, at the top edge of the instrument panel.

The engine number is stamped on the generator support flange as shown in the figure. Note the code letter preceding the numbers.

Figures 1A through 1E show all changes which occurred from 1961 to the present. But remember, the presence of one or more of these changes does not identify a particular model year. Parts are very easily changed, and the previous owner may have updated his Beetle. Uses Figures 1-1E as a guide. Then check chassis *and* engine number.

Table 1   GENERAL SPECIFICATIONS

	1961-1966	1967
Overall length		
Sedan & Convertible	160" (4070mm)	160" (4070mm)
Karmann Ghia	163" (4110mm)	163" (4110mm)
Super Beetle (Sedan & Convertible)	— — —	— — —
Overall width		
Sedan & Convertible	60.6" (1540mm)	60.6" (1540mm)
Karmann Ghia	64.3" (1634mm)	64.3" (1634mm)
Super Beetle (Sedan & Convertible)	— — —	— — —
Wheelbase		
Sedan, Karmann Ghia, & Convertible	94.5" (2400mm)	94.5" (2400mm)
Super Beetle (Sedan & Convertible)	— — —	— — —
Track		
Sedan, Karmann Ghia, & Convertible		
Front	51.4" (1305mm)	51.4" (1305mm)
Rear	51.2" (1300mm)	51.2" (1300mm)
Track		
Super Beetle (Sedan & Convertible)		
Front	— — —	— — —
Rear	— — —	— — —
Turning Circle		
Sedan, Karmann Ghia, & Convertible	34'6" (10.5m)	34'6" (10.5m)
Super Beetle (Sedan & Convertible)	— — —	— — —
Ground clearance (fully laden)	6" (152mm)	6" (152mm)
Curb weight		
Sedan	1720 lb (780 kg)	1764 lb (800 kg)
Convertible (all)	1808 lb (820 kg)	1852 lb (840 kg)
Karmann Ghia	1830 lb (830 kg)	1852 lb (840 kg)
Super Beetle (Sedan)	— — —	— — —
Maximum load		
Sedan	838 lb (380 kg)	838 lb (380 kg)
Convertible (all)	794 lb (360 kg)	794 lb (360 kg)
Karmann Ghia	727 lb (330 kg)	727 lb (330 kg)
Super Beetle (Sedan)	— — —	— — —
Maximum total weight		
Sedan	2556 lb (1160 kg)	2602 lb (1180 kg)
Convertible (all)	2600 lb (1180 kg)	2645 lb (1200 kg)
Super Beetle (Sedan)	— — —	— — —

Table 1   GENERAL SPECIFICATIONS (continued)

	1968	1969
Overall length		
Sedan & Convertible	158.6" (4030mm)	158.6" (4030mm)
Karmann Ghia	163" (4110mm)	163" (4110mm)
Super Beetle (Sedan & Convertible)	— — —	— — —
Overall width		
Sedan & Convertible	60.6" (1540mm)	61" (1550mm)
Karmann Ghia	64.3" (1634mm)	64.3" (1634mm)
Super Beetle (Sedan & Convertible)	— — —	— — —
Wheelbase		
Sedan, Karmann Ghia, & Convertible	94.5" (2400mm)	94.5" (2400mm)
Super Beetle (Sedan & Convertible)	— — —	— — —
Track		
Sedan, Karmann Ghia, & Convertible		
Front	51.6" (1310mm)	51.6" (1310mm)
Rear	53.2" (1350mm)	53.2" (1350mm)
Track		
Super Beetle (Sedan & Convertible)		
Front	— — —	— — —
Rear	— — —	— — —
Turning circle		
Sedan, Karmann Ghia, & Convertible	34'6" (10.5m)	34'6" (10.5m)
Super Beetle (Sedan & Convertible)	— — —	— — —
Ground clearance (fully laden)	6" (152mm)	6" (152mm)
Curb weight		
Sedan	1812 lb (822 kg)	1808 lb (820 kg)
Convertible (all)	1922 lb (872 kg)	1918 lb (870 kg)
Karmann Ghia	1918 lb (870 kg)	1918 lb (870 kg)
Super Beetle (Sedan)	— — —	— — —
Maximum load		
Sedan	838 lb (380 kg)	838 lb (380 kg)
Convertible (all)	794 lb (360 kg)	794 lb (360 kg)
Karmann Ghia	727 lb (330 kg)	727 lb (330 kg)
Super Beetle (Sedan)	— — —	— — —
Maximum total weight		
Sedan	2646 lb (1200 kg)	2646 lb (1200 kg)
Convertible (all)	2712 lb (1230 kg)	2712 lb (1230 kg)
Super Beetle (Sedan)	— — —	— — —

15

Table 1   GENERAL SPECIFICATIONS (continued)

	1970	1971-1974
Overall length		
Sedan & Convertible	158.6" (4030mm)	158.6" (4030mm)
Karmann Ghia	163" (4110mm)	162.6" (4140mm)
Super Beetle (Sedan & Convertible)	— — —	160.6" (4080mm)
Overall width		
Sedan & Convertible	61" (1550mm)	61" (1550mm)
Karmann Ghia	64.3" (1634mm)	64.3" (1634mm)
Super Beetle (Sedan & Convertible)	— — —	62.3" (1585mm)
Wheelbase		
Sedan, Karmann Ghia, & Convertible	94.5" (2400mm)	94.5" (2400mm)
Super Beetle (Sedan & Convertible)	— — —	95.3" (2420mm)
Track		
Sedan, Karmann Ghia, & Convertible		
Front	51.6" (1310mm)	51.6" (1310mm)
Rear	53.2" (1350mm)	53.2" (1350mm)
Track		
Super Beetle (Sedan & Convertible)		
Front	— — —	54.1" (1375mm)
Rear	— — —	53.1" (1350mm)
Turning circle		
Sedan, Karmann Ghia, & Convertible	34'6" (10.5m)	34'6" (10.5m)
Super Beetle (Sedan & Convertible)	— — —	31'5" (9.6m)
Ground clearance (fully laden)	6" (152mm)	6" (152mm)
Curb weight		
Sedan	1808 lb (820 kg)	1808 lb (820 kg)
Convertible (all)	1918 lb (870 kg)	2028 lb (920 kg)
Karmann Ghia	1918 lb (870 kg)	1918 lb (870 kg)
Super Beetle (Sedan)	— — —	1918 lb (870 kg)
Maximum load		
Sedan	838 lb (380 kg)	838 lb (380 kg)
Convertible (all)	794 lb (360 kg)	794 lb (360 kg)
Karmann Ghia	727 lb (330 kg)	727 lb (330 kg)
Super Beetle (Sedan)	— — —	881 lb (400 kg)
Maximum total weight		
Sedan	2646 lb (1200 kg)	2646 lb (1200 kg)
Convertible (all)	2712 lb (1230 kg)	2821 lb (1280 kg)
Super Beetle (Sedan)	— — —	2799 lb (1270 kg)

Table 1   **GENERAL SPECIFICATIONS** (continued)

1975 ON	
Overall length	
Sedan & Convertible	163.4″
Karmann Ghia	——
Super Beetle (Sedan & Convertible)	164.8″
Overall width	
Sedan & Convertible	61.0″
Karmann Ghia	——
Super Beetle (Sedan & Convertible)	62.4″
Wheelbase	
Sedan, Karmann Ghia, & Convertible	94.5″
Super Beetle (Sedan & Convertible)	95.3″
Track	
Sedan, Karmann Ghia, & Convertible	
Front	51.5″
Rear	53.1″
Track	
Super Beetle (Sedan & Convertible)	
Front	54.9″
Rear	53.1″
Turning circle	
Sedan, Karmann Ghia, & Convertible	36.0 ft.
Super Beetle (Sedan & Convertible)	31.5 ft.
Ground clearance (fully laden)	5.9″
Curb weight	
Sedan	1,973 lb.
Convertible (all)	2,127 lb.
Karmann Ghia	——
Super Beetle (Sedan)	2,072 lb.
Maximum load	
Sedan	735 lb.
Convertible (all)	715 lb.
Karmann Gha	——
Super Beetle (Sedan)	735 lb.
Maximum total weight	
Sedan	2,712 lb.
Convertible (all)	2,844 lb.
Super Beetle (Sedan)	2,844 lb.

15

Table 2 ENGINE AND CHASSIS NUMBERS

Year	Chassis Number	Engine Number	Disp.	HP
1961	3,192,507 - 4,010,994	5,000,001 - 8,309,892		
1962	4,010,995 - 4,846,835			
1963	4,846,836 - 5,677,118		1200	40
1964	5,677,119 - 6,502,399			
1965	115 000 001 -		1200	40
	145 000 001 -	D		
1966	116 000 001 -		1300	50
	146 000 001 -	F		
1967	117 000 001 -			
	147 000 001 -			
1968	118 000 001 -			
	148 000 001 -	H	1500	53
1969	119 000 001 -			
	149 000 001 -			
1970	1102 000 001 -		1600	57
	1402 000 001 -	B		
1971	1112 000 001 -		1600	60
	1412 000 001 -	AE		
1972	1122 000 001 -			
	1422 000 001 -			
1973	1132 000 001 -		1600	46
	1432 000 001 -	AH		
1974	1142 000 001 -			
	1442 000 001 -			
1975	1152 000 001 -		1600	48
	1352 000 001 -			
1976	1162 000 001 -			
1977	1172 000 001 -			
1978*	1582 000 001 -			
1979*	1592 000 001 -			

* Convertible only

1976-1977 BEETLE AND SUPER BEETLE

(1) A

1. New speedometer with outer scale in miles per hour and inner scale in kilometers per hour (on most 1976 models)
2. Redesigned front seats with improved back adjustment, for added comfort and body support
3. 2-speed fresh air blower
4. All trim components chrome-plated
5. Automatic Stick Shift (option) discontinued
6. Standard rear window defogger
7. Standard sports-style wheel rims and full carpeting
8. High altitude kit on 1977 models that will be operated at altitudes over 4,000 ft. above sea level.

1975 BEETLE AND SUPER BEETLE

1. Electronic fuel injection, with "fuel injection" insignia on rear deck lid
2. Single tailpipe
3. Increased horsepower; 48 hp, up from 46 (SAE net)
4. Clutch pedal pressure eased
5. Larger exhaust valve stems for better heat transfer
6. New heat exchangers for greater heater output
7. Installation of battery ground cable with diagnosis contact for more accurate computer analysis readings

8. Odometer triggers red warning light "EGR" in speedometer to notify driver of service requirements
9. California models with catalytic converter require lead-free gasoline; fuel filler neck has smaller opening for nozzle
10. Maintenance intervals extended to 15,000 miles

15

① B

1974 BEETLE AND SUPER BEETLE

1. New windshield wiper arms.
2. Redesigned dash.
3. Improved transmission mounts.
4. Parking lock on Automatic Stick Shift.
5. Reinforced side guard doors.

6. Exhaust gas recirculation modifications.
7. Larger taillights.
8. Curved windshield.
9. Improved fresh air ventilation.

1973 BEETLE AND SUPER BEETLE

1. Energy absorbing bumpers.
2. Safety interlock seat belts.
3. Modified exhaust gas recirculation.

4. TDC sensor flywheel.
5. Negative steering roll radius (113 only).
6. New cylinder head alloy.

1972 BEETLE AND SUPER BEETLE

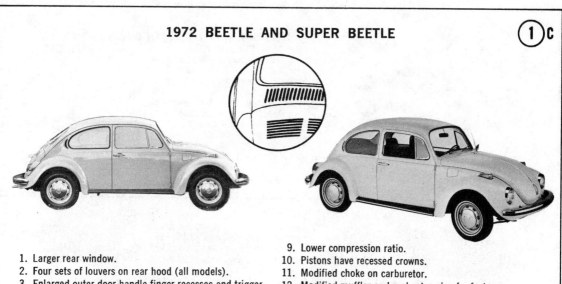

1. Larger rear window.
2. Four sets of louvers on rear hood (all models).
3. Enlarged outer door handle finger recesses and trigger.
4. Lid over rear luggage area.
5. New safety steering wheel.
6. Rubber body mounts to reduce noise.
7. Windshield wiper switch on steering column.
8. Modified brake warning light circuit.
9. Lower compression ratio.
10. Pistons have recessed crowns.
11. Modified choke on carburetor.
12. Modified muffler and preheater pipe for faster preheating.
13. Preheated air controlled by temperature and engine vacuum.
14. Special system on automatic stick shifts to reduce nitrogen oxides.

1971 BEETLE

1. Increased horsepower, from 57 to 60.
2. Flow-through ventilation with exhaust ports behind rear side windows.
3. Headlights automatically go off and parking lights stay on when ignition is turned off.
4. Larger taillights.

1971 SUPER BEETLE

1. In addition to major improvements built into the 1971 Beetle, the Super Beetle features fan-powered flow-through ventilation.
2. Nearly double the trunk space of the Beetle. Spare tire positioned horizontally under trunk floor.
3. New coil spring front suspension giving the car a wider front track and tighter turning circle.
4. Carpeted floors.
5. Rubber bumper inserts.

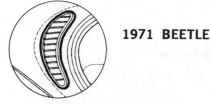

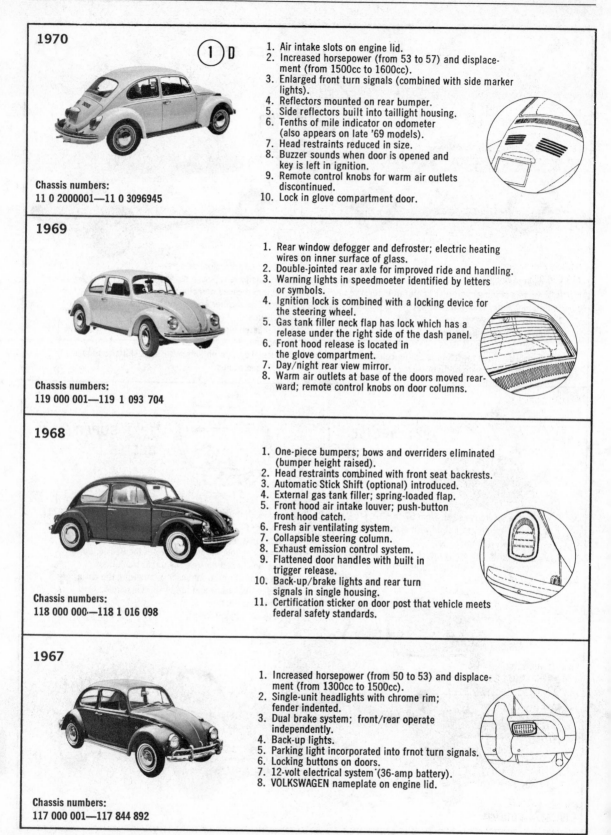

1970

1. Air intake slots on engine lid.
2. Increased horsepower (from 53 to 57) and displacement (from 1500cc to 1600cc).
3. Enlarged front turn signals (combined with side marker lights).
4. Reflectors mounted on rear bumper.
5. Side reflectors built into taillight housing.
6. Tenths of mile indicator on odometer (also appears on late '69 models).
7. Head restraints reduced in size.
8. Buzzer sounds when door is opened and key is left in ignition.
9. Remote control knobs for warm air outlets discontinued.
10. Lock in glove compartment door.

Chassis numbers:
11 0 2000001—11 0 3096945

1969

1. Rear window defogger and defroster; electric heating wires on inner surface of glass.
2. Double-jointed rear axle for improved ride and handling.
3. Warning lights in speedmoeter identified by letters or symbols.
4. Ignition lock is combined with a locking device for the steering wheel.
5. Gas tank filler neck flap has lock which has a release under the right side of the dash panel.
6. Front hood release is located in the glove compartment.
7. Day/night rear view mirror.
8. Warm air outlets at base of the doors moved rearward; remote control knobs on door columns.

Chassis numbers:
119 000 001—119 1 093 704

1968

1. One-piece bumpers; bows and overriders eliminated (bumper height raised).
2. Head restraints combined with front seat backrests.
3. Automatic Stick Shift (optional) introduced.
4. External gas tank filler; spring-loaded flap.
5. Front hood air intake louver; push-button front hood catch.
6. Fresh air ventilating system.
7. Collapsible steering column.
8. Exhaust emission control system.
9. Flattened door handles with built in trigger release.
10. Back-up/brake lights and rear turn signals in single housing.
11. Certification sticker on door post that vehicle meets federal safety standards.

Chassis numbers:
118 000 000—118 1 016 098

1967

1. Increased horsepower (from 50 to 53) and displacement (from 1300cc to 1500cc).
2. Single-unit headlights with chrome rim; fender indented.
3. Dual brake system; front/rear operate independently.
4. Back-up lights.
5. Parking light incorporated into frnot turn signals.
6. Locking buttons on doors.
7. 12-volt electrical system (36-amp battery).
8. VOLKSWAGEN nameplate on engine lid.

Chassis numbers:
117 000 001—117 844 892

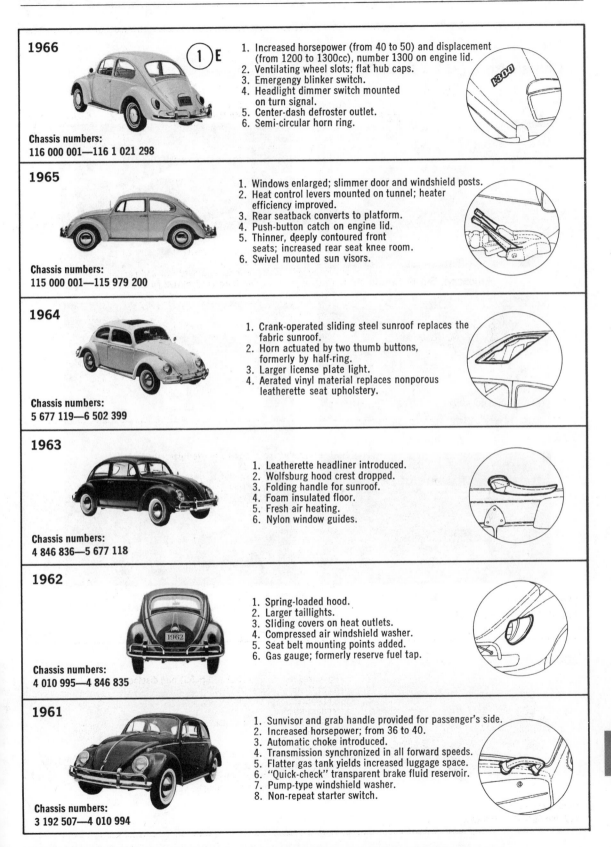

1966

1. Increased horsepower (from 40 to 50) and displacement (from 1200 to 1300cc), number 1300 on engine lid.
2. Ventilating wheel slots; flat hub caps.
3. Emergengy blinker switch.
4. Headlight dimmer switch mounted on turn signal.
5. Center-dash defroster outlet.
6. Semi-circular horn ring.

Chassis numbers:
116 000 001—116 1 021 298

1965

1. Windows enlarged; slimmer door and windshield posts.
2. Heat control levers mounted on tunnel; heater efficiency improved.
3. Rear seatback converts to platform.
4. Push-button catch on engine lid.
5. Thinner, deeply contoured front seats; increased rear seat knee room.
6. Swivel mounted sun visors.

Chassis numbers:
115 000 001—115 979 200

1964

1. Crank-operated sliding steel sunroof replaces the fabric sunroof.
2. Horn actuated by two thumb buttons, formerly by half-ring.
3. Larger license plate light.
4. Aerated vinyl material replaces nonporous leatherette seat upholstery.

Chassis numbers:
5 677 119—6 502 399

1963

1. Leatherette headliner introduced.
2. Wolfsburg hood crest dropped.
3. Folding handle for sunroof.
4. Foam insulated floor.
5. Fresh air heating.
6. Nylon window guides.

Chassis numbers:
4 846 836—5 677 118

1962

1. Spring-loaded hood.
2. Larger taillights.
3. Sliding covers on heat outlets.
4. Compressed air windshield washer.
5. Seat belt mounting points added.
6. Gas gauge; formerly reserve fuel tap.

Chassis numbers:
4 010 995—4 846 835

1961

1. Sunvisor and grab handle provided for passenger's side.
2. Increased horsepower; from 36 to 40.
3. Automatic choke introduced.
4. Transmission synchronized in all forward speeds.
5. Flatter gas tank yields increased luggage space.
6. "Quick-check" transparent brake fluid reservoir.
7. Pump-type windshield washer.
8. Non-repeat starter switch.

Chassis numbers:
3 192 507—4 010 994

15

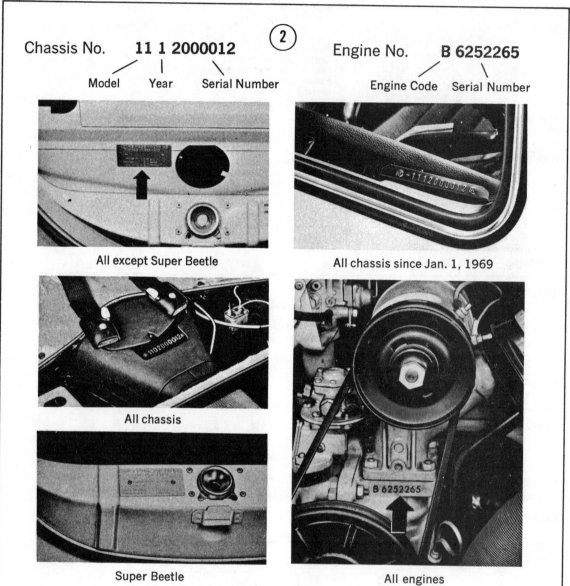

Chassis No. **11 1 2000012** ②   Engine No. **B 6252265**

Model   Year   Serial Number   Engine Code   Serial Number

All except Super Beetle

All chassis since Jan. 1, 1969

All chassis

Super Beetle

All engines

INDEX

16

V

W

16

NOTES

NOTES

NOTES

NOTES

NOTES

NOTES

LIST OF WIRING DIAGRAMS

1961 BEETLE

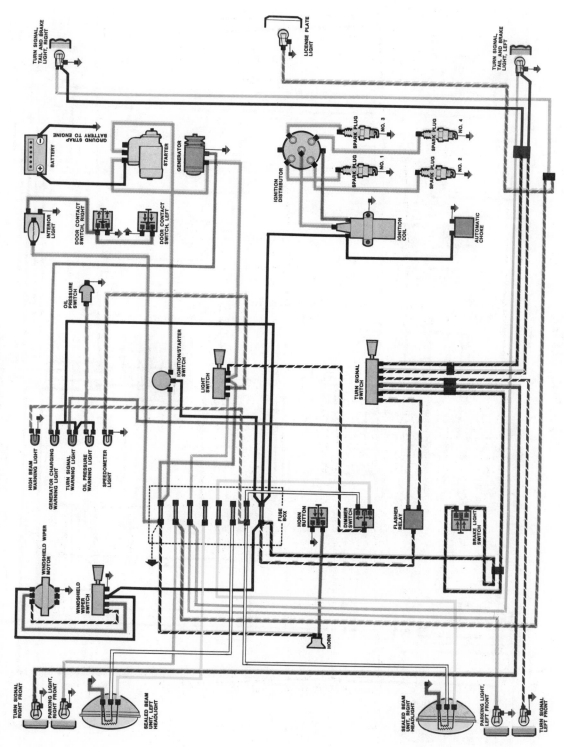

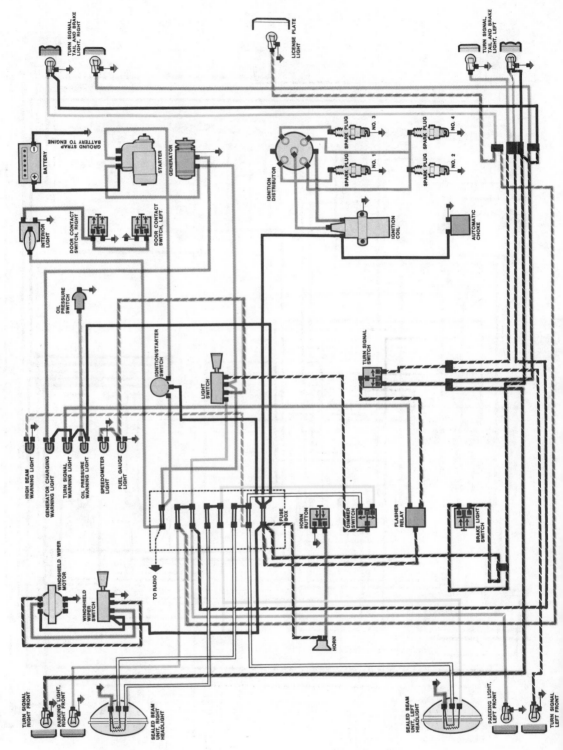

1962-1965 BEETLE

TURN SIGNAL, TAIL AND BRAKE LIGHT, RIGHT

LICENSE PLATE LIGHT

TURN SIGNAL, TAIL AND BRAKE LIGHT, LEFT

BATTERY

GROUND STRAP BATTERY TO ENGINE

STARTER

GENERATOR

IGNITION DISTRIBUTOR

SPARK PLUG NO. 3

SPARK PLUG NO. 1

SPARK PLUG NO. 4

SPARK PLUG NO. 2

INTERIOR LIGHT

DOOR CONTACT SWITCH, RIGHT

DOOR CONTACT SWITCH, LEFT

IGNITION COIL

AUTOMATIC CHOKE

OIL PRESSURE SWITCH

IGNITION/STARTER SWITCH

LIGHT SWITCH

TURN SIGNAL SWITCH

HIGH BEAM WARNING LIGHT

GENERATOR CHARGING WARNING LIGHT

TURN SIGNAL WARNING LIGHT

OIL PRESSURE WARNING LIGHT

SPEEDOMETER LIGHT

FUEL GAUGE LIGHT

FUSE BOX

HORN BUTTON

DIMMER SWITCH

FLASHER RELAY

BRAKE LIGHT SWITCH

WINDSHIELD WIPER MOTOR

WINDSHIELD WIPER SWITCH

TO RADIO

HORN

TURN SIGNAL RIGHT FRONT

PARKING LIGHT, RIGHT FRONT

SEALED BEAM UNIT RIGHT HEADLIGHT

SEALED BEAM UNIT, LEFT HEADLIGHT

PARKING LIGHT, LEFT FRONT

TURN SIGNAL LEFT FRONT

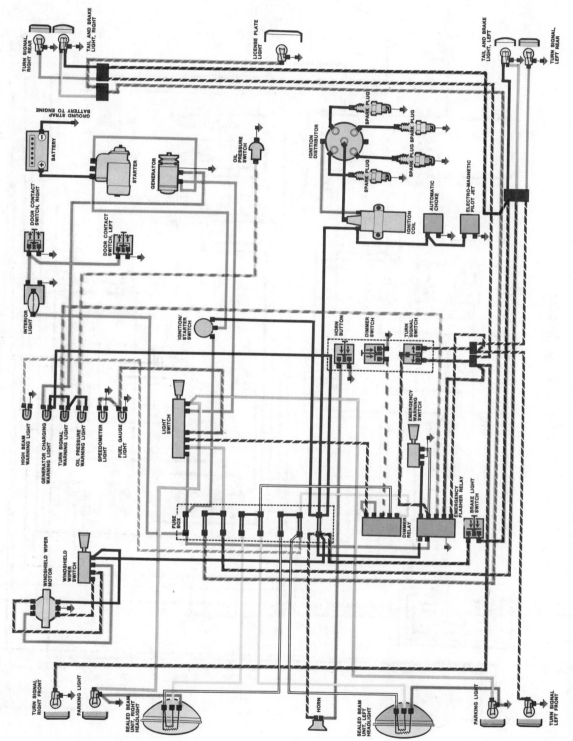

1966 BEETLE

TURN SIGNAL RIGHT REAR

TAIL AND BRAKE LIGHT, RIGHT

LICENSE PLATE LIGHT

TAIL AND BRAKE LIGHT, LEFT

TURN SIGNAL LEFT REAR

GROUND STRAP BATTERY TO ENGINE

BATTERY

STARTER

GENERATOR

OIL PRESSURE SWITCH

IGNITION DISTRIBUTOR

SPARK PLUG

SPARK PLUG

SPARK PLUG

SPARK PLUG

SPARK PLUG

IGNITION COIL

AUTOMATIC CHOKE

ELECTRO-MAGNETIC PILOT JET

DOOR CONTACT SWITCH, RIGHT

DOOR CONTACT SWITCH, LEFT

INTERIOR LIGHT

IGNITION/STARTER SWITCH

HORN BUTTON

DIMMER SWITCH

TURN SIGNAL SWITCH

EMERGENCY WARNING SWITCH

HIGH BEAM WARNING LIGHT

GENERATOR CHARGING WARNING LIGHT

TURN SIGNAL WARNING LIGHT

OIL PRESSURE WARNING LIGHT

SPEEDOMETER LIGHT

FUEL GAUGE LIGHT

LIGHT SWITCH

FUSE BOX

DIMMER RELAY

EMERGENCY FLASHER RELAY

BRAKE LIGHT SWITCH

WINDSHIELD WIPER MOTOR

WINDSHIELD WIPER SWITCH

TURN SIGNAL RIGHT FRONT

PARKING LIGHT

SEALED BEAM UNIT, RIGHT HEADLIGHT

HORN

SEALED BEAM UNIT, LEFT HEADLIGHT

PARKING LIGHT

TURN SIGNAL LEFT FRONT

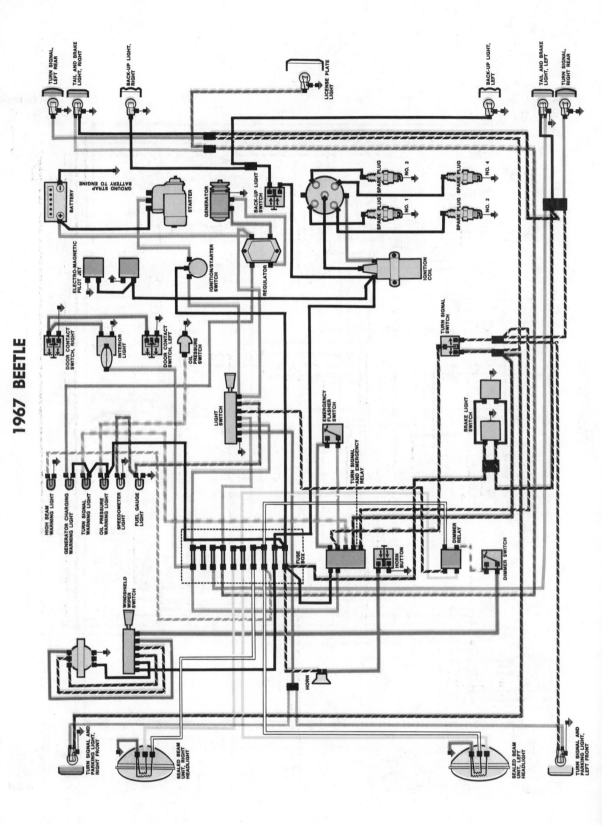

1967 BEETLE

TURN SIGNAL, LEFT REAR
TAIL AND BRAKE LIGHT, RIGHT
BACK-UP LIGHT, RIGHT
LICENSE PLATE LIGHT
BACK-UP LIGHT, LEFT
TAIL AND BRAKE LIGHT, LEFT
TURN SIGNAL, RIGHT REAR

BATTERY
GROUND STRAP BATTERY TO ENGINE
STARTER
GENERATOR
BACK-UP LIGHT SWITCH
SPARK PLUG NO. 3
SPARK PLUG NO. 4
SPARK PLUG NO. 1
SPARK PLUG NO. 2

ELECTRO-MAGNETIC PILOT JET
IGNITION/STARTER SWITCH
REGULATOR
IGNITION COIL

DOOR CONTACT SWITCH, RIGHT
INTERIOR LIGHT
DOOR CONTACT SWITCH, LEFT
OIL PRESSURE SWITCH
TURN SIGNAL SWITCH

LIGHT SWITCH
EMERGENCY FLASHER SWITCH
TURN SIGNAL AND EMERGENCY RELAY
BRAKE LIGHT SWITCH

HIGH BEAM WARNING LIGHT
GENERATOR CHARGING WARNING LIGHT
TURN SIGNAL WARNING LIGHT
OIL PRESSURE WARNING LIGHT
SPEEDOMETER LIGHT
FUEL GAUGE LIGHT

FUSE BOX
HORN BUTTON
DIMMER RELAY
DIMMER SWITCH

WINDSHIELD WIPER SWITCH
HORN

TURN SIGNAL AND PARKING LIGHT, RIGHT FRONT
SEALED BEAM UNIT, RIGHT HEADLIGHT
SEALED BEAM UNIT, LEFT HEADLIGHT
TURN SIGNAL AND PARKING LIGHT, LEFT FRONT

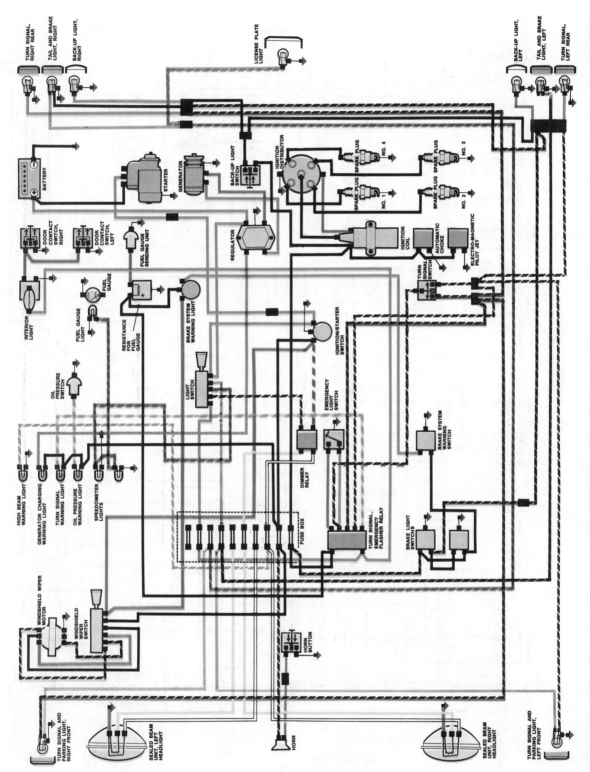

1968 BEETLE

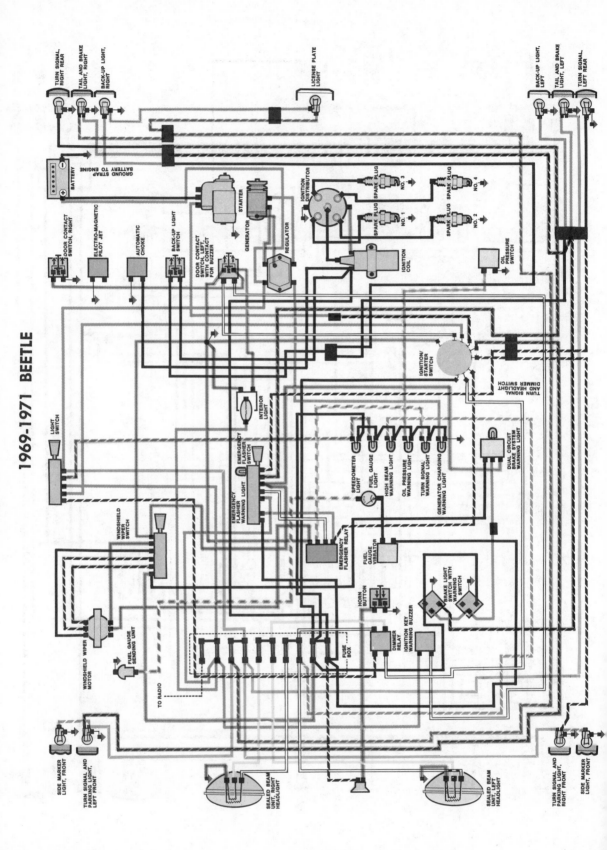

1969-1971 BEETLE

TURN SIGNAL, RIGHT REAR
TAIL AND BRAKE LIGHT, RIGHT
BACK-UP LIGHT, RIGHT
LICENSE PLATE LIGHT
BACK-UP LIGHT, LEFT
TAIL AND BRAKE LIGHT, LEFT
TURN SIGNAL, LEFT REAR

BATTERY
GROUND STRAP BATTERY TO ENGINE
STARTER
GENERATOR
REGULATOR
IGNITION DISTRIBUTOR
SPARK PLUG NO. 3
SPARK PLUG NO. 4
SPARK PLUG NO. 1
SPARK PLUG NO. 2
IGNITION COIL
OIL PRESSURE SWITCH

DOOR CONTACT SWITCH, RIGHT
ELECTRO-MAGNETIC PILOT JET
AUTOMATIC CHOKE
BACK-UP LIGHT SWITCH
DOOR CONTACT SWITCH, LEFT WITH CONTACT FOR BUZZER

IGNITION/STARTER SWITCH
TURN SIGNAL AND HEADLIGHT DIMMER SWITCH

LIGHT SWITCH
INTERIOR LIGHT
EMERGENCY FLASHER SWITCH
EMERGENCY FLASHER WARNING LIGHT

SPEEDOMETER LIGHT
FUEL GAUGE LIGHT
HIGH BEAM LIGHT
OIL PRESSURE WARNING LIGHT
TURN SIGNAL WARNING LIGHT
GENERATOR CHARGING WARNING LIGHT
DUAL CIRCUIT BRAKE SYSTEM WARNING LIGHT

WINDSHIELD WIPER SWITCH
EMERGENCY FLASHER RELAY
FUEL GAUGE VIBRATOR

BRAKE LIGHT SWITCH WITH WARNING SWITCH

WINDSHIELD WIPER MOTOR
FUEL GAUGE SENDING UNIT
TO RADIO

HORN BUTTON
FUSE BOX
DIMMER RELAY
IGNITION KEY WARNING BUZZER

SIDE MARKER LIGHT, FRONT
TURN SIGNAL AND PARKING LIGHT, LEFT FRONT
SEALED BEAM UNIT, RIGHT HEADLIGHT
SEALED BEAM UNIT, LEFT HEADLIGHT
TURN SIGNAL AND PARKING LIGHT, RIGHT FRONT
SIDE MARKER LIGHT, FRONT

Page 6

1970-1971 BEETLE SUPPLEMENT
(Automatic Stick Shift & Rear Window Defogger)

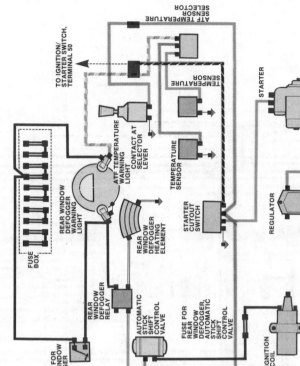

1971 SUPER BEETLE SUPPLEMENT
Automatic Stick Shift, Rear Window Defogger, Fresh Air Fan)

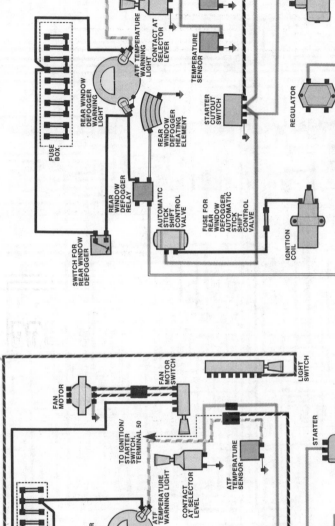

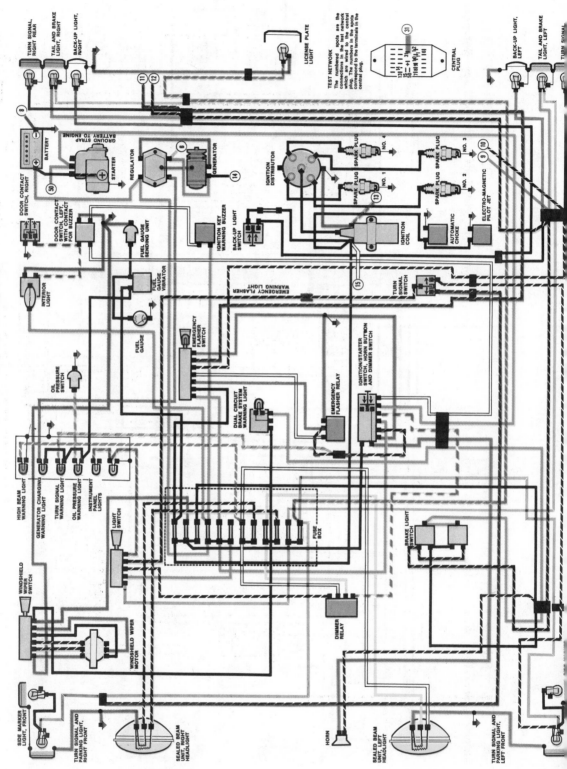

1971 SUPER BEETLE

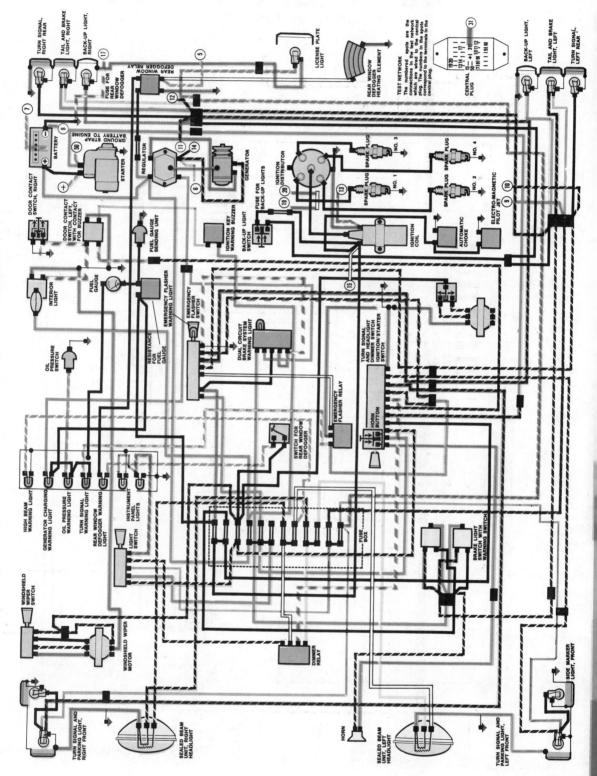

1972 BEETLE AND SUPER BEETLE

1972 BEETLE AND SUPER BEETLE SUPPLEMENT
(Automatic Stick Shift)

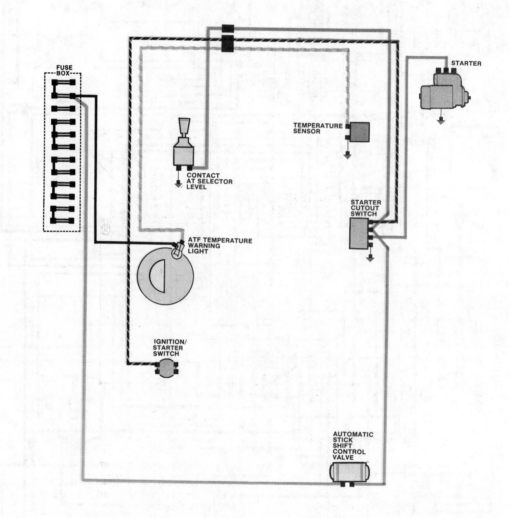

FUSE
BOX

STARTER

TEMPERATURE
SENSOR

CONTACT
AT SELECTOR
LEVEL

STARTER
CUTOUT
SWITCH

ATF TEMPERATURE
WARNING
LIGHT

IGNITION/
STARTER
SWITCH

AUTOMATIC
STICK
SHIFT
CONTROL
VALVE

HOW TO READ 1973 AND LATER DIAGRAMS

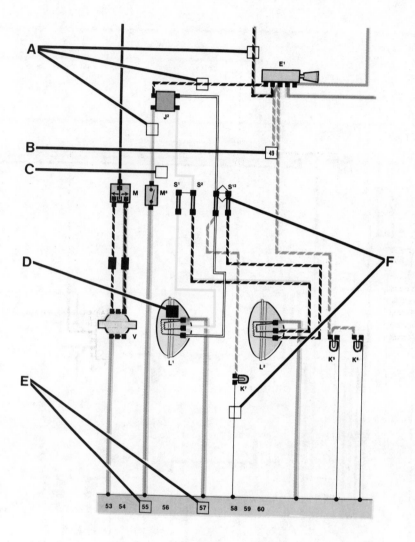

A. **Wire color** (corresponds with color in vehicle)

B. **Current track continuance designation.** No. indicates this wire continues on and can be found at this current track location. In this example track No. 49.

C. **Part designation.** Helps you to find, in the legend, the part which the symbol in the diagram belongs to, e.g. E^9 = switch for fan motor.

D. **Symbol** (here: headlamp)

E. **Current tracks** with track numbers to facilitate finding of part in diagram (see legend).

F. **Internal connections** (thin lines). These are not actual wires but ground connections which go through parts such as bulb holders for example.

1973 AND LATER BEETLE — PART I
(See Page 11 for Explanation of Wiring Diagram Symbols;
See Page 15 for List of Components)

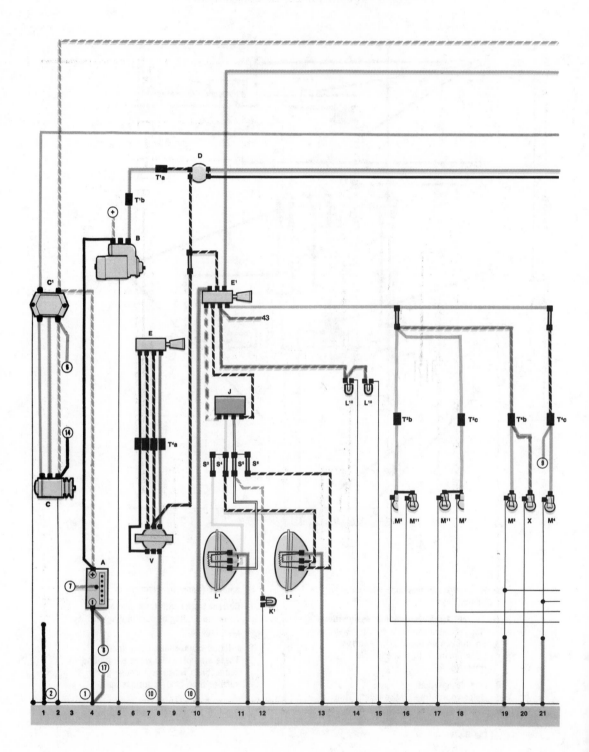

1973 AND LATER BEETLE — PART II
(See Page 11 for Explanation of Wiring Diagram Symbols;
See Page 15 for List of Components)

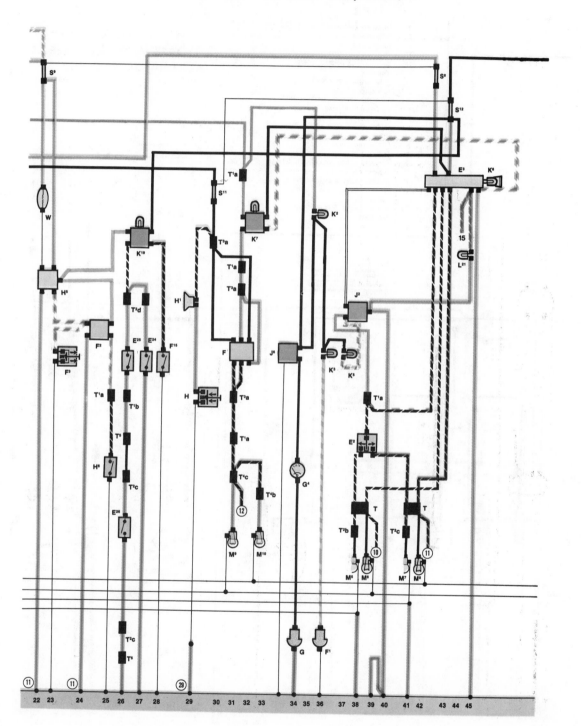

1973 AND LATER BEETLE — PART II

(See Page 11 for Explanation of Wiring Diagram Symbols; See Page 15 for List of Components)

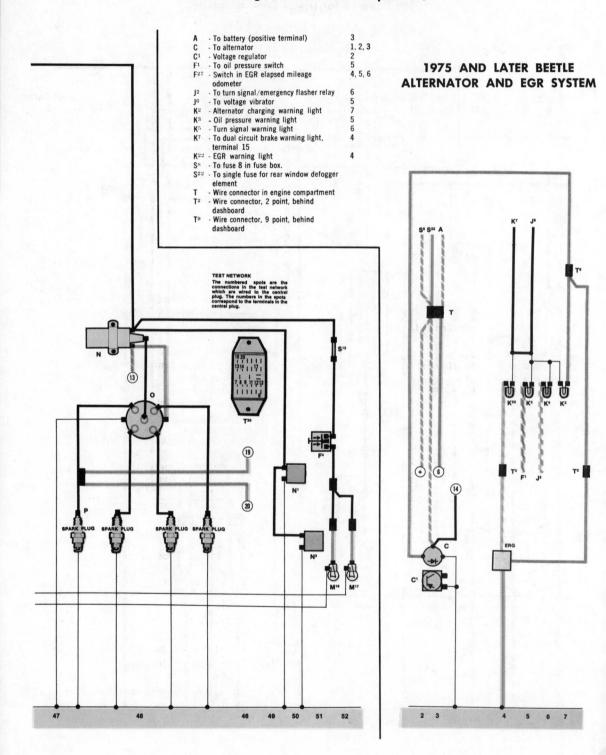

A	- To battery (positive terminal)	3
C	- To alternator	1, 2, 3
C^1	- Voltage regulator	2
F^1	- To oil pressure switch	5
F^{27}	- Switch in EGR elapsed mileage odometer	4, 5, 6
J^2	- To turn signal/emergency flasher relay	6
J^6	- To voltage vibrator	5
K^2	- Alternator charging warning light	7
K^3	- Oil pressure warning light	5
K^5	- Turn signal warning light	6
K^7	- To dual circuit brake warning light, terminal 15	4
K^{22}	- EGR warning light	4
S^8	- To fuse 8 in fuse box.	
S^{22}	- To single fuse for rear window defogger element	
T	- Wire connector in engine compartment	
T^2	- Wire connector, 2 point, behind dashboard	
T^9	- Wire connector, 9 point, behind dashboard	

1975 AND LATER BEETLE ALTERNATOR AND EGR SYSTEM

TEST NETWORK
The numbered spots are the connections in the test network which are wired to the central plug. The numbers in the spots correspond to the terminals in the central plug.

1973 AND LATER BEETLE

Description	current track	Description	current track
A - Battery	4	M9 - Brake light, left	30
B - Starter	5, 6	M10 - Brake light, right	33
C - Generator	1, 2, 3	M11 - Side marker light, front	16, 17
C1 - Regulator	1, 2, 3	M16 - Back-up light, left	51
D - Ignition/starter switch	10	M17 - Back-up light, right	52
E - Windshield wiper switch	9	N - Ignition coil	48
E1 - Light switch	11	N1 - Automatic choke	49
E2 - Turn signal and headlight dimmer switch	38, 39	N3 - Electromagnetic pilot jet	50
E3 - Emergency flasher switch	42, 43, 44, 45	O - Distributor	48
		P - Spark plug connectors	48
E24 - Safety belt lock, left	27	Q - Spark plugs	48
E25 - Safety belt lock, right	26	S1	
E26 - Contact strip in passenger seat	26	to - Fuse box	10, 11, 12
F - Brake light switch	31, 32	S12	22, 42, 43
		S13 - Fuse for back-up light (8 amp)	51
F1 - Oil pressure switch	36	T - Wire connector (close to fuse box)	
F2 - Door contact and buzzer alarm switch, left	24, 25	T1 - Wire connector, single	
F3 - Door contact switch, right	23	a - close to fuse box	
F4 - Back-up light switch	51	b - below rear seat bench	
F15 - Transmission switch for safety belt warning system	28	c - behind the engine compartment insulation, front	
G - Fuel gauge sending unit	34	T2 - Wire connector, double	
G1 - Fuel gauge	34	a - in engine compartment lid	
G4 - Ignition timing sensor	46	b - in luggage compartment, front, left	
H - Horn button	29	c - in passenger seat	
H1 - Horn	29	d - below rear seat bench	
H5 - Ignition key warning buzzer	22, 23	T3 - Wire connector, triple	
H6 - Steering lock contact for ignition key warning system	25	a - in luggage compartment, front, left	
		T4 - Wire connector, four connections	
J - Dimmer relay	10, 11	a - close to fuse box	
J2 - Emergency flasher relay	37, 38	b - behind engine compartment insulation, right	
J6 - Fuel gauge vibrator	34	c - behind engine compartment insulation, left	
K1 - High beam warning light	12		
K2 - Generator charging warning light	35	T5 - Wire connector, double on passenger seat rail	
K3 - Oil pressure warning light	36		
K5 - Turn signal warning light	37	T20 - Test network, test socket	46
K6 - Emergency flasher warning light	45	V - Windshield wiper motor	7, 8
K7 - Dual circuit brake warning light	32	W - Interior light	22
K19 - Safety belt warning system light	27	X - License plate light	20
L1 - Sealed beam unit, left headlight	11		
L2 - Sealed beam unit, left	13	① - Ground strap from battery to frame	4
L10 - Instrument panel light	14, 15	② - Ground strap from transmission to frame	1
L21 - Light for heater lever illumination	44	④ - Ground wire on steering coupling	29
M2 - Taillight, right	19	⑩ - Ground connector, dashboard	
M4 - Taillight, left	21	⑪ - Ground connector, speedometer	
M5 - Turn signal and parking light, front, left	15, 38		
M6 - Turn signal, rear, left	39		
M7 - Turn signal and parking light, front, right	18, 41		
M8 - Turn signal, rear, right	42		

1973 SUPER BEETLE — PART I
(See Page 11 for Explanation of Wiring Diagram Symbols;
See Page 19 for List of Components)

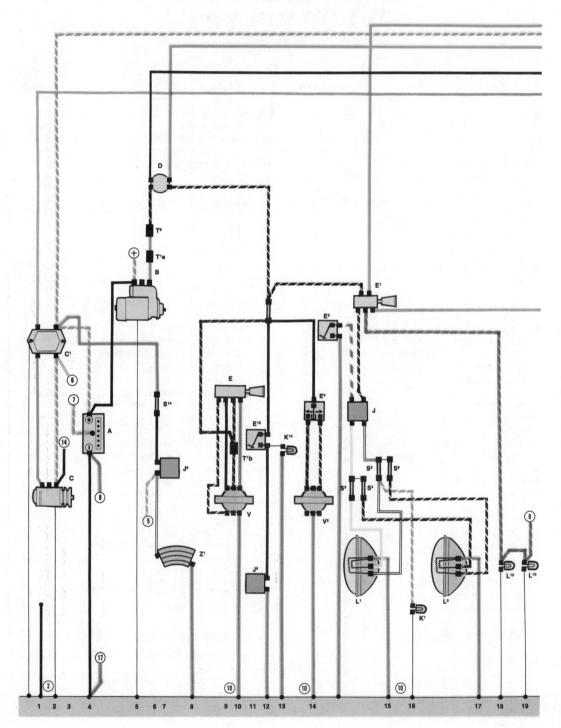

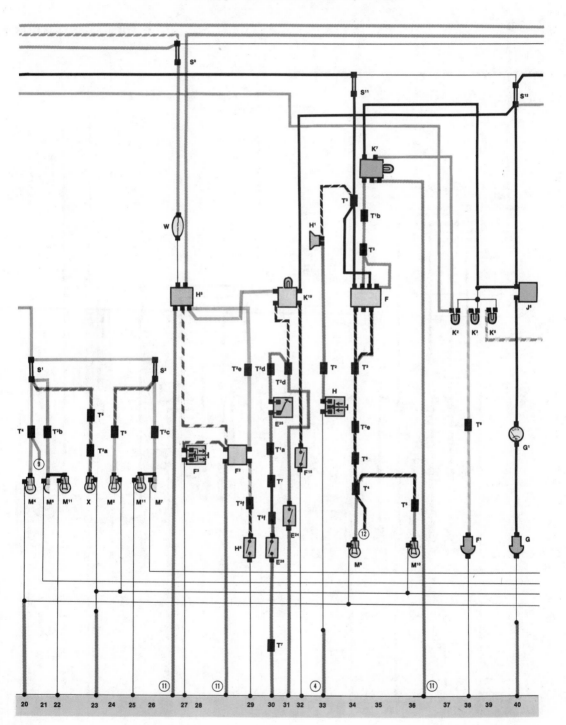

1973 SUPER BEETLE — PART III
(See Page 11 for Explanation of Wiring Diagram Symbols;
See Page 19 for List of Components)

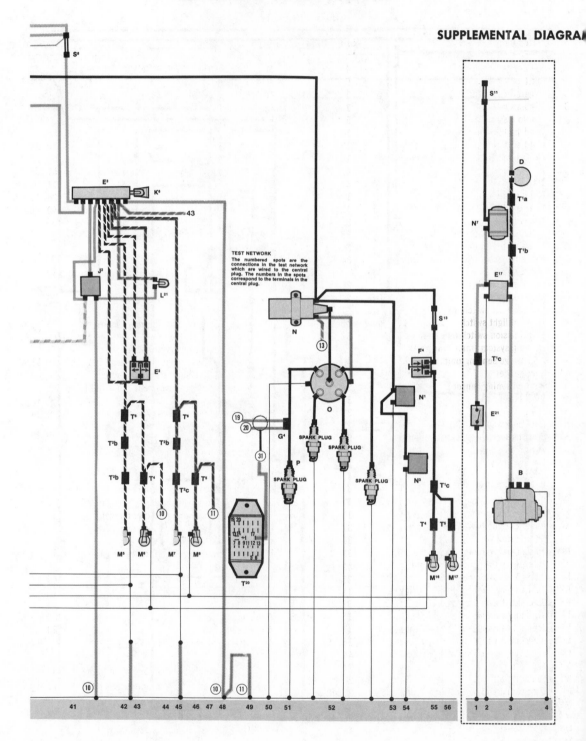

SUPPLEMENTAL DIAGRAM

TEST NETWORK
The numbered spots are the connections in the test network which are wired to the central plug. The numbers in the spots correspond to the terminals in the central plug.

Key To
1973 SUPER BEETLE
(See Pages 16-18)

Description	current track	Description	current track
A - Battery	4	M11 - Side marker light, front left + right	22, 25
B - Starter	5, 6	M16 - Back-up light, left	55
C - Generator	1, 2, 3	M17 - Back-up light, right	56
C1 - Regulator	1, 2, 3	N - Ignition coil	52
D - Ignition/starter switch	5	N1 - Automatic choke	53
E - Windshield wiper switch	10	N3 - Electromagnetic pilot jet	54
E1 - Light switch	15	O - Distributor	50, 52
E2 - Turn signal and headlight dimmer switch	14	P - Spark plug connectors	51, 52
E3 - Emergency flasher switch	41, 42, 43, 44	Q - Spark plugs	51, 52
E9 - Fan motor switch	14	S1	14, 15, 20,
E15 - Rear window defogger switch	12	to - Fuse box	26, 27, 34,
E24 - Safety belt lock, left	31	S12	40, 41
E25 - Safety belt lock, right	30	S13 - Fuse for back-up light (8 amp.)	55
E26 - Contact strip in passenger seat	30	S14 - Fuse for rear window defogger, (8 amp.)	6
F - Brake light and dual circuit warning light switch	34, 35, 36	T1 - Wire connector, single	
		a - below rear seat bench	30
F1 - Oil pressure switch	38	b - one connector of the eight terminals (strip) behind the dashboard	10
F2 - Door contact and buzzer alarm switch, left	29		
F3 - Door contact switch, right	27	c - behind the engine compartment insulation	55
F4 - Back-up light switch	55		
F15 - Transmission switch for safety belt warning system (man. transm.)	32	T2 - Wire connector, double, one of the eight terminals (strip)	33
G - Fuel gauge sending unit	40	a - in engine compartment lid	23
G1 - Fuel gauge	40	b - in luggage compartment, front, left two of the eight terminals (strip)	21, 42, 45
G4 - Ignition timing sensor	51		
H - Horn button	33	c - in luggage compartment, front, right	26
H1 - Horn	33	d - below rear seat bench	30, 31
H5 - Ignition key warning buzzer	28	e - two of the eight terminals (strip) behind the dashboard	29, 34
H6 - Steering lock contact for ignition key warning system	29		
		f - in passenger seat	29, 30
J - Dimmer relay	15	T3 - Wire connector, triple, in luggage compartment, front, left	
J2 - Emergency flasher relay	41	T4 - Wire connector, four connections, behind engine compartment insulation, left	
J6 - Fuel gauge vibrator	40		
J9 - Rear window defogger relay	7	T5 - Wire connector, five connections, behind engine compartment insulation, right	
K1 - High beam warning light	16		
K2 - Generator charging warning light	37	T6 - Wire connector, six connections, above fuse box, left	
K3 - Oil pressure warning light	38		
K5 - Turn signal warning light	39	T7 - Wire connector, double, on passenger seat rail	
K6 - Emergency flasher warning light	43		
K7 - Dual circuit warning light	35	T20 - Test network, test socket	49
K10 - Rear window defogger warning light	13	V - Windshield wiper motor	10
K19 - Safety belt warning system light	31, 32	V2 - Fan motor	14
L1 - Sealed beam unit, left headlight	15	W - Interior light	27
L2 - Sealed beam unit, right headlight	17	X - License plate light	23
L10 - Instrument panel light	18, 19	Z1 - Rear window defogger heating element	8
L21 - Light for heater lever illumination	44		
M2 - Taillight, right	24	① - Ground strap from battery to frame	4
M4 - Taillight, left	20	② - Ground strap from transmission to frame	1
M5 - Turn signal and parking light front, left	21, 42		
M6 - Turn signal, rear, left	43	④ - Ground cable on steering coupling	33
M7 - Turn signal and parking light front, right	26, 45	⑩ - Ground connector, dashboard	
M8 - Turn signal, rear, right	46	⑪ - Ground connector, speedometer housing	
M9 - Brake light, left	34		
M10 - Brake light, right	36		

1974 AND LATER SUPER BEETLE AND LA GRANDE BUG—PART I
(See Page 11 for Explanation of Wiring Diagram Symbols;
See Page 23 for List of Components)

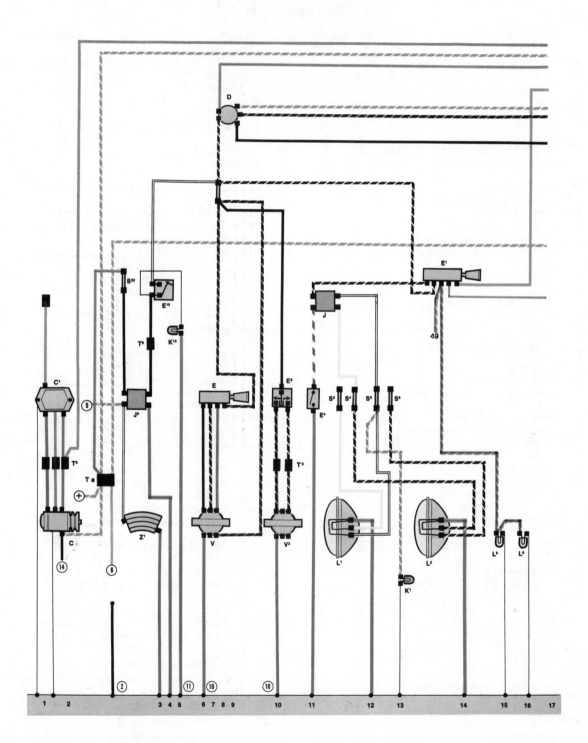

1974 AND LATER SUPER BEETLE AND LA GRANDE BUG — PART II
(See Page 11 for Explanation of Wiring Diagram Symbols;
See Page 23 for List of Components)

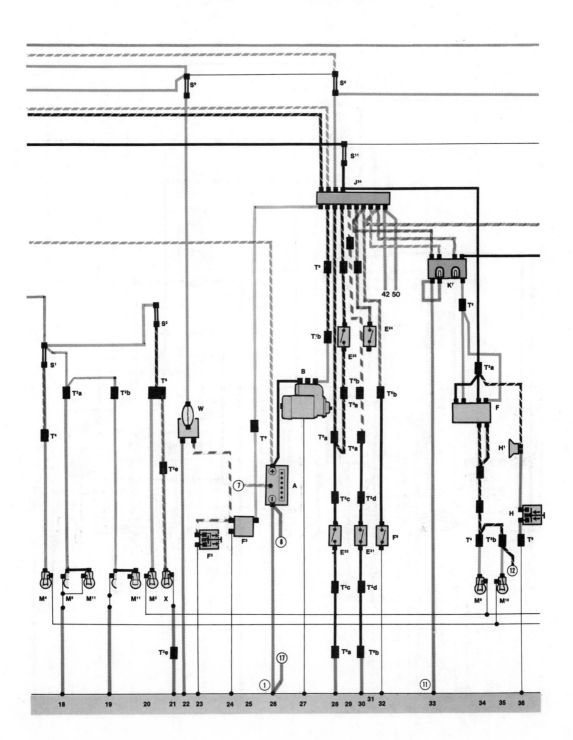

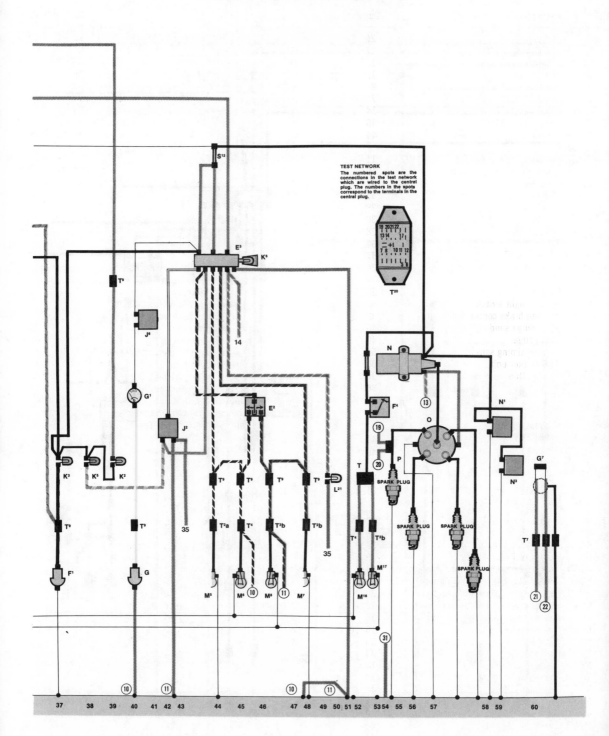

TEST NETWORK
The numbered spots are the connections in the test network which are wired to the central plug. The numbers in the spots correspond to the terminals in the central plug.

Description	Current track	Description	Current track
A - Battery	26	M[11] - Side marker light front, left and right	19, 20
B - Starter	27	M[16] - Backup light, left	52
C - Alternator	1, 2	M[17] - Backup light, right	53
C[1] - Regulator	1, 2	N - Ignition coil	55
D - Ignition/starter switch	8	N[1] - Automatic choke	58
E - Windshield wiper switch	7, 9	N[3] - Electromagnetic cutoff valve	59
E[1] - Light switch	14	O - Ignition distributor	57
E[2] - Turn signal switch	46	P - Spark plug connectors	55, 56, 57
E[3] - Emergency flasher switch	44,	Q - Spark plugs	55, 56, 57
		S[1] to S[12] } Fuses in fuse box	8, 12, 14, 17, 20, 22, 30, 31, 40
E[4] - Headlight dimmer switch	11		
E[9] - Fresh air fan motor switch	10	S[21] - Fuse for backup lights (8 amps)	53
E[15] - Rear window defogger switch	4	S[22] - Fuse for rear window defogger (8 amp)	3
E[24] - Safety belt lock, left	31		
E[25] - Safety belt lock, right	29	T - Cable adapter, behind insulation in engine compartment	
E[31] - Contact strip in driver seat	30	a - under rear seat bench	
E[32] - Contact strip in passenger seat	28	T[1] - Wire connector, single	
F - Brake light switch	34, 35	a - behind instrument panel	
F[1] - Oil pressure switch	37	b - under rear seat bench	
F[2] - Door contact and buzzer alarm switch, left	24, 25	T[2] - Wire connector, double	
		a - in luggage compartment, left	
F[3] - Door contact switch, right	23	b - in luggage compartment, right	
F[4] - Backup light switch	52	c - under passenger seat	
F[9] - Parking brake control light switch	32	d - under driver's seat	
G - Fuel gauge sending unit	40	e - in hood of engine compartment	
G[1] - Fuel gauge	40	T[3] - Wire connector, 3 point	
G[4] - Ignition timing sensor	54	a - in luggage compartment, left	
G[7] - TDC marker unit	60	b - behind insulation in engine compartment, right	
H - Horn button	36		
H[1] - Horn	36	T[4] - Wire connector, 4 point, behind insulation in engine compartment, left	
J - Dimmer relay	11	T[5] - Wire connector, single	
J[2] - Emergency flasher relay	42	a - behind instrument panel	
J[6] - Voltage vibrator	40	b - on passenger seat rail	
J[9] - Rear window defogger relay	3	T[6] - Wire connector, double	
J[34] - Safety belt warning system relay	28, 29, 30, 31, 32	a - under passenger seat	
		b - under driver's seat	
K[1] - High beam warning light	13	T[7] - Wire connector, 3 point, in engine compartment	
K[2] - Alternator charging warning light	39	T[8] - Wire connector, 4 point, under rear seat bench	
K[3] - Oil pressure warning light	37		
K[5] - Turn signal warning light	38	T[9] - Wire connector, 8 point, behind instrument panel	
K[6] - Emergency flasher warning light	51		
K[7] - Dual circuit breaker warning and safety belt interlock warning system	33	T[20] - Test network, test socket	55
		V - Windshield wiper motor	6
L[1] - Sealed beam unit, left headlight	12	V[2] - Fresh air motor	10
L[2] - Sealed beam unit, right headlight	14	W - Interior light	22
L[6] - Speedometer light	15, 16	X - License plate light	21
L[21] - Light for heater lever illumination	50	Z[1] - Rear window defogger heating element	3
M[2] - Taillight, right	20		
M[4] - Taillight, left	18		
M[5] - Parking light, front, left	18	① - Ground strap from battery to frame	
M[5] - Turn signal, front, left	44	② - Ground strap from transmission to frame	
M[6] - Turn signal, rear, left	45		
M[7] - Parking light, front, right	19	⑩ - Ground connection on instrument panel	
M[7] - Turn signal, front, right	48		
M[8] - Turn signal, rear, right	47	⑪ - Ground connection on speedometer	
M[9] - Brake light, left	34		
M[10] - Brake light, right	35		

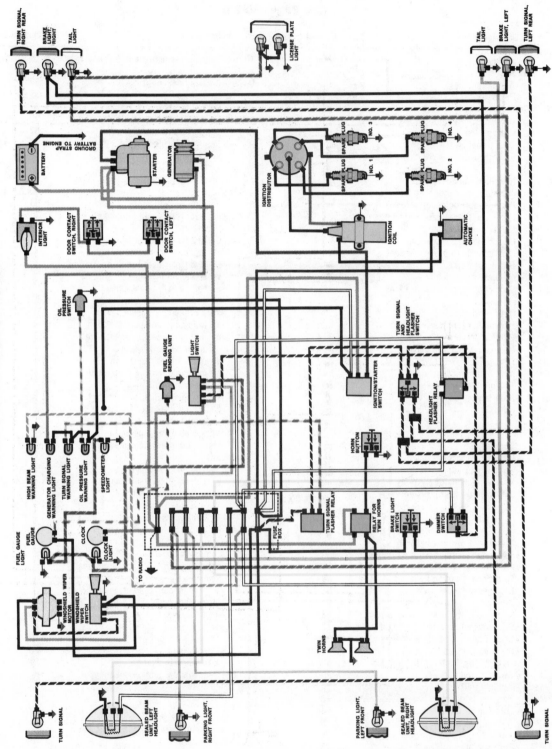

1961-1966 KARMANN GHIA

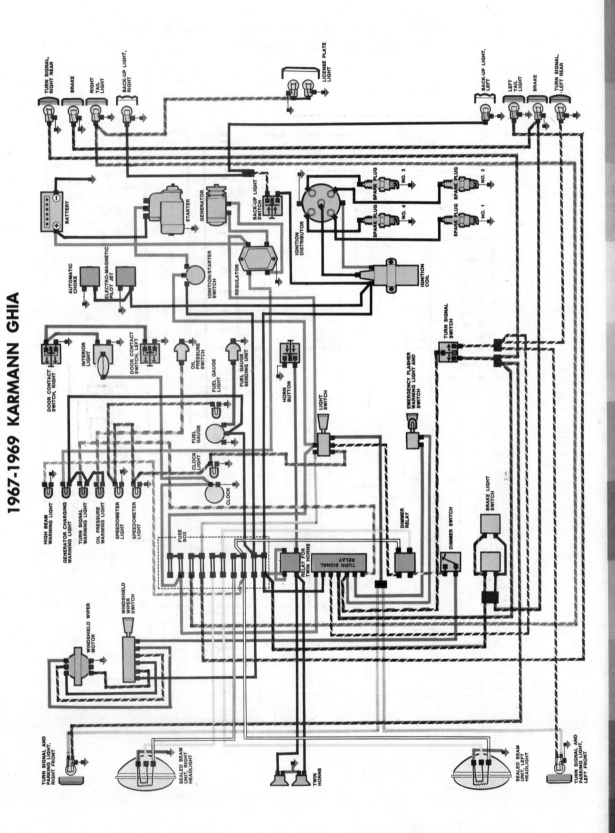

1967-1969 KARMANN GHIA

1969-1972 KARMANN GHIA SUPPLEMENT
(Automatic Stick Shift & Rear Window Defogger)

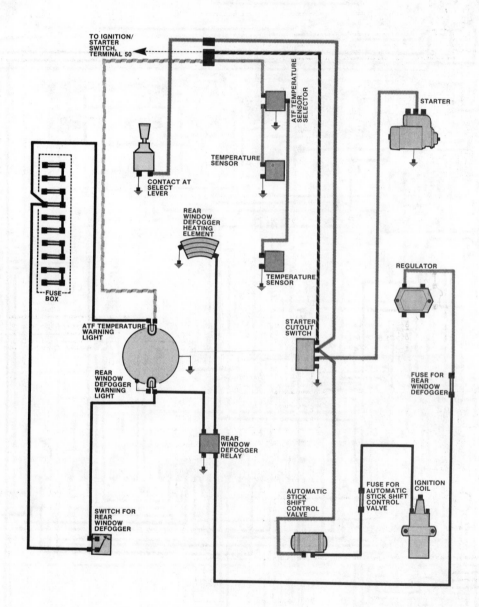

TO IGNITION/
STARTER
SWITCH,
TERMINAL 50

ATF TEMPERATURE
SENSOR
SELECTOR

TEMPERATURE
SENSOR

CONTACT AT
SELECT
LEVER

REAR
WINDOW
DEFOGGER
HEATING
ELEMENT

TEMPERATURE
SENSOR

STARTER

REGULATOR

ATF TEMPERATURE
WARNING
LIGHT

STARTER
CUTOUT
SWITCH

REAR
WINDOW
DEFOGGER
WARNING
LIGHT

FUSE FOR
REAR
WINDOW
DEFOGGER

FUSE
BOX

REAR
WINDOW
DEFOGGER
RELAY

AUTOMATIC
STICK
SHIFT
CONTROL
VALVE

FUSE FOR
AUTOMATIC
STICK SHIFT
CONTROL
VALVE

IGNITION
COIL

SWITCH FOR
REAR
WINDOW
DEFOGGER

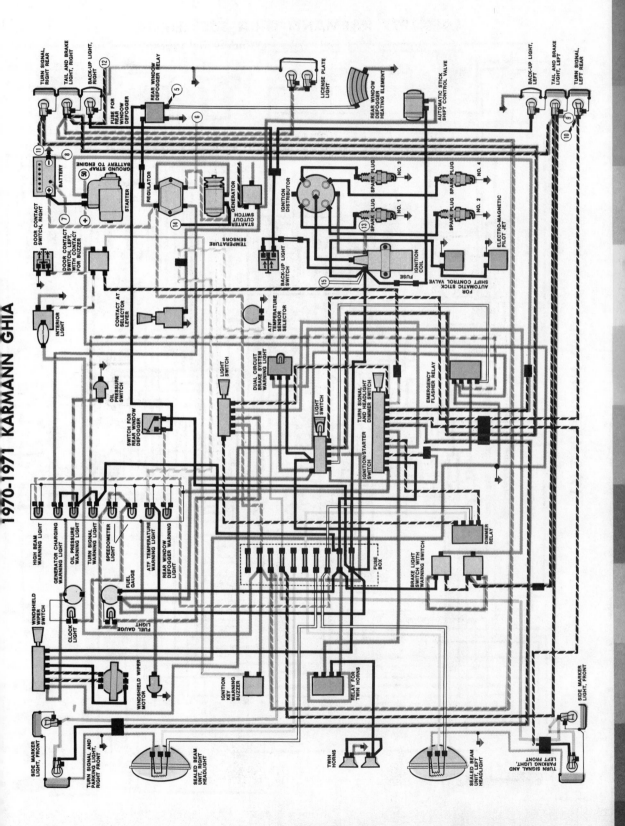

1970-1971 KARMANN GHIA

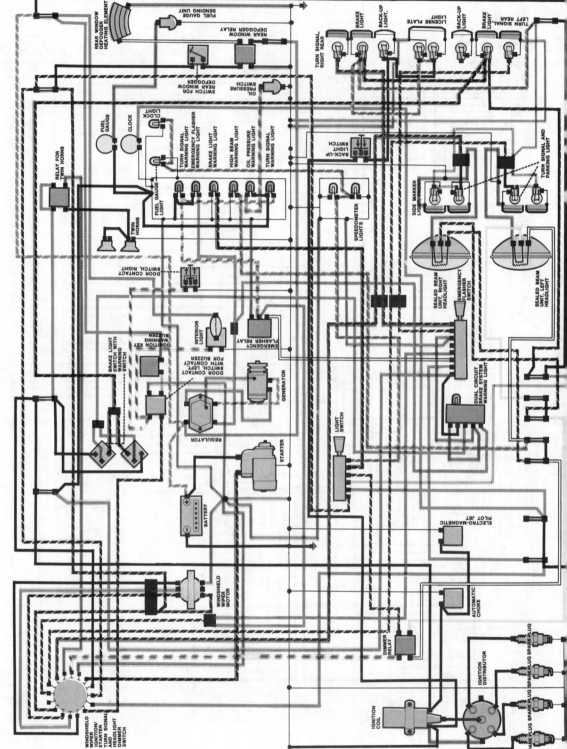

1972 KARMANN GHIA